HAZEL CLEMENT

CW01584184

Introductory Business Statistics With Microsoft Excel

Introductory Business Statistics With Microsoft Excel

Andrew J Robson

Business Education Publishers 1999

© Andrew J Robson

ISBN 1 901888 15 0

First published 1999

Published in Great Britain by
Business Education Publishers Limited
The Teleport
Doxford International
Sunderland
SR3 3XD

Tel: 0191 5252400
Fax: 0191 5201815

All rights reserved. No part of this publication may be reproduced, stored in a retrieval system, or transmitted, in any form or by any means, electrical, mechanical, photocopying, recording or otherwise, without the prior permission of Business Education Publishers Limited.

British Cataloguing-in-Publications Data
A catalogue record for this book is available from the British Library

Printed in Great Britain by Athenaeum Press, Gateshead

Preface

The objective of this book is to introduce a range of statistical techniques regularly used by business decision makers. In describing these techniques, business related examples will be used and the necessary manual calculations described. In addition, reference will be also made to their spreadsheet solution, by making reference to one particular spreadsheet, namely Microsoft Excel 97. For both manual and spreadsheet solution of the various examples, emphasis will be given to the interpretation of the results obtained rather than any rigorous proof of the statistical methods used. *The built-in tabular, graphical and statistical functions provided within Excel 97 are directly transferable to other (i.e. earlier) versions of the software, and as a consequence, users of versions 4, 5 and 7 of Excel should have little trouble following the computer based examples in this text.*

This material is aimed at those students undertaking introductory courses in Business Statistics at either higher national, undergraduate or postgraduate conversion level. Detail will be given in the computer examples on how to activate the appropriate tools and any assumptions made by Microsoft Excel. The examples considered will be further supported by referring to appropriate screen diagrams.

The statistical concepts are introduced in this book in a sequential manner, chapter by chapter. At the end of each chapter, the author has provided questions which aim to test the reader's understanding of these concepts. In most cases, the quantitative questions provided should first be attempted by hand and the results verified by using the relevant tools offered by Excel. After the completing the book, it is hoped that the students will have gained an understanding of the role of statistical analysis in the business decision making and the support which can be provided by a popular IT application.

Contents

Part 2 - Summary Statistics

Introductory Business Statistics With Microsoft Excel

Part 1
Data Collection and Organisation

Chapter 1

Introduction, Types of Data and Methods of Collection

Learning Outcomes

In this chapter you will be made aware of the sources of data available to a business decision maker and you will distinguish between the various types of data collected. You will see the different ways in which data may be collected and will discuss the relevance of sampling.

After completing this chapter you will be able to:

- Define the term 'statistics'.
- Understand the differences between primary and secondary data.
- Distinguish between qualitative and quantitative data.
- Recognise the benefits and disadvantages of using various methods of collecting primary data.
- Be able to develop an effective questionnaire using a suitable mix of multiple choice and open-ended questions.
- Understand the need to pilot a survey.
- Distinguish between a census and a survey.
- Recognise the suitability of various sampling techniques.
- Recognise the potential errors in survey data.

Introduction

To run a business effectively, you require information. Some of this information will be generated from numbers which must be collected, organised, analysed and their properties understood. The process described here is statistical analysis. The data referred to may be collected inside an organisation, covering issues such as factory output, rates of staff sickness or levels of stock. Alternatively, a set of data may be collected outside of the business and relate to issues such as market share of a product or the behaviour of a particular consumer group.

Studying a course in statistical analysis provides you with an awareness of the process of data collection, organisation, analysis and understanding. In reading this book, you will take a sequential approach in following the relevant material, and emphasis will be placed on analysis and understanding (i.e. interpretation) of the output from both manual calculations and from a spreadsheet such as Excel.

In this chapter, you will consider various data sources and the types of data which may be collected. Consideration will also be given to the various ways in which data can be collected. Moreover, you will be made aware of the role of sampling and recognise the potential errors which may appear in survey data.

Primary and Secondary Data

Business data can be generated from a variety of sources. These sources may include the results of a market research survey into the viability of a new product or service, the output generated during a quality control exercise or the monthly sales figures recorded during the last financial year. Whatever the origin of a business data set, it falls into one of two categories; namely **primary** and **secondary** data.

Primary Data

Data collected as 'new' which refers to a particular product, process or project is called primary data. The data collected via a market research survey aimed at determining the viability of a new product or service represents the collection of primary data, and likewise, a work study exercise measuring the waiting and service times of customers in a bank involves the collection of primary or 'new' data.

To collect data in a market research survey, the population or subject of interest has to be identified, questions need to be formulated and personnel trained to collect and process the relevant data. This process is expensive, and as a consequence, it limits the number of organisations who can survey in this way.

However, the data which is collected (providing the exercise is properly planned and carried out) will be both up to date and relevant to the project or process under consideration. The data will also be accurate, and as a consequence, will potentially generate reliable business information.

Secondary Data

In any large organisation data has been collected already and perhaps may have been stored on a computer or manual database and even have been presented by table, graph or statistics in various reports. This data may be used (again) within the organisation. This is known as secondary data. If a bank carries out a market research project to determine the viability of a new personal loan, primary data will be collected comprising of personal and financial details of the survey respondents. Once this data is recorded, either manually or electronically on a spreadsheet or database, it represents potential secondary data. If these respondents are used in any additional mail order survey, then the data used (i.e. the data regarding their personal finance) represents the use of secondary data.

If a council plans to build a new secondary school, data collected in the last Government Census may be used to determine the numbers of 11-18 year olds in the district, and in turn, this secondary data may be used to establish the school's size and actual location.

Examples of secondary data available to you from a University library include company accounts and reports as well as monthly and quarterly publications from the UK Government.

The advantage of using secondary data sources are that they are easily accessible (say from your library or via the internet) and cover a variety of subjects. As a consequence, using secondary data incurs little or no cost and the data are easy to collate. However, many secondary data sources may be dated or incomplete with regard to their subsequent use. As a consequence, the data are unlikely to have the same degree of accuracy and relevance as that provided by a primary data set. For example, the last Government Census was undertaken in 1991. If this secondary data is used to plan education provision in a city, it may be highly inaccurate if the districts under consideration have been subject to major shifts in population.

Census and Surveys

If data is collected from all of the subjects of interest or **population**, a census has been undertaken. The most widely known census in the UK is that undertaken every decade by the Government which provides a demographic analysis of the UK, considering factors such as the population's age profile, working practices and standards of living. When referring to the term **population**, you are likely to imagine all of the people living in a city or country (as in the UK census), every employee working at a factory or each student attending a university. However, the term can also refer to objects such as all cars leaving an assembly line.

Whilst accurate measures can be made from data collected in a census, project costs can be very high and it may take too long to target all of the population. Instead, it may be more appropriate to collect data from a **subset** or **sample** of the population. If data are collected from a sample, a survey will have been undertaken. For reasons of both cost and being practical, you will generally undertake a survey rather than a census. When you collect data from a sample, it must be **representative** of the population. For example, if you interview only senior managers in a survey investigating public sector pay, the data collected is not likely to be representative of the population of all public sector employees. In this case the sample rather than being **representative**, is likely to be **biased**.

Data Classification

Although data can be collected from a variety of primary and secondary sources, it can be classified in one of two ways, namely as qualitative or quantitative data.

Qualitative Data

Qualitative data is non-quantifiable and either words or numbers are used to describe the different observations in a data set. The type of car owned by a sample of new customers recorded by an insurance company (Saloon, Sports, etc.) is an example of a qualitative data set, where each category of car is defined by labels (words) rather than by numbers.

There are two subgroups of categorical data:

Nominal Data

Data consisting of non-numeric categories like the example described above is known as nominal data. Other examples include type of car owned, favourite football team or spreadsheet most often used by a set of management accountants. If this type of data is collected, it is obvious that quantitative measures cannot be calculated. In order to identify a typical category (rather than value) for the data set, it would be appropriate to indicate the (named) category or categories which occur most often (descriptive statistics will be introduced in Chapter 4).

If a large data set is collected, it is likely that it will be analysed using computer software such as Excel. To make coding easier (and guarantee the accuracy of the data entered into the spreadsheet), the names of each category in the data set (Saloon, Sports, etc.) could be replaced by labels 1, 2, 3, etc. However, when you are presenting and analysing the data, you must be aware that these numbers represent labels rather than actual values and should not be processed as if they were quantitative data.

Ordinal Data

Ordinal data is categorical data where numbers or words are used as relative measures which are known as ranks. A training manager may ask staff attending a course on spreadsheet modelling to rank the quality of the course from 1 to 5, where '1' represents excellent and '5' represents poor. In this type of data set, no quantitative relationship exists between the responses, so that the response '1' does not represent an opinion which is twice as good as the response '2'. Again, the typical value in the data set is the rank that occurs most often, and additionally, the 'middle' score is that rank which can be determined once the labels and their corresponding frequencies are ordered in size. Figure 1.1 displays an ordinal data set. The respondents in a public opinion poll were asked to list the most important issues that need to be tackled by the Government. Inspection of Figure 1.1 indicates the most important issue is Europe, followed by Unemployment and then Education.

Top ten priorities for the Government (Poll - December 1994)

1. Europe
2. Unemployment
3. Education
4. Crime and Drugs
5. Pensions
6. Racism
7. NHS
8. Environment
9. Transport
10. Defence

Figure 1.1 - An ordinal data set based on ranks

Quantitative Data

In contrast to qualitative data, quantitative data can be measured or counted, and as a consequence, this type of data consists of numerical values. These numerical values indicate quantity or size rather than the ranked order indicated by the ordinal data set.

There are also two subgroups of quantitative data:

Continuous Data

This is the type of quantitative data where you can record any value (or alternatively, a large number of values) over a continuous range. Examples of continuous data include height, weight and time related data (including age). Figure 1.2 shows a continuous data set displaying the age of a group of 550 people living in a small mining village. In this example, the age of an individual resident can be recorded as any value between 0 and 100.

Age distribution in a mining village

Age	Number of residents
0 -	62
16 -	68
24 -	45
30 -	61
40 -	89
50 -	112
60 -	71
70 -	29
80 - < 100	13
Total	550

Figure 1.2 Distribution of ages (continuous, quantitative data)

Discrete Data

With certain quantitative data you can record specific values only (in many examples these specific values will be integers or whole numbers) over a given range. Examples include the number of children per family resident on a housing scheme where you can record integer values only, i.e. 0, 1, 2, 3, etc. or UK adult shoe sizes which include non-integer values, i.e. 4, 4½, 5, 5½ etc. However, if a discrete data set is grouped over a wide range, e.g. number of customer complaints recorded daily may be grouped 0 - < 5, 5 - < 10 etc., then the grouping of the data converts into a continuous data set.

Unlike qualitative data, it is possible to calculate quantitative statistics from discrete or continuous data sets, and specifically, you will be able to calculate typical measures and determine potential associations which may exist between different variables. The term variables refer to the different subjects which are recorded in a data set. For example, you may consider customers opening a new bank account. They may record their age, salary and weekly rent. The three measurements here are variables. Throughout this book a number of statistical techniques will be introduced, and in general, these will be considered with reference to 'variables' which may be either qualitative or quantitative.

Methods of Collecting Primary Data

If you wish to collect primary data, there are four main ways in which this can be achieved. The four main methods of data collection are face to face interview, observation, postal and telephone surveys.

Face to Face Interview

Interviews involve an individual interviewer or (perhaps) a team of interviewers asking a set of pre-defined questions to a targeted audience. This target audience may be named individuals or a group identified on the basis of their age, gender, colour or class. This method of collecting data may be used by market researchers working for a company interested in launching a new product or an opinion pollster interested in predicting the outcome of a national election. If the interviewers are experienced, they can actively promote interviewee co-operation, and as a result, deliver accurate and plentiful responses. Any problems resulting from 'difficult' questions may be minimised with the presence of interview personnel. The interviewer may be able to identify specific answers or unanticipated replies to particular questions and be able to raise supplementary issues, thus enhancing the quality of the data collected. However, there is a trade-off in collecting high volume and high quality data with expense, because of the costs involved in supporting an interview team. The problem of cost may be accentuated further if the target audience is dispersed, e.g. in a general election opinion poll.

Observation

Examples of primary data collected via observation may include surveying customers queuing and being served in a bank in order to determine cashier requirements at various times of the working day, or identifying the age and gender mix of people using a shopping centre at specific times of the week. The success of collecting accurate data by observation depends upon the observer's ability to identify all of the features of the system under consideration and the method can be particularly expensive if it covers long or ad-hoc time periods. If the survey considers an organisation's employees, e.g. the work study involving the bank's cashiers, then the observer's common sense is particularly important. In this type of survey, the presence of a stop-watch and clip-board in a work place may result in a bias with regard to any data collected or records made. That is the times recorded to serve a customer may in fact be significantly quicker than the 'true' times because the staff concerned may (wrongly) believe they are being assessed as individuals for efficiency rather than the system or process that they are part of.

Other ways of collecting data via the method of observation include monitoring activities and making records in a diary. The length of time and frequency of diary records will depend upon the nature of the survey.

Postal Surveys

A well known example of the postal survey is the Government Census which is carried out every ten years. Other examples include customer profiles used by banks, credit card companies and department stores. Postal surveys are a particularly useful method of data collection if the population is dispersed (as in any of the examples described), and is less expensive than carrying out face to face interviews because the cost of supporting an interview team will be reduced. Another advantage of the postal survey over using face to face interviews, is that many questions in a survey cannot be answered 'off-the-cuff' and require the respondent to recollect or research the required answers. The postal survey is also particularly useful because the audience are usually given a pre-defined length of time in which they can reply. However, it can cause problems if any questions are unclear or certain answers need to be expanded upon. There is usually little chance to raise supplementary issues with an individual respondent who provides fascinating or 'one-off' answers to particular questions. As a consequence, the postal survey achieves its best results when it presents short, simple questions which require short answers. The biggest disadvantage of using this particular technique is the low level of response.

Telephone Surveys

If you want to target a dispersed audience as cheaply as possible, it may be useful to use telephone surveys. The telephone survey is a cheaper than using face to face interviews, but the method still aims to promote communication between the researcher and the target audience. Using this method of data collection, the interviewer must be positive and enthusiastic but attempt to keep the survey time as short as possible. However, the method can be limited if technical responses are needed to certain questions and bias can occur if a significant and well defined group within the population cannot be accessed by telephone, e.g. those who have ex-directory numbers or exclusively use mobile telephones instead.

A similar method of interview is used in larger organisations, namely **video interview**, whereby interviewer and respondent use video booths which are linked together. In practice, this requires more of the skills described under face to face interviews and is particularly advantageous if the interviewer and respondent are located in different parts of the country.

Designing Effective Questionnaires

Many business surveys use questionnaires and this is particularly true for those surveys which make use of face to face interviews, the post and the telephone.

To increase the chance that a survey is successful, it is good practice to undertake a 'pilot' survey at various stages in the design of the questionnaire by referring to a limited section of the potential target audience. Doing this helps you to identify any problems in the presentation of the questions on the questionnaire and to make sure that most responses can be accounted for by the questionnaire. If questions can be simplified, they not only have more chance of being answered, but the subsequent results may be easier to code, and in turn, analyse. The pilot survey can be used to assess the capability of the 'proper' or resultant survey, or in the example of market research, the viability of the product to be launched. If a pilot survey for a market research exercise indicates little or no interest in the new product, both the actual survey and product development can be scrapped or redirected, thus saving an organisation valuable time and money.

It should also be apparent that the survey process may often be iterative rather than sequential. That is, a questionnaire can be designed and tested on a pilot audience. The individual questions can be assessed for wording, ambiguity and relevance whilst the responses generated can be analysed. This process can be repeated, perhaps with the same pilot audience, until the survey team are confident about the performance of the questionnaire and the survey process as well as the viability of the analysis or product. At this stage the 'proper' survey can commence.

The author has supervised many student projects which have involved questionnaire design. Many students regard this process as being simple, and as a consequence, pay little attention to how the questions may be answered, the range of responses or the subsequent coding. In order to design a questionnaire you will now consider the kinds of question which may be employed, and some of the major issues regarding their validity and application. Whilst not exhaustive, these represent the main issues which can arise in the simplest of questionnaires.

Types of Question

There are two kinds types of question which can be used; multiple choice and open-ended questions.

Multiple Choice Questions

The simplest multiple choice questions which are often called dichotomous questions permit you to choose one option from two pre-defined answers, e.g. Pass or Fail, Yes or No. Figure 1.3 shows three examples of a dichotomous question:

Which spreadsheet do you use?	Lotus 1-2-3 ❑	Excel ❑
Have you had any formal PC training?	Yes ❑	No ❑
Did you enjoy the training course?	Enjoy ❑	Didn't Enjoy ❑

Figure 1.3 - Examples of dichotomous questions

The advantage of using this simplest type of multiple choice question is that they are easy to answer and easy to code onto a computer if a large data set is to be collected. In particular, answers to the question 'Which spreadsheet do you use?' can be coded as 1 for Lotus 1-2-3 and 2 for Excel on a spreadsheet, where each column refers to a question and each row to an individual respondent.

Whilst this type of question is easy to answer and process, it does not allow the respondent to justify a response or express an alternative opinion, e.g. someone who uses Quattro Pro instead of Lotus 1-2-3 or Excel. Also, it should not be used if the pre-defined responses are polarised like 'Enjoy' and 'Didn't Enjoy', because many respondents may have an opinion which is somewhere between the extremes offered. Moreover, if someone answers 'Didn't Enjoy' to the question ' Did you enjoy the training course?' it may be useful to determine why (i.e. get the respondent to expand upon the answer provided).

More often the multiple choice question will permit you to choose (one or more responses) from more than just than two options. Figure 1.4 shows two multiple choice questions:

What is your age?		**How long have you used spreadsheets?**	
16 - 23	❑	Less than 6 months	❑
24 - 29	❑	6 months up to a year	❑
30 - 39	❑	1 to 2 years	❑
40 - 49	❑	More than two years	❑
50 - 64	❑		

Figure 1.4 - Multiple choice questions

You must define the options offered in a multiple choice question so that they cover all possible responses and each option should be distinct. Common mistakes are encountered on age related questions, where the question may give options 16 - 24, 24 - 30, 30 - 34, 40 - 50, and 50 - 60. Obviously, these groups overlap since those respondents who are aged 24, 30, 40 and 50 can tick one of two boxes. Instead, this question should be presented like its equivalent in Figure 1.4. Where a lot of possible responses are available, the category '**Other**' may be used as shown in Figure 1.5.

Which software do you use most often at work?	
Word processor	❑
Spreadsheet	❑
Database	❑
Other	❑

Figure 1.5 - Use of 'Other' in a multiple choice question

Whilst the option 'Other' can be used to count those responses which may not fit into what are considered to be the 'likely' answers, it is not desirable if 'Other' becomes a category with one of the biggest frequencies. This would give you either misleading or meaningless data. For example, if you are interviewed staff at an Engineering Consultancy, you may find that 20% use the word processor most often, 35% the spreadsheet, 15% the database and 30% use project management software more than any other application. The last statistic would not become apparent from the question listed in Figure 1.5, since the 30% would be categorised as 'Other'.

As suggested earlier, the multiple choice questions listed above are easy to code on a computer. For example, the age responses in Figure 1.4 could be coded as 1, 2, 3, 4 and 5 respectively.

Multiple choice questions can also be used to determine the opinion of each individual in a target audience on a particular issue. If the question is to be used in this way, it is important to offer balance (and as a consequence, avoid ***biasing*** the responses in either a negative or a positive way) by offering an equal number of 'positive' and 'negative' alternatives. Figure 1.6 shows two possible ways of asking the same question with multiple choice responses. The first may possibly give biased results because it contains a majority of positive options. The bias here could either involve prompting respondents to unwillingly provide a positive answer or failing to determine the degree of negativity amongst those who use the lone negative option provided by the list of choices.

There is also a difference of opinion amongst decision makers regarding the provision of an odd or even number of alternatives in a ranking multiple choice question. The advantage of the even number is that it prevents the respondent from selecting the 'middle' alternative. However, this 'middle' is considered by many people as a genuine option. Often this type of question is presented as a numbered scale between two extremes such as Poor and Excellent.

What did you think of the spreadsheet training course?

Excellent ❑

Good ❑ Unbalanced choice, 2 positive options and 1 negative option. Such a choice may bias the 'neutral' or

Average ❑ 'negative' respondent towards giving a positive response

Poor ❑

What did you think of the spreadsheet training course?

Very Good ❑

Good ❑

Average ❑ More balanced, 2 positive, 2 negative options and a 'middle' or 'neutral' option

Poor ❑

Very Poor ❑

Figure 1.6 - Multiple choice involving ranked opinions

Again, the second question in Figure 1.6 can be coded 1, 2, 3, 4, and 5 for the purposes of analysis by computer. However, you should remember that the data is qualitative and this will influence the types of statistics calculated.

It is always useful to cater for potential "Don't Know" or "No Opinion" responses in a multiple choice question. In the questions presented in Figure 1.6, any respondent who was not interested in the training course, may have answered 'Average' to the question rather than 'No Opinion'. The revised question presented in Figure 1.7 would take account of such a response.

What did you think of the spreadsheet training course?	
Very Good	❑
Good	❑
Average	❑
Poor	❑
Very Poor	❑
No Opinion	❑

Figure 1.7 - Taking account of No Opinion Response

Finally, the multiple choice question can be used to ask a respondent to rank choices, say from 'best' to 'worst'. For example, the question in Figure 1.8 asks the respondent to rank the most difficult aspects of a spreadsheet training course.

Rank the most difficult aspects (1 = Hardest, 2 = Next Hardest and so on - only rank those responses which apply)	
Graphs	❑
Formulae	❑
Printing	❑
Macros	❑
Analysis Toolpak	❑
Sorting Data	❑

Figure 1.8 - Ranking multiple choice responses

In this type of question, the respondent should be allowed to finish ranking and not assign scores to options where no difficulty arises. In the question displayed in Figure 1.8, a respondent may find macros most difficult, followed by graphs but everything else simple. The six boxes would be labelled ***2, blank, blank, 1, blank and blank*** respectively. Providing the respondent with clear instructions should increase the chance that the questions listed in the questionnaire are answered properly, e.g. when only one response is required, the appropriate instruction should be provided.

Moreover, when coding responses to this question you should be aware that it requires six columns of the spreadsheet (Excel say) to code each response to the question presented in Figure 1.8, i.e. 1 column for each option. Any blank options may be given a blank or unique number when coded, since by default, this represents a response, i.e. the respondent (in this case the spreadsheet user) finds no difficulty with that particular feature.

For example, a review of a spreadsheet training course may involve 3 questions with the associated responses, listed in Figure 1.9.

1. Which spreadsheet do you use most (select one only)?

   Excel ❑ *Lotus 1-2-3* ❑

2. How often do you use the spreadsheet at work?

   Rarely ❑ *Occasionally* ❑ *Often* ❑ *Major part of work* ❑

3. Which internal spreadsheet courses have you attended?

   Introductory ❑ *Intermediate* ❑ *Advanced* ❑

Figure 1.9 - An example of a course feedback questionnaire

To code these questions you could use labels 1 and 2 for the respective choices in question 1 and the labels 1, 2, 3 and 4 for the possible responses to question 2. However, an individual respondent may have attended any combination of the three internal courses provided. As a consequence, labels 0 and 1 could be used for the responses No and Yes for each course and the subsequent coding will require three columns on the spreadsheet. Figure 1.10 shows how this data could be coded in Excel. Each respondent is provided with their own ID and their responses are recorded in each row of the spreadsheet. The columns represent the questions;

columns B and C represent questions 1 and 2, whilst columns D, E and F represent the responses to question 3.

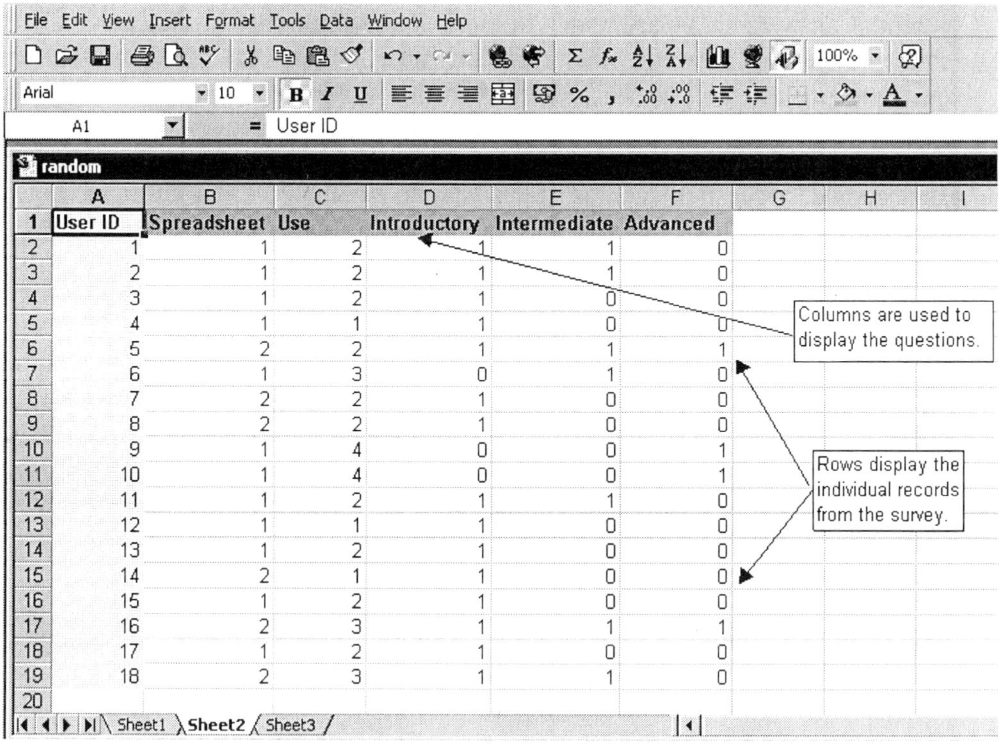

	A	B	C	D	E	F
1	User ID	Spreadsheet Use		Introductory	Intermediate	Advanced
2	1	1	2	1	1	0
3	2	1	2	1	1	0
4	3	1	2	1	0	0
5	4	1	1	1	0	0
6	5	2	2	1	1	1
7	6	1	3	0	1	0
8	7	2	2	1	0	0
9	8	2	2	1	0	0
10	9	1	4	0	0	1
11	10	1	4	0	0	1
12	11	1	2	1	1	0
13	12	1	1	1	0	0
14	13	1	2	1	0	0
15	14	2	1	1	0	0
16	15	1	2	1	0	0
17	16	2	3	1	1	1
18	17	1	2	1	0	0
19	18	2	3	1	1	0

Figure 1.10- Coding questionnaire responses using Excel

Open Ended Questions

In an open ended question, you can collect more detailed responses rather than say 'Yes' or 'No', 'Like' or 'Dislike' or by selecting or ranking choices from a pre-defined list of options. This type of question is useful because it permits a range of different responses, some of which you may expect but others may be useful or surprising. Conversely, this also represents the main problem of including open ended questions, since the varying responses can be difficult to organise and interpret. As a consequence, you should limit, if possible, the number of open ended questions you use, especially if the size of target audience is going to be large, and if the survey involves a voluntary postal questionnaire.

The open ended question can be effective in the following situations:

- **In the pilot stage of a survey**, where it can be used to determine the range of potential answers to a particular question. If the pilot survey indicates only a small range of answers, the resultant question on the 'proper' survey questionnaire can perhaps be presented in the simpler multiple choice format, which makes it easier to answer and its responses easier to code.

  For example, a question such as age is easy to present (see the multiple choice question in Figure 1.4), but you may not be aware of all the possible responses to questions such as 'Which spreadsheet do you regularly use at work?' or 'Which features of the spreadsheet cause you problems?'

- **As a supplementary question**, in order to generate additional data in relation to the answer to an associated (multiple choice) question. For example, a question 'What did you think of the spreadsheet training course?' could be followed by an open ended question 'Please explain your answer' or 'If you responded *Poor* or *Very Poor*, what problems did you encounter'? These supplementary questions may be positioned to gather comments on answers to specific questions or as an overview to the whole survey.

In conclusion, it is useful to consider a number of issues when designing a questionnaire. You will consider these issues by means of reference to the questionnaire in Figure 1.11. Some aspects of this questionnaire are good, whilst others could be improved. Comments will be made as appropriate.

Review of Spreadsheet Training

1. What is your staff grade?

M1 - M3	❑	M4 - M6	❑	E1 - E4	❑
C1 - C4	❑	T1 - T3	❑		

2. What is your age?

16 - 23	❑	24 - 29	❑	30 - 39	❑
40 - 49	❑	50 - 64	❑		

3. Have you attended the introductory course?

Yes ❑ No ❑
If you have responded 'No', do to question 5.

4. How did you relate the delivery of the course

	1	2	3	4	5	
Excellent	❑	❑	❑	❑	❑	Poor

5. Have you attended the intermediate course?

Yes ❑ No ❑
If you have responded 'No', do to question 7.

6. How did you relate the delivery of the course

	1	2	3	4	5	
Excellent	❑	❑	❑	❑	❑	Poor

7. Have you attended the advanced course?

Yes ❑ No ❑
If you have responded 'No', do to question 9.

8. How did you relate the delivery of the course

	1	2	3	4	5	
Excellent	❑	❑	❑	❑	❑	Poor

9. If you responded 4 or 5 to any of questions 4, 6 and 8, please give reasons why.

....

....

....

Figure 1.11 - A questionnaire using a mix of the three types of question

- The shorter the questionnaire, the greater the response. Longer questionnaires and more complex questions will deter your audience if they are used in postal or telephone surveys. Questions 1, 2, 3, 5 and 7 in Figure 1.11 use multiple choice questions which are easy to answer. Questions 4, 6 and 8 may be re-written to account for those with no opinion.

- The questions should, if possible, avoid being technical particularly if they are to be used in face to face or telephone interviews.

- Questions should avoid relying heavily on the respondent's ability to recall, since they may not have access during the survey to the relevant information. Questions 3 to 8 in Figure 1.11 involve the respondent having to recall past events. These questions may be improved by imposing a time limit, e.g. question 3 may be re-written as 'Have you attended the introductory course in the last twelve months?'

- Questions involving personal information should be diplomatically presented, e.g. age, salaries and health. In particular, these questions can be presented using the multiple choice format described earlier which was illustrated in questions 1 and 2 in Figure 1.11 which avoid the respondent having to supply specific answers.

- Questions need to be sensibly listed within the questionnaire. In Figure 1.11, questions 1 and 2 are job related, whilst questions 3 to 9 discuss the spreadsheet training. Moreover, the questions pertaining to the different levels of training are grouped together.

- Finally, when designing a questionnaire, you must pay attention to the coding and analysis of the data collected. It is worth remembering that there is usually a trade-off between accurate, detailed information and the ease of coding and subsequent analysis. In particular, open ended questions provide a variety of detailed, in depth information, but their responses (especially for a large number of returned questionnaires) can prove problematic to summarise. In this example, only one question out of 9 is open ended. This question is situated at the end of the questionnaire and inspection of the questionnaire would suggest that it is unlikely to deter many respondents given that it asks specifically about poor training.

Sampling Techniques

Earlier in the chapter a distinction was made between a census and a survey. A census takes place when you collect data from the whole of a population (i.e. group of interest), whilst a survey involves collecting data from a sample, which will ***hopefully*** be representative of the population. Figure 1.12 shows the relationship between a population and a sample.

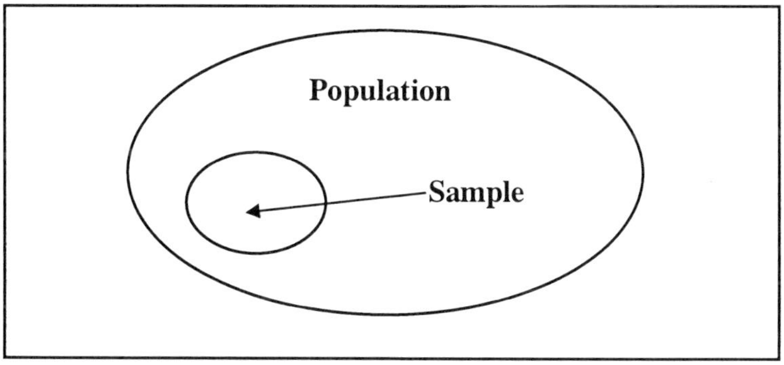

Figure 1.12 - The relationship between population and sample

In general, a survey is undertaken instead of a census because you need to control costs and the research must be undertaken as efficiently as possible. For a university consisting of 17,000 students, it would be more efficient to quantify the extent of student debt by considering a representative subset of the student population because of the cost and time which it would take to interview and analyse the records of the whole population.

If you read a newspaper or access the internet you will see data published on issues such as trends in wages, employment, prices and personal expenditure. Much of this data are collected using various types of survey. Although these surveys involve collecting large quantities of data, the data collected within each is likely in practice to only represent a small proportion of the population. Therefore, you may ask if the size of the sample used in the research important? Although the proportion of data collected in the examples listed above will be small compared to the various populations, the actual sample sizes are large enough to obtain representative data. The increased cost of collecting additional data (by increasing the size of the various samples) may have only a marginal effect on the accuracy of the data collected. As described earlier in the chapter, there may be a trade-off in a survey between data accuracy and time and cost. This is often not a problem because even if your data set is small, any extra data collected may not significantly improve the accuracy of the statistics generated provided that the sample you have targeted is representative of its population.

There are a number of sampling techniques available which can be used collect a representative sample. The methods considered in this chapter are:

- Simple Random Sampling
- Stratified Sampling
- Systematic Sampling
- Quota Sampling

In turn, each technique will be illustrated using simple business examples.

Simple Random Sampling

If a simple random sample is to be collected, then it must be possible for you to identify all of the population, and in turn, each individual must have the same probability of being chosen as part of the sample.

For a large population, each individual can be given a unique code (e.g. a student's registration number at University) and by using random numbers in association, a simple random sample may be collected. Spreadsheets can be used to assist in the collection of random samples because many now include a built-in random number function. In particular, Excel contains the **RAND()** function which generates uniform random numbers from 0 up to less than 1. In the table below in Figure 1.13, the personnel details of thirty employees working for a chain of shops have been recorded.

No.	Shop	Job Category	Sex	Age
1	B	Part-Time Assistant	Female	52
2	B	Full-Time Assistant	Female	26
3	C	Full-Time Assistant	Female	26
4	A	Part-Time Assistant	Female	39
5	C	Full-Time Assistant	Male	37
6	A	Full-Time Assistant	Female	22
7	A	Full-Time Assistant	Female	25
8	B	Junior Manager	Male	38
9	B	Full-Time Assistant	Male	38
10	C	Junior Manager	Male	22
11	A	Junior Manager	Female	31
12	A	Manager	Male	47
13	B	Junior Manager	Male	25
14	C	Manager	Male	38
15	C	Part-Time Assistant	Female	34
16	B	Manager	Male	43
17	A	Full-Time Assistant	Male	19
18	A	Junior Manager	Male	29
19	C	Full-Time Assistant	Female	24
20	A	Full-Time Assistant	Female	29
21	A	Full-Time Assistant	Male	37
22	B	Full-Time Assistant	Female	32
23	B	Full-Time Assistant	Male	19
24	A	Part-Time Assistant	Female	51
25	A	Part-Time Assistant	Female	28
26	B	Full-Time Assistant	Male	17
27	B	Part-Time Assistant	Female	46
28	C	Part-Time Assistant	Female	41
29	B	Part-Time Assistant	Male	34
30	B	Part-Time Assistant	Female	22

Figure 1.13 - Personnel records of thirty employees

Suppose you wish to collect a random sample of twelve employees. Inspection of the table in Figure 1.10 indicates that each employee has been given an individual employee number, i.e. 1, 2, 3, etc. up to 30. This reference may be used in combination with random numbers generated, say, by Excel. Figure 1.14 displays an Excel screen where a set of random numbers have been generated.

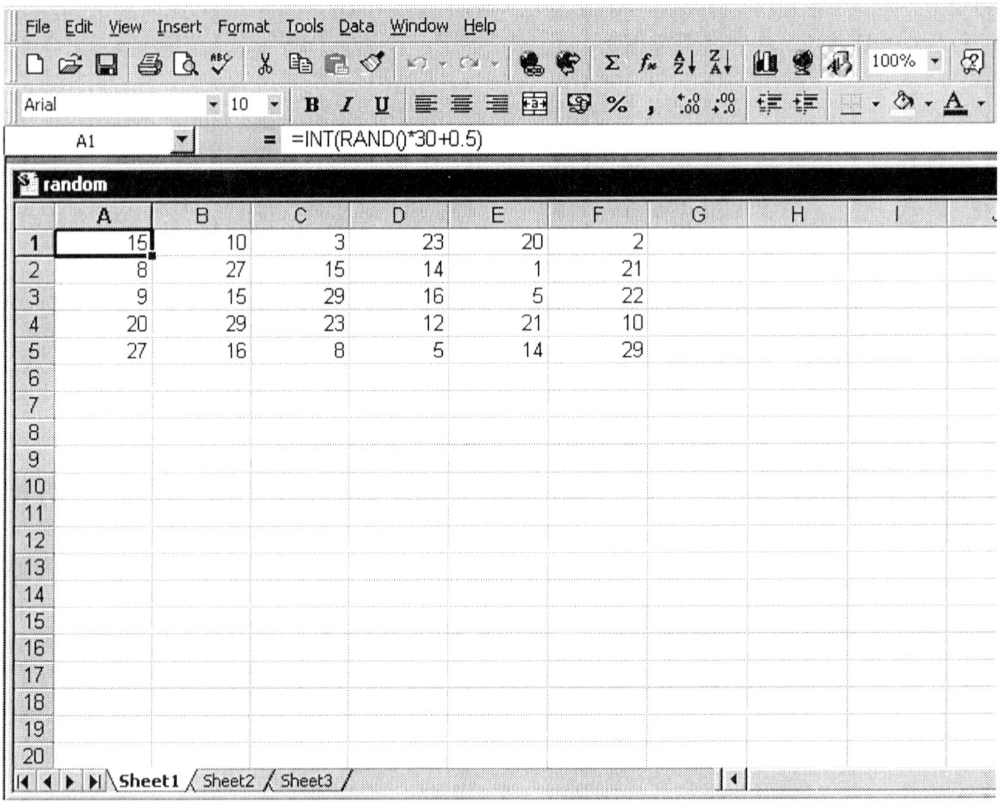

Figure 1.14 - Random numbers generated by Excel

Since the employee reference number are recorded between 1 and 30 inclusive, it would be useful to use random numbers of the same range of values. Each active cell on the worksheet displayed in Figure 1.11 contains the formula:

=INT(RAND()*30+0.5)

where the random number of value between 0 up to 1 (generated using **RAND()**) has been multiplied by 30 (because there are thirty values in the population). The value 0.5 has been added so that when Excel truncates to get a random integer (using **INT()**), the random number 30 can still be generated.

Alternatively, the following formula could be applied instead:

=ROUND(RAND()*30,0)

This function should provide all 30 employees with an equal probability of being chosen to be in the sample because the uniform numbers generated using **RAND()** assume a uniform distribution.

Inspection of the random numbers show that the first value generated is 15, so employee 15 is the first member of the sample. The next number (working left to right) is 10, so employee 10 is the second sample member. If the random numbers stored in rows 1 and 2 are applied, the number 15 is repeated. However, the relevant employee should only be selected once for your sample, and as a consequence, the second random number 15 will not be used. The sample of data collected is displayed in Figure 1.15.

No.	Shop	Job Category	Sex	Age
15	C	Part-Time Assistant	Female	34
10	C	Junior Manager	Male	22
3	C	Full-Time Assistant	Female	26
23	B	Full-Time Assistant	Male	19
20	A	Full-Time Assistant	Female	29
2	B	Full-Time Assistant	Female	26
8	B	Junior Manager	Male	38
27	B	Part-Time Assistant	Female	46
14	C	Manager	Male	38
1	B	Part-Time Assistant	Female	52
21	A	Full-Time Assistant	Male	37
9	B	Full-Time Assistant	Male	38

Figure 1.15 - Random sample of twelve employees

There are a number of advantages in collecting a random sample. The sample is unbiased since each population member has the same probability of being chosen.

However, the method may prove problematic if the population covers a dispersed area or if certain members of the population are difficult to identify. If the pre-defined sample size is small, an unrepresentative sample may be collected. For example, it is possible that you could have randomly selected a sample above with 10 out of 12 sample members being female, compared to 16 out of a population of 30 workers. In this case you may have a **unrepresentative** rather than a **representative** sample. If the sample of workers are interviewed regarding conditions of employment, equality of opportunity and career development then an unrepresentative company profile may be generated.

Stratified Sampling

To counter the problem of a simple random sample being unrepresentative, the sample can be split into sub-populations. The method of splitting a population into sub-groups in this way is known as stratification. In the example above, the chain of shops employ 30 staff, 16 female and 14 male. If the sample of staff to be surveyed needs a representative number of men and women, then the population could be split into two strata, and an appropriate number of employees could be randomly selected from each. If a sample of 15 employees was required, then 8 would be selected randomly from the strata of women employees and 7 from the male strata using random numbers using the method presented in Figures 1.14 and 1.15. Figure 1.16 illustrates the process of stratified sampling.

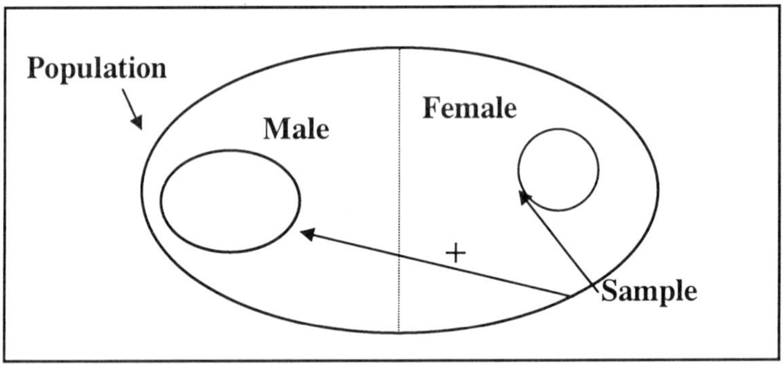

Figure 1.16 - Selecting a stratified sample

Stratified random sampling is reasonably unbiased, since each significant sub-group in the population is represented proportionately within the sample. This can be done even for small samples like the one described above.

However, you must have detailed information about the make up of the population in order to select the strata. These strata are often chosen in a biased way, e.g. should the population described above be necessarily be stratified into male and female employees? Perhaps, the population should have been stratified by shop and job grade, which although potentially more representative, makes the sampling process more complicated. If the latter was chosen, the number of strata would have been 12, i.e. 3 shops x 4 job categories. The extra complexity should be evident!

Systematic Sampling

If you are employing this sampling technique, you select every n^{th} member of the (randomly ordered) population where n is equal to **size of population size / size of required sample.**

To select a systematic sample of 10 employees from the population listed in Figure 1.13, it is possible to start arbitrarily with employee 2 and pick every 3rd (30/10) employee, i.e. 2, 5, 8 etc. The systematic sample is listed in Figure 1.17.

No.	Shop	Job Category	Sex	Age
2	B	Full-Time Assistant	Female	26
5	C	Full-Time Assistant	Male	37
8	B	Junior Manager	Male	38
11	A	Junior Manager	Female	31
14	C	Manager	Male	38
17	A	Full-Time Assistant	Male	19
20	A	Full-Time Assistant	Female	29
23	B	Full-Time Assistant	Male	19
26	B	Full-Time Assistant	Male	17
29	B	Part-Time Assistant	Male	34

Figure 1.17 - Systematic sample of 10 employees

The main advantage of a systematic sample is that it is easy to understand and a sample is easy to identify even compared the simple random and stratified sampling techniques and its main application is in the area of telephone or electoral register surveys, where every n^{th} (say every 100th) population member is selected from an alphabetic list.

Quota Sampling

When face to face interviews are the principal method of data collection, importance is placed on the interviewer obtaining a representative data set. In practice, the interviewer will have created or have been provided with a 'pre-defined' quota of people to interview. These quota may be in proportion to the population of interest for a by-election opinion poll, or alternatively, it may target specific sub-groups within the population if it forms part of a market research survey connected with the launch of a new product.

To collect the relevant data, the interviewer will identify and target an appropriate number of potential respondents for each sub-quota.

This particular technique could be used by an opinion pollster wishing to determine the outcome of a parliamentary by-election. Using this sampling technique, the population may be split by age and gender (and also perhaps by social class and postal code) and an appropriate (and in this case, proportionate) quota for each sub-group can be defined. Figure 1.18 shows electorate profile of constituency X by age and gender.

Profile of electorate - constituency X

	Gender		
Age	Male	Female	Total
18 -	2000	**1800**	3800
24 -	3500	4000	7500
30 -	8500	7200	15700
45 -	7700	6800	14500
60 +	4300	4200	8500
Total	26000	24000	**50000**

Figure 1.18 - Profile of a population by age and gender

The electorate shown above totals 50,000. If the pollster wished to predict the outcome of a by-election, a representative sample of voters must be selected. Supposing the sample size was pre-defined to be *1000* voters. This sample group can be selected by using a quota sample which consists of the appropriate number of each sub-group, e.g. 18 - < 24 year old females, 60+ males etc. In this sample the appropriate number of the former would be **1800** x *1000* / **50000** = 36. The size of each quota is presented in Figure 1.19.

Size of Quota sample - constituency X

Age	Gender: Male	Female
18 -	40	36
24 -	70	80
30 -	170	144
45 -	154	136
60 +	86	84
Total	520	480

Figure 1.19 - Size of each category in the quota sample

Because face-to-face interviews are conducted, the level of response is usually high and if the interviewer is experienced, he or she is likely to interview enough people to meet the pre-defined quotas.

However, the collection of a representative data set is perhaps too dependent upon the interviewer and is also non-random. For example, to fill the quota of young people, the interviewer may simply stand outside a college or university. This may potentially lead to bias among that particular age group for the sample of data collected. Specifically, no working 18 to 24 year olds would have been considered and this group may collectively have a different opinion to that expressed by those who were interviewed.

Survey Error

Whatever sampling technique is employed (as opposed to undertaking a census), the resultant survey of any population is unlikely to achieve totally accurate results. A number of different factors result in errors, and in general, they fall into one of three categories; unrepresentative sampling, those who don't supply information and recording mistakes.

Unrepresentative sampling

Sampling errors will occur whenever the sample selected is unrepresentative of its population. For example, you are likely to encounter **bias** if you interview a sample consisting solely of part-time female employees regarding employment conditions if the population of employees consists of equal numbers of males and females and a majority of full-time staff. These errors are generally minimised by the appropriate use of the various sampling techniques described. Equally, a public opinion pollster would not restrict their survey during a UK General Election to Northern England.

No return of information

It is likely in a survey involving people that a proportion cannot or will not take part or reply. Certain sample members may be reluctant to answer questions regarding age, personal finance or politics. Others may have moved house (but are part of a sample because they appear on the electoral register) whilst others have ex-directory telephone numbers. The latter two cannot take part in the survey. This can prove problematic if the sample consists of a relatively high proportion of people who do not answer your questions, e.g. in 1992 a number of opinion polls close to the General Election ignored a significant number of 'Don't Knows'.

Recording mistakes

Mistakes (i.e. those not caused by inappropriate sampling or by members of the target audience who don't supply information) occur from one or more of the following parts of the recording process:

- inexact reporting by the interviewer or the survey respondent completing a questionnaire.
- inaccurate coding of data in a spreadsheet or other statistical software.
- unclear questions, whose meaning may be interpreted incorrectly either by the interviewer or the respondent. This type of problem is potentially prevalent amongst postal questionnaires. However, if a survey questionnaire or interview schedule is properly piloted, any potential problems with regard to misleading questions can be highlighted, and in turn, these can be avoided during the actual survey.

Conclusions

In this chapter, you have been introduced to three particular concepts:

- types of data and sources of information
- methods of collecting primary data
- sampling techniques

Business data can be generated in a variety of ways, from a market research exercise, investigation into the proportion of defective items leaving an assembly line or the analysis of a company's major competitors. Whatever the source of this information, business data can be classified as **primary** or **secondary**.

Primary data is 'new', up to date data which has been collected regarding a particular product or project. As a consequence, primary data is relevant to your research but its collection can involve long periods of time and specialist individuals which may incur high costs. Secondary data has already been collected, and has perhaps been organised and published or is available on a database. Because of its existence, it provides inexpensive data which can be used to make decisions in business. However, this data is potentially dated, less accurate and perhaps less relevant to a particular project than the new primary data.

Whatever the origin of a business data set, it may consist of two types of variable; qualitative or quantitative. Qualitative data is non-numeric whilst quantitative data, as the name suggests is numerical. You need to be aware of the distinction between the two types of variable, and this should be taken into consideration when a data set is coded (say by using a spreadsheet like Excel) and subsequently analysed.

If data is collected from the whole of a population (subject of interest), a **census** has been carried out. For reasons of time and associated cost, it is unlikely that you will undertake a census. Data will usually be collected from a representative subset or **sample** of the population, and in doing so, you will have carried out a **survey**. In general, your data will be more representative if it collected from a big sample rather than a small sample. There are a number of different methods in which a sample can be defined, and the choice of sampling technique should be influenced by the population and the method of data collection.

If a primary data set is being collected by means of a questionnaire, and you are writing the questions, then you must be aware of the needs of the decision maker, the abilities and limitations of the target audience and the practicalities of coding and analysing the data. To assist in the latter, multiple choice questions are particularly useful, but don't generally provide the target audience with much opportunity for providing additional opinion or explanation. This can be overcome by including open ended questions in the questionnaire. However, organising and analysing the responses to an open ended question is more difficult, and as a consequence, the use of this type of question should be limited on an individual survey.

Learning Outcomes Checklist

After completing this chapter you should have an understanding of the following concepts, calculations and functions:

- The term 'statistics'.
- The difference between nominal, ordinal, continuous and discrete data.
- The difference between primary and secondary data.
- The issues involved in designing a questionnaire.
- The terms census and survey.
- The need to use pilot surveys.
- The sampling techniques; simple random, stratified random, systematic and quota samples.
- Excel's **RAND()** function.

Make sure that you understand these concepts before progressing to Chapter 2.

Chapter Case Question

The data set below contains the details of 80 public houses owned by a national chain.

Category	Location	Turnover	Beers	Promotions	Capacity	Decorated	Months
Family	Country	109500	3	2	210	Yes	18
Family	Town	73500	3	2	80	Yes	33
Family	Country	98750	3	1	80	No	33
Restaurant	Country	113750	4	2	160	No	9
Family	Country	100500	4	2	100	Yes	33
Family	Country	91500	2	2	70	No	3
Family	Country	108000	5	1	160	No	42
Family	Town	79750	3	1	60	No	1
Restaurant	Town	109500	4	3	300	No	8
Restaurant	Country	115500	4	1	200	Yes	34
Restaurant	Country	108750	4	2	150	No	25
Family	Town	67750	3	1	50	No	2
Family	Town	77750	4	2	80	Yes	25
Family	Country	107750	5	1	150	Yes	23
Restaurant	Town	111500	3	2	100	No	23
Restaurant	Country	89750	2	1	100	No	13
Restaurant	Country	93500	3	2	90	Yes	13
Restaurant	Country	90500	2	1	170	Yes	28
Family	Town	85000	3	1	80	No	11

Family	Country	105000	4	2	110	No	8
Family	Town	89750	5	1	90	Yes	27
Family	Town	78750	3	1	90	No	14
Family	Town	71250	3	2	70	Yes	21
Restaurant	Town	85000	3	1	70	Yes	43
Family	Town	58500	2	2	50	No	35
Family	Town	87500	3	3	60	Yes	22
Family	Country	95750	5	2	140	Yes	26
Family	Town	85250	3	1	80	No	18
Restaurant	Country	122500	4	3	260	Yes	21
Restaurant	Town	101000	3	1	160	No	6
Restaurant	Town	85500	3	1	70	No	17
Restaurant	Country	109750	3	1	160	No	1
Restaurant	Town	100500	4	2	200	Yes	21
Restaurant	Country	106250	4	2	150	No	23
Family	Country	103000	4	2	160	No	1
Restaurant	Country	134500	6	2	300	No	12
Family	Country	97500	3	1	160	Yes	32
Family	Town	85000	2	2	60	No	5
Family	Town	89250	4	1	70	Yes	28
Restaurant	Country	122500	4	1	260	No	28
Restaurant	Country	118750	3	1	200	No	15

Restaurant	Country	100000	3	2	170	No	2
Family	Town	91250	4	2	80	No	20
Family	Town	86500	2	2	70	Yes	13
Family	Town	86500	3	1	80	No	11
Family	Country	91250	3	2	130	Yes	19
Family	Town	85250	3	1	70	No	3
Restaurant	Country	123500	4	1	180	Yes	45
Restaurant	Town	80250	3	1	100	Yes	26
Restaurant	Country	101000	3	2	200	No	16
Family	Town	91000	3	1	90	No	33
Family	Country	103500	3	2	170	No	41
Family	Country	110000	5	2	100	No	16
Family	Town	92000	3	1	90	No	52
Restaurant	Country	110000	4	1	140	No	7
Family	Town	75500	4	1	60	No	13
Family	Town	88500	4	2	60	Yes	17
Restaurant	Town	112750	4	1	110	Yes	14
Restaurant	Town	87250	3	2	80	Yes	14
Restaurant	Town	93500	3	2	110	Yes	33
Family	Town	64250	3	2	50	No	20
Family	Town	91250	3	2	70	No	6
Family	Town	68250	2	2	30	No	4

Restaurant	Country	120500	3	2	200	Yes	22
Family	Town	80000	4	1	50	No	27
Restaurant	Country	125500	5	2	230	Yes	30
Restaurant	Country	91250	3	2	160	Yes	39
Restaurant	Town	119000	4	3	160	No	21
Family	Town	71000	3	1	40	Yes	25
Family	Town	89000	3	2	80	No	2
Restaurant	Country	121500	5	3	190	Yes	35
Restaurant	Country	93500	3	2	120	No	35
Restaurant	Country	118000	4	2	200	No	35
Restaurant	Town	101500	3	1	220	No	10
Family	Country	101000	4	1	120	No	38
Restaurant	Country	105000	4	2	140	Yes	11
Family	Town	75250	4	2	50	No	2
Family	Country	94500	3	1	80	No	7
Family	Town	71000	2	1	20	Yes	30
Family	Town	81250	3	2	60	Yes	14

- You are required to enter the data into the Excel spreadsheet into columns A to H respectively.
- Save the Excel file as **CHAP01.XLS**
- ***Reference will be made throughout the text to this data set.***
- On a separate sheet of paper describe the type of data stored in each column of the spreadsheet.

Column A	Type of Public house (i.e. Restaurant or Family pub)
Column B	Location (i.e. Town or Country)
Column C	Average monthly turnover (1997)
Column D	Number of guest beers per month
Column E	Number of drinks promotions per month
Column F	Capacity of the public house
Column G	Has it been decorated in the last 3 years (Yes or No)?
Column H	Number of months the landlord has been in post

Supplementary Questions

1. How are primary and secondary data different? Describe the advantages and disadvantages of using both types of data.

2. How are qualitative and quantitative data different? Give examples of both types of data.

3. Decide whether the following data sets are nominal, ordinal, continuous or discrete:

   (a) Makes of car sold by a motor dealer.

   (b) Number of new customers recorded monthly by a building society.

   (c) Types of mortgage offered by the building society.

   (d) Weights of jars of coffee selected from a production line.

   (e) World men and women's tennis ranking.

   (f) Ages of citizens of Birmingham.

   (g) Number of complaints recorded daily by a bus operator.

   (h) Degree classification obtained by a cohort of graduates.

4. A supermarket wishes to relocate and open a new store at an out-of-town shopping centre and is keen to determine its viability. What data needs to be collected and what method of collection should be used?

5. For a parliamentary by-election, an opinion poll was carried out using a telephone survey. What are the advantages and disadvantages of using this method of data collection? If the survey was carried out between 9am and 5pm, would this improve the quality of the data collected?

6. An engineering company wishes to profile the lifestyle of its employees. Among the questions listed on a questionnaire were:

   (a) Do you smoke?

   (b) Do you drink?

   (c) Do you take exercise?

   (d) Have you visited your doctor in the last 12 months?

   What problems may occur from asking these questions? Re-write these questions bearing in mind the type of respondent and the method of analysis is by spreadsheet. You may need to use more than 4 questions in your re-write.

7. What is the difference between a survey and a census? Why is it necessary to collect data from a representative sample? Describe the possible sampling techniques which can be used, outlining their positive and negative aspects.

8. Describe the most appropriate method of sampling for the following situations:

   (a) Determining the proportion of 'light' and 'heavy' bags of sugar from a production line.

   (b) Quantifying the public attitude towards a single European Market.

   (c) Measuring the attitude of students towards leaving the NUS.

   (d) Determining the viability of a new low alcohol lager.

9. A mail order company has 100,000 customers which have been broken down in percentage form by age and gender below:

Age	Gender	
	Male	Female
18 -	11	15
24 -	12	16
30 -	9	12
40 -	6	7
50 -	3	4
60 +	1	4

The company wants to introduce a new method of payment and wishes to measure the opinions of its customers. A budget has been agreed which would allow 2000 customers to be contacted.

(a) Describe the advantages in using a quota sample.

(b) Referring to the answer above, what is the profile of the sample selected?

10. Why is it important to pilot a survey? Describe the benefits gained from a pilot study.

11. The NE Lending Co. offers financial advice and loans for the personal market. It operates 40 offices in the North East of England. The locations are listed below:

Location of offices - NE Lending Co.

1.	Annfield Plain	21.	Morpeth
2.	Ashington	22.	Newcastle upon Tyne
3.	Birtley	23.	Newton Aycliffe
4.	Blyth	24.	North Shields
5.	Boldon	25.	Peterlee
6.	Chester-le-Street	26.	Redcar
7.	Consett	27.	Saltburn *
8.	Darlington	28.	Seaham
9.	Durham	29.	Sedgefield *
10.	Eaglescliffe	30.	South Shields
11.	Easington	31.	Spennymoor
12.	Gateshead	32.	Stanley
13.	Hartlepool	33.	Stockton
14.	Hebburn	34.	Sunderland
15.	Hexham	35.	Tynemouth
16.	Houghton-le-Spring	36.	Wallsend
17.	Jarrow	37.	Washington
18.	Killingworth	38.	Whitburn *
19.	Lanchester	39.	Whitley Bay *
20.	Middlesbrough	40.	Yarm

The General Manager wishes to determine the volume of new business by analysing the records of a sample of offices.

(a) With the aid of the random numbers listed below, identify a random sample of 10 branches.

7	15	1	1	1	2	6	13	5	5	13	11
4	12	3	3	7	12	15	9	8	11	2	13
19	10	11	20	8	2	20	7	14	20	2	8
0	13	3	14	7	10	14	12	18	8	12	18
8	7	4	9	16	17	13	19	14	10	6	3

(b) Generate another set of random numbers using Excel and repeat the sampling exercise described above.

(c) The asterisk (*) next to the name of certain offices signifies that these are small outlets. The remaining offices are assumed to be standard. Using the stratified technique, identify a sample of 10 offices for the General Manager.

(d) Identify a systematic sample of ten branches.

(e) Which method gives the most appropriate sample? Give reasons for your answer.

Chapter 2

Using Tables to Simplify a Data Set

Learning Outcomes

In this chapter you will see a number of ways in which a primary data set can be converted into meaningful information. It will be shown how simple techniques such as sorting and tabular summary can enhance the presentation of a business data set.

After completing this chapter you will be able to:

- Sort a data set to enhance its presentation and make the data more manageable.
- Simplify a primary data set using one and two variable tables.
- Compute simple summary measures such as totals for one and two variable tables.
- Identify the most important features of a data set by inspection of its tabular presentation.
- Create frequency and cumulative frequency distributions for continuous data.
- Use the built-in facilities offered by Excel to sort a data set, produce two variable tables and generate both frequency and cumulative frequency distributions.

Introduction

Once a primary data set has been collected, it is may well have to be presented in a more readable and meaningful way. A small set of business data is displayed in

Figure 2.1, which refers to the personnel details of the thirty employees who work for a chain store called *Ideal World*. This chain consists of three shops. From the data set listed in Figure 2.1, it is not easy to determine by quick inspection the number of males and females employed by the chain, let alone quantify the age range of the various employees. In this chapter, you will consider this data set and determine how even a relatively small amount of data can be converted into meaningful information.

In particular, a variety of tables will be generated, paying attention to whether the variables under consideration are categorical, ordinal, discrete or continuous. The type of data will determine the intervals or categories used in the tabular presentation of the data.

The data set presented consists of four variables:

- The shop at which the employee works (i.e. shop A, B or C).

- The employees job category (Manager, Junior Manager, Full-Time Assistant or Part-Time Assistant).

- The employee's sex.

- The employee's age (between a minimum of 16 and maximum of 60, the company's retirement age).

Shop	Job Category	Sex	Age
B	Part-Time Assistant	Female	52
B	Full-Time Assistant	Female	26
C	Full-Time Assistant	Female	26
A	Part-Time Assistant	Female	39
C	Full-Time Assistant	Male	37
A	Full-Time Assistant	Female	22
A	Full-Time Assistant	Female	25
B	Junior Manager	Male	38
B	Full-Time Assistant	Male	38
C	Junior Manager	Male	22
A	Junior Manager	Female	31
A	Manager	Male	47
B	Junior Manager	Male	25
C	Manager	Male	38
C	Part-Time Assistant	Female	34
B	Manager	Male	43
A	Full-Time Assistant	Male	19
A	Junior Manager	Male	29
C	Full-Time Assistant	Female	24
A	Full-Time Assistant	Female	29
A	Full-Time Assistant	Male	37
B	Full-Time Assistant	Female	32
B	Full-Time Assistant	Male	19
A	Part-Time Assistant	Female	51
A	Part-Time Assistant	Female	28
B	Full-Time Assistant	Male	17
B	Part-Time Assistant	Female	46
C	Part-Time Assistant	Female	41
B	Part-Time Assistant	Male	34
B	Part-Time Assistant	Female	22

Figure 2.1 - Raw data set consisting of personnel information

Sorting a Data Set

Before creating any tables to summarise this data set, the appearance of the personnel records can be greatly simplified if they are sorted, perhaps either by shop or job category. Sorting the data in order to make it more meaningful is a reasonable approach for this particular example because the data set is small. For larger data sets you would need to go one step further and use tabular presentation. This will be addressed shortly.

Figure 2.2 shows the sorted list, where the personnel details have been sorted first by shop and then by job category for each shop in the chain.

Shop	Job Category	Sex	Age
A	Manager	Male	47
A	Junior Manager	Female	31
A	Junior Manager	Male	29
A	Full-Time Assistant	Female	22
A	Full-Time Assistant	Female	25
A	Full-Time Assistant	Male	19
A	Full-Time Assistant	Female	29
A	Full-Time Assistant	Male	37
A	Part-Time Assistant	Female	39
A	Part-Time Assistant	Female	51
A	Part-Time Assistant	Female	28
B	Manager	Male	43
B	Junior Manager	Male	25
B	Junior Manager	Male	38
B	Full-Time Assistant	Female	26
B	Full-Time Assistant	Male	38
B	Full-Time Assistant	Female	32
B	Full-Time Assistant	Male	19
B	Full-Time Assistant	Male	17
B	Part-Time Assistant	Male	34
B	Part-Time Assistant	Female	22
B	Part-Time Assistant	Female	52
B	Part-Time Assistant	Female	46
C	Manager	Male	38
C	Junior Manager	Male	22
C	Full-Time Assistant	Female	24
C	Full-Time Assistant	Female	26
C	Full-Time Assistant	Male	37
C	Part-Time Assistant	Female	34
C	Part-Time Assistant	Female	41

Figure 2.2 - Raw data set sorted by shop and job category

By sorting the data you have obtained a clearer indication of the staffing levels at the three shops, e.g. each shop employs a similar number of staff on managerial grades. You can now use the sorted data set to produce the various tabular information. Before any tables are created, there are a number of important points which should be considered.

Rules for Tabulating Data

When tabulating a data set, you must ensure the rules listed below are obeyed when determining the categories or class intervals to be used:

- the table consists of an exhaustive range of categories or intervals.
- the categories or intervals are distinct.
- the number of categories is not excessive.

If you are creating a table, the chosen categories (for nominal data) or intervals (for quantitative data) must be exhaustive so that every label or value in the data set is recorded in the resultant table. If the number of categories is large, those categories which are only marginally represented can be combined to form an individual category called **'Other'**, and in doing so, simplify the appearance of the tabular summary. This is illustrated in the by-election result pictured in Figure 2.3 where the votes obtained by the bottom six parties represent only about 0.7% of the total votes cast. Replacing them with the label **'Others'** has simplified the table of results, without hiding the most significant statistic in the table, namely that Labour won the by-election with a majority in excess of 14,000 votes.

By-Election - Seaport West	
Labour	26253
Conservative	12008
Liberal Democrat	4105
Green	495
UK Independence	103
Loony	57
Workers Party	55
Independent	42
Natural Law	41
Death off the Roads	18

By-Election - Seaport West	
Labour	26253
Conservative	12008
Liberal Democrat	4105
Green	495
Others	316

Figure 2.3 - Simplifying tabular output

However, if the category 'Other' is used in a table, then you should ensure that its frequency is not too large relative to the size of the data set. If the Liberal Democrat and Green votes were included in the 'Other' category, it would consist of 11.4% of the total votes cast and as a consequence, potentially useful information is lost from the display of the election result.

When intervals are included on a table, they must be distinct. For those responsible for collecting, recording and analysing the data, there should be no confusion about where to record each data value. You must be precise when you are recording continuous data, examples including the salaries for the staff employed by a retailer or the ages of a group canvassed by a market researcher. A table recording the ages of the group of employees listed in Figure 2.1 should **not** be 16-20, 20-30, 30-40 and so on, because confusion would occur when recording the age of respondents who are exactly 20, 30 or 40 years old. In this case the age groups used are not distinct, i.e. they overlap. A more suitable classification would be 16-19, 20-29, 30-39, because none of the age intervals overlap. These problems don't usually occur so often with categorical data.

Finally, the number of categories or intervals should not be excessive. For the age data displayed in Figure 2.1, 5 to 10 classes could be used. If too many categories or intervals are used on a table, the resultant presentation may well be little different to the raw data set. However, if too few classes are used then a lot of useful information may be lost in the simplification.

Creating One and Two Variable Tables

Considering the personnel records for the chain of shops you can summarise the data by using a number of simple one and two variable tables. Figure 2.4 displays two tables which summarise the staff separately by gender and job category. Both data sets are similar in that they consist of categorical data. To complete the tables you must total all of the staff who fall into the respective categories.

Table A - Sex of Staff

Sex	Frequency (No. of Staff)
Male	14
Female	16
TOTAL	30

Table B - Job Category of Staff

Job Category	Frequency
Manager	3
Junior Manager	5
Full-Time Assistant	13
Part-Time Assistant	9
TOTAL	30

Source: Staff Records, Ideal World

Figure 2.4 - Frequency Tables for Categorical Data

It is important to note that both tables in Figure 2.4 contain a meaningful title whilst each column and row have been given meaningful headings in both tables. The heading 'Frequency' refers to the number of staff who fall into each category.

Additionally, both tables display column totals which represent the total number of staff employed by the company and the origin of the personnel information has been included underneath the tables, i.e. Staff Records, Ideal World.

From a decision maker's perspective, these two simple tables provide useful personnel information. For example, Table A indicates that the company employs an almost equal number of males and females, whilst Table B suggests the biggest category of employee is full-time assistant and 30% of the staff (i.e. 9 out of 30) are part-time.

The next variable to consider is staff age which is an example of continuous, quantitative data. As a **raw** data set (i.e. when the individual ages of the employees are presented, as shown in Figure 2.1), the distribution of this type of data is generally the hardest to explain by simple inspection. Once quantitative data is sorted into classes (known as intervals) the individual values may be unavailable and the grouped data will not provide you with as much information as the raw data set. In short, there is a trade-off between making continuous data more presentable and manageable with the loss of specific information.

To decide on the class intervals in which to divide a continuous data set, it is useful to initially determine the minimum and maximum values of the data set. For the personnel records listed above the minimum and maximum ages are 17 and 52 respectively. The intervals you should use on this table must cover all of this range.

A useful set of classes may be 16-19, 20-29, 30-39, 40-49, 50-59, which are continuous, non-overlapping and as suggested, cover all possible ages between 16 and 59 inclusive. Using 5 intervals for the size of data set is also reasonable. This choice of classes demonstrates that the selected intervals **don't necessarily have to be of equal width**.

Now that the intervals have been selected it is necessary to consider each value individually and use ***tally marks*** to count the number of employees whose age falls in each of the intervals listed. The resultant frequency distribution table is displayed in Figure 2.5. The notation '- <' used in each row of the table means up to but not including and you should note that this table contains a meaningful title, labels for each row and column, a summary total of staff and a reference to the data's origin.

Table C - Distribution of Staff Ages

Staff Age (Years)	**Tally**	**Frequency**
16 - < 20	1 1 1	3
20 - < 30	1 1 1 1 1 1 1 1 1 1 1	11
30 - < 40	1 1 1 1 1 1 1 1 1 1	10
40 - < 50	1 1 1 1	4
50 - < 60	1 1	2
TOTAL		30

Source: Staff Records, Ideal World.

Figure 2.5 - Frequency distribution of staff ages

Inspection of the frequency distribution tells us that the most common age group is 20 to less than 30 and that 70% (21 out of 30) of the staff are aged between 20 and 40. An additional method of displaying quantitative data is by using a cumulative frequency table. The cumulative frequency table shows that the total number of staff who are below a certain age, and is displayed in Figure 2.6. The cumulative frequency indicates the number of values in a data set which lie below pre-defined limits and you can use the upper class boundaries of the intervals used in the frequency distribution for the value of the limits. It should be noted the cumulative frequency for the first interval is zero (i.e. the number of staff less than the age of the youngest employee) and 30 (the total number of values in the data set) for the final interval.

Table D - Cumulative Distribution of Staff Ages

Staff Age (Years)	Cumulative Frequency
Less than 16 (or < 16)	0
Less than 20	3
Less than 30	14
Less than 40	24
Less than 50	28
Less than 60	30

Source: Staff Records, Ideal World.

Figure 2.6 - Cumulative frequency distribution of staff ages

Again, useful observations can be made from this table. For example, 24 out of the 30 staff (which represents 80% of the company's employees) are aged under 40. This information could be used to make decisions regarding short term and long term recruitment and promotion opportunities within the organisation.

Tabulation of Two Variables

It is often appropriate to tabulate two variables on an individual table. A table which consists of two or more variables is referred to as a **cross-tabulation**. Figure 2.7 displays a cross-tabulation of shop by job category. Included on the table are sub-totals for each shop and job category and a **cross-total** which represents the total number of employees. Inspection of the table suggests that the distribution of staff by grade is **similar** for all three shops.

Table E - Grade of Staff by Shop

			Job Category		
Shop	**Manager**	**Junior Manager**	**Full-Time Assistant**	**Part-Time Assistant**	**TOTAL**
A	1	2	5	3	11
B	1	2	5	4	12
C	1	1	3	2	7
TOTAL	3	5	13	9	30

Source: Staff Records, Ideal World.

Figure 2.7 - Cross-tabulation of shop data

The principal of tabulation may also be applied to three or more variables. However, increasing the number of variables considered may make the table hard to read and potentially useful information may be lost or hidden. In general, it is usually better to display the data using a number of the simpler one and two variable tables rather than provide a business decision maker with one large and relatively complex display.

Finally, you may wish to compare data from two or more separate data sets. If the data sets are of similar size then comparison can be made using actual frequencies. However, if the data sets are significantly different in size a better comparison may be made if percentage frequencies are used instead. In Figure 2.8, the results of two by-elections are presented as frequency of votes and percentage of votes cast. Comparison of the performance of the respective parties is much easier when considering the percentages, since the total number of votes cast in the two campaigns are quite different in size. However, if the total number of votes were 43500 and 44100 respectively, a comparison of either frequencies or percentage frequencies would be reasonable.

Votes cast at two by-elections (frequencies)

	Election A	**Election B**
Labour	26253	31348
Conservative	12008	14256
Liberal Democrat	4105	10778
Green	495	375
Others	316	100
Totals	43177	56857

% Votes cast at two by-elections (percentage frequencies)

	Election A	**Election B**
Labour	60.8%	55.1%
Conservative	27.8%	25.1%
Liberal Democrat	9.5%	19.0%
Green	1.1%	0.7%
Others	0.7%	0.2%

Figure 2.8 - Comparing frequencies and percentage frequencies

Using the Facilities Offered by Excel to Summarise a Data Set

Sorting Data

Sorting a data set in Excel is an easy task to undertake. All of the data, *including the titles*, must first be highlighted by dragging with the mouse. If you consider the personnel records described so far in the chapter, you would have to highlight four columns of data, namely shop, job category, sex and age, including the column titles, which may have been typed into the spreadsheet. To sort the data set, you must activate:

Data
Sort

This produces the window pictured in Figure 2.9. In the first key box (labelled **Sort By**), you need to select a row heading from the menu (hence it is useful to include titles on the worksheet and as a consequence, the facility **Header Row** is applied in the sort box below)

From this menu, you can choose Shop so that all records for A are stored together, followed by those for shops B and C respectively. Specifically, you have chosen to sort in **Ascending** order, i.e. alphabetic order for textual data and smallest to largest value for quantitative data, so that shop A appears at the top of the list. The **Then By** field represents the next variable which you sort by, i.e. job category. Again, you will sort in alphabetic order. By clicking OK you produce the sorted list shown in Figure 2.9, where the employees of Shop A are listed together and within this sub list, they are sorted by job-grade. The same follows for employees at shops B and C.

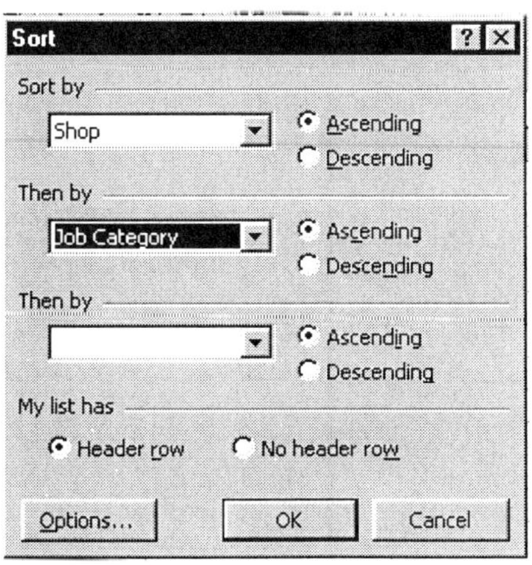

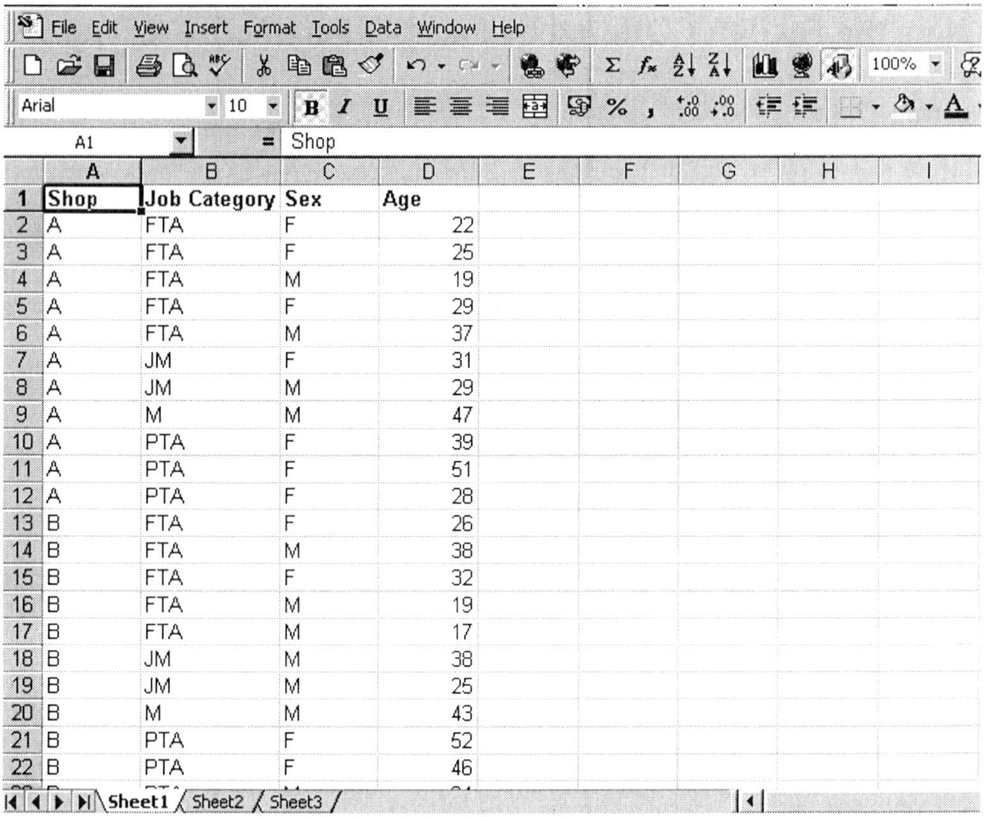

	A	B	C	D
1	Shop	Job Category	Sex	Age
2	A	FTA	F	22
3	A	FTA	F	25
4	A	FTA	M	19
5	A	FTA	F	29
6	A	FTA	M	37
7	A	JM	F	31
8	A	JM	M	29
9	A	M	M	47
10	A	PTA	F	39
11	A	PTA	F	51
12	A	PTA	F	28
13	B	FTA	F	26
14	B	FTA	M	38
15	B	FTA	F	32
16	B	FTA	M	19
17	B	FTA	M	17
18	B	JM	M	38
19	B	JM	M	25
20	B	M	M	43
21	B	PTA	F	52
22	B	PTA	F	46

Figure 2.9 - Excel's Data Sort box and a sorted data set

Generating two variable tables

Excel also allows us to generate two variable tables using the **pivot table** facility. To activate this routine, you must select:

> **Data**
> **PivotTable Report**

which results in the menu routine displayed step-by-step in Figure 2.10.

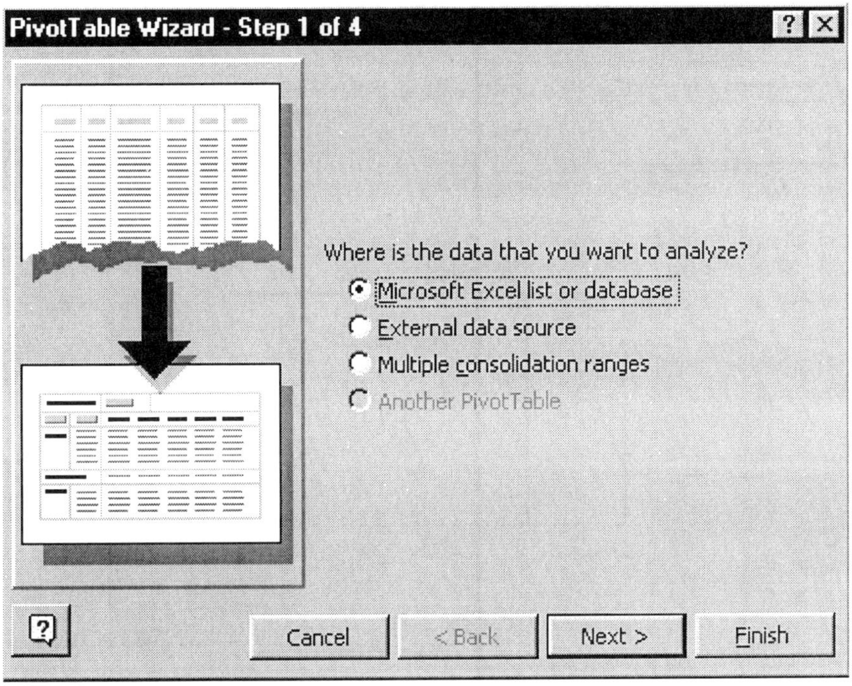
PivotTable Wizard - Step 1 of 4
Where is the data that you want to analyze?
Microsoft Excel list or database
External data source
Multiple consolidation ranges
Another PivotTable
Cancel
< Back
Next >
Finish

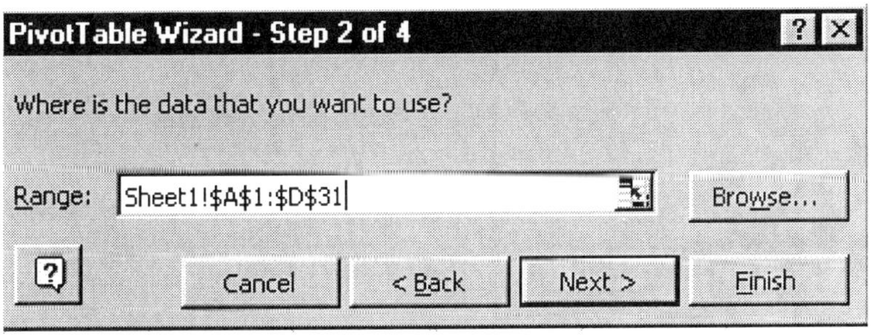
PivotTable Wizard - Step 2 of 4
Where is the data that you want to use?
Range:
Sheet1!$A$1:$D$31
Browse...
Cancel
< Back
Next >
Finish

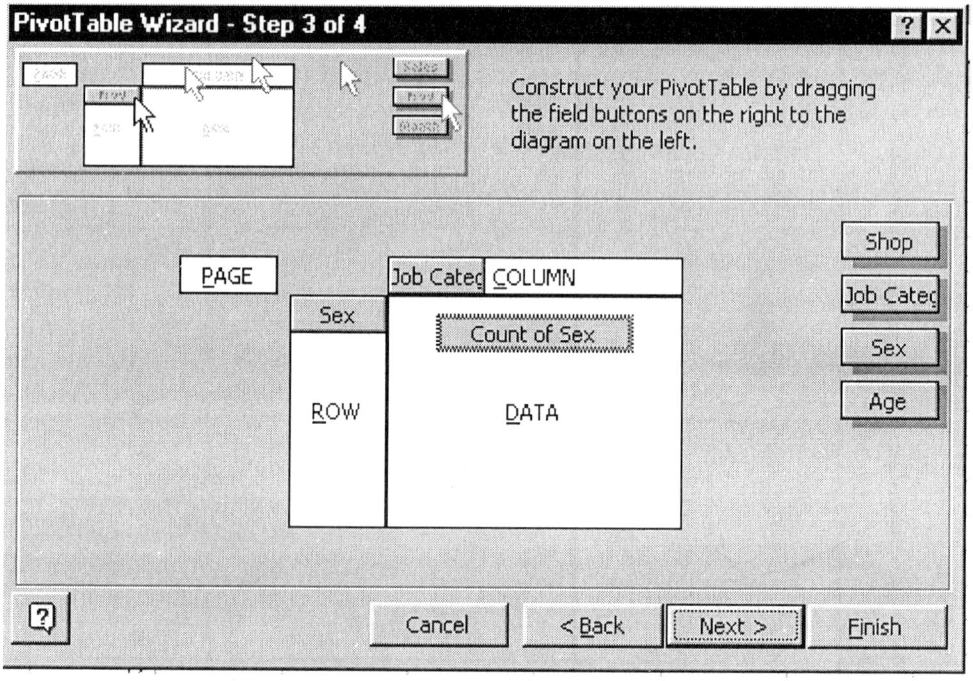

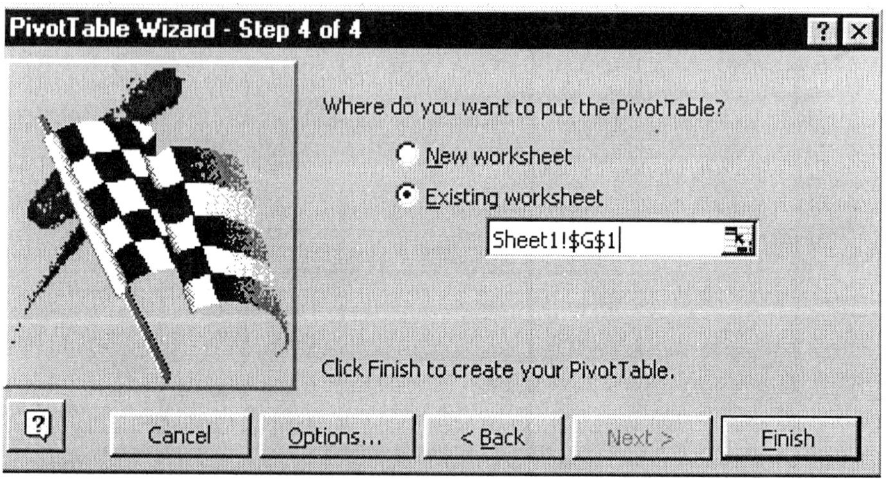

Figure 2.10 - Excel's PivotTable menu

On entering the PivotTable menu you want to create a new table from data stored in a Microsoft Excel list, i.e. the default option.

By selecting **Next**, you can define the data range which **includes *the single row of titles in row 1***, i.e. Shop, Job Category, Sex and Age. Including the row headings ensures that the field buttons take on the column titles.

Clicking on **Next** again, Excel asks you to define the row fields, column fields and data by dragging and dropping the field name (i.e. Shop, job Category, Sex and Age) buttons into the customised fields diagram given in step 3. In this case, our row field was **sex**, the column field **job category** and the data count was **sex** (i.e. how many of each gender work in each job category).

Clicking on **Next** takes us to the end of the PivotTable. Here, you can define the location for printing the table. Clicking on **Finish** will create the table as shown in Figure 2.11. The output created is numerical rather than as formulae. Therefore, if any changes are made to the data set, the pivot table process would have to be repeated to create an updated table.

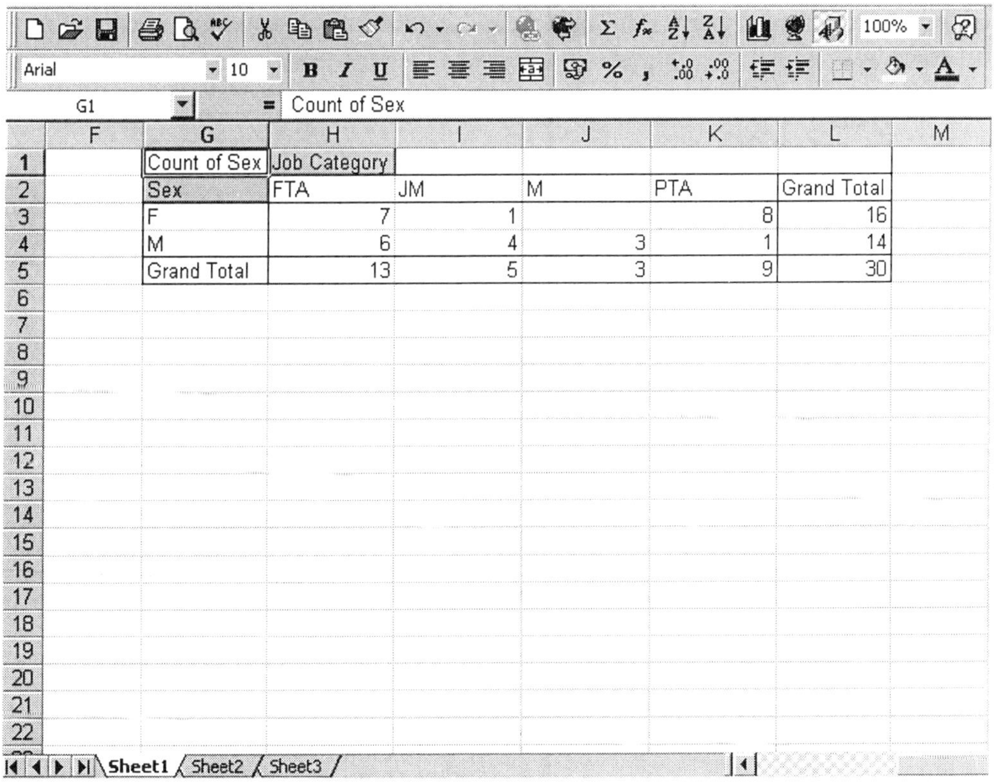

Count of Sex	Job Category				
Sex	FTA	JM	M	PTA	Grand Total
F	7	1		8	16
M	6	4	3	1	14
Grand Total	13	5	3	9	30

Figure 2.11 - Table generated by PivotTable

Inspection of the table above suggests that all managers are Male as are 4 of the 5 Junior Managers. The table also suggest that a majority of both categories of assistant are Female. This information may have implications on future recruitment and promotions.

Finally, if you wanted to generate a two variable table which includes either one or two quantitative variables, these must be converted into named groups (i.e. into nominal data) if they contain a wide range of values before activating PivotTable Report as shown above. An example of categorising a quantitative variable may be categorising number of days sick leave at a factory (which is a discrete quantitative variable) as 1 - 10 days, 11 - 20 days and so on which may be named Minor to Serious say, and then cross-tabulated against a categorical variable such as department name, e.g. engineering, administration etc.

Creating frequency and cumulative frequency tables using Excel

For a continuous data set such as employee age in the previous example, you can create frequency and cumulative frequency tables using a specific built-in facility offered by the spreadsheet. Both tables can be generated automatically using Excel by activating:

> **Tools**
> **Data Analysis**

and selecting the **Histogram** facility.

You can consider the following example. A medium sized manufacturing company wants to determine the typical amount of expenses claimed by its sales and administration team. Data was collected from the staff for one month and is shown in Figure 2.12.

Monthly Expenses (£) - June 1994

96	23	7	55	36	23	22	18	56	45
37	39	67	43	9	69	27	58	51	30

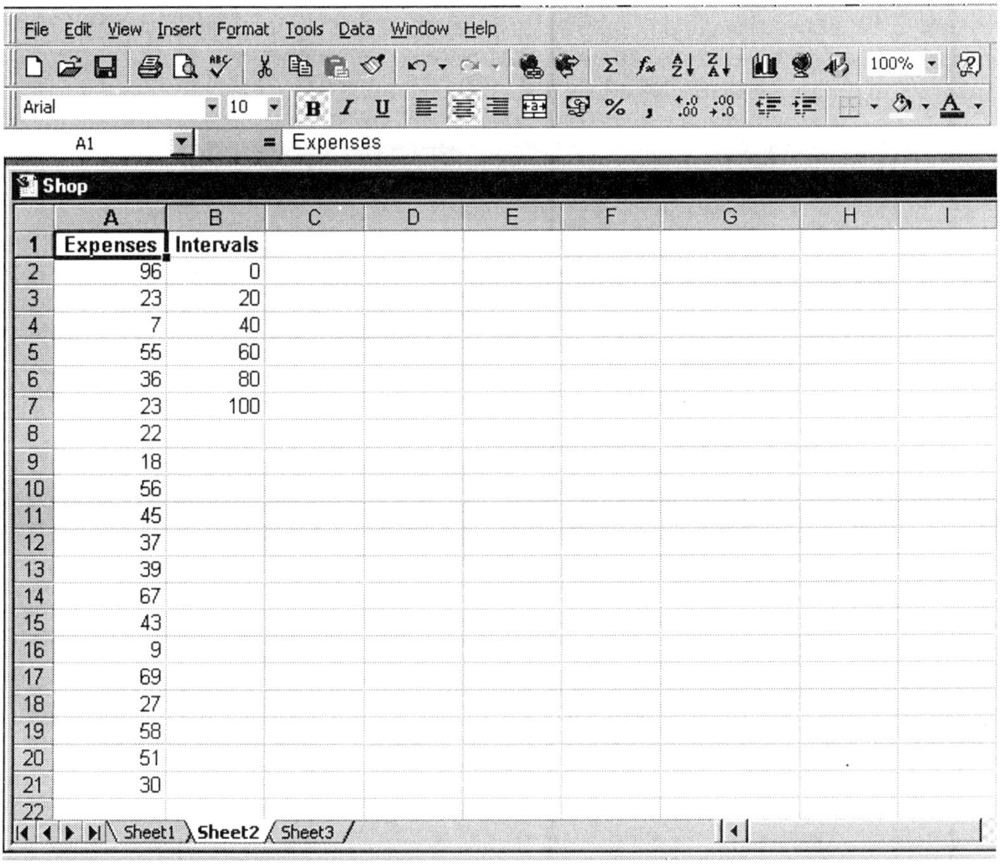

	A	B
1	Expenses	Intervals
2	96	0
3	23	20
4	7	40
5	55	60
6	36	80
7	23	100
8	22	
9	18	
10	56	
11	45	
12	37	
13	39	
14	67	
15	43	
16	9	
17	69	
18	27	
19	58	
20	51	
21	30	

Figure 2.12 - Monthly expenses and the corresponding Excel worksheet

To create a frequency table you have to first decide on the intervals. These intervals are optional, but if not defined, Excel will create equally spaced intervals between the minimum and maximum values in the data set. In other words, for the expense data shown above the first interval would start at the value 7. In Figure 2.12, the column labelled '**Intervals**' represent the class intervals. The first interval defined in Figure 2.12 represents all expense claims which are less than or equal to £0, the next interval will consist of claims which are greater than £0 but less than or equal to £20, and so on.

After activating the Histogram facility, the box presented in Figure 2.13 appears. For the expenses data the input range is **A2:A21** (the expense claims) and the interval range is **B2:B7**. The output range, given by cell reference **E1** has been chosen so that the resultant table does not overwrite any of the data set and you have selected to calculate the cumulative percentage (as indicated by the **tick** in the relevant box).

Figure 2.13 shows the tabular output. Inspection of this table suggest that the most common level of monthly expense is £20-40 and the cumulative percentage table suggests that 85% of staff claim less than £60 per month.

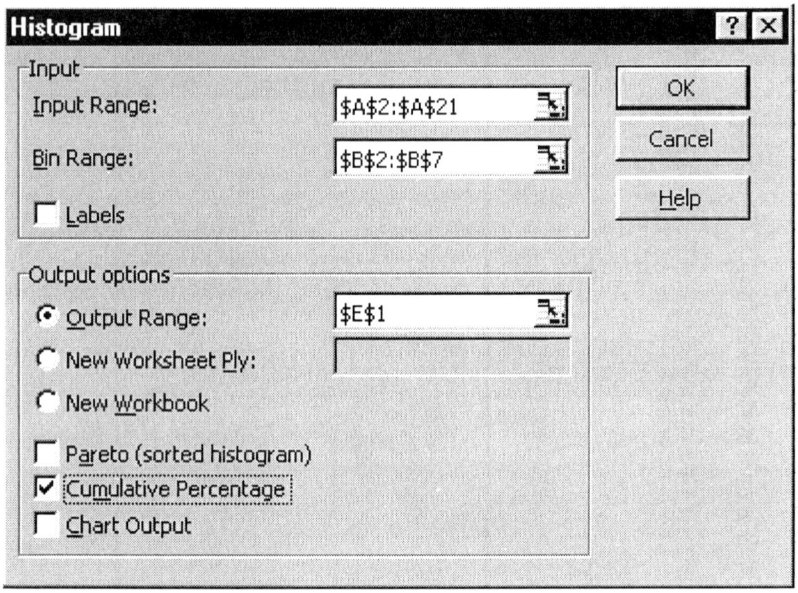

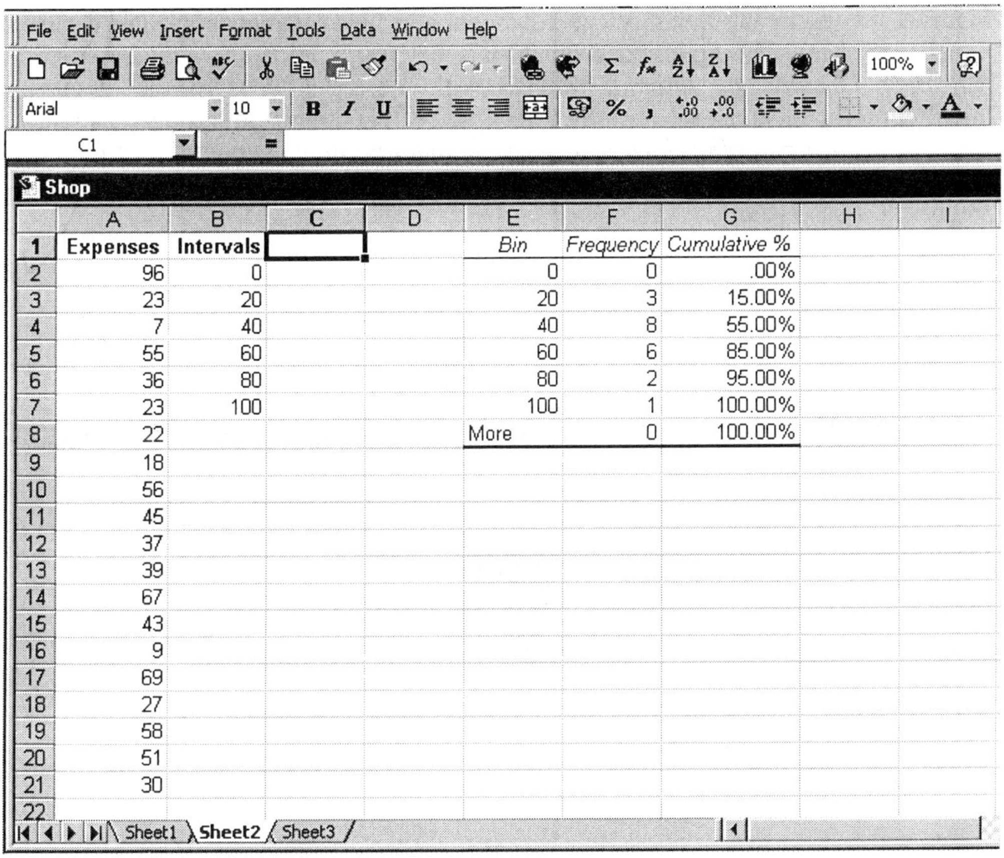

	Expenses	Intervals		Bin	Frequency	Cumulative %
2	96	0		0	0	.00%
3	23	20		20	3	15.00%
4	7	40		40	8	55.00%
5	55	60		60	6	85.00%
6	36	80		80	2	95.00%
7	23	100		100	1	100.00%
8	22			More	0	100.00%
9	18					
10	56					
11	45					
12	37					
13	39					
14	67					
15	43					
16	9					
17	69					
18	27					
19	58					
20	51					
21	30					

Figure 2.13 - Frequency distribution table generated by Excel's histogram facility

The method you have seen above is simple to use but creates numerical rather than formula based output. Any changes to the data will not be updated automatically in the frequency table. An alternative way of generating frequency and cumulative frequency distributions which are responsive to changes in the data is to activate the array command **FREQUENCY()**. This command has the structure:

FREQUENCY(data,intervals)

where:

data corresponds to the data to be tabulated (numerical data only)which is cell referenced as a block.

intervals corresponds to the predetermined intervals

Figure 2.14 shows the monthly expenses data and interval ranges displayed on the Excel worksheet. The highlighted block of cells (*which must be equal in length to the block housing the interval ranges*) will subsequently store the frequency distribution for this data set once the FREQUENCY() command has been activated. ***This block must be highlighted before the command name is entered into Excel. If it is not highlighted, then the FREQUENCY() command will not generate the frequency distribution.***

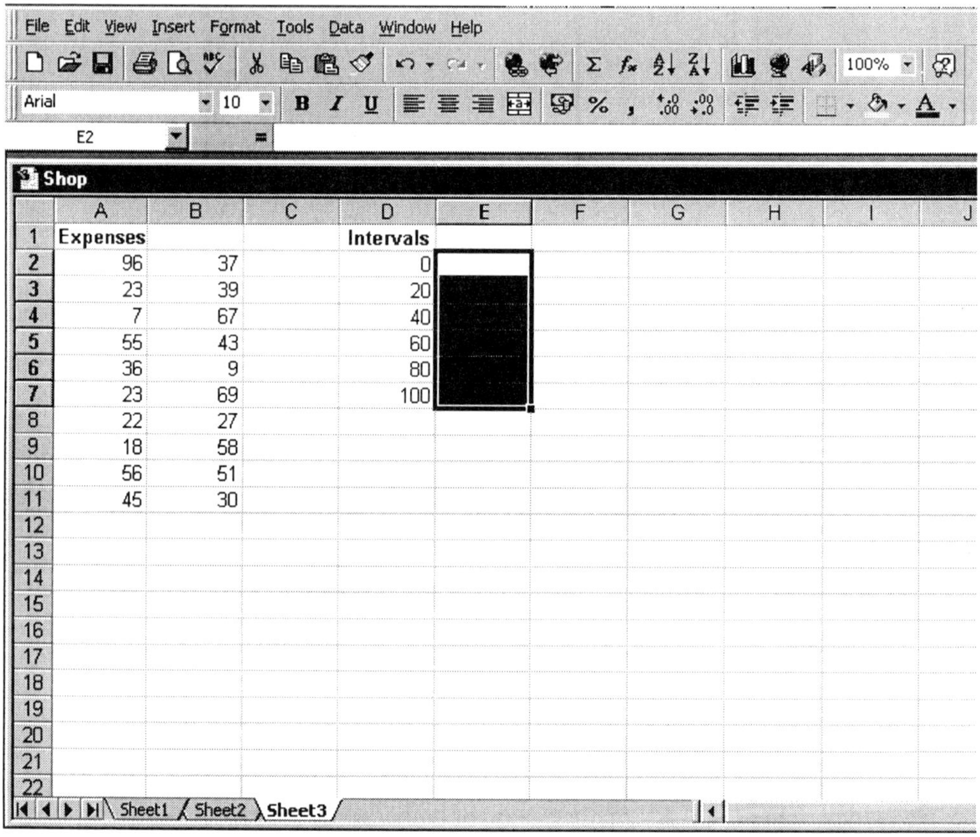

Figure 2.14 - Data set and interval range entered into Excel

In order to generate the frequency distribution, the following command should be typed into cell **E2** (i.e. the top cell in the highlighted block):

=FREQUENCY(A2:B11,D2:D7)

where:

A2:B11 represents the expenses data (i.e. the data range)

D2:D7 represents the intervals

Since you are using an array command, this should be entered into Excel after typing by pressing **CTRL SHIFT RETURN** rather than simply RETURN. The appearance off the command on the formula bar will resemble:

{=FREQUENCY(A2:B11,D2:D7)}

where the braces **{}** signify an array command has been activated.

Figure 2.15 pictures the frequency distribution generated. The first value 0 indicates that no expense claims are less than or equal to £0 (≤ 0), whilst the second value 3 tells us that you have 3 claims which are greater than £0 but less than or equal to £20 (i.e. 0 < x ≤ 20, so they don't include £0, ensuring the intervals are non-overlapping).

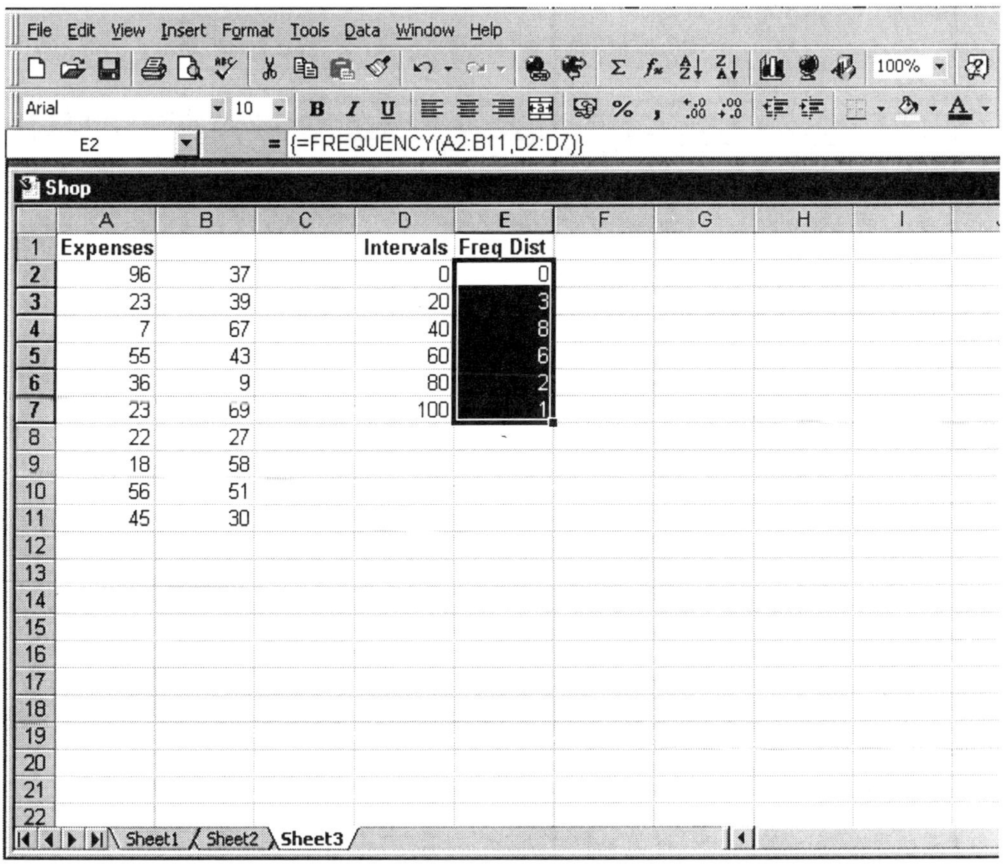

Figure 2.15 - Frequency distribution generated by Excel

However, if you want to create a frequency table with intervals < 20, 20 - < 30, 30 - < 40 etc., the interval range would have to be 19, 29, 39 and so on (since you are dealing with whole numbers in this example) given that Excel counts all values up to an including those equal to the top of the interval range.

Finally, to generate the cumulative frequency distribution,

=FREQUENCY($A$2:$B$11,D2)

was entered into cell **F2** this time be simply pressing **RETURN**. The absolute referencing (signified by the dollar signs) fixes the data array reference and can be added by pressing the **F4** key after highlighting the relevant range. The formula can be copied by dragging with the mouse to the appropriate cells below.

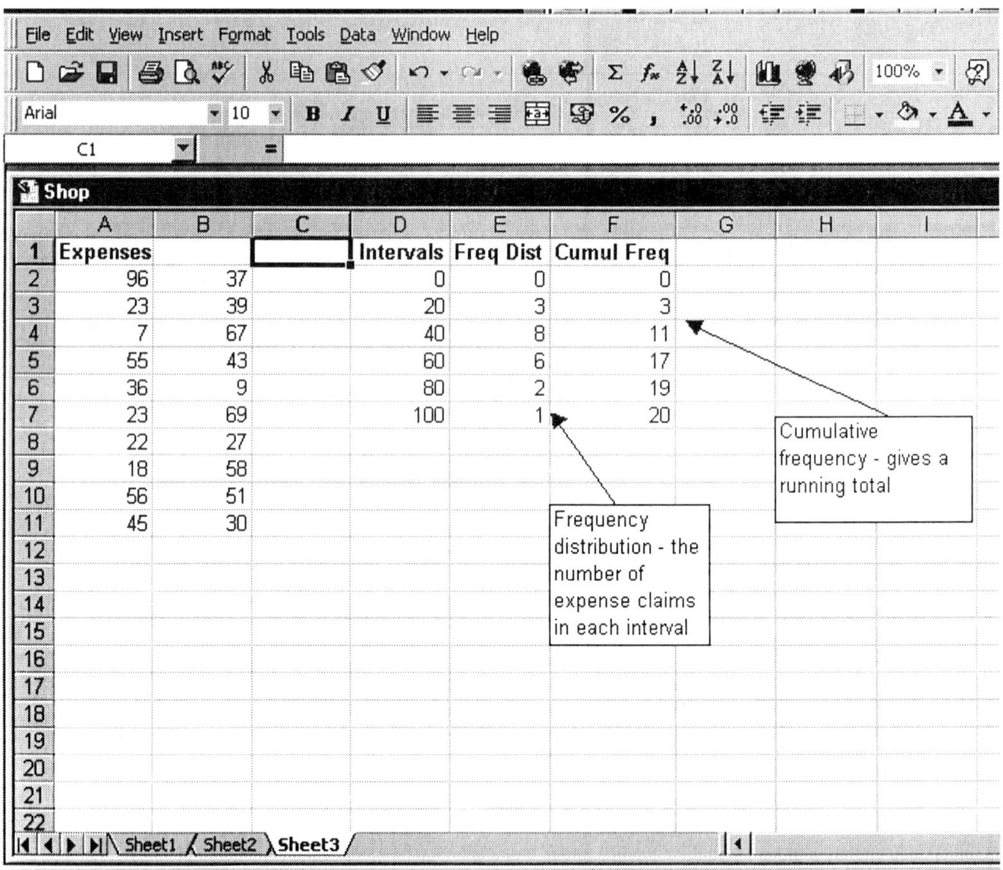

Figure 2.16 - Cumulative frequency distribution

Inspection of the cumulative frequency table in figure 2.16 tells us that 17 out of the 20 sales representatives have a monthly expense claim of less than or equal to £60. The advantage of using the **FREQUENCY()** command is that it provides functional rather than numerical output. As a consequence, its output will update automatically to any changes made to the data array.

Conclusions

In this chapter you have seen how a raw data set can be converted into meaningful information using simple techniques such as sorting and tabular summary.

In particular, four powerful facilities offered by Excel have been described. These are **Data Sort, Data PivotTable** which can be used to generate tables for one or two categorical variables, whilst **Histogram** and the built-in **FREQUENCY()** function can generate frequency and cumulative frequency tables for numerical data.

Whether tables are generated manually or by using Excel, they should always be titled. Additionally, each row should be provided with meaningful labels and if appropriate, summary totals should be provided. If a data source has been used it is often useful to mention this underneath the table together with any other information you may consider useful or relevant.

The PivotTable facility is particularly powerful and allows tables to be created which consist of more than two variables. However, for most decision makers the simpler one and two variable representations will generally prove more useful for displaying business information.

Learning Outcomes Checklist

After completing this chapter you should have an understanding of the following concepts, calculations and functions:

- Creating one and two variable tables.
- Understand the need to include meaningful titles, summary totals and sources on a table.
- Ensure that the categories or intervals on a table account for each observation in the data set.
- Ensure the intervals are non-overlapping.

- Be able to sort a data set in Excel.

- Use Excel's **FREQUENCY()**, **Histogram** and **PivotTable** facilities to create one and two variable tables.

Ensure that you understand these concepts before progressing to Chapter 3.

Chapter Case Question

- Open the file **CHAP01.XLS**

- Using Excel's **FREQUENCY()** command, create a frequency table for the number of guest beers per month in the sample of public houses. Use the '**intervals**' 2, ,3, 4, 5 and 6, which must be entered as a column on your spreadsheet.

- Using Excel's **FREQUENCY()** command, create a frequency table for the monthly turnover of the public houses. Use the '**intervals**' 60000, 80000, 100000, 120000 and 140000, which again, must be entered as a column on your spreadsheet.

- Using Excel's **FREQUENCY()** command, create a cumulative frequency table for the monthly turnover of the public houses. Use the '**intervals**' 60000, 80000, 100000, 120000 and 140000, which must be entered as a column on your spreadsheet.

- Using the **PivotTable** facility, count the number of public houses falling into the following categories:

	Restaurant	**Family**	**Total**
Country			
Town			
Total			

- Save the amended file as **CHAP02.XLS**

- For each of the tables created above, identify the most important features of the data, e.g. biggest category of public house, typical number of guest beers etc.

Supplementary Questions

1. List the essential features of a table.

2. Why is it better to use one and two variable tables than a cross-tabulation involving multiple variables?

3. What is the difference in the output provided by Excel's **FREQUENCY()** function and its **Histogram** facility?

4. If you want to categorise age data into intervals < 16, 16 - , 24 - , 44 - and 65 - < 80 using either of these facilities, what interval range would you use?

5. The length of service of 50 employees at a computer factory were recorded in years:

10	9	3	4	2	2	1	8	7	4
11	12	6	2	3	5	5	1	12	9
6	7	4	4	12	14	10	5	7	3
3	5	4	4	7	5	2	1	1	9
9	8	4	4	5	6	2	7	10	6

   (a) Present the data as a frequency distribution using the intervals 0-, 2-, 4-, etc.

   (b) Display the data using a cumulative frequency distribution.

   (c) Check your answers using Excel.

   (d) What is the typical length of service?

   (e) What proportion of employees have worked at the factory for less than 6 years?

   (f) How many workers does this represent?

6. A record company surveyed 25 sixth formers with respect to musical preferences. The respondents were asked to describe their favourite types of music and asked whether they usually purchase LPs, CDs or cassette tapes. The following data was collected:

Respondent	Type of Music	Type of Purchase
1	Indie	CD
2	Chart	CD
3	Dance	CD
4	Dance	Cassette
5	Chart	CD
6	Chart	Cassette
7	Chart	CD
8	Dance	Cassette
9	Dance	CD
10	Chart	CD
11	Chart	LP
12	Indie	CD
13	Indie	CD
14	Chart	CD
15	Rock	LP
16	Chart	Cassette
17	Dance	CD
18	Chart	CD
19	Dance	Cassette
20	Indie	Cassette
21	Indie	CD
22	Chart	CD
23	Rock	CD
24	Chart	LP
25	Indie	CD

(a) Present the type of music as frequency distribution using PivotTable. What types of music are the most and least popular among the respondents?

(b) Present the type of purchase as frequency distribution using PivotTable (i.e. CD, LP or Cassette). What are the most and least popular?

(c) Either by hand or using Excel's PivotTable, create a two variable table for the data set listed above.

7. An opinion poll was conducted on the voting intentions of a group of people at the forthcoming parish council elections. The following votes were recorded:

Lab, Con, Con, Lab, Ind, Lab, Lib, Lab, Con, Lab, Ind, Con, Con, Lab, Lab, Lib, Ind, Lab, Con, Lib, Lab, Lab, Lab, Lab, Con, Lab, Lab, Ind, Lib, Con, Lab, Lib, Con, Con, Ind, Lab, Lab, Ind, Con, Con, Con, Con, Con, Con, Con, Lab, Lib, Con, Lib, Lab

(a) Create a frequency table using PivotTable for the data set.

(b) What outcome for the election is suggested by the opinion poll?

(c) If 600 people vote, how many votes are each party likely to receive?

(d) If the poll is correct, what will be the likely majority of the winning party?

(e) Describe the limitations of the data provided.

8. For a small Northern village, the number of young unemployed people (aged 16 to 21 inclusive) are recorded below:

Sex	Age	Length of unemployment (months)
M	19	16
F	21	8
F	20	7
M	16	4
M	17	11
F	17	3
F	18	12
M	16	2
M	16	3
M	19	10
F	20	12
F	21	3
M	18	11
M	17	12
F	20	7
M	19	2
M	16	3
F	16	3
M	18	5
F	16	3

(a) Create the following single variable tables by hand:

Sex
Age of respondent (use categories 16, 17, 18, etc.)

(b) Using the Histogram facility offered by Excel, present the data relating to the length of unemployment as a frequency distribution and a cumulative frequency distribution. Use the intervals 0- months, 2- months, etc.

(c) What is the typical length of unemployment?

(d) What proportion of the village's unemployed youth have been unemployed for more than a year?

9. The mileage (in thousands of miles) was recorded for 25 truck drivers by a haulage company in 1993.

55	75	79	80	32	29	57	60	39	58
29	65	26	44	50	32	56	33	77	29
45	37	39	29	61					

(a) Using Excel present the data as a frequency and a cumulative frequency distribution.

(b) What proportion of drivers have recorded in excess of 55,000 miles?

(c) What proportion have driven less than 30,000 miles?

(d) What is the typical number of miles (by interval) recorded by the truck drivers?

10. A small computer software house employs twenty people. Their annual salaries for 1997 are recorded (in thousands of pounds) below:

8	12	16	7	20	75	16	16	25	18
17	15	22	11	18	22	27	18	17	19

(a) Using Excel present the data as a frequency and a cumulative frequency distribution using the intervals 5-, 10-, 15-, 20-, 25- and 30+

(b) What is the most typical salary range for 1997?

(c) What proportion of staff earn less than £15,000?

(d) Comment on the presence of the salary £75,000.

11. Twenty five students were selected randomly on a university campus and asked about their opinions of the university's catering facilities. The following responses were made, where Good, OK and Poor are the possible descriptions about the catering and M and F refer to the respondent's gender:

M(OK), F(Poor), F(Good), F(Good), F(Poor), M(Good), M(Good), F(Poor), F(Poor), M(Good), M(OK), M(Poor), M(Good), M(OK), F(OK), F(OK), M(Poor), M(Good), M(OK), F(OK), F(Good), M(Good), F(Good), M(Poor), F(Poor)

(a) Using Excel's PivotTable facility, present the data using the following tables:

A one variable table counting the number of male and female respondents.

A one variable table counting the number of respondents who answer 'Good', 'OK' and 'Poor'.

A two variable table of gender by opinion of catering.

(b) Is there any evidence to suggest that males and females hold a different opinion regarding the standard of catering available?

Chapter 3

Using Graphs to Represent Data

Learning Outcomes

In this chapter you will see how various types of data recorded by a business decision maker can be represented graphically. In particular, the ChartWizard facility offered by Excel will be used and referred to throughout the chapter.

After completing this chapter you will be able to:

- Recognise the appropriate types of graphical display for categorical, ordinal, discrete quantitative and continuous quantitative data.
- Activate the ChartWizard facility offered by Excel and produce the various types of graphical display.
- Recognise the need for each graph to include a meaningful title.
- Recognise the importance of using sensible scales and titles on each axis of the graph.
- Understand the need to distinguish between data sets on a graph containing two or more groups, and be able to include a legend on a chart (graph) generated using ChartWizard.

Be able to identify the main features of a data set from its graphical display.

Introduction

As you saw in the last chapter, the first step in converting primary data into useful business information involves simplifying and enhancing its appearance. This data can be simplified by using tables which in turn may be used to highlight the main features of typically one or two variables in the data set.

An alternative way of presenting business data is in the form of a chart or graph. There are a number of different types of graph which can be used to represent a data set.

However, it is important that the appropriate type of graph is chosen to display the data under consideration. In particular:

Categorical data - should be represented either by a bar chart or pie chart.

Ordinal data - by a bar chart.

Discrete data - by a bar chart.

Continuous data - by a line graph (frequency polygon) or a histogram. (or grouped discrete - see the comments about grouping discrete data in Chapter 1)

In this chapter, you will see how each of these charts can be generated using Excel, and more importantly, understand how each representation is suitable for the type of data under consideration.

Essential Features of a Graph

Whether a graph is drawn by hand or generated using a spreadsheet it should contain the following features:

- An informative title.
- Informative labels and a reasonable scale for each axis.
- A legend to distinguish between the lines and bars if two or more data sets are being represented by the same graph.

If a graph contains the features listed above, it will provide an understandable display of the data under consideration, even if the corresponding data values are not provided. An absence of any of the features listed, may make the graph either difficult to read or worse still, may make the graphical display meaningless.

Creating a Graph (Chart) Using Excel

Creating a graph (or chart as it is referred to by the spreadsheet) is an easy task using Excel. Figures 3.1 to 3.8 inclusive show the step-by-step method of creating a graph using the built-in ChartWizard facility offered by Excel. You should be aware that slight differences exist between this version (i.e. Excel 97) and previous versions of Excel. The data below in Figure 3.1 refers to the number of students enrolled in each faculty at the University of Redcar in the academic year 1998.

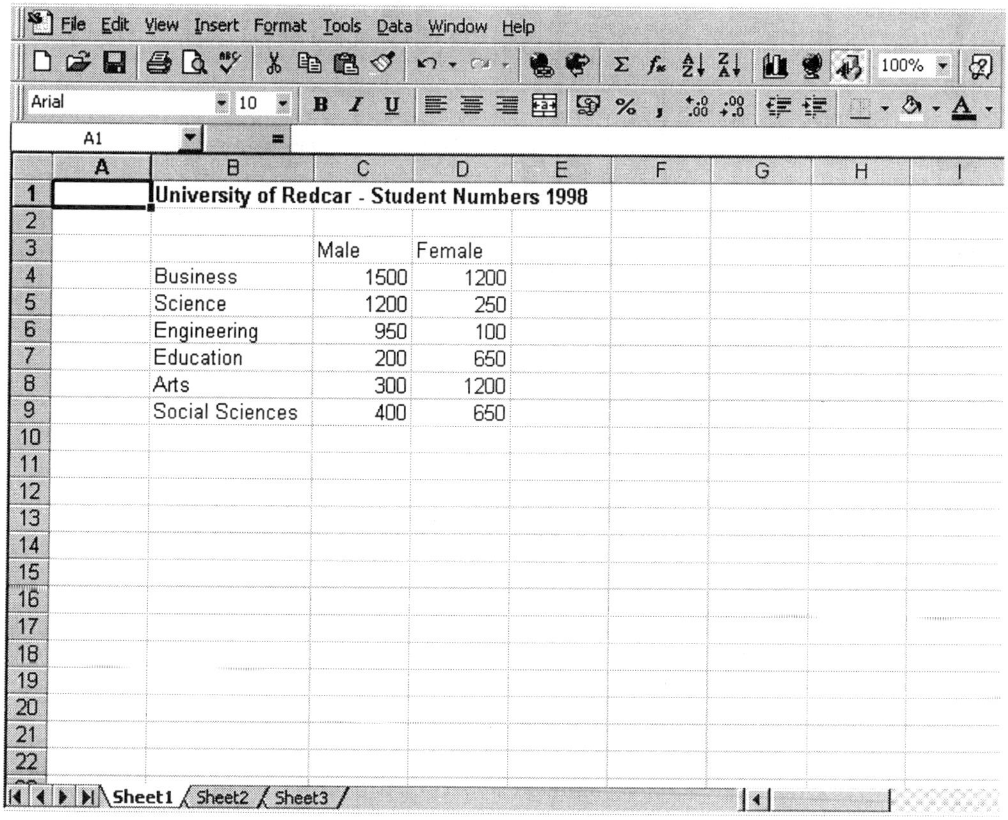

University of Redcar - Student Numbers 1998

	Male	Female
Business	1500	1200
Science	1200	250
Engineering	950	100
Education	200	650
Arts	300	1200
Social Sciences	400	650

Figure 3.1 - Student enrolment data

To create a chart for this data, you must highlight the block of cells **B3:D9** and click on the ChartWizard icon  which is located on the Excel toolbar. This range includes the labels Male and Female in row 3 and the faculty names in column B, and the reason for including the former will become evident shortly.

ChartWizard will now be active. You will need to go through the following steps, step 1 being shown in Figure 3.2.

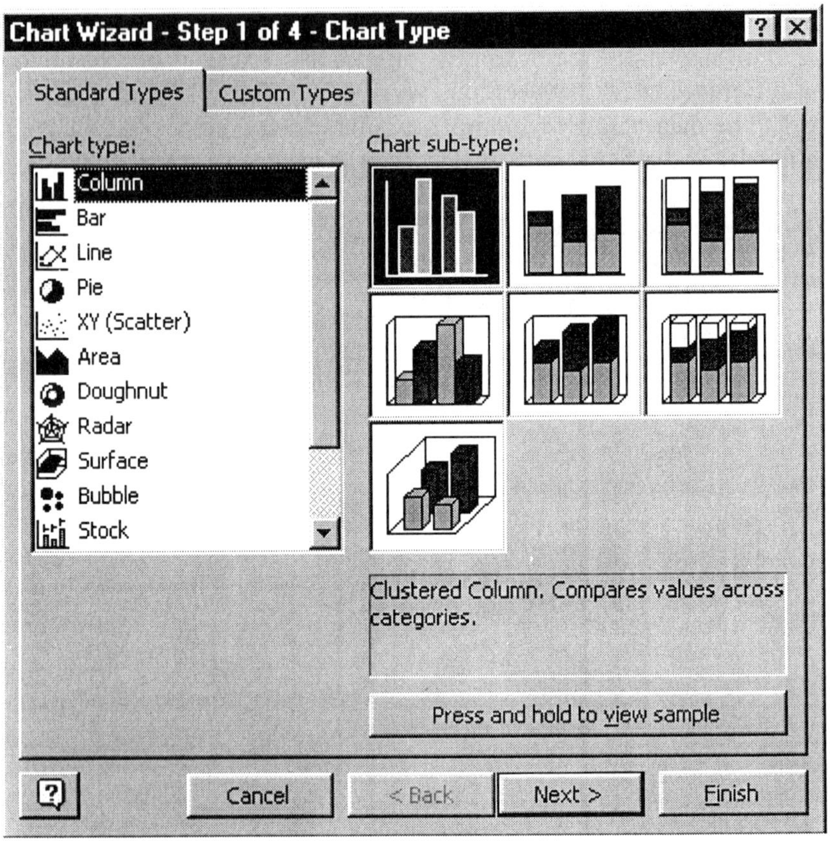

Figure 3.2 - Selection of chart type in Step 1 of ChartWizard

At this stage you must select the appropriate type of graph. In this example the default chart type **Column** is appropriate for the categorical data set under consideration. You must then click **Next**.

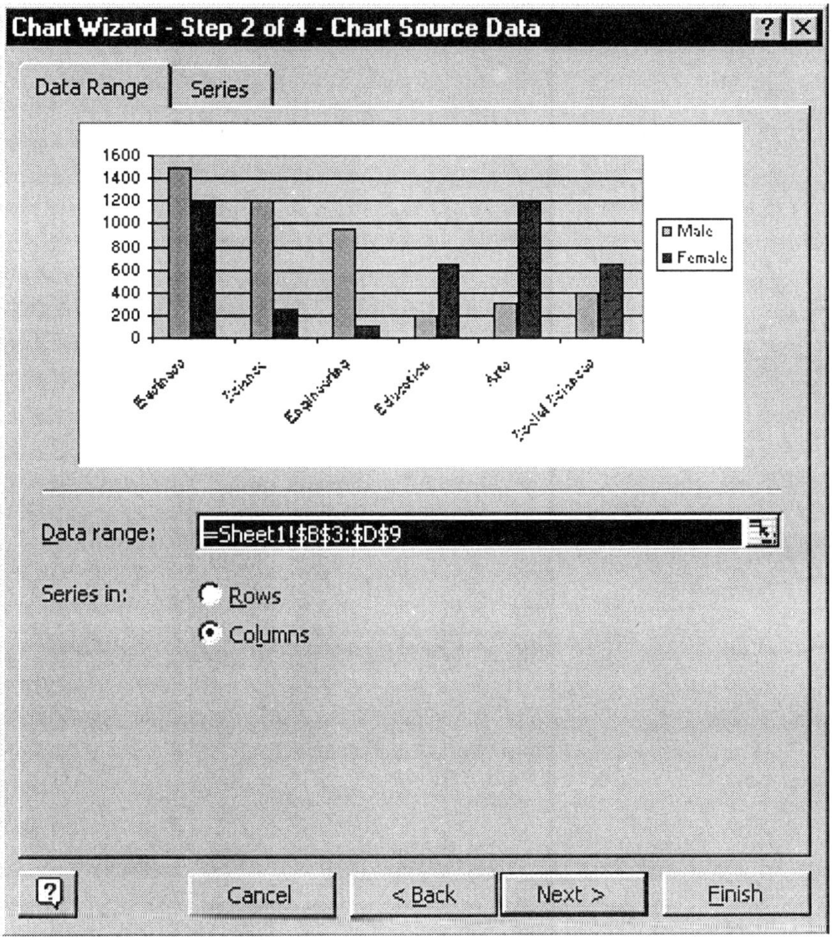

Figurc 3.3 - The suggested graph displayed by ChartWizard

At this stage, you have a suggested graph as shown in Figure 3.3. By highlighting the labels **Male** and **Female** before activating ChartWizard, an appropriate **Legend** is included on the graph, to distinguish between the two groups of students. This graph is OK, so again you can click on **Next**.

However, if you were considering *quantitative data* where the frequencies were located, say in cells C35:C40, and the corresponding interval values were stored in the range B35:B40 you must highlight the former as the data range as suggested prior to Figure 3.2, and define in Step 2 the **Category (X) axis Labels** by clicking on the **Series tab** at the top of the dialogue box and defining B35:B40 as shown in Figure 3.4. Once this has been done, you can click back on the **Data Range** tab (at the to of the box) and then select **Next**.

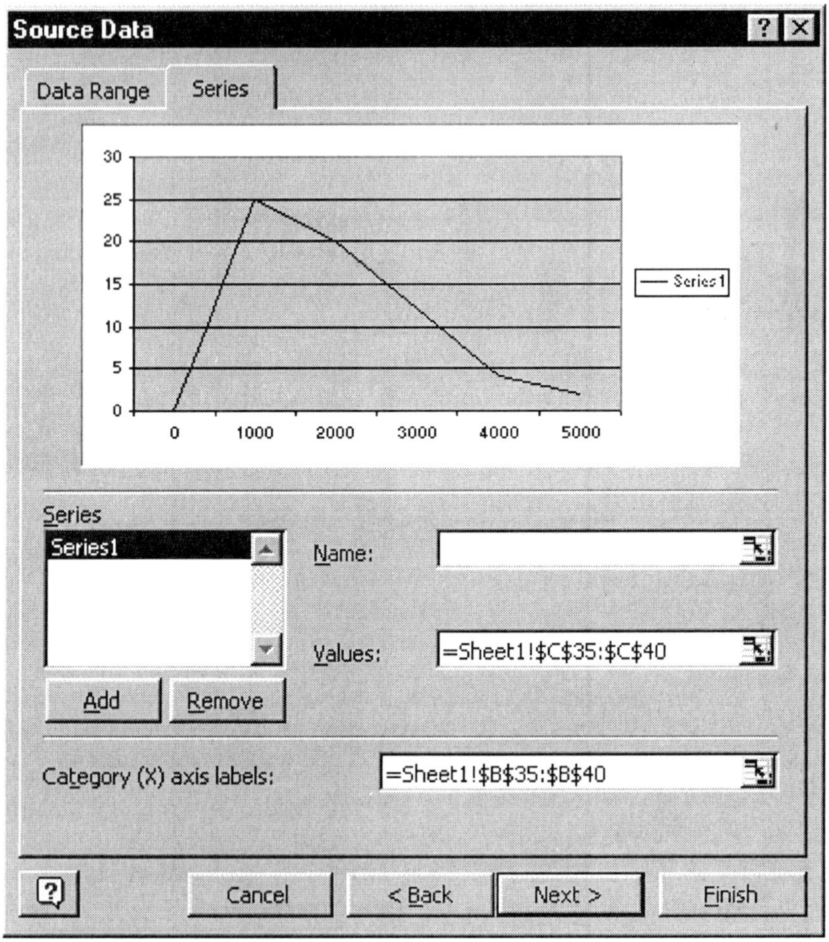

Figure 3.4 - Defining the Category (X) Axis Range for a quantitative data set

Step 3 is shown below in Figure 3.5. At this step within ChartWizard you can define the chart titles and if appropriate, the legend information to be used on your chart.

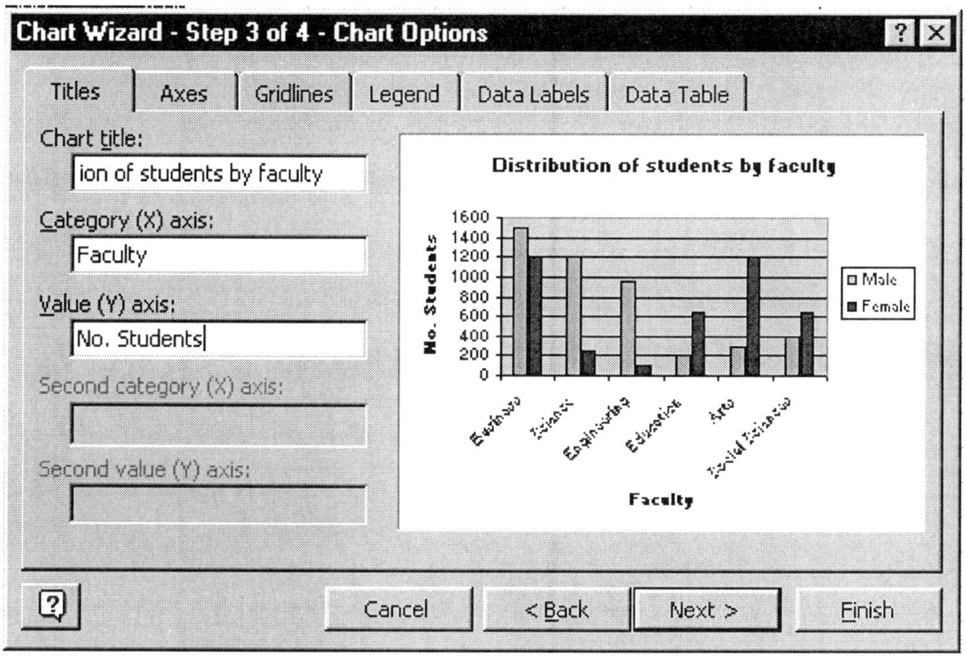

Figure 3.5 - Selecting Chart options (titles and legends)

If you had only one set of data values on a graph, the legend would not really be necessary because the title should indicate the meaning of the graph and you don't have to distinguish between two or more data sets. However, if you do wish to use the legend, include meaningful labels from the spreadsheet (these being selected as part of the data range as indicated after Figure 3.1) to ensure that the legend applied to your chart is not the meaningless default of **Series 1**. Alternatively, if you want to switch off the Legend facility, click on the **Legend tab** at the top of the Step 3 dialogue box, and switch off the default **Show Legend** as shown in Figure 3.6. You can then click back on the **Titles** tab to return to the view shown in Figure 3.5.

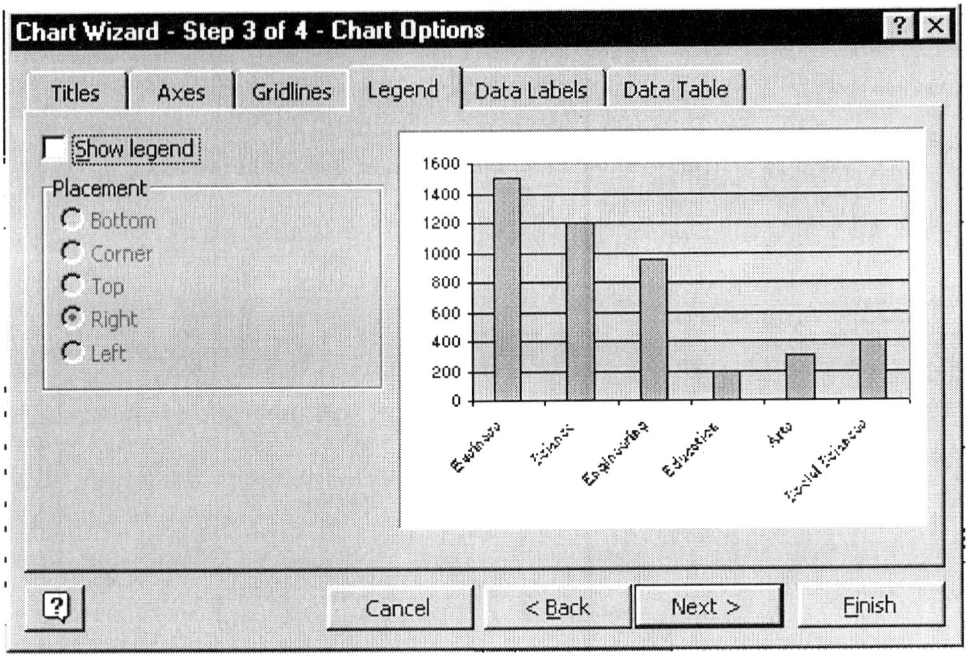

Figure 3.6 - The Legend facility in ChartWizard

Once you have added the relevant titles and labels in step 3, you can click on **Next**.

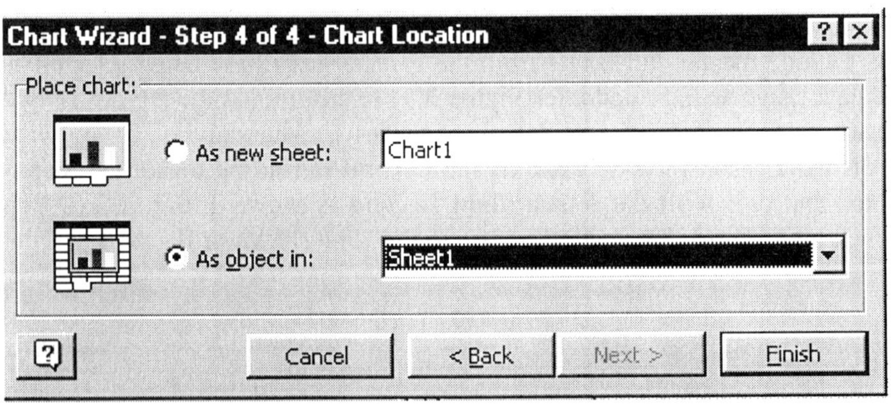

Figure 3.7 - Defining the chart's location

Finally, in step 4, you can define where the new graph is to be located as shown in Figure 3.7. In this example, the resultant graph will be located on the same worksheet as its data set. You can click on **Finish** to produce the graph.

The completed graph resembles Figure 3.8.

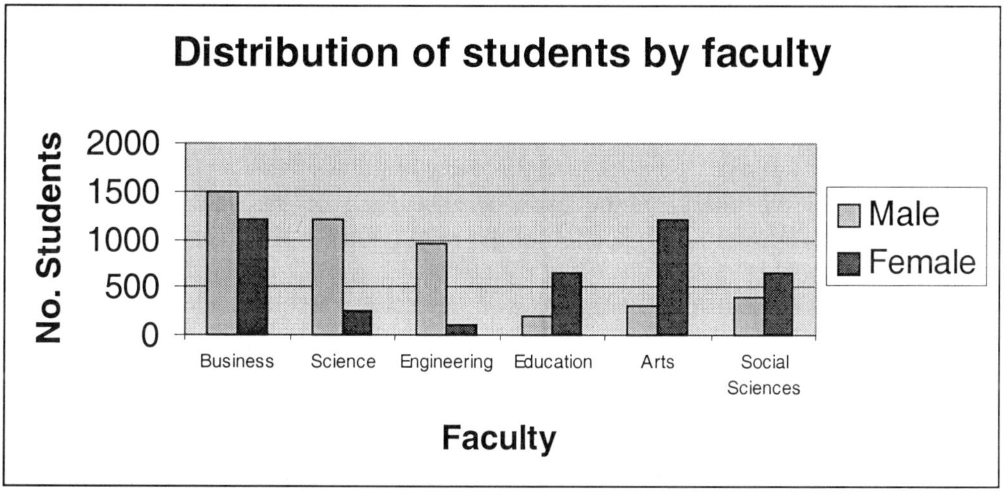

Figure 3.8 - The completed Column Chart

If the graph produced isn't big enough, it can be extended, by dragging on a corner and moving in an outward direction. This can be achieved since the graph is active, i.e. it has handles around its border (these handles resemble small squares). Also, by pointing in the middle of the chart and dragging with the mouse, you can define the location of the chart on your worksheet. To make the worksheet active again, simply click anywhere on the grid. The chart handles will disappear.

Now that you have seen how ChartWizard can be activated, consideration will be given to the presentation of each type of data.

Representing Categorical Data Using a Pie Chart

If a data set consists of a number of *categories where each represents a proportion of the total data*, then a pie chart can be used to display the data graphically. Suppose that at a medium sized manufacturing company, the personnel manager wishes to analyse the reasons why employees have left posts on the shop-floor. The reasons for leaving have been calculated as a percentage of the total number of resignations and are shown below:

Reason for leaving	Proportion of Staff
Other company	27%
Retirement	35%
Redundancy	10%
Promotion	20%
Education	8%

In this case, a pie chart can be used because each of the categories listed are exhaustive and represent a proportion of the total (value of the) data set.

The whole data set is displayed as a pie (i.e. a circle) which is made up of a number of slices of varying and proportionate size which represent each of the categories.

The size of each slice is determined by the size of the angle in the centre of the circle. The total pie consists of 360°, and the bigger the proportion a particular category is of the total data set, the bigger the angle is in its slice of the pie.

For the category 'Other company' listed above, the slice of the pie representing this group of workers has an angle $0.27 \times 360^o = 97.2^o$. The angles for each category in the data set under consideration are:

Reason for leaving	Size of angle (^{o})
Other company	97.2
Retirement	126.0
Redundancy	36.0
Promotion	72.0
Education	28.8
TOTAL	360.0

Using these angles, the pie chart can be drawn. The chart produced by Excel is shown in Figure 3.9.

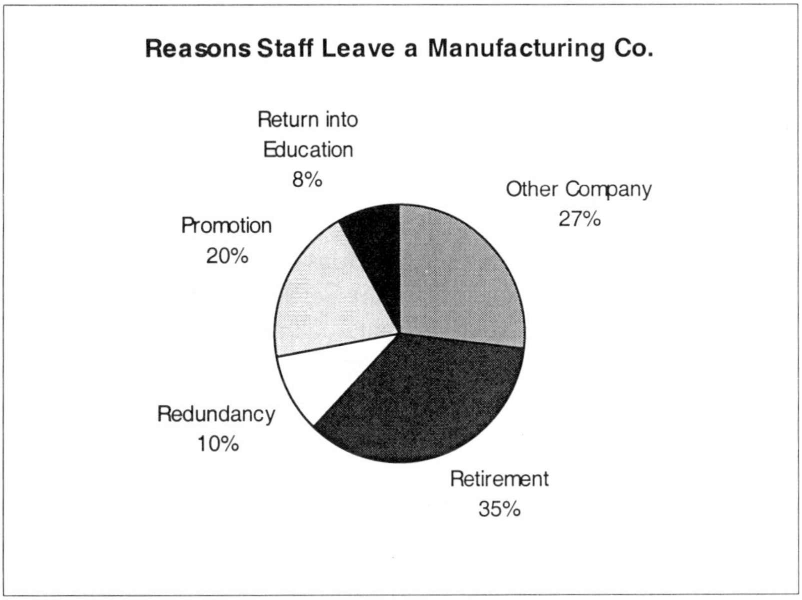

Figure 3.9 - Pie chart generated by Excel

The pie chart indicates the biggest reason for leaving this company is Retirement, and this category is displayed by the largest slice of the pie.

The pie chart presented is a useful display because only a small number of categories (in this example 6 categories) have been included, each representing a reasonable proportion of the total data set. Therefore, comparing the size of each category is easy. However, if a data set consists of a large number of categories, say more than 10, or if an individual category is small, i.e. less than 1% of the total data set, then it may be useful to combine groups (for example into a category called 'Other') before creating this type of chart.

Finally, one common mistake is to consider the pie chart to be suitable for all types of categorical data. This is *not* true, the pie chart should only be used if the categories considered add up to the total value of the data.

Representing Categorical and Discrete Data Using a Bar Chart

There may be occasions when categorical data is encountered where the separate categories do not represent a proportion of a 'total' amount or value. If you consider the earnings in 1994 of the chairmen of the UK's top ten companies, the data is categorical (where the chairmen identified by company or name represent the categories), but their earnings do not represent the total earnings by all chairmen for the particular year.

In this example, an alternative type of graphical display must be used and this is called the bar chart. On this chart each individual category is displayed using a separate bar (specifically, all of the bars are separated by spaces on the chart). The height (for Excel's column chart) or length (for Excel's bar chart) of these bars indicate the frequency or size of the respective categories and the chart provides a useful comparison of the individual frequencies. Figure 3.10 shows two types of bar chart, which can be produced by activating the bar and column options respectively from Excel's ChartWizard menu. It should be apparent that, by default, Excel has provided a reasonable scale for the frequency axis on both charts. In both bar charts, typical weekly expenditure for a group of students is considered. On these charts, the categories of expenditure consist of items such as food, rent and clothing. Inspection of each chart suggests rent is the biggest weekly expenditure since it is represented by the longest bar.

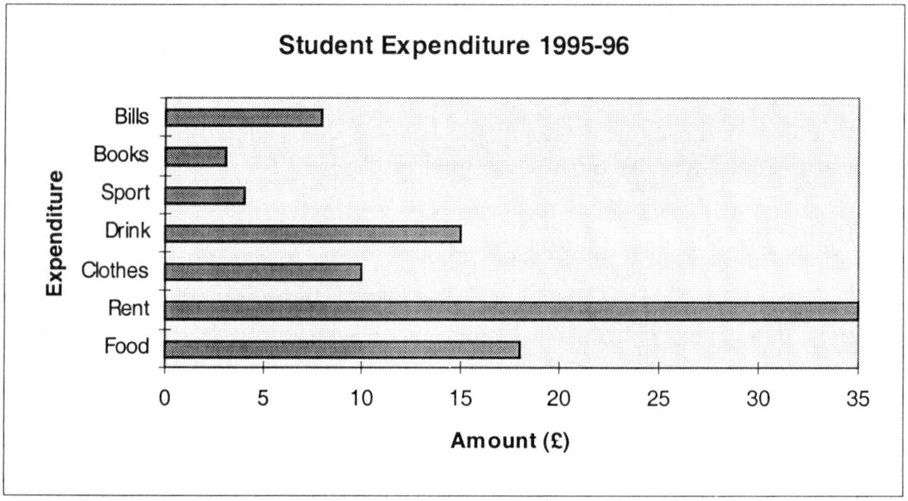

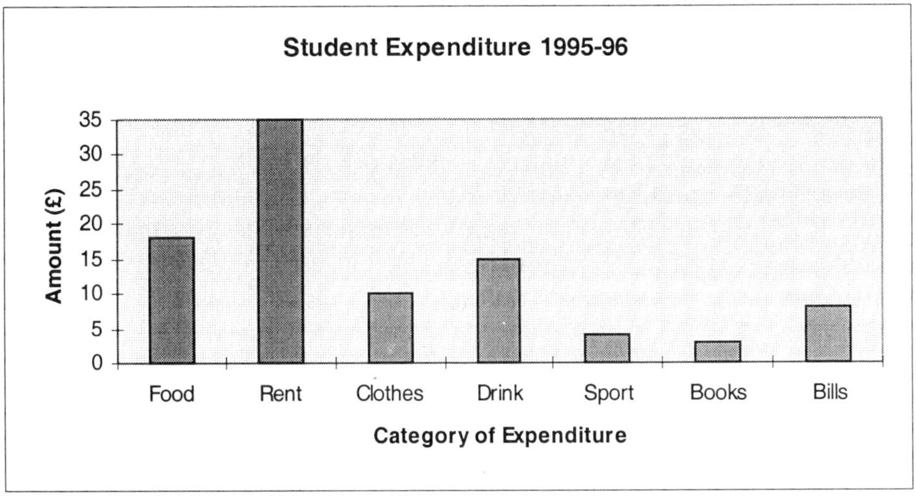

Figure 3.10 - Bar charts provided by Excel

If a comparison has to be made between two or more (categorical or discrete) data sets, this can achieved by using a **multiple bar chart**. In Figure 3.11, a multiple bar chart has been used to compare typical weekly expenditure for a group of male and female students. Again, this graph shows that the biggest weekly outgoing for both sexes is rent. To distinguish between the sexes, the graph includes a **legend**.

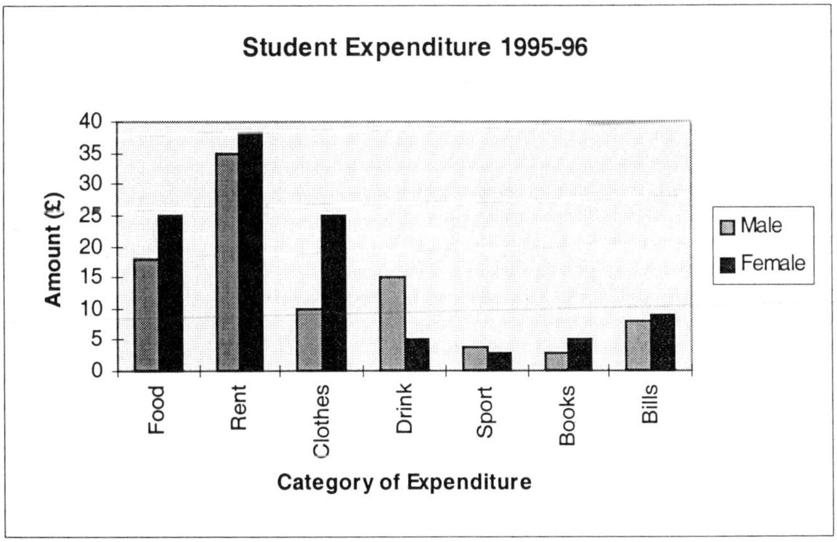

Figure 3.11 - A multiple bar chart created by Excel

Also, when two groups of data are being compared, it may be more appropriate to consider percentage frequencies rather than actual frequencies if the total value or size of the two data sets are significantly different. Figure 3.12 shows the same data except percentage of expenditure has been used for each item. Whilst Figure 3.11 indicated that on average, female students spend more on rent per week than male students, they actually spend less on rent than males as a proportion of their total expenditure. However, inspection of Figure 3.12 indicates that whilst the biggest proportion of expenditure for both sexes is rent, the biggest difference in percentage expenditure between the two groups is clothes.

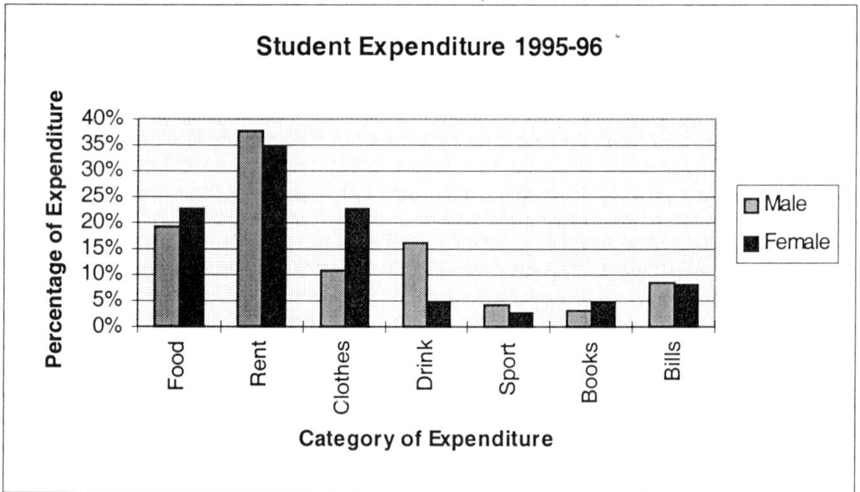

Figure 3.12 - A multiple bar chart which uses percentage frequencies

The final type of bar chart which can be used to represent two or more data sets is the **stacked bar chart**. On this chart, the total height of each bar represents the total frequency of each category, but each bar is made up of a number of components or sub-groups, where the height of each component represents the sub-total for each particular category. In Figure 3.13, the height of each bar represents the total sales of baby buggies in five sales regions. It should be clear that the biggest sales are recorded in the South, since this bar is the tallest. However, the sales presented are made up of sales of single and double buggies and the bars representing one type of buggy are stacked on top of the bars representing the other category. Again, the biggest sales of double buggies (one of the two categories) is in the southern region.

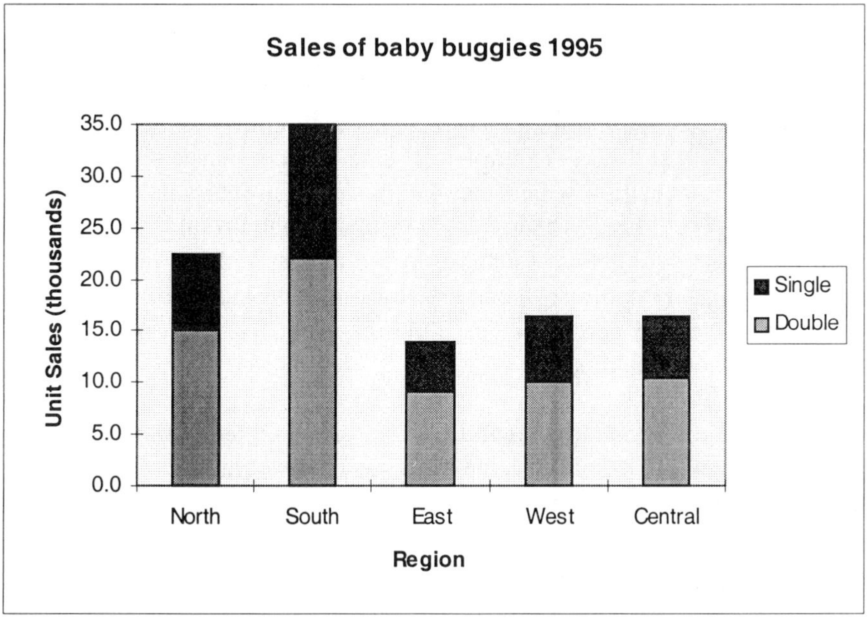

Figure 3.13 - A stacked bar chart

In each of the three examples considered above, categorical data sets have been represented by the bar graphs in Figures 3.10, 3.11, 3.12 and 3.13. Equally, the various displays can be used to represent discrete quantitative data. An example of this type of data could be the number of pairs of shoes (recorded by size) held in stock by a department store. The number of pairs by size could be represented by a bar chart, a comparison of male and female stock could be made using the multiple bar chart and the total stock for a chain of stores by size could be displayed using the stacked bar chart where each sub-group in the stacked bar represents an individual store, and the height of the bar represents the total stock held for each size.

Representing Continuous Quantitative Data

Three types of display will be considered for continuous, quantitative data; the histogram, the frequency polygon and the cumulative frequency polygon (ogive).

The Histogram

An initial inspection of the histogram may suggest that it is similar in appearance to the bar chart. However, the horizontal or x axis of the histogram represents continuous data rather than separate values or categories, and therefore, the sections (bars) on this graph are continuous rather than separate bars as seen on the bar chart. You need to be aware that it is the **area** of each bar on the histogram which indicates the frequency of each class interval rather than the height. This is particularly useful because many continuous data sets may consist of unequal class intervals. Perhaps the most likely example of data which consists of unequal intervals is age related information which may be presented in intervals such as 0 -, 16 -, 25 -, 45 - and 65+. It is reasonable to use unequal groups in this way, because each of the chosen groups have a sensible and understandable meaning, i.e. children, young adults etc. In contrast, using equal group intervals 0 -, 10 -, etc. for age may prove problematic, in particular including the group 10 - < 20 which will consist of children and young adults.

On a histogram, the height of each bar is indicated by its **frequency density** which equals **frequency/class width**. Consider the data set below which consists of the expenses claimed in a typical month by a group of sales managers.

Expenses(£)	Frequency	Class Width	Frequency Density
0 -	20	100	20/100 = 0.20
100 -	12	50	12/50 = 0.24
150 -	20	50	20/50 = 0.40
200 -	28	50	28/50 = 0.56
250 -	10	50	10/50 = 0.20
300 - < 400	10	100	10/100 = 0.10

The corresponding histogram is shown in Figure 3.14, where expense forms the continuous scale on the x axis and frequency density is recorded on the y axis. The most typical monthly expense bill is in the interval £200 to £250 since this group has the **highest frequency** density, and is therefore the **modal group**. In contrast, the least common group is £300 to £400 since this interval has the smallest frequency density.

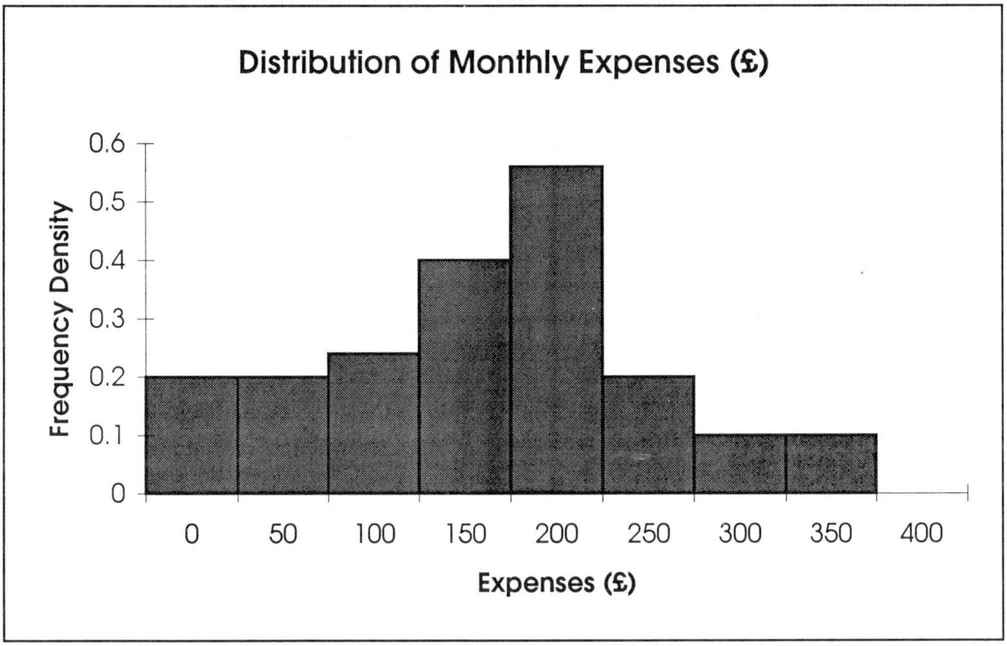

Figure 3.14 - The Histogram representing monthly expenses

One problem which you may encounter if you wish to represent a continuous data set is that most spreadsheets do not include facilities which can be used to create a 'proper' histogram. Excel offers a **Histogram** facility included as part of its **Analysis Toolpak** (see Chapter 2 for details of its application) and Figure 3.15 shows a graph provided by this facility. The graph has not had the general headings modified, and is shown here to indicate the potential limitation of this histogram display.

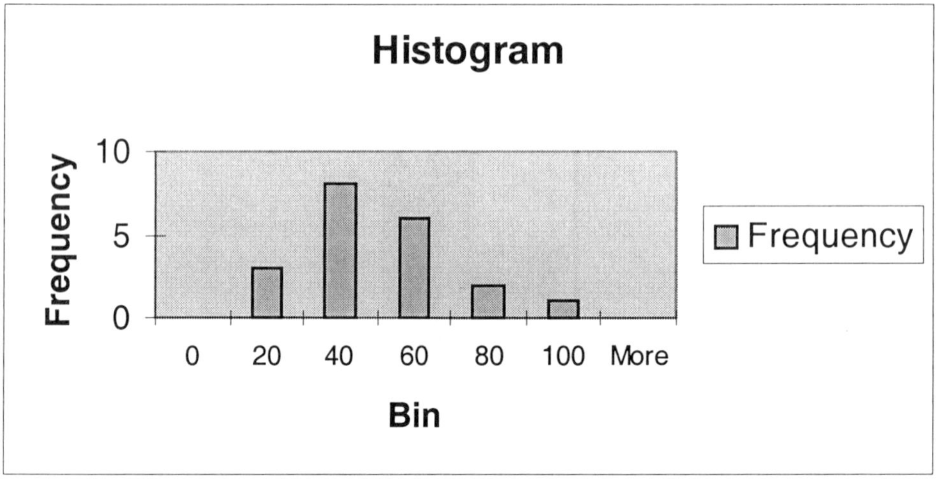

Figure 3.15 - Graphical output provided by Excel's Histogram Tool

The 'histogram' pictured in Figure 3.15 is in fact a bar chart and not a histogram since the blocks included on the graph are separated by spaces rather than continuous. As a consequence, this display may at times provide an inaccurate representation of the data set. This can resolved to some extent by double clicking on the centre of the chart in order activate **Format Data Series**. Within this facility, if you select Options, you can set the **Gap Width** equal to 0. The amended chart is shown in Figure 3.16.

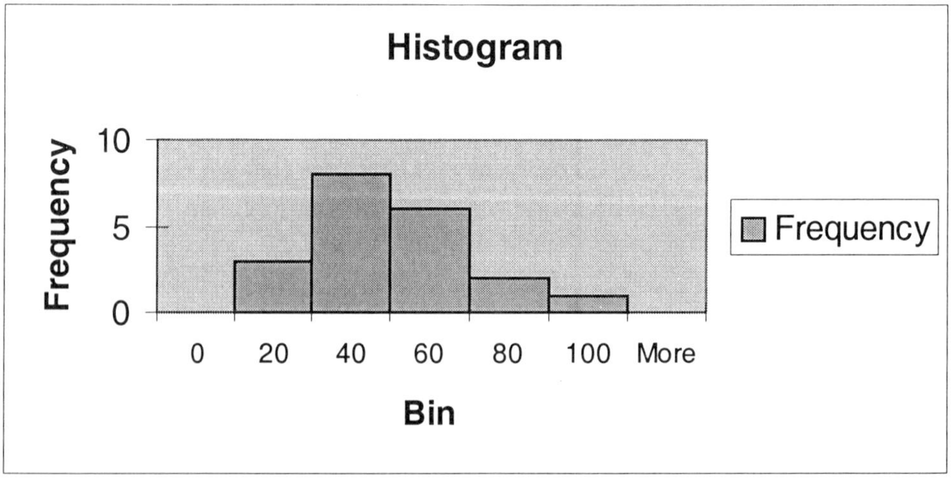

Figure 3.16 - The modified histogram provided by Excel

The Frequency Polygon

If you require a graphical display for an individual continuous data set or wish to compare two or more continuous data sets on the same graph, then a **frequency polygon** can be created using Excel. In Figure 3.17 the bonuses earned by salesmen in the North are compared with those earned by salesmen in the South. The frequency polygon was generated by choosing the **XY Scatter** graph facility offered by ChartWizard, and then by selecting an appropriate display under this menu option (i.e. a display such as Chart 2 where the points are joined by a line). The reason for this will be given shortly.

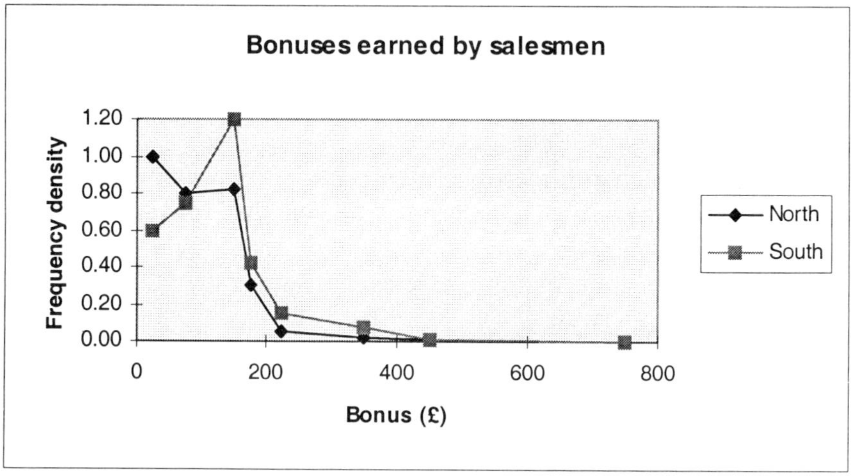

Figure 3.17 - Frequency polygon generated using Excel

The frequency values (or if appropriate percentage frequencies for two or more data sets of vastly different size or value) are paired with the mid-point values for each defined class on the frequency polygon. Given that the data is continuous, these points are joined together by a line. Comparison of the two (or more) data sets is then quite straightforward. In this example, the peak bonus for the two sets of salesmen is represented by the interval £100 to £150.

To account for the unequal class widths in the frequency data represented in Figure 3.17, the appropriate graphical display was created by selecting **XY (Scatter)** from the ChartWizard menu and selecting the line option at Step 3. If the data was allocated to equal class intervals, a Line graph can also be activated. The Line graph facility in the latter can **only** be used for data allocated to equal sized intervals. If it had been used for the data set presented above, the values in the X range, i.e. 25, 75, 150, 175, 225 etc. would be evenly spaced, hence potentially hiding the non-symmetric shape of the data which is portrayed in Figure 3.17.

If you are using a spreadsheet, the frequency polygon can be used to overcome the problems associated with the histogram. Additionally, comparing two or more data sets using a histogram is virtually impossible, because this display unlike the bar chart uses continuous rather than separate bars.

The Cumulative Frequency Polygon (Ogive)

The final type of plot which can be used for a continuous data set is the **cumulative frequency polygon** or **ogive**. Again, this can be generated (in the example below) using the **Line** graph facility provided by the ChartWizard, since the intervals are of equal size. The ogive can be used to indicate the number of observations in a continuous data set which are located below a group of pre-defined intervals. The graph can be used to estimate various statistics such as the median and quartiles (see Chapters 4 and 5).

In Chapter 2 you have seen how to calculate a cumulative frequency distribution manually and have also seen how it could be generated using the **Histogram** facility offered by Excel. To plot this distribution, the cumulative frequency is represented by the vertical or y axis of the graph and the value of the data by the graph's x axis. The points displayed on the graph are joined by a line. The ogive representing the number of visits to customers in a certain week by 80 insurance sales representatives is shown in Figure 3.18.

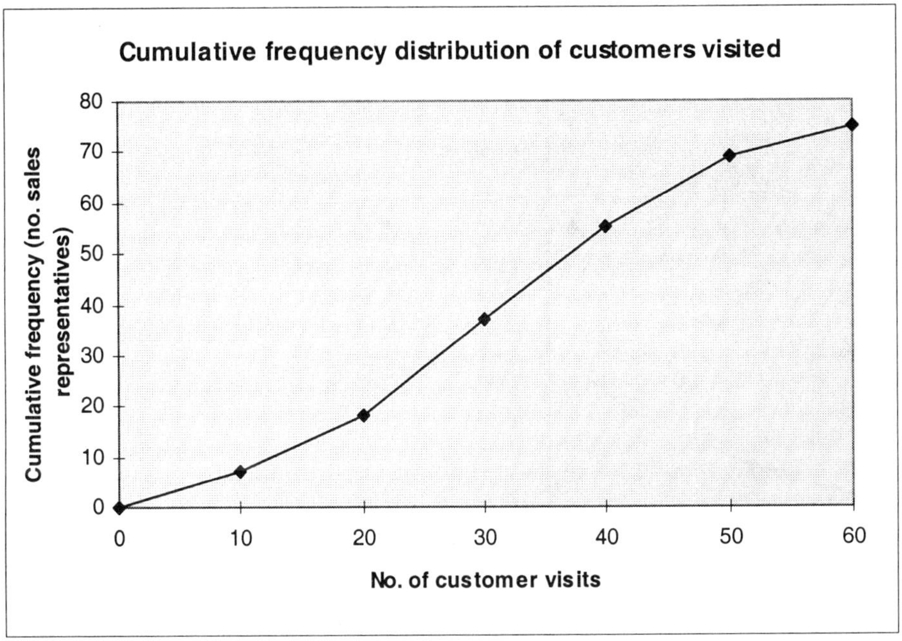

Figure 3.18 - Cumulative Frequency Graph (Ogive) generated using Excel

Now that the ogive has been drawn you can answer questions like 'Estimate the number of sales representatives who visit less than 25 customers per week'. To do this you read 25 off the x axis and draw a vertical line until it meets the ogive, as shown in Figure 3.19. You then draw a horizontal line and read the estimate of the number of sales representatives from the y axis. For this data set, you can estimate that 28 sales representatives make less than 25 visits per week.

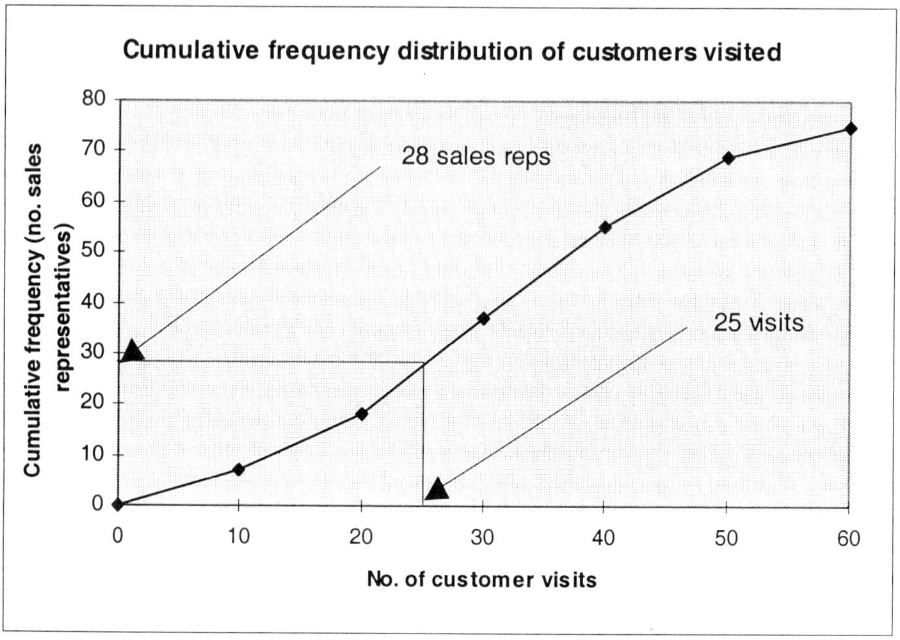

Figure 3.19 - Using the Ogive for estimation

Other Types of Graphical Display

Most of the popular types of graphical display have now been considered in this chapter. However, you may encounter two other types of graphical display and these are considered later in greater detail in this book. These graphs are the **time series plot** and the **scatter diagram**.

The Time Series Plot

If the average price of a three bedroom house in London or the output from a factory has been recorded at regular intervals of time, for example, monthly for the former and weekly for the latter, it may be useful to plot a graph to record this data to determine whether any underlying trend exists. The type of graph which should be used is the **Line** graph. On this graph time is recorded on the x axis, price or output is recorded on the y axis and the points on the graph are joined by a line. A line graph is used for this type of data because time is a continuous variable. The resultant graph is known as a **time series plot**. If the graph contains an identifiable pattern, there are a number of time based models which can be used to forecast future values of the data set by taking into account the exact nature of the pattern identified. Time based models will be considered in Chapters 14 and 15.

In Figure 3.20 a time series plot has been used to represent the index of factory output from 1987 to 1994 inclusive. This plot indicates that output at the factory increased from 1989 to 1992, but this was followed by a sharp decrease during 1993. Output then increased in 1994 compared to the previous year. If a time series plot is created, the decision maker may be able to link its shape to various historical events. For example, the sharp decrease in production recorded in 1993 may have been caused by industrial action.

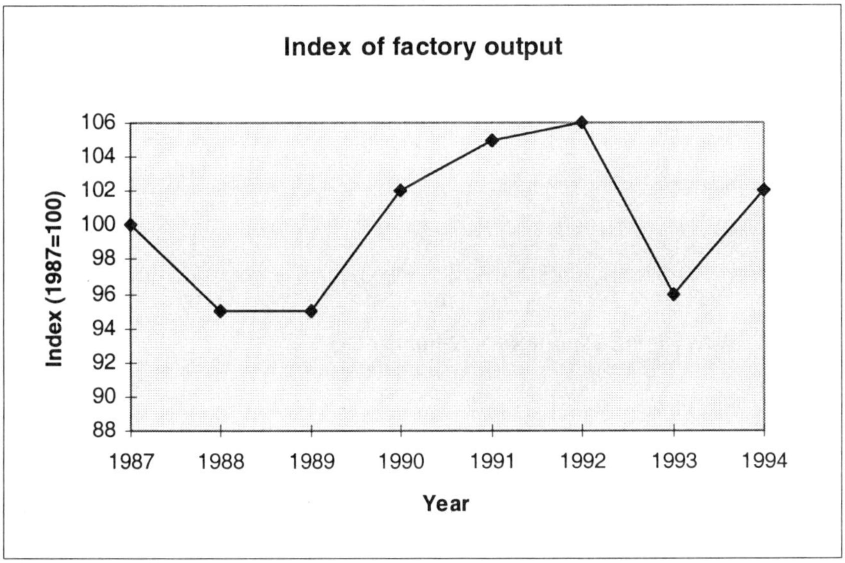

Figure 3.20 - Using a line graph to plot time related data

The Scatter Diagram

It may be reasonable to assume that in certain data sets, the behaviour of two or more variables may be related. For example, it would be reasonable to suggest for fast moving consumables such as food and drink, sales and price are related, i.e. as price increases, sales decrease. Again, a specific type of graphical display can be used to represent this type of data set. The graphical display is called a **scatter diagram** (generated using the **XY Scatter** option from the ChartWizard menu). The points on the scatter diagram are **not** connected by a line, but the overall shape suggested by the points can be used to indicate the strength and nature of any relationship that may exist between the variables under consideration.

In Figure 3.21, advertising expenditure and corresponding sales were recorded by a mail order company. As expected, the greater the level of advertising, the higher the value of sales. This is suggested by the positive or upward slope of the points on the scatter diagram.

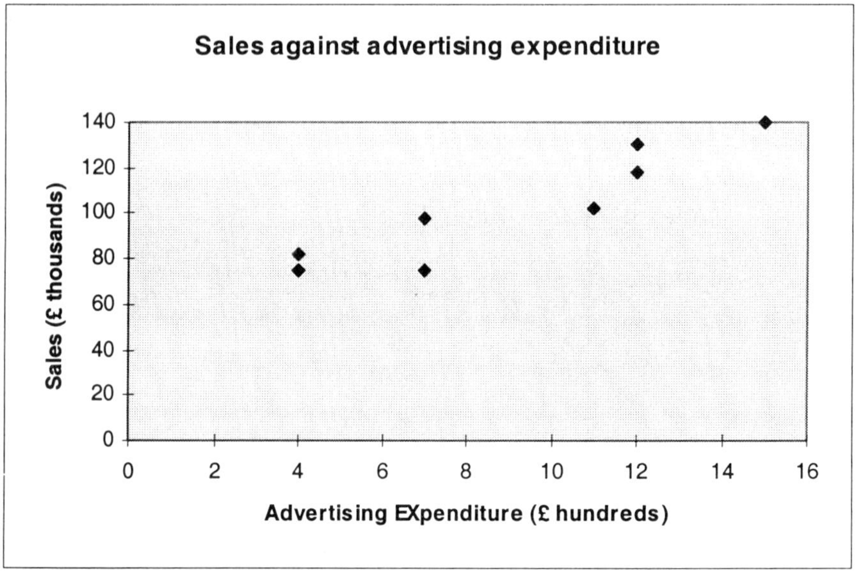

Figure 3.21 - A scatter diagram generated by Excel

In Chapters 12 and 13 you will consider the strength of such associations between variables, and where appropriate, you will make forecasts with regard to the variables under consideration.

Review

To create a graph using Excel, you should undertake the following steps:

1. Highlight the data set on the worksheet. If a legend needs to be added to the graph, the data set highlighted should include titles.

2. Activate ChartWizard by clicking on the relevant icon on the standard Excel toolbar.

3. Drag the mouse to define the frame which will contain the resultant chart.

4. From the ChartWizard, select an appropriate graphical display, i.e. for **categorical data** select either a bar chart or a pie chart, for **ordinal** or **discrete**

data select the bar chart, and finally, for grouped discrete or **continuous data**, use the line graph to create a frequency polygon.

5. Ensure that the data has been interpreted properly by Excel. For example, if two sets of numeric data have been highlighted, ensure, if appropriate, that Excel interprets the first column of data as Category (X) Axis labels rather than an individual data series. This issue was addressed in Figure 3.4.

6. To ensure that the graph is useful, add a relevant chart title and axes titles. As a default, Excel provides reasonable scales for each axis.

Conclusions

In this chapter you have seen how Excel can be used to generate charts (graphs) in order to represent a variety of data sets which may be collected by a business decision maker. You should now be aware of the specific type of graphs which can be used for the different types of data which may be collected.

Once an appropriate type of chart has been created, it can provide you with a useful facility for summarising a data set in a simple yet meaningful way. In particular the shape of the graph produced will reflect the features of the data collected. By looking at a graph and identifying its main features, you can obtain an overview of the data collected which cannot be readily gained by inspection of a set of raw numbers or labels.

Learning Outcomes Checklist

After completing this chapter you should have an understanding of the following concepts, calculations and functions:

- Nominal, ordinal, discrete and continuous data are represented by specific types of graph.

- The features of the bar chart, pie chart, histogram, frequency polygon and ogive.

- The existence of other types of graphical display such as the scatter graph and time series plot.

- How to identify the key features of a data set from the shape of its graphical display.

- How to activate Excel's **ChartWizard** facility to produce the various graphs described above.

Ensure that you understand these concepts before progressing to Chapter 4.

Chapter Case Question

- Open the file CHAP02.XLS
- Represent the frequency table for the number of guest beers per month in the sample of pubs using an appropriate graphical display. Remember this data set is discrete.
- Represent the cumulative frequency table for the monthly turnover for the sample of pubs using an ogive.
- Use the ogive to determine the number of pubs with a monthly turnover of less than £95,000.
- Represent the number of pubs falling into the following categories using a multiple bar chart. Comment on the main features of the graph.

	Restaurant	**Family**	**Total**
Country			
Town			
Total			

- Ensure each graph is properly titled and labelled.
- Save the amended file as CHAP03.XLS

Supplementary Questions

1. Describe the following types of data and suggest suitable graphical displays:

   (a) The proportion of graduates leaving a university by the sector of their first job.

(b) Sales of a chocolate bar by region.

(c) Sales of a chocolate bar in the UK measured on an annual basis.

(d) Typical weekly expenditure by item for a UK family.

(e) The relationship between sales and price for a UK toy manufacturer.

(f) Monthly sales generated by a group of managers.

(g) Distribution of age for a group of university teachers.

2. Give examples where the following types of graph may be used:

(a) Stacked bar chart.

(b) Frequency polygon.

(c) Scatter diagram.

3. Why is it important for certain graphs to display a legend?

4. What are main differences between a bar chart and a histogram?

5. Thirty clerical officers at a local authority were asked to record their length of service in years. The values recorded were:

15	9	3	6	11	10	17	1	7	11
12	2	4	9	10	17	25	2	8	14
13	22	21	5	3	13	6	2	14	26

(a) By hand, present the data as a frequency distribution, using six intervals of equal width.

(b) What type of data set is under consideration?

(c) Represent the data using an appropriate graph.

(d) Using Excel, repeat parts a) and c).

6. The table provided shows the average monthly bonuses earned by 50 sales representatives working for a national organisation.

Bonus (£)	Number of representatives
< £50	5
£50 - < £75	15
£75 - < £100	10
£100 - < £125	9
£125 - < £150	8
£150 - < £200	3

(a) Present this data set using a histogram.

(b) Determine the cumulative frequency distribution and create an ogive.

(c) Using the ogive, estimate the number of representatives earning an average bonus of less than £80 and the number earning a bonus exceeding £160.

7. At a small Northern college, the following number of male and female students were recorded by faculty:

Faculty	Male	Female
Business	657	539
Catering	182	451
Engineering	551	78
Physical Education	220	197
Science	255	325

Using Excel produce two different types of graphical display which can be used to compare the number of students by faculty.

8. The number of contracts won by an IT consultancy group have been recorded quarterly over the past 5 years:

Year	Q1	Q2	Q3	Q4
1	28	17	19	30
2	25	16	19	26
3	23	15	18	25
4	20	14	16	22
5	18	13	15	20

(a) Using Excel present the data using a time series plot and describe its shape. At what time of the year do the maximum sales and minimum sales occur?

(b) What is indicated by the overall trend in the data?

9. A department store has recruited 30 new staff in the northern region over the last year. The ages of these staff were:

25	42	16	16	18	21	23	25	22	24
49	18	22	25	22	28	32	32	37	22
53	21	23	22	32	21	19	20	24	26

Use Excel to:

(a) Present the data as a frequency distribution using the intervals: 15 -, 20 -, 25 -, 30 -, 40 -, 50 -.

(b) Present the data as a cumulative frequency distribution for this data set.

(c) Present the data as a frequency polygon.

(d) Present the data using an ogive.

(e) Use the ogive to estimate the number of new employees aged 22 or less and the number aged between 35 and 45.

10. The number of small businesses which failed in a small Northern town were recorded monthly over the last two years:

0	3	5	2	3	2	1	4	2	5	6	2
1	2	1	4	2	5	2	3	4	0	2	1

(a) By hand, tabulate this data as a frequency distribution.

(b) Present the data using a bar chart.

(c) What is the typical number of failed businesses recorded each month?

(d) Repeat parts a) and b) using Excel.

Part 2

Summary Statistics

Chapter 4

Measures of Average

Learning Outcomes

In this chapter you will be introduced to a number of summary statistics which offer 'representative' values for a data set. These 'representative' values, which are known as measures of average, are the **mode**, **median** and **mean**. Each measure will be described and calculated, and by reference to specific data sets, you will see when their application is suitable. Reference will also be made to the built-in facilities offered by Excel.

After completing this chapter you will be able to:

- Define the terms mode, median and mean.
- Understand the term 'ordered array'.
- Calculate the mode, median and mean for both raw and grouped data.
- Recognise the strengths and limitations of each summary measure.
- Understand the term 'skewness'.
- Distinguish between a symmetrical and a skewed frequency distribution.
- Recognise the appropriate measure of average for symmetrical data and the best measure for a skewed frequency distribution.
- Compute the mode, median and mean using the built-in facilities offered by Excel.
- Appreciate the properties of three additional summary measures; the trimmed mean, percentile and quartile.

Introduction

Once a data set has been collected and organised, it may be appropriate for you to compute a suitable measure of average. The measure of average is the value which is most 'typical' of the data. Alternatively, this typical measure can be regarded as the value which is similar in size to a significant amount of the data under consideration. There are three statistics which are regarded as 'typical' values for a data set:

- Mode
- Median
- Mean

In this chapter you will consider the properties of all three measures, and by making reference to specific data sets, you will see how each summary measure can be computed for raw data (where each individual value is available) and grouped data.

In addition to calculating the mode, median and mean, a description will be given of the relative advantages and disadvantages of using each measure to represent certain types of data.

Towards the end of the chapter, distinction will be made between symmetrical and skewed frequency distributions by reference to a number of graphical displays. Once this distinction has been made, an indication will be made about which measures of average provide the most appropriate representative summary for both data types.

While the mode, median and mean are arguably the measures of average appreciated the most be decision makers, three additional measures are considered at the end of the chapter (see Additional Concepts). These three lesser used measures are:

- Trimmed Mean
- Percentiles
- Quartiles

Finally, the you will be made aware of how all of the measures described can be computed both quickly and accurately using the built-in facilities offered by Excel. Again, reference will be made to specific business examples.

The Mode

The **mode** is the value or values in the data set which occur more regularly than any other. For a data set where one value occurs more often than any other, the data is said to be **unimodal**. In contrast, if two values with equal occurrence are more common than any other, the data set is considered to be **bimodal**. Finally, there may occasions, particularly in small data sets, when all of the values are different. For these types of data, **no mode** exists.

Examples 1: Calculating the mode for different categories of data

(a) Finding the mode for discrete data

The number of children per household were recorded for nine families selected at random.

No of children: 2 4 4 2 1 3 0 2 0

From the data presented above, the modal value is 2 children per household, since this value occurs most often, i.e. three times. Only one mode exists, so the data set can be described as unimodal.

In contrast, a separate data set showing the number of children per household was collected and is listed below. In this data set **two modes** exist, namely no children and two children, both values occurring three times. This data set can be described as **bimodal**. If a large number of modes exist, then the data could be called multimodal

No of children: **2** 0 4 **2** 1 3 0 **2** 0

In the last discrete data set listed below, again recording the number of children per household, each value is different and therefore **no mode** exists.

No of children: 0 4 5 2 1 3 (**no mode**)

(b) Finding the mode for a frequency distribution

For a data set consisting of discrete data which has been presented in the form of a frequency distribution table, the modal value or values is the group or groups which occur most often, i.e. the value or category with the biggest frequency. In the example below, the number of accidents at a cross roads in a small town have been recorded weekly over a two year period.

No. of Accidents	Frequency (no of weeks)
0	78
1	16
2	6
3	3
4	1
	Total: 104

For this data set, the **modal** number of accidents per week is **zero**. This value corresponds to the group with the largest frequency, i.e. no accidents occur in 78 weeks over the two year period.

(c) Finding the mode for a continuous data set

For a continuous data set presented in the form of a histogram or frequency distribution table, the modal class or interval can be identified in the same way as shown for a grouped discrete data set. In the table below, the annual salaries of 25 manual workers were recorded by a government agency monitoring low pay.

Salary (£000s)	No. of Workers
9 -	2
10 -	7
11 -	10
12 -	4
13 -14	2
	Total: 25

Inspection of this data set tells us that the modal salary range is **£11,000 - <£12,000**. This represents the group with the highest frequency. If the data is presented as a frequency distribution where the intervals are of **unequal width**, then the interval with the **highest frequency density** (see Chapter 3 with reference to the histogram) will represent the **modal class**.

For a continuous data set, a **point estimate** for the mode can be obtained by drawing a histogram. From the histogram, the modal class should be identified (i.e.

the tallest bar on the histogram), and by drawing a line between the opposite corners on the modal bar as shown, a point estimate of the mode can be obtained. This has been illustrated in Figure 4.1 for the data set corresponding to the salaries of the manual workers.

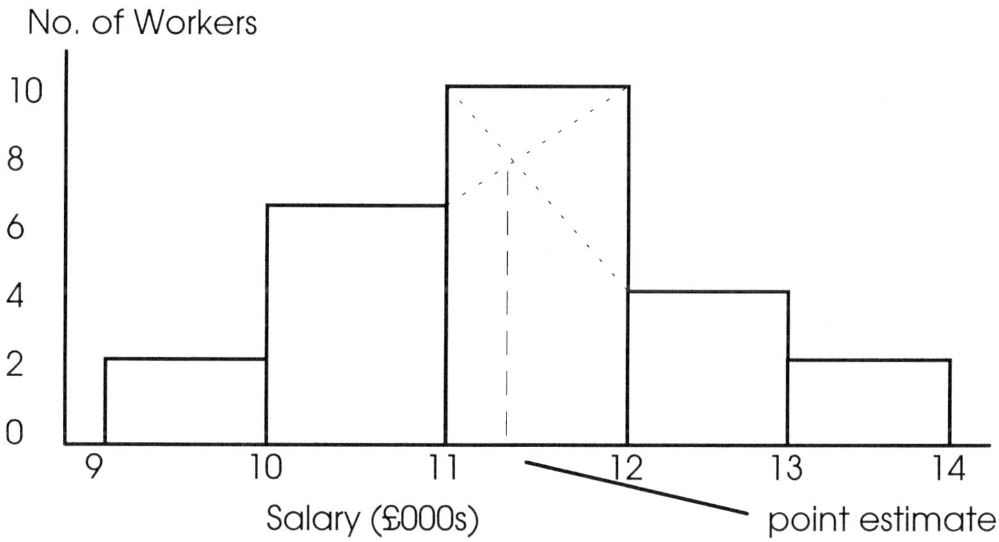

Figure 4.1 - Estimating the mode for a continuous data set

From the histogram presented in Figure 4.1, the point estimate of the modal salary is £11,300. Since the salaries in the original data set are presented to the nearest thousand pounds, the point estimate of the mode has been presented to one more significant figure, i.e. to the nearest hundred pounds. When estimating any of the summary measures described in this chapter, care should always be taken not to give 'too accurate' an estimation.

The Median

When all of the observations in a data set have been listed in either ascending or descending order, an **ordered array** has been created. The **median** value of the data set is defined as the value which lies in the '**middle**' of the ordered array. If a data set contains an even number of values, the median is calculated by averaging of the **two middle values in the ordered array**.

Examples 2: Calculating the median for different categories of data

(a) Finding the median for discrete data

The number of children per household were recorded for nine families selected at random.

No of children: 2 4 4 2 1 3 0 2 0

To determine the median value for the data set, the values must be presented as an **ordered array**. The ordered array for the data set is:

0 0 1 2 **2** 2 3 4 4

Since you have an odd number of values in the data set, the median value is represented by ordered value **(n+1)/2**, where **n** equals nine. In this example, (n+1)/2 is equal to 5, and so the fifth ordered value represents the median. For this data set, the median number of children per household is 2.

In another data set, the number of children per household were recorded for ten families. The **ordered array** is shown below.

No of children: 0 0 1 2 **2** **3** 3 3 3 4

In this case, there are an **even** number of observations, so the median is taken as the average of the 'middle' two values. The **two middle** values are **2** and **3**, so the median number of children per household is **2½**. This example is useful because it shows that the median does not have to take a value that can be observed in the data set, i.e. you cannot observe 2½ children!

(b) Finding the median for a continuous data set

To find the median for continuous, grouped data you can use a cumulative frequency ogive to determine an 'estimate' for the 'middle' value. It is necessary to estimate in this case, because the individual, raw data values are not available. In calculating an estimate for the median in this way, you are assuming that all of the values located in the interval containing the median are *evenly distributed*. The tables below show the frequency distribution of the annual salaries of 25 manual workers and the corresponding cumulative frequency distribution.

Salary (£000s)	No. of Workers
9 -	2
10 -	7
11 -	10 (Frequency Distribution)
12 -	4
13 -14	2
	Total: 25

Salary (£000s)	No. of workers
< 9	0
<10	2
<11	9 (Cumulative
<12	19 Frequency Distribution)
<13	23
<14	25

The cumulative frequency graph for this data set is illustrated in Figure 4.2. Since there are 25 values in the data set, the median is given by ordered value (25+1)/2, i.e. value 13.

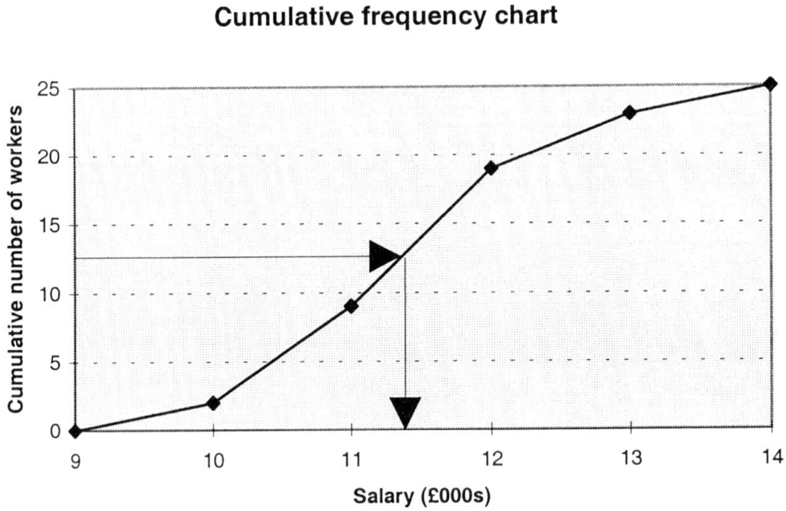

Figure 4.2 - Estimating the median for a continuous data set

From the graph presented in Figure 4.2, you can *estimate* the median to be **£11,400**.

A number of textbooks describe methods in which you can estimate the median by formula. Given you are estimating, the simpler approach is the one described above.

The Mean

The **mean** of a data set is equal to the total of the values divided by the number of values. You will often refer to the mean as the **average**. If the mean is calculated for a population (see Chapter 1), then it is represented by the Greek letter μ (mu). Alternatively, if the mean is calculated for a sample of data, then it is represented by $\bar{x}$ (x bar). Irrespective of whether the mean represents a population or a sample of data, it can be calculated using the formula:

$$\bar{x} = \frac{\sum x}{n}$$

where:

Σx represents the sum of the values of x
i.e. $x_1 + x_2 + ... + x_n$

and

n is equal to the number of values in the data set

In this case, you are considering the **arithmetic mean** of a data set. Other types of means which can be calculated for a data set include the **geometric mean** and the **harmonic mean**. These statistics will not be considered here.

Examples 3: Calculating the mean for different categories of data

(a) Finding the mean for discrete data

Again, you shall consider the data set corresponding to the number of children per household. The data set and the calculation of the mean are shown below:

No of children	2	4	4	2	1	3	0	2	0

$$\bar{x} = \frac{2 + 4 + 4 + 2 + 1 + 3 + 0 + 2 + 0}{9}$$

$\bar{x}$ = **2.0 children**

Therefore, the sample of households considered contain an average of 2.0 children.

(b) Finding the mean for grouped discrete data

If the data set is presented in the form of a grouped frequency distribution table, the mean can be calculated using the formula for the mean of grouped data which is written as:

$$\bar{x} = \frac{\Sigma fx}{\Sigma f}$$

where:

n will be used if the data is calculated from a population.

Σfx represents the sum of the grouped values of x, i.e. **Σfx** equals the total value of the data set for grouped discrete data and provides an *estimate* of the total value of the data set for grouped *continuous* data
$\Sigma fx = f_1x_1 + f_2x_2 + \dots + f_nx_n$

and

Σf is equal to the number of values in the data set (**Σf** is the same as **n**)

The number of accidents recorded weekly at a cross roads in a small town over a two year period are given below.

No. of Accidents (x)	No of Weeks (f)	fx	
0	78	0	(78 x 0)
1	16	16	(16 x 1)
2	6	12	(6 x 2)
3	3	9	(3 x 3)
4	1	4	(1 x 4)

$\Sigma f = 104 \qquad \Sigma fx = 41$

Using the values of Σfx and Σf calculated above, the average number of accidents per week is given by:

$$\bar{x} = \frac{\Sigma fx}{\Sigma f} = \frac{41}{104} = \mathbf{0.39\ accidents\ (2dp)}$$

This calculation shows that the mean value for a data set is not necessarily observable, i.e. you cannot record 0.39 accidents for any individual week.

(c) Finding the mean for continuous data

If a data set is presented in the form of a histogram or grouped frequency distribution, the mean value must be estimated using the formula described in Example 3b). The only difference in this calculation is that the observations in each interval of the frequency distribution must be **approximated** by a single value. The value used to represent each class interval is its **mid-point**. By using such a value to represent each interval, you are making the assumption that the values in a given interval are evenly distributed, as in the estimation of the median. In the table shown below, the annual salaries were recorded as a frequency distribution for 25 manual workers.

Salary (£000s)	**No. of workers** (f)	**Mid-** (x)	fx	
9 -	2	9500	19000	(2 x 9500)
10 -	7	10500	73500	(7 x 10500)
11 -	10	11500	115000	(10 x 11500)
12 -	4	12500	50000	(4 x 12500)
13 - 14	2	13500	27000	(2 x 13500)

$\Sigma f = 25 \qquad \Sigma fx = 284500$

Using the values of **Σfx** and **Σf** shown above, the average annual salary for the group of workers is estimated to be:

$$\bar{x} = \frac{\Sigma fx}{\Sigma f} = \frac{284500}{25} = £11{,}380$$

Comparison of the Main Measures of Average

Since you have been introduced to three statistics in this chapter, the next section will give you a comparison of their properties. In practice, you will only use of one these measures to describe a data set.

The Mode

Since the mode is the most regularly occurring value in a data set, it by definition will not be affected by the presence of any 'one-off' extreme data points. As a consequence, it can provide a representative measure of average. However, a data set can have more than one modal value. If two modes exist, the data is **bimodal**, and if there are more than two modes, the data can be referred to as being **multimodal**. Moreover, in many data sets containing only a small number of observations, the mode may not even exist.

The types of data set where the mode is a useful measure of average are those which consist of only a limited number of possible values. Such a data set was considered in Example 1a) when the number of children per household were recorded. If a local authority or housing association wishes to build new houses, then the modal number of children per household provides a suitable summary measure which can be used in the planning of the mix of properties to be built. In contrast, where a data set contains a much bigger range of possible values, for example the salaries of employees within a large multi-disciplinary organisation such as a university, then the mode may be unsuitable because its value is much less likely to be unique.

The Median

The **median** value of the data set is defined as the value which lies in the '**middle**' of the ordered array, i.e. 50% of the data set lies to the left of the median and 50% to the right. Since the median is the 'middle' value of a data set, its value is not influenced by the presence of 'one-off' extreme values. In another way, the median has a similar property to the mode that in it *explicitly* uses only one or two values in its calculation, and hence, may not be considered as being truly representative of the whole data set.

The Mean

The **mean** of a data set is equal to the total of the values divided by the number of values present, and you will know it as the **average**. The mean is in the 'centre' of a data set because the sum of the deviations of values to its left (i.e. pertaining to those values which are smaller than the mean) **is always** equal to the sum of the deviations of values to its right (i.e. the deviations corresponding to those values which are greater than the mean). The term deviation refers to the difference between the data value and the mean. The (arithmetic) mean considers **every** data value in an equal way, and as a consequence, it is representative of all of the data under consideration. However, by taking all values into account, it will be influenced by 'one-off' extreme values in a data set. When extreme values are present, the mean may have a value which has no similarity to any of the data. However, the properties and application of the mean are accepted more than those of the mode and median by most business decision makers.

Unlike the mode, it is always possible to calculate a unique value for the median and mean. Additionally, both the median and mean can be used for any type of data.

Identifying the Shape of a Frequency Distribution

In Chapter 2 you saw how a data set could be summarised into a table or graph known as a frequency distribution. If a frequency distribution has only one peak or modal class and is **symmetrically** shaped (i.e. the modal class is in the centre), the modal class, median and mean values will be 'roughly' equal in size. A symmetric distribution resembles diagram (a) in Figure 4.3 below.

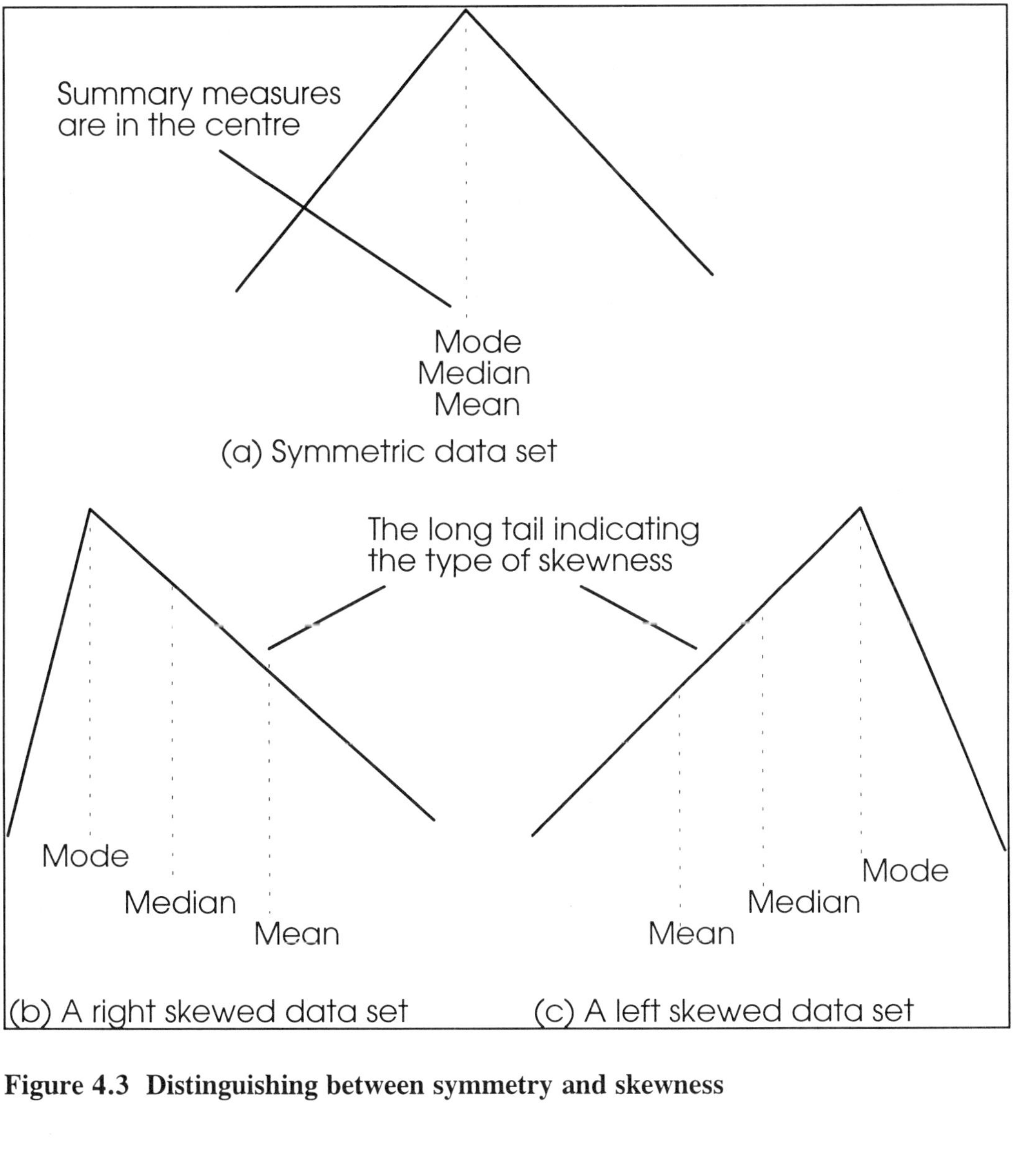

Figure 4.3 Distinguishing between symmetry and skewness

If the modal class of the frequency distribution does not tie close to the centre of the distribution, then its distribution is called **skewed**. As a consequence, the distribution has a long tail and a shorter opposite tail on either side of the modal class. The position of the long tail indicates the type of skewness, if it is to the right of the modal class, the frequency distribution has a right or positive skew and if it is to the left of the modal class the frequency distribution left or negative skew. Diagrams (b) and (c) in Figure 4.4 illustrate distributions which are right and left skewed respectively. Positive skewness occurs with salary data, where a small minority of individuals (such as leaders of major companies and stars of sport and entertainment) earn significantly more than the 'typical' earnings for the data set as a whole.

In general, the creation of a histogram or bar chart will provide sufficient evidence to suggest whether a data set is symmetrical or skewed in shape. Additionally, the degree of skewness can be quantified using a statistic called the **skewness coefficient**. This coefficient may be calculated using Excel and will be described in the next chapter. The formula used by Excel is rather complex, and as a consequence, will not be provided in this text. However, interpretation of the value it generates is very straightforward. Specifically, the coefficient generated by Excel's **SKEW()** function will fall into one of three categories:

Values ≤ -1	indicate recognisable left skewness
Values between -1 and +1	indicate a 'roughly' symmetric distribution
For perfect symmetry, the coefficient will be zero	
Values ≥ 1	indicate recognisable right skewness

Moreover, it should be obvious that the greater the degree of skewness shown by a data set, the greater the negative or positive value displayed by the skewness coefficient.

Whether it be to the left or the right, the skewed shape of a frequency distribution is caused by the presence of certain values which are either much larger (in the case of positive skewness) or much smaller (in the case of negative skewness) than the majority of values present in the data set. Values which are much smaller or larger than the majority of observations in a data set are known as **extreme** values or **outliers**. The main property of the mean is that it considers <u>all</u> data points. As a consequence, if extreme values are present, the mean may have no similarity with any of the data collected. In such a situation, the mean will not provide a representative measure of average. In this case, the median will provide a much more 'typical' value for the data under consideration. This problem is illustrated in Example 4.

Example 4: Comparing the value of the mean and median for a skewed data set.

At a Northern IT consultants, the salaries were recorded for ten employees. The salaries are presented below in the form of an ordered array.

Salaries: (£000s)	7	9	11	12	12	14	14	15	18	125

By inspection of the data set, it is apparent that one extreme value is present. This is the annual salary of £125,000. To compute the mean of the data set, this extreme observation will be included in the calculation. The mean value is calculated to be £23,700. Comparing the value of the mean with the ordered data set listed above, it should be apparent that nine of the values are lower than the mean and therefore this statistic is unrepresentative of the data set as a whole. In contrast, the median salary is £13,000, which is much more representative. Indeed, inspection of the data indicates that six out of the ten salaries are in the range £11,000 to £15,000. Unlike the mean, the value of the median is not affected by the extreme observation, and as a consequence, it can be considered as a more representative or typical value of the data set. In short, the median is the most appropriate measure of average.

In conclusion, if a data set is **symmetrical**, then either the **mean** or the **median** may be used as an appropriate measure of average, since both measures will be similar in value. However, it is arguable that for many decision makers the **mean** is more suitable since it can be used in further calculations and its properties are more widely understood.

In contrast, if a data set is recognisably **skewed**, then the **median** is the most appropriate summary measure to use, since the extreme values are ignored by the median which is calculated from the values in the middle of the distribution. As a consequence, the **median** remains representative of the majority of values in the data set.

In the case of a bimodal frequency distribution, it is best to summarise this data by using the two modal values. If these two modal values are polarised, e.g. circulation of a broadsheet newspaper amongst a group of Business undergraduates, the mean and median values may have values which are untypical of the data set.

Using Excel to Compute Measures of Average

For a raw data set (i.e. where each individual value is available), the built-in facilities offered by Excel may be used to compute the main measures of average both quickly and accurately. These measures can be determined by using the functions:

MODE()

MEDIAN()

AVERAGE()

In all three functions, the data set can be listed as individual values or as an array of cells. Figure 4.4 illustrates their application to a data set consisting of the weights of twenty '50g packets of peanuts' selected at random during a quality control exercise.

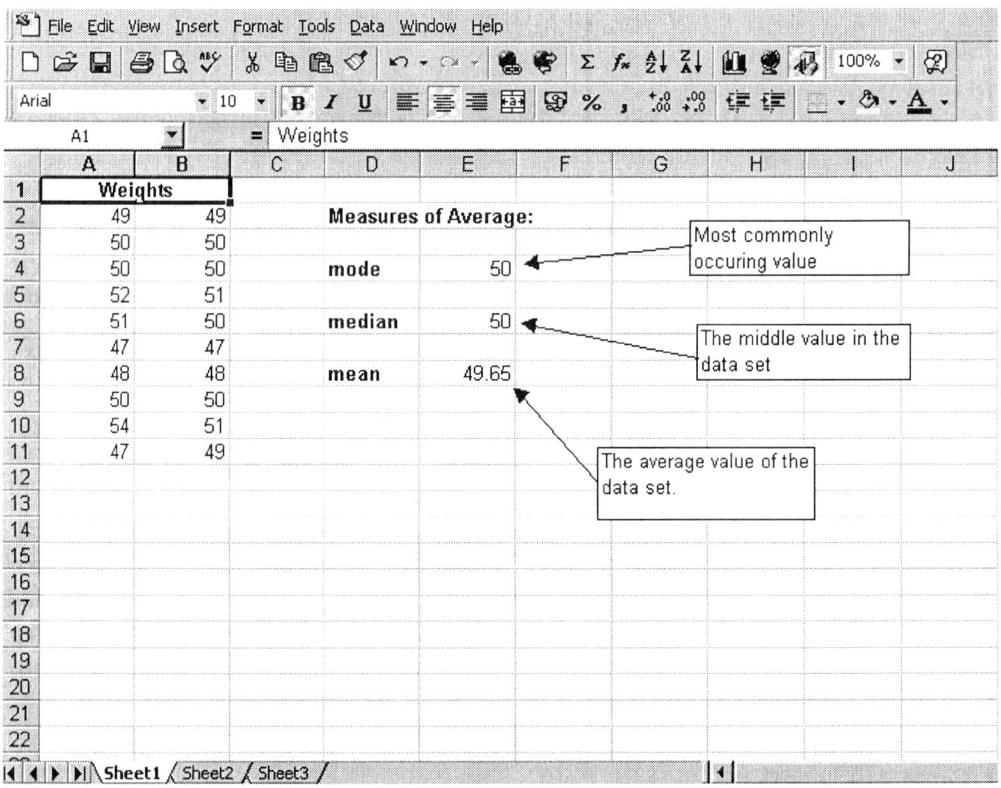

Figure 4.4 - Generating measures of average using Excel

The measures of average are recorded in cells **E4**, **E6** and **E8**. These cells contain the following formulae:

E4 - =MODE(A2:B11)

E6 - =MEDIAN(A2:B11)

E8 - =AVERAGE(A2:B11)

If **no mode** exists in the data set, the function returns the statement **#N/A**. In contrast, for **bimodal** or **multimodal** data, Excel returns only one of the modal values. Specifically, it returns the first modal value identified from the array, after inspecting the data from top to bottom. Also, all three functions listed above ignore blank cells in a specified array, i.e. it treats them as 'missing' values rather than zeros.

Alternatively, when a number of measures need to be calculated, it may be more efficient to use the **Descriptive Statistics** facility which is present in Excel's toolpak. This facility provides both measures of average and dispersion and will be described in the next chapter after a number of the commonly applied measures of dispersion have been considered.

Although Excel does not provide built-in facilities which compute summary measures for grouped data, it may be used to create the necessary graphs and formulae both quickly and accurately. An example is provided in Chapter 5 which illustrates how Excel may be used to calculate the mean and standard deviation for a grouped data set and creating graphs in Excel has been described in Chapter 3.

Additional Concepts

The mode, median and mean described earlier in this chapter are the best known measures of average. However, a number of other measures can be quantified for a data set and are perhaps worth considering. Three additional (but arguably less appreciated) measures of average are:

- Trimmed Mean
- Percentiles
- Quartiles

These three measures are described below by making reference to the built-in facilities offered by Excel.

The Trimmed Mean

The **trimmed mean** of a data set is similar to the mean in terms of calculation except a pre-defined proportion of the smallest and largest values are ignored. For example, the **95% trimmed mean** is calculated by ignoring the smallest 2½% and largest 2½% of values present in a data set.

For a set of values which are **symmetrical** in distribution, the mean and trimmed mean will be **similar** in value. In contrast, if a data set is **skewed**, then it must contain a number of **extreme** observations, and as a consequence, the values of the mean and trimmed mean may be quite different.

Excel offers a built-in facility for calculating the trimmed mean, namely the function:

TRIMMEAN()

Figure 4.5 below shows how this facility has been used. Comparison has been made between the mean and trimmed mean for two data sets each containing the salaries (in £000s) of twenty employees selected at random. For both data sets, the mean and trimmed mean have been computed using the built-in functions AVERAGE() and TRIMMEAN(). The Excel worksheet illustrated in Figure 4.6 contains the following formulae:

D5 - =AVERAGE(A3:B12)

D7 - =TRIMMEAN(A3:B12,0.1)

H5 - =AVERAGE(E3:F22)

H7 - =TRIMMEAN(E3:F22,0.1)

Both C7 and F7 contain the values of the 90% trimmed mean, since 10%, i.e. the largest 5% and the smallest 5% (selected by using the value 0.1 inside the function), of both data sets have been ignored. In this example the values ignored represent the lowest and highest salaries in each sample. Whereas the first data set contains no extreme values, the second contains one extreme value (a salary of £85,000 stored in cell F4) which causes the relatively large difference in the value of the two means.

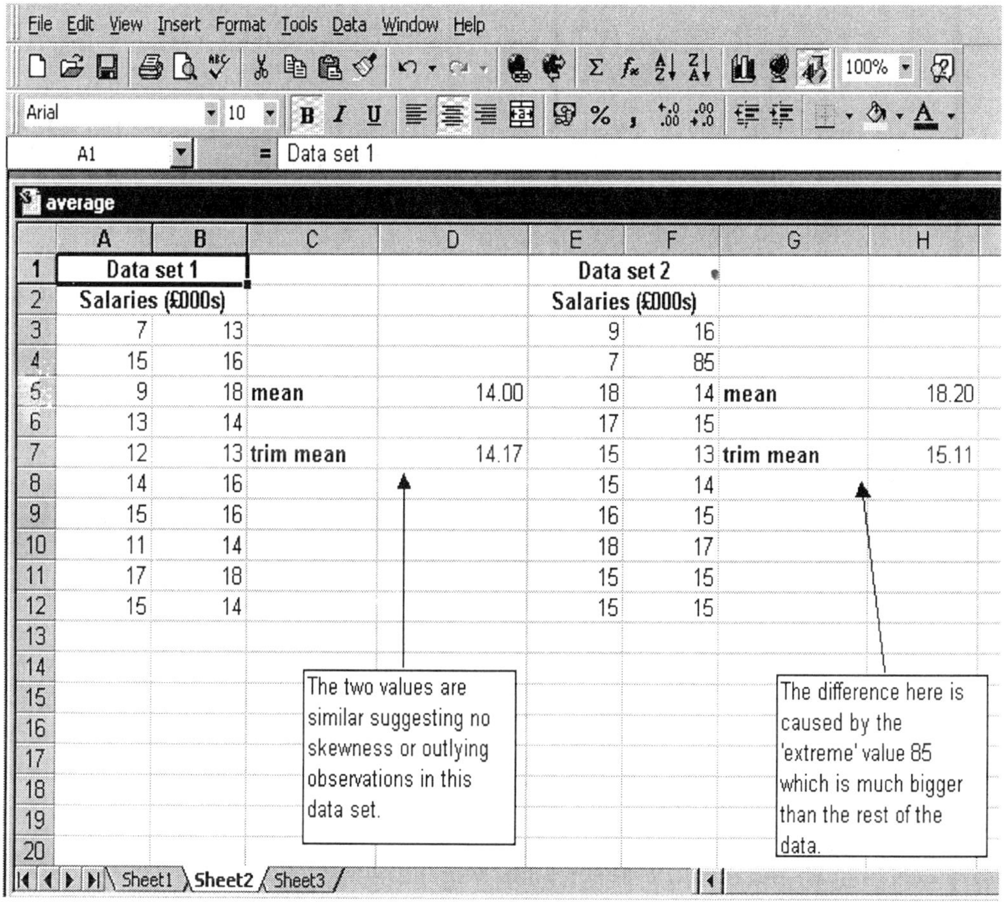

Figure 4.5 - Computing means and trimmed means using Excel

Quartiles and Percentiles

The **quartiles** divide a data set into four parts. The first quartile Q_1, is the value below which twenty five percent of the data values are located and the third quartile Q3, is the value above which twenty five percent of the data can be found.

For a data set stored in cells **A1:A20** on an Excel worksheet, the first quartile can be computed by typing:

=QUARTILE(A1:A20,1)

where:

1 represents the required quartile. Here any integer between 0 and 4 inclusive can be used to define the required quartile.

Where the **quartiles** divide the data set into four equal quarters, the **percentile** points divide a data set into a hundred equal parts. For example, the tenth percentile, is the value below which the **bottom** or **smallest** ten per cent of the values are located in the data set.

Percentiles can be computed easily using Excel. For a data set stored in cells **A1:A20** of a worksheet, the **40th percentile** (i.e. the value above which 40% of the data is located) can be calculated by typing:

=PERCENTILE(A1:A20,0.4)

where:

0.4 represents the required percentile. Any value between 0 and 1 inclusive can be used inside the built-in function.

It should also be apparent from the definitions of the percentile and quartile that the **median** is a special example of both measures. In other words, the median can be written as P_{50} (the fiftieth percentile) or Q_2 (the second quartile). Additionally, the quartiles are useful summary measures since the range of values lying between them often provide a suitable measure of spread or dispersion for a data set. In Chapter 5, you will consider the properties of the quartiles in greater detail, by showing how they can quantify the measure of spread or variability for a data set.

Review

To compute the most appropriate measures of average for a data set, you should undertake the following steps:

1. Inspect the data to determine the number of different values present. If the number of values is small, e.g. the data represents the number of children per household resident on a particular housing estate, then any of the three statistics described as the measure of average can be used.

2. For data sets containing a large number of possible values, create a (grouped) frequency distribution then a graphical display to identify the shape of the distribution, and also note the existence of any extreme values. Finally, compute the **skewness coefficient** to confirm symmetry or skewness.

3. If the data is roughly **symmetrical**, use the **mean** or the **median** as the measure of average. Alternatively, if the data is recognisably **skewed**, use the **median** as the summary measure.

4. For raw data, use the built-in facilities offered by Excel to carry out the steps described above both quickly and accurately.

5. If the data has been grouped, use Excel to undertake the necessary calculations or draw the relevant graphs to ***estimate*** the various measures described in this chapter.

Conclusions

In this chapter you became familiar with the three main measures of average, the mode, median and mean. The most accepted measure of average is the **mean**. However, in skewed data sets, its value may not be representative of the data. In contrast, the mode or median may provide a more suitable measure.

Moreover, by drawing a suitable graph for a data set, it is possible to determine whether the data is symmetrical or skewed. Once this has been determined, a suitable summary measure can then be calculated.

Finally, for raw data, each of the three summary measures described can be computed quickly and accurately using built-in functions offered by Excel.

Learning Outcomes Checklist

After completing this chapter you should have an understanding of the following concepts, calculations and functions:

- The mode, median and mean.
- How to calculate each measure for raw data.
- How to estimate each measure for grouped data.
- The additional summary measures trimmed mean, quartile and percentile.
- How to use the built-in Excel functions **MODE()**, **MEDIAN()**, **AVERAGE()** and how they are applied to raw data.

- An awareness of the Excel functions **TRIMMEAN()**, **QUARTILE()** and **PERCENTILE()**.

- The difference between symmetrical and skewed data.

Ensure that you understand these concepts before progressing to Chapter 5.

Chapter Case Question

- Open the files **CHAP01.XLS** and **CHAP02.XLS**

- Copy the following table from **CHAP02.XLS** into **CHAP01.XLS** and close **CHAP02.XLS**

	Restaurant	Family	Total
Country			
Town			
Total			

- Sort the data by property type and then by location (i.e. Sort By and Then By fields).

- Using Excel's built-in function, complete the following table regarding monthly turnover:

	Reataurant Country	Restaurant Town	Family Country	Family Town
Mean				
Median				
Trimmed Mean (95%)				
Number				

- Save the amended file as **CHAP04.XLS**

Supplementary Questions

1. Describe the mode, median and mean. Describe their advantages and disadvantages as measures of average for a data set.

2. Describe the difference between a symmetric and skewed distribution. Sketch a distribution which is:

   (a) Symmetric

   (b) Left skewed

   (c) Right skewed

3. For each graph in question 2, state which measure of average is the most appropriate.

4. What is meant by the term extreme observation? Describe how they cause a data set to be skewed? Use business examples to support your answer.

5. A quality controller measured the weights of 25 '1 kg' bags of sugar. The following weights (in kg) were recorded:

0.97	0.99	1.00	1.00	1.01
1.05	1.00	1.03	0.96	0.99
0.99	1.00	1.00	1.00	1.01
1.04	1.01	1.00	0.98	0.97
1.00	1.01	1.01	0.97	0.96

   (a) Use a grouped frequency distribution to form a histogram. Describe the shape of the distribution.

   (b) Find the mode, the median and mean for the data using manual calculations.

   (c) Which is the most appropriate measure of average? Give reasons for your answer.

   (d) Check your values for the mode, median and mean using Excel.

6. From a sample of nine employees randomly selected at a manufacturing company, the following annual salaries (in thousands of pounds) were recorded:

   7.6 9.8 10.8 11.2 12.4 13.0 16.0 16.1 78.5

   (a) Find the mean and median salary using the data provided using manual calculations.

   (b) Why is there a difference in the values of the two measures of average? Which is the most appropriate measure? Give reasons for your answer.

   (c) Check your values for the two measures of average using Excel.

7. A northern city council plans to re-house residents on a particular estate. To assist in this relocation of its tenants, the council officers wish to determine a profile regarding the number of children per household. A sample of twenty households was considered. The number of children per household is recorded below:

   0 0 2 3 1 1 3 2 2 2 3 1 2 0 0 1 1 2 3 1

   (a) Present the data in the form of a frequency distribution table. Describe the distribution of children per household.

   (b) Find the mode, median and mean for the data collected using manual calculations.

   (c) Which is the most appropriate measure of average? Give reasons for your answer.

   (d) Check your values for the three measures of average using Excel.

8. As part of a local awareness campaign regarding alcohol consumption, the local Health Council wished to measure the average weekly consumption of beer or lager among young people. A sample of nine youngsters provided the information which is given below:

   No of pints/week: 4 6 11 10 8 12 14 15 9

   (a) Explain why the mode would be an unsuitable measure of average for this data set.

(b) Find the mean and median for the data provided using manual calculations. Compare the values of the two summary statistics. Which is the more representative of the data collected?

(c) Check your values for the two measures of average using Excel.

9. The salaries awarded to 100 company chairmen was recorded as a frequency distribution and are shown below:

Salary (£000s)	Number of chairmen
0 -	2
50 -	11
100 -	17
150 -	35
200 -	18
250 -	12
300 - < 400	5

(a) Present the data using a suitable graphical display. What is the shape of the distribution?

(b) Using the relevant graphs and calculations, estimate the mode, median and mean for this data set.

(c) What is the most appropriate summary measure? Give reasons for your answer.

10. The number of customers using the car park at an 'out of town' shopping centre were recorded weekly over the period of a year. The data set is shown below:

Number of customers	**Number of weeks**
0 -	1
1000 -	33
2000 -	10
3000 -	5
4000 -	2
5000 - < 6000	1

(a) Present the data using a suitable graphical display. What is the shape of the distribution?

(b) Using the relevant graphs and calculations, estimate the mode, median and mean for this data set.

(c) What is the most appropriate summary measure? Give reasons for your answer.

Chapter 5

Measures of Dispersion

Learning Outcomes

In Chapter 4 you were introduced to a number of statistics which offer 'representative' values for a data set. In this chapter you will see how the 'spread' of values or variability in a data set may be quantified. There are several different ways of measuring this variation, the main measures being the **range**, **inter-quartile range**, **mean absolute deviation** and the **standard deviation**. You will be able to describe and calculate each measure, and by reference to specific data sets, suggest when their application is appropriate. Reference will also be made to built-in facilities offered by Excel.

After completing this chapter you will be able to:

- Define the terms range, inter-quartile range, mean absolute deviation, variance and standard deviation.
- Calculate these measures for both raw and grouped data.
- Recognise the strengths and limitations of each summary measure.
- Recognise the appropriate measure of dispersion for symmetrical data and the best measure for a skewed data set.
- Compute the range, inter-quartile range, mean absolute deviation, variance and standard deviation using built-in facilities offered by Excel.

Introduction

While measures of average provide you with values which are 'representative' of a data set, it is also necessary to measure the 'spread' or 'variability' of the data. The statistics which indicate the variability in a data set are described as **measures of variability or dispersion**. This measure of dispersion will also give you an indication of how well the chosen average will represent the data, i.e. if the variability or dispersion of the data is low, the average measure is likely to be representative. There are a number of techniques which can be used to quantify spread and you will consider the four main measures:

- Range
- Inter-quartile range
- Mean absolute deviation
- Standard deviation

In this chapter you will become aware of the properties of all four measures, and by making reference to specific data sets, illustrate how each measure of dispersion can be computed for discrete and continuous data.

In addition to calculating the range, inter-quartile range, mean absolute deviation and standard deviation, you will see the relative advantages and disadvantages of using each measure to represent certain types of data. The suitability of each measure of dispersion will be considered with respect to symmetrical and skewed distributions.

Finally, you will see how all of the measures described can be computed both quickly and accurately using the built-in facilities offered by Excel. Additionally, reference will be made to the **Descriptive statistics** facility offered as part of the spreadsheet's toolpak. This facility will be illustrated by making use of a specific business example.

The Range

The range is the simplest measure of dispersion to calculate and is:

RANGE = MAXIMUM - MINIMUM

Examples 1: Calculating the range for different categories of data

(a) Finding the range for raw data

The number of children per household were recorded for nine families selected at random.

No of children: 2 4 4 2 1 3 0 2 0

From the data presented above, the **maximum** value is **4** children and the **minimum** value is **0**. Therefore, the range is:

maximum - minimum = **4 - 0 = 4**

(b) Finding the range for a grouped discrete data set

For a data set consisting of discrete data which has been presented in the form of a frequency distribution table, the range can be calculated in the same way as shown in Example 1a). The range is the value of the largest group minus the value of the smallest. In the example below, the number of accidents at a cross roads in a small town have been recorded weekly over a two year period.

No. of Accidents	Frequency (no of weeks)
0	78
1	16
2	6
3	3
4	1
	Total: 104

For this data set, the **maximum** number of accidents per week is **4** and the **minimum** number is **0**. The range of number of accidents over the two year period is:

maximum - minimum = **4 - 0 = 4**

(c) Finding the range for a continuous data set

For a continuous data set presented in the form of a histogram or frequency distribution table, the range can be quantified in a similar way to that shown for a grouped discrete data set. In the table below, the annual salaries of 25 manual workers were recorded by a government agency monitoring low pay.

Salary (£000s)	No. of workers
9 -	2
10 -	7
11 -	10
12 -	4
13 - < 14	2
	Total: 25

For a continuous data set, the **maximum** value is estimated as the upper value of the final interval and the **minimum** value as the lower value of the first interval. For the table presented above, the maximum value is £14,000 and the minimum value is £9,000. The range of salaries is given by:

maximum - minimum = **£14,000 - £9,000** = **£5,000**

Although the range is easy to calculate for all types of data, often it is not a very representative measure of variability because it only involves the two **extreme** observations (the **maximum** and **minimum**), and as a consequence, it is not influenced by any of the values within these extremes. This is illustrated below by comparing two data sets with identical ranges but vastly different distributions.

Example 2: Comparing the ranges for two data sets

For two different districts in a city (labelled A and B), the number of children per household were recorded, and their distributions are compared by the graph in Figure 5.1.

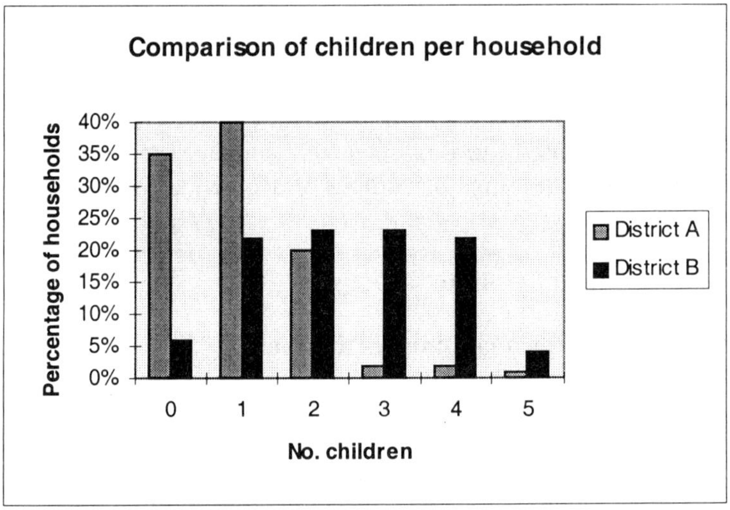

Figure 5.1 - Comparing two distributions with the same range

Both distributions cover exactly the same range, i.e. 0 to 5 children per household. However, inspection of the graph indicates that the two distributions are not the same. The number of children per household in District A are peaked around the modal value of 1, with a recognisable right skew. In comparison, the number of children per household District B are more evenly distributed (compared to District A) between the extreme values zero and five. A much better measure of dispersion is given by the inter-quartile range which measures the variability of a data set within the two extremes described already.

The Inter-Quartile Range

In many ways the interquartile range is similar to the median in the way the quartiles divide a data set specifically, the **quartiles** divide a data set into four parts. The **first or lower** quartile Q_1, is the value *below* which twenty five percent of the data values are situated.

Using the same principle the **third or upper** quartile Q_3, is the value *above* which twenty five percent of the data values and below which seventy five percent of the data values are situated.

The range between Q_3 and Q_1 measures the dispersion of the **middle 50%** of the data and is called the **inter-quartile range**.

INTER-QUARTILE RANGE = UPPER QUARTILE - LOWER QUARTILE

The concept of the inter-quartile range is illustrated by diagram in Figure 5.2. The advantage of using this measure instead of the range is that its value is not affected by extreme observations, and as a consequence, it provides a more representative measure of dispersion than the range.

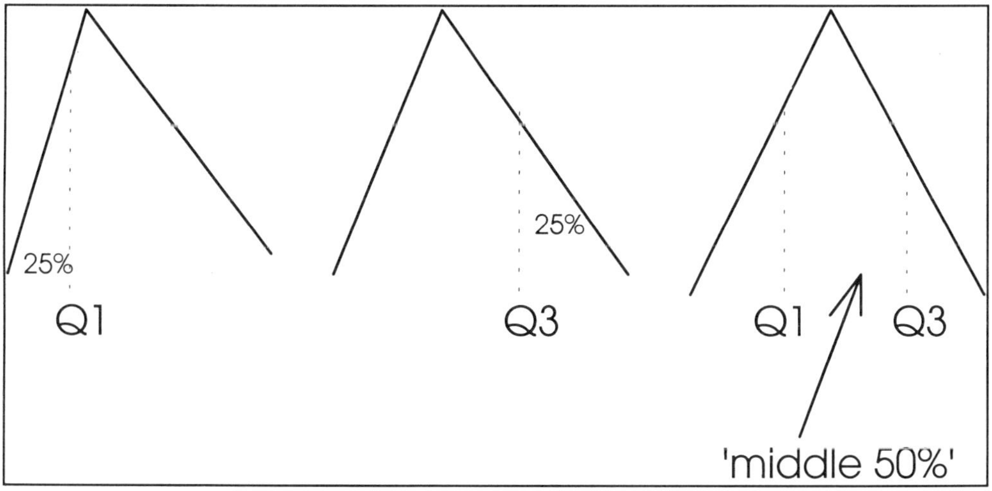

Figure 5.2 - Diagram illustrating the inter-quartile range

Examples 3: Calculating the inter-quartile range for different categories of data

(a) Finding the inter-quartile range for discrete data

The number of children per household were recorded for nine families selected at random.

No of children: 2 4 4 2 1 3 0 2 0

To determine the inter-quartile range for the data set, the values must be initially listed as an **ordered array**. The ordered array for the data set is:

0 0 1 2 2 2 3 4 4

The first or lower quartile Q_1 is given by ordered observation (n+1)/4, where n represents the number of values. In this data set you have nine values, so (n+1)/4 equals 2½. From the data set:

Ordered value 2 = 0
Ordered value 3 = 1, thus ordered observation 2½ is estimated as ½ (since this 'value' is in-between 0 and 1).

$\mathbf{Q_1}$ = ½.

The third or upper quartile Q_3 is given by ordered observation 3(n+1)/4. Since **n** is equal to nine, 3(n+1)/4 equals 7½. From the data set:

Ordered value 7 = 3
Ordered value 8 = 4, thus ordered 'observation' 7½ is estimated as 3½.

$\mathbf{Q_3}$ = **3½**.

The inter-quartile range is given by $Q_3 - Q_1$
= 3½ - ½ = **3**

This measure tells you that the middle 50% of households (ordered in size) have a range of ½ to **3½** children.

(b) Finding the inter-quartile range for a continuous data set

To find the inter-quartile range for a continuous data set the easiest way is to draw a cumulative frequency graph to determine an 'estimate' for the lower and upper quartiles. In calculating an estimate for the quartiles in this way, you are assuming that the values located in the intervals containing both Q_1 and Q_3 are *evenly distributed.* The tables below show the frequency distribution of the annual salaries of 25 manual workers and the corresponding cumulative frequency distribution.

As suggested in Chapter 4 on the discussion of the median, you must estimate the quartiles for the grouped data set because the process of grouping the data results in the individual data values no longer being available.

(Frequency Distribution)

Salary (£000s)	No. of workers
9 -	2
10 -	7
11 -	10
12 -	4
13 - < 14	2
	Total: 25

(Cumulative Frequency Distribution)

Salary (£000s)	No. of workers
< 9	0
<10	2
<11	9
<12	19
<13	23
<14	25

The cumulative frequency graph for this data set is illustrated in Figure 5.3. Since there are 25 values in the data set, the lower quartile Q_1 is given by ordered value $(25+1)/4$, i.e. value 6½, and the upper quartile Q_3 is given by order value $3(25+1)/4$, i.e. value 19½.

Like the estimate of the median for a continuous data set which was described in Chapter 4, the values of Q_1 and Q_3 can be estimated from the cumulative frequency graph. To estimate Q_1, you must read 6½ from the y axis and draw a straight line until it meets the ogive. You then draw a vertical line from the ogive to the x axis which gives you the estimate. The upper quartile is determined in the same way, except you start from the value 19½ on the y axis. Once determined, the difference between Q_3 and Q_1 provides an estimate of the inter-quartile range.

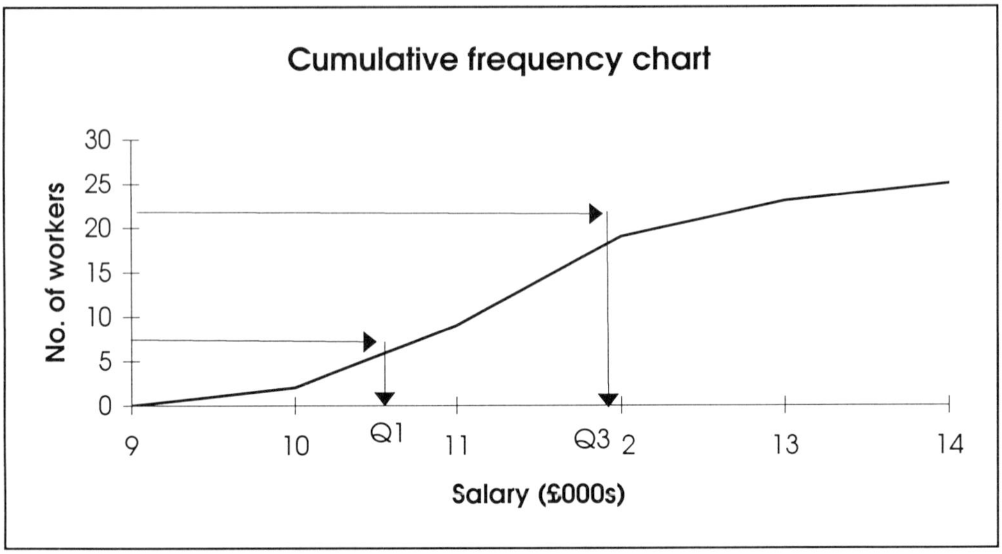

Figure 5.3 - Estimating the upper and lower quartiles

From the graph presented in Figure 5.3, you can *estimate* Q_1 to be £10,600 and Q_3 to be £11,900. The inter-quartile range can then be estimated as:

$$Q_3 - Q_1 = £11{,}900 - £10{,}600 = \mathbf{£1{,}300}$$

By measuring the dispersion of the middle 50% of observations, the inter-quartile range gives a much more representative measure of dispersion than the range since it is not influenced by extreme observations. This principle is illustrated in Example 4 where a data set containing one extreme observation is considered.

Example 4: Comparing the value of the range and inter-quartile range for a data set containing extreme values

At an IT software house, the salaries were recorded for ten employees. The salaries are presented below in the form of an ordered array.

Salaries: (£000s)	7	9	11	12	12	14	14	15	18	125

By inspection of the data set, it is apparent that one extreme value is present, namely the annual salary of £125,000. To compute the range of the data set, this extreme observation will be included in the calculation. The range is equal to £118,000. The lower quartile Q_1, is £10,500 (given by ordered value $2^3/_4$) and the upper quartile Q_3, is £15,750 (given by ordered value 8¼). The inter-quartile range

$Q_3 - Q_1$, is equal to £5,250, the value of which is clearly not influenced, unlike the range, by the presence of a single, extremely large salary in the data set.

The Mean Absolute Deviation

In Chapter 4 you were made aware that the mean is the 'centre' of a data set, i.e. sum of the deviations to the left of the mean are **always** equal to the sum of the deviations to its right. Since this property is true for all data sets, the sum of the deviations

$$\Sigma(x - \bar{x})$$

will always be equal to zero. In the example shown in Figure 5.4, the deviations are -3, -1, -1, 2 and 3. These add up to zero. To calculate an average measure of dispersion for a data set *compared* to their mean, you can measure the **average or mean absolute deviation** instead. This is a potentially useful measure because each deviation from the mean is considered as the same. By calculating absolute values, the positive and negative deviations don't nullify each other, and you are given a measure of how the data varies. For any number, the absolute value is found by disregarding its sign. For example,

the absolute value of 5 is 5 while the absolute value of -3 is 3.

Usually, the absolute value of a number is denoted by $| \; |$, e.g. $|-3| = 3$. The mean absolute deviation can therefore be expressed by the formula:

$$\text{MAD} = \frac{\Sigma|(x - \bar{x})|}{n}$$

where $\bar{x}$ is the mean of the data set
n is equal to the number of values

The concept of the mean absolute deviation is illustrated below in Figure 5.4, with the actual deviations given in brackets (), with their corresponding absolute values being adjacent. The diagram further illustrates the idea of the mean being at the 'centre' of the data set.

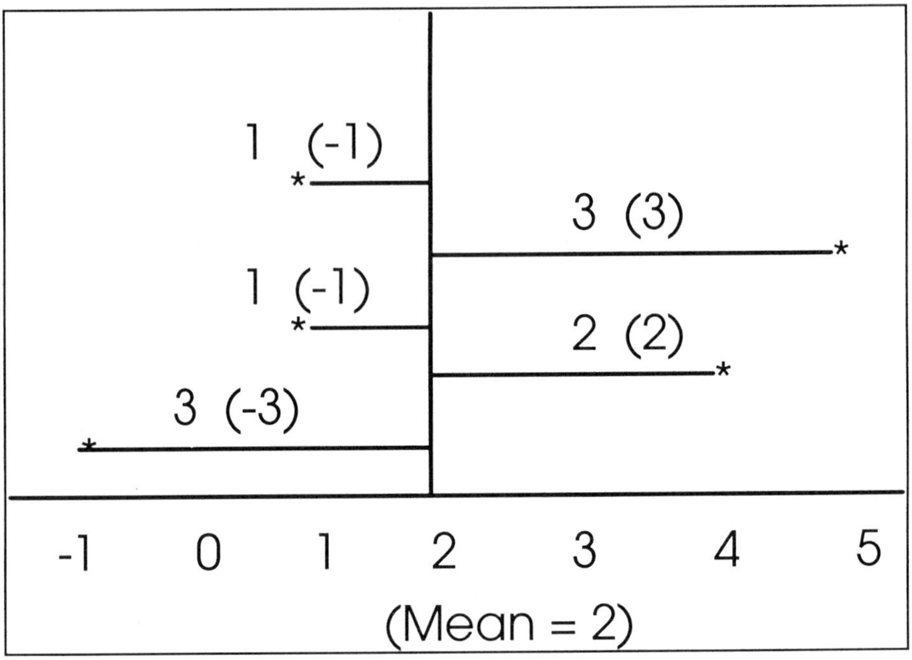

Figure 5.4 - Diagram illustrating the mean absolute deviation

The calculation of the mean absolute deviation is shown below by considering a number of different data sets. The more dispersed the data, the bigger the value of the mean absolute deviation.

Examples 5: Calculating the mean absolute deviation for different categories of data

(a) Finding the mean absolute deviation for discrete data

Again our discrete data set consists of the number of children per household in a small street. The data set and their mean value are shown below:

No of children	2	4	4	2	1	3	0	2	0

Mean $\bar{x}$ = **2.0 children**

x:	2	4	4	2	1	3	0	2	0	Total
$x - \bar{x}$:	0	2	2	0	-1	1	-2	0	-2	
$\|x - \bar{x}\|$:	0	2	2	0	1	1	2	0	2	10

Therefore, the mean absolute deviation = 10/9 = **1.11 children (2dp)**.

(b) Finding the mean absolute deviation for grouped discrete data

If the data set is presented in the form of a grouped frequency distribution table, the mean absolute deviation can be calculated using the formula:

$$\textbf{MAD} = \frac{\sum f|x - \bar{x}|}{\sum f}$$

where:

$\sum f|x - \bar{x}|$ represents the sum of the weighted deviations from the mean

and

$\sum f$ is the number of values in the data set ($\sum f$ is the same as n)

The number of accidents recorded weekly at a cross roads in a small town over a two year period are given below.

Mean $\bar{x} = \frac{\sum fx}{\sum f} = \frac{41}{104} =$ **0.39** accidents (2dp), as shown in Chapter 4.

No. of Accidents (x)	No of weeks (f)	$x - \bar{x}$	$f\lvert x - \bar{x}\rvert$	
0	78	-0.39	30.42	78 x abs(-0.39)
1	16	0.61	9.76	16 x abs(0.61)
2	6	1.61	9.66	
3	3	2.61	7.83	
4	1	3.61	3.61	

$\sum f = 104 \qquad \sum f|x - \bar{x}| = 61.28$

Using the values of $\sum f|x - \bar{x}|$ and $\sum f$ calculated above, the average absolute deviation for the number of accidents per week is given by:

$$\textbf{MAD} = \frac{\textbf{61.28}}{\textbf{104}} = \textbf{0.59 accidents (2dp)}$$

(c) Finding the mean absolute deviation for continuous data

If a data set is presented in the form of a histogram or continuous frequency distribution table, the method used to calculate the mean absolute deviation will be similar to that illustrated above. For a continuous data set, you must determine **one** value of x to represent each class interval in the frequency distribution. The values you use are the **mid-points** of the intervals defined on the frequency distribution. By using this mid-point, reasonable *estimates* can be obtained both for the mean and the mean absolute deviation. This assumption was made and illustrated in Chapter 4 when you calculated the mean for grouped, continuous data.

The Standard Deviation

Like the mean absolute deviation, the **standard deviation** considers the deviation or distance of each value in a data set from their mean value, and the more dispersed the data is from the mean, the greater the standard deviation. Because it measures variability from the mean and is used in specific statistical tests, the standard deviation is used more than the other statistics described in this chapter. Before calculating the standard deviation, a statistic called the **variance** must be determined.

As you saw earlier in the chapter, the average deviation of a data set from its mean is always equal to zero. To calculate an average measure of dispersion for a data set from their mean, the **average absolute deviation** can be used. The **average squared deviation** of a data set provides another way of measuring the dispersion from their mean. Squaring the deviations guarantees the negative and positive values do not nullify each other, so you a provided with a meaningful measure of dispersion. This average squared deviation is known as the **variance** of a data set.

To calculate the variance, two different formulae may be used. The application of either formula will depend upon whether the data represents a **population** or whether it is collected from a **sample**. The relationship between a population and a sample was described in Chapter 1.

The population variance is denoted by σ^2 (sigma squared) and is given by:

$$\sigma^2 = \frac{\Sigma(x - \mu)^2}{n}$$

(this formula shows the sum of the squared deviations divided by the number of values, hence providing a measure of the average squared deviation)

where μ (mu) represents the mean of the data set.

However, the calculation of the variance can be simplified for the purpose of calculations by re-arranging the formula above to give:

$$\sigma^2 = \frac{\Sigma x^2 - n(\mu)^2}{n} \quad \text{or} \quad \sigma^2 = \frac{\Sigma x^2}{n} - (\mu)^2$$

which is a much easier formula to use.

If the data is collected as a sample, the formula for the sample variance is denoted by s^2 and is given by:

$$s^2 = \frac{\Sigma x^2 - n(\bar{x})^2}{n - 1}$$

where $\bar{x}$ represents the sample mean.

By inspecting the formulae for the population and sample variances, it should be apparent that the difference in the two equations is that you divide by **n** for the population parameter and by **n-1** for the sample statistic. You can accept this difference, and should be aware that Excel offers two built-in functions for calculating standard deviations. ***In either case it is important to note that the mean has to be determined before the variance can be evaluated.***

However, there are problems in using the variance as a measure of dispersion. When you measure the **average squared deviation** from the mean, you are calculating a measure of dispersion which cannot be represented in consistent units. If a data set consists of the salaries of a group of employees at an organisation, then each salary (as well as their mean) may be recorded in pounds (£). As a consequence, the units of the variance will be £^{2}. To ensure that the statistic measuring dispersion is recorded in consistent units, you can calculate **the square root of the variance**, to provide a statistic which is called the **standard deviation**.

Although the standard deviation is widely used, its formula and meaning can be quite difficult to understand. Certainly its equivalent measure of average, the mean, is much easier to understand both mathematically and conceptually and so is the mean absolute deviation as an equivalent measure of dispersion. The standard deviation is the square root of the average squared deviation from the mean. This statistic provides an additional average measure of the variability of the data from their mean value and like the mean absolute deviation, it considers every member of the data set in an equal way.

Examples 6: Calculating the variance and standard deviation for different categories of data

(a) Finding the variance and standard deviation for discrete data

Being consistent with the previous measures of dispersion, you can consider the data set corresponding to the number of children per household. The data set and the calculation of the mean are shown below:

No of children	2	4	4	2	1	3	0	2	0

Mean $\bar{x}$ = **2.0 children** and the size of the sample **n = 9**

x:	2	4	4	2	1	3	0	2	0	Total
x^2:	4	16	16	4	1	9	0	4	0	54

Once the mean has been calculated, you can determine the variance. In this example, you are assuming that the data corresponds to a *sample*. Using the values of Σx^2 and the mean gives:

$$\text{Variance } s^2 = \frac{\Sigma x^2 - n(\bar{x})^2}{n - 1}$$

$$= \frac{54 - 9(2)^2}{8}$$

$$s^2 = 2.25 \text{ children}^2$$

Now the variance has been calculated, you must find its square root to give the standard deviation.

$$\text{Standard deviation } s = \sqrt{2.25}$$
$$= \mathbf{1.5 \text{ children}}$$

This tells us that on average, the deviation of children per household from the mean is 1.5.

(b) Finding the variance and standard deviation for a frequency distribution

If the data set is presented in the form of a grouped frequency distribution table, the sample variance can be calculated using the formula for the variance of grouped data which is written as:

$$\text{Variance } s^2 = \frac{\Sigma fx^2 - \Sigma f(\bar{x})^2}{\Sigma f - 1}$$

where:

Σfx^2 represents the sum of the weighted values of x^2
i.e. $f_1x_1^2 + f_2x_2^2 + ... + f_nx_n^2$

You should note in this calculation, it is the <u>x values only</u> that are squared.

and

> Σ**f** represents the number of values in the data set (Σf is equal to n)

The number of accidents recorded weekly at a cross roads in a small town over a two year period are given below. The bold and italics indicate which numbers have been multiplied together in each row of the table.

No. of Accidents (x)	**No of weeks** (f)	fx	fx^2
0	78	**0** (78 x *0*)	0 (**0** x *0*)
1	16	**16** (16 x *1*)	16 (**16** x *1*)
2	6	**12** (6 x *2*)	24 (**12** x *2*)
3	3	**9** (3 x *3*)	27 (**9** x *3*)
4	1	**4** (1 x *4*)	16 (**4** x *4*)
	$\Sigma f = 104$	$\Sigma fx = 41$	$\Sigma fx^2 = 83$

Using the values of Σfx and Σf calculated above, the mean number of accidents per week is 0.39, as found earlier.

Using the value of the mean to determine the variance:

$$\text{Variance} \quad s^2 = \frac{\Sigma fx^2 - \Sigma f\,(\bar{x})^2}{\Sigma f - 1} = \frac{83 - 104(0.39)^2}{103}$$

$$= \mathbf{0.6522\ (4dp)}$$

Standard deviation $s = \sqrt{0.6522}$
$= \mathbf{0.81\ accidents\ (2dp)}$

(c) Finding the variance and standard deviation for continuous data

If a data set is presented in the form of a histogram or grouped frequency distribution, the method used to estimate the standard deviation is similar to that described above, except the values in each interval must be approximated by a single value. The values used are the **mid-points** for each interval defined in the frequency distribution. In the table shown below, the annual salaries were recorded as a frequency distribution for 25 manual workers. Again, the bold and italics indicate which numbers have been multiplied together in each row of the table.

Salary (£000s)	**Workers**	**Mid-point**		
(x)	(f)	(x)	fx	fx^2
9 -	2	*9.5*	**19.0** (2 x *9.5*)	180.50 (**19.0** x *9.5*)
10 -	7	*10.5*	**73.5** (7 x *10.5*)	771.75 (**73.5** x *10.5*)
11 -	10	*11.5*	**115.0** (10 x *11.5*)	1322.50 (**115.0** x *11.5*)
12 -	4	*12.5*	**50.0** (4 x *12.5*)	625.00 (**50.0** x *12.5*)
13 - 14	2	*13.5*	**27.0** (2 x *13.5*)	364.50 (**27.0** x *13.5*)
	$\Sigma f = 25$		$\Sigma fx = 284.5$	$\Sigma fx^2 = 3264.25$

Using the values of Σfx and Σf shown above, an *estimate* of the average annual salary for the group of workers is:

$$\textbf{Mean } (\bar{x}) = \frac{\Sigma fx}{\Sigma f} = \frac{284.50}{25} = \pounds 11.38 \text{ (£ in thousands)}$$

Using the values of Σfx^2, Σf and $\bar{x}$, *estimates* of the variance and standard deviation are given by:

$$\text{Variance} \quad s^2 = \frac{\Sigma fx^2 - \Sigma f(\bar{x})^2}{\Sigma f - 1} = \frac{3264.25 - 25(11.38)^2}{24}$$

$$= \mathbf{1.11}$$

Standard deviation $s = \sqrt{1.11}$
= **1.054 (£ thousands)**
= **£1,054**

Comparison of the Main Measures of Dispersion

You have been introduced to four statistics in this chapter, which indicate the dispersion in a data set. In this section you will be given a comparison of their properties. In practice, you will only use of one these measures to describe a data set.

The Range

The range is the simplest measure of dispersion to calculate and is the difference between the maximum and minimum values in a data set. Although it is easy to calculate, the range is limited in its application because it considers the two extremes, and as a consequence, it is highly influenced by 'one-off' outlying observations. Moreover, the range gives no indication about the values which are located between the two extreme observations.

However, the range does provide a useful measure of dispersion for data sets which consist of only a small number of possible values. Such a data set was considered in Example 1a) where the number of children per household were recorded.

The Inter-quartile range

In the same way as the median divides a data set in half, the **quartiles** divide a data set into four parts. The **first or lower** quartile Q_1, is the value *below* which twenty five percent of the data values are located and the **third or upper** quartile Q_3, is the value *above* which twenty five percent of the data values are situated. The range between Q_3 and Q_1 indicates the dispersion of the middle 50% of the data and is called the **inter-quartile range**.

Unlike the range, the inter-quartile range is not influenced by extremes in a data set since the largest and smallest twenty five percent of observations are ignored. As a consequence, it is a much more representative measure of dispersion, particularly when a data set is skewed. However, the inter-quartile range is similar to the range in that only two values of a data set are explicitly considered in its calculation.

The Mean Absolute Deviation

The **mean absolute deviation** of a data set is equal to the average of the absolute deviations from the mean. Since the mean is a data set's 'centre', this measure provides an indication of the average deviation of each observation from the 'centre' value. The mean absolute deviation uses **every** data value in its calculation, and as a consequence, it will be influenced by the presence of 'one-off' high or low values. When extreme values are present, the value of the mean absolute deviation may not provide a representative measure of dispersion, unlike the inter-quartile range described above.

The Standard Deviation

The **variance** of a data set is equal to the average of the squared deviations from the mean for each value in a data set. Since this measure considers squared deviations, the units are not the same as those of the actual data. By taking the square root of the variance, a statistic called the **standard deviation** is calculated. The standard deviation has consistent units with the data set, and like the mean absolute deviation provides an indication of the average deviation from the mean or 'centre' value. Because each value in a data set is considered, its value may not provide a representative measure of dispersion when extreme observations are present. Compared to the mean absolute deviation, the standard deviation is a much harder concept to grasp for many business students. Inspection of the respective formulae would suggest the former is a simpler measure of dispersion to calculate.

However, the standard deviation is a useful statistical measure in the area of inferential statistics which will be described in Chapters 9 and 10. Its value (along with the mean) are used to determine the shape of a special statistical distribution, called the normal distribution. This distribution is considered in various statistical tests which are regularly used by decision makers in business.

Finally, it should be apparent that the greater the spread of a data set, the greater the value of each of the four measures of dispersion described in this chapter. This is illustrated below in Figure 5.5, where the graph of two data sets are compared. Both data sets have a mean value of 450, but the respective standard deviations are 15 and 35. Inspection of the two graphs indicates the latter has the greater dispersion of values, as expected.

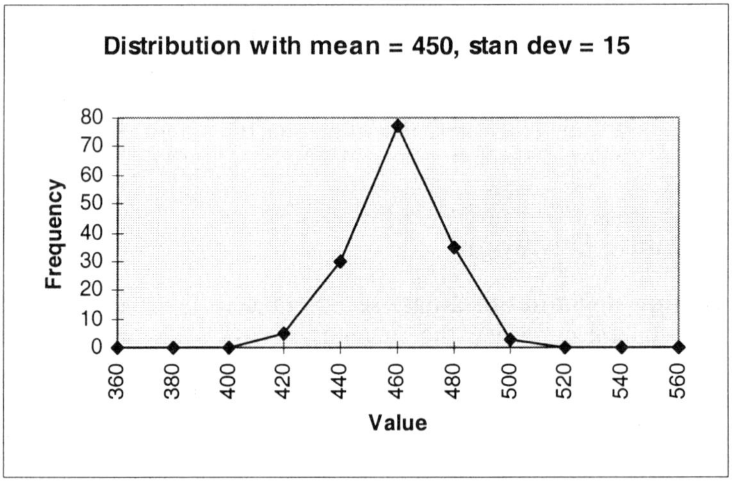

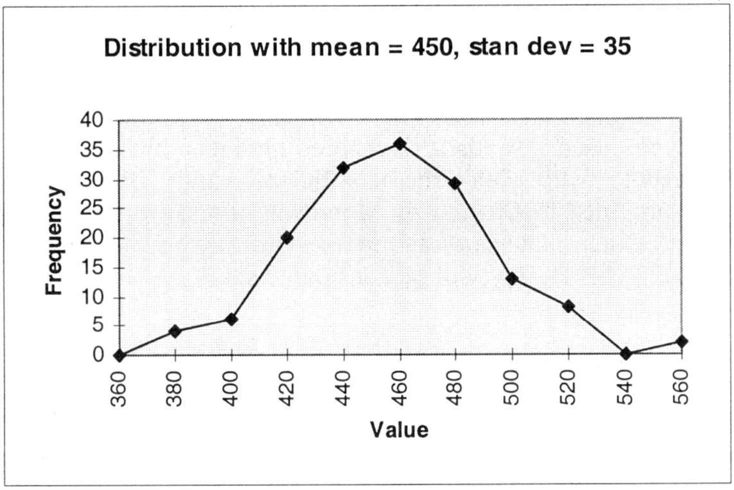

Figure 5.5 - Comparison of two data sets with different standard deviations

Quantifying the Level of Skewness in a Frequency Distribution

In Chapter 4 this concept was introduced and a distinction was made between frequency distributions which are symmetrical in shape and those which are skewed. Certain measures of average are appropriate for symmetrical data, while others are more suitable for asymmetrical or skewed data sets. Similarly, certain measures of dispersion are most suitable for the different types of data.

If a data set is **symmetrical**, then it is likely that it contains no extreme values. As a consequence, either the **mean absolute deviation** or **standard deviation** should be used as an appropriate measure of dispersion, since both consider every value in the data set and measure the spread of the data compared to their mean. Using the same principles, the **mean** represents the most appropriate measure of average (see Chapter 4). However, it is arguable that for many decision makers the **standard deviation** is more suitable than the **mean absolute deviation** since the former can be used in additional analysis (in particular when inferences are made about population means - see Chapters 9 and 10) and as a consequence, its properties are more widely accepted.

Finally, for any data set whose distribution has a identifiable **skew**, the **inter-quartile range** is the most suitable summary measure to use, because the extreme values which have resulted in the skewed distribution are not considered in this measure of dispersion. The inter-quartile range indicates the spread of only the 'middle 50%' of values in the data set, and as a consequence, it ignores any outlying observations. The equivalent measure of average for this type of data is of course, the **median**.

To measure the degree of skewness in a raw data set, Excel's built-in **SKEW()** command can be used. If data is stored in the block **A1:A100**, typing **=SKEW(A1:A100)**, will yield the coefficient value. Interpretation of this coefficient was provided in Chapter 4. Moreover, the skewness coefficient is also provided as part of the output provided by the **Descriptive Statistics** facility found in Excel's toolpak. This facility will be considered shortly.

Using Excel to Compute Measures of Dispersion

For a discrete data set, the built-in facilities offered by Excel may be used to compute the main measures of dispersion both quickly and accurately. These measures can be determined by using the functions:

MAX() and MIN()
QUARTILE()
VAR()
STDEV()
AVEDEV()

In all the functions listed above, the data set can be listed as individual values or as an array of cells. Figure 5.6 illustrates their application to a *sample* consisting of the weights of twenty '50g packets of peanuts' selected at random during a quality control exercise.

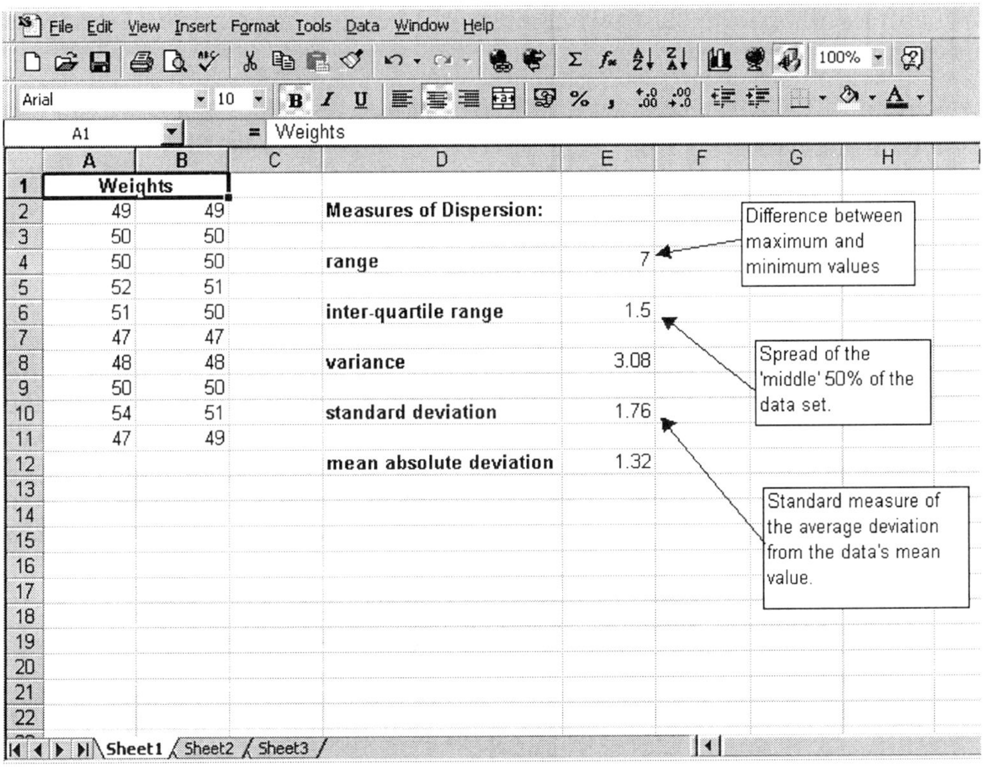

Figure 5.6 - Generating measures of dispersion using Excel

The measures of dispersion are recorded in cells **E4**, **E6**, **E8**, **E10** and **E12**. These cells contain the following formulae:

E4 - **=MAX(A2:B11)-MIN(A2:B11)**
E6 - **=QUARTILE(A2:B11,3)-QUARTILE(A2:B11,1)**
(NB: the arguments 3 and 1 indicate the required quartiles, i.e. Q_3 and Q_1 respectively)
E8 - **=VAR(A2:B11)**
E10 - **=STDEV(A2:B11)**
E12 - **=AVEDEV(A2:B11)**

When a number of measures need to be calculated, it may be more efficient to use the **Descriptive Statistics** facility which is present in Excel's **toolpak**. As stated in Chapter 4, this facility provides both measures of average and dispersion, providing numerical rather than formula based output. If the data regularly updates on the spreadsheet, e.g. output from a quality control exercise input onto a pre-defined spreadsheet at the end of each production run, application of the built-in statistical functions described in the last two chapters will be more appropriate. To activate this facility, you must select:

Tools
Data Analysis

followed by **Descriptive Statistics**.

The dialogue box corresponding to this facility is shown in Figure 5.7. To activate the tool, the 'input range' and the 'output range' must be defined. The 'input range' is the data to be analysed. If the data is entered as a block, then Excel will assume the separate columns represent different samples of data, and as a consequence, will compute summary statistics for each. **If the block represents a single data set, the values should be moved into a single column before this facility is activated.** The 'output range' is given by a single cell reference indicating the top left hand corner of the cells which will store the computed statistics. To compute these statistics, the 'Summary Statistics' button also needs to be clicked on as shown below.

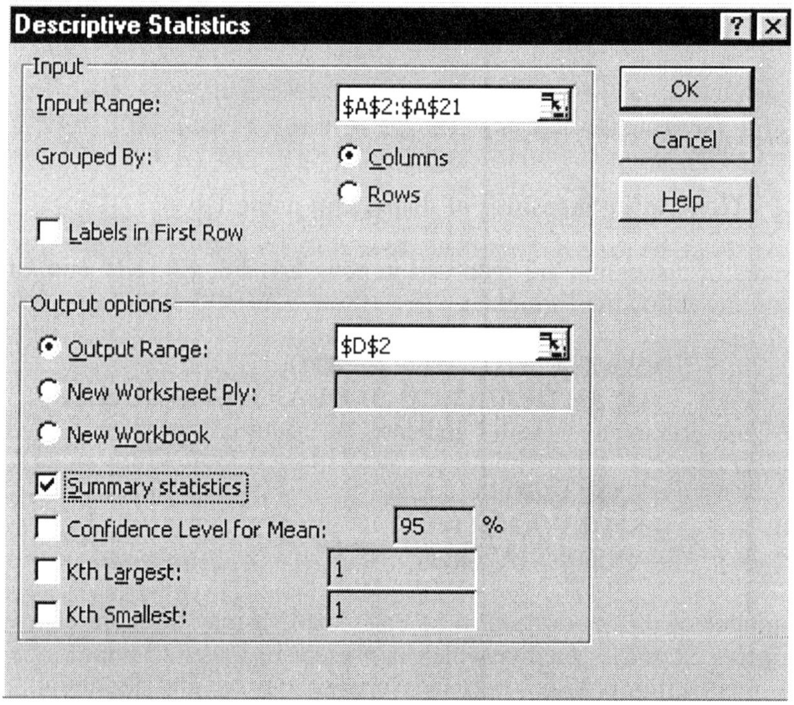

Figure 5.7 - The dialogue box for Excel's Descriptive statistics tool

The output generated by this facility is shown in Figure 5.8.

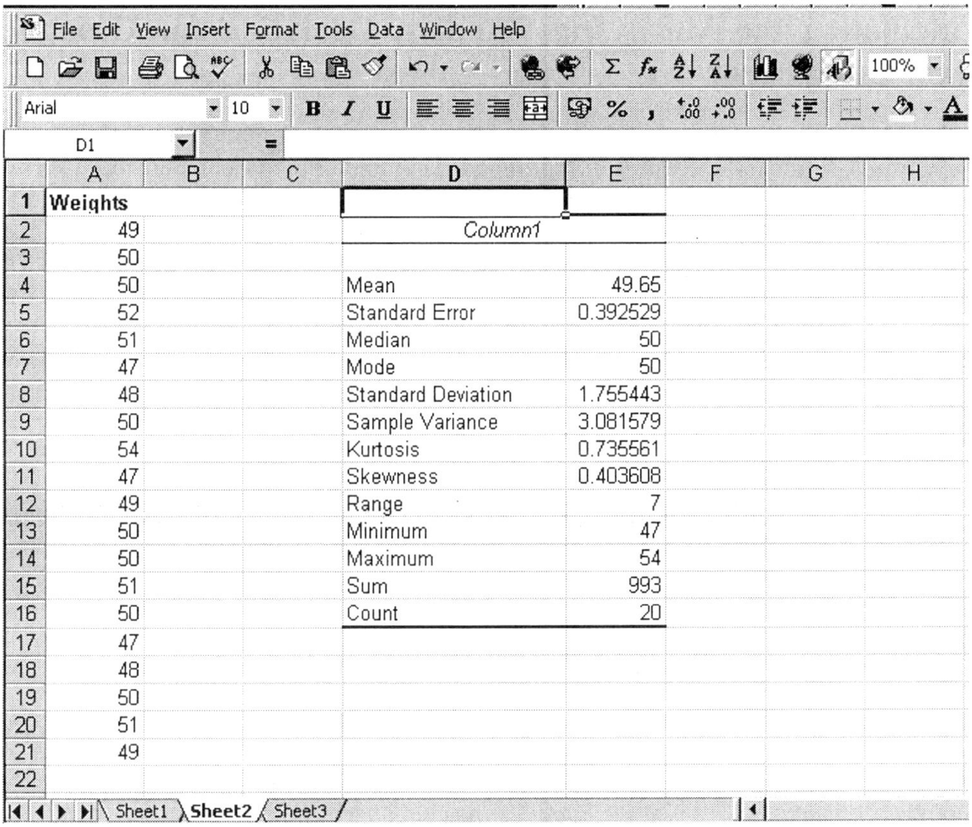

	A	B	C	D	E	F	G	H
1	**Weights**							
2	49			*Column1*				
3	50							
4	50			Mean	49.65			
5	52			Standard Error	0.392529			
6	51			Median	50			
7	47			Mode	50			
8	48			Standard Deviation	1.755443			
9	50			Sample Variance	3.081579			
10	54			Kurtosis	0.735561			
11	47			Skewness	0.403608			
12	49			Range	7			
13	50			Minimum	47			
14	50			Maximum	54			
15	51			Sum	993			
16	50			Count	20			
17	47							
18	48							
19	50							
20	51							
21	49							
22								

Figure 5.8 - Output from the Descriptive statistics option in Excel

An important note to make is that the variance and standard deviation provided as part of the output in Figure 5.8 represent sample statistics. If the data corresponded to a population, the two parameters could be computed in Excel by using the built-in population functions:

VARP()
STDEVP()

Most of the output provided by this facility should be self explanatory at this stage with the exception of two measures; the standard error and kurtosis. Kurtosis is considered to be beyond the scope of this book. The **standard error** is given by the formula **s/√n** (i.e. the standard deviation of a data set divided by the square root of the number of observations). The chief application of the standard error is in the area of inferential statistics and this statistic will be introduced formally in Chapters 9 and 10.

Calculating the Mean and Standard Deviation for Grouped Data Using Excel

Although Excel does not provide built-in facilities which compute the ***estimates*** of the various summary measures for grouped data, the spreadsheet may be used to draw the necessary graphs and formulae both quickly and accurately. Figure 5.9 shows how Excel may be used to compute the mean and standard deviation for a grouped data set. The data relates to the number of new sales recorded by 75 salesmen. It has been assumed that the data set represents a population.

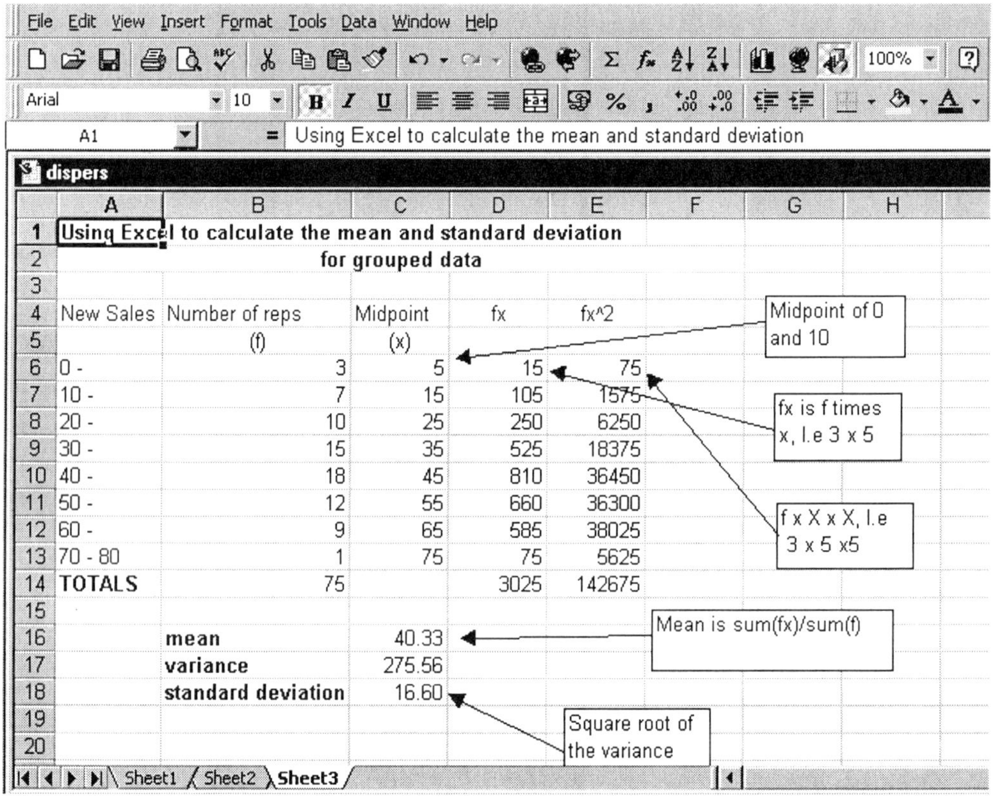

	A	B	C	D	E
1	**Using Excel to calculate the mean and standard deviation**				
2			**for grouped data**		
3					
4	New Sales	Number of reps	Midpoint	fx	fx^2
5		(f)	(x)		
6	0 -	3	5	15	75
7	10 -	7	15	105	1575
8	20 -	10	25	250	6250
9	30 -	15	35	525	18375
10	40 -	18	45	810	36450
11	50 -	12	55	660	36300
12	60 -	9	65	585	38025
13	70 - 80	1	75	75	5625
14	TOTALS	75		3025	142675
15					
16		**mean**	40.33		
17		**variance**	275.56		
18		**standard deviation**	16.60		
19					
20					

Figure 5.9 - Calculating measures for grouped data using Excel

The output illustrated in Figure 5.9 contains three formulae which are recorded in cells **C16**, **C17** and **C18**.

C16 - =D14/B14
C17 - =E14/B14-(C16*C16)
C18 - =SQRT(C18)

where B14 = $\sum f$, D14 = $\sum fx$ and E14 = $\sum fx^2$, each cell making use of Excel's **sum()** function.

Moreover, if the estimate of the median and inter-quartile range were required. these statistics could be estimated from an ogive as demonstrated in the last two chapters. The ChartWizard facility offered by Excel can be used to produce this type of graph.

Review

To compute the most appropriate measures of dispersion for a data set, you should undertake the following steps:

1. Inspect the data to determine the number of different values present. If the number of possible values the data set is limited, e.g. the data represents the number of children per household resident on a particular housing estate, use any of the four measures described in this chapter.

2. For data sets containing a large number of values, draw a suitable graph or table to identify the shape of the frequency distribution, and also note the existence of any extreme values. Finally, compute the **skewness coefficient** (described in Chapter 4) to confirm symmetry or skewness.

3. If the data is **symmetrical**, use the **mean absolute deviation** or the **standard deviation** as the measure of dispersion. If the data is **skewed**, use the **inter-quartile range** as the summary measure.

4. Use the built-in facilities offered by Excel to carry out the steps described above both quickly and accurately.

It should be obvious that the more dispersed an individual data set is, the greater the values of each of the four measures of variability considered in this chapter.

Conclusions

In this chapter you were introduced to the four main measures of dispersion, the range, inter-quartile range, mean absolute deviation and the standard deviation. The **standard deviation** is used more than the other statistics considered. However, in skewed data sets, its value may not be representative of the data, and as a result, the **inter-quartile** range may provide a more suitable measure.

By drawing a suitable graph for a data set or using **SKEW()**, it is possible to determine whether the data is symmetrical or skewed. Once this has been determined, a suitable measure of dispersion can then be calculated.

If data is collected and presented in a raw form, each of the four summary measures described can be computed quickly and accurately using the built-in facilities offered by Excel. For a grouped data set, the environment offered by Excel can be used in the creation of the necessary graphs and formulae required to estimate the value of the most appropriate measure.

Learning Outcomes Checklist

After completing this chapter you should have an understanding of the following concepts, calculations and functions:

- The statistics range, inter-quartile range, mean absolute deviation, variance and standard deviation..
- How to calculate each measure for raw data.
- How to estimate each measure for grouped data.
- How to use the built-in Excel functions **MIN()**, **MAX()**, **QUARTILE()**, **AVEDEV()**, **VAR()** and **STDEV()** and how they are applied to raw data.
- An awareness of the different Excel functions for calculating the variance and standard deviation for population and sample data.
- How to determine the degree of skewness for a raw data set using Excel's **SKEW()** function.
- Symmetrical, well-behaved data are summarised by the mean and standard deviation, whilst a data set with a recognisable skew is summarised by the median and inter-quartile range.

Ensure that you understand these concepts before progressing to Chapter 6.

Chapter Case Question

- Open the file **CHAP04.XLS**
- Create the following table with regard to monthly turnover:

	Restaurant Country	Restaurant Town	Family Country	Family Town
Minimum				
Maximum				
Range				
Upper Quartile				
Lower Quartile				
Inter-Quartile Range				
Mean Absolute Deviation				
Variance				
Standard Deviation				
Skewness Coefficient				

- Identify the most appropriate summary measures for each of the four data sets.

- Save the amended file as **CHAP05.XLS**

Supplementary Questions

1. Describe the range, inter-quartile range, mean absolute deviation and standard deviation.

2. Describe the advantages and disadvantages of using the statistics described in Question 1 as measures of dispersion for a data set.

3. Why is the inter-quartile range a more suitable measure of dispersion than the range?

4. Which are the most suitable measures of dispersion for:

   (a) symmetrical data set

   (b) skewed data set?

   Give reasons for your answer.

5. A quality controller measured the weights of 25 '1 kg' bags of sugar. The following weights (in Kgs) were recorded:

0.97	0.99	1.00	1.00	1.01
1.05	1.00	1.03	0.96	0.99
0.99	1.00	1.00	1.00	1.01
1.04	1.01	1.00	0.98	0.97
1.00	1.01	1.01	0.97	0.96

(a) Find range, inter-quartile range, mean absolute deviation and standard deviation for the data collected using manual calculations.

(b) Which is the most appropriate measure of dispersion? Give reasons for your answer by considering the graph created in Ch4 Q5.

(c) Check your values for the four measures of dispersion using Excel.

6. From a sample of nine employees randomly selected at a manufacturing company, the following annual salaries (in thousands of pounds) were recorded:

   7.6 9.8 10.8 11.2 12.4 13.0 16.0 16.1 78.5

   (a) Find the range, inter-quartile range, mean absolute deviation and standard deviation using the data provided using manual calculations.

   (b) Why are big differences in the values of the four measures of dispersion? Which is the most appropriate measure? Give reasons for your answer by considering the graph created in Ch4 Q6.

   (c) Check your values for the four measures of dispersion using Excel.

7. A northern city council plans to re-house residents on a particular estate. To assist in this relocation of its tenants, the council officers wish to determine a profile regarding the number of children per household. A sample of twenty households were considered. The number of children per household are recorded below:

   0 0 2 3 1 1 3 2 2 2 3 1 2 0 0 1 1 2 3 1

   (a) Find the range, inter-quartile range, mean absolute deviation and standard deviation for the data collected using manual calculations.

   (b) Which is the most appropriate measure of dispersion? Give reasons for your answer by considering the frequency distribution table created in Ch4 Q7.

(c) Check your values for the four measures of dispersion using Excel.

8. As part of a local awareness campaign regarding alcohol consumption, the local Health Council wished to measure the average weekly consumption of beer or lager among young people. A sample of nine youngsters provided the information which is given below:

No of pints/week: 4 6 11 10 8 12 14 15 9

(a) Find the range, inter-quartile range, mean absolute deviation and standard deviation using manual calculations.

(b) Which is the most suitable measure of dispersion for this data set? Give reasons for your answer by considering the frequency distribution table created in Ch4 Q8.

(c) Check your values for the four measures of dispersion using Excel.

9. The salaries awarded to a sample of 100 company chairmen was recorded as a frequency distribution and are shown below:

Salary (£000s)	**Number of chairmen**
0 -	2
50 -	11
100 -	17
150 -	35
200 -	18
250 -	12
300 - < 400	5

(a) Using the relevant graphs and calculations, estimate the range, inter-quartile range, mean absolute deviation and standard deviation for this data set.

(b) What is the most appropriate summary measure? Give reasons for your answer by considering the graph created in Ch4 Q9.

10. The number of customers using the car park at an 'out of town' shopping centre were recorded weekly over the period of a year. The data set is shown below:

Number of customers	Number of weeks
0 -	1
1000 -	33
2000 -	10
3000 -	5
4000 -	2
5000 - < 6000	1

(a) Using the relevant graphs and calculations, estimate the range, inter-quartile range, mean absolute deviation and standard deviation for this data set.

(b) What is the most appropriate summary measure? Give reasons for your answer by considering the graph created in Ch4 Q10.

Part 3

Applying Probability To Business Decision Making

Chapter 6

An Introduction To Probability

Learning Outcomes

In this chapter you will be introduced to the concept of probability, and in doing so, you will be shown a number of laws of probability. Throughout the chapter, you will be shown how the laws of probability can applied to specific business problems.

After completing this chapter you will be able to:

- Understand the terms 'event', 'trial' and 'probability'.
- Recognise the existence of two main branches of measurable probability, namely 'classical', and 'experimental' probability.
- Calculate the probability of a particular outcome taking place.
- Understand certain rules of classical probability; including the range of values a measure of probability can take, expected number of events, the multiplicative law and the additive law.
- Understand the terms 'exclusive' and 'exhaustive'.
- Distinguish between independent and dependent events.
- Use a tree diagram to represent the number of possible events from a trial and display the corresponding probabilities.
- Draw a venn diagram.

Introduction

In everyday life you will encounter problems which involve uncertainty. The 1990s have seen the introduction in the UK of the **National Lottery** in which anyone purchasing a lottery ticket has a probability (albeit very small) of winning a multi-million pound jackpot prize. The theory of probability is often presented by making reference to gaming, in particular referring to throwing dice and selecting playing cards since these applications are easy to understand and will have been introduced to many readers via Mathematics courses at school. You will also consider this type of example, although where possible, reference will be made to business problems in order to show that the techniques presented have applications in business decision making. For example, the laws of probability can be used to measure the likelihood of faulty components leaving a production line, or the probability that a borrower may default on a loan taken out with a credit agency.

The laws of probability allow you to measure the likelihood that an event will take place. An example of an event is throwing a dice and recording a six, whilst the action of throwing a dice is often called a **trial** or **experiment**.

In this text you will consider two important branches of measurable probability; classical probability and probability distributions.

Classical probability involves calculating the probability of a particular outcome occurring by using a number of simple laws. Examples may include selecting a faulty TV from a production line, as well examples relating to gaming such as throwing a coin and recording a head, of throwing a dice and scoring a six, where the probabilities of an individual outcome occurring are either known or can be calculated. ***The calculation of a particular probability is measured on a scale from 0 to 1 inclusive, where values close to zero suggest that the event will rarely if ever happen (e.g. winning the jackpot in the national lottery), whilst values close to 1 suggest that there is almost certainty that the outcome under consideration will take place***. The rules of classical probability will be introduced in this chapter using a number of gaming and business examples.

In addition to the classical examples of probability, certain business processes may display behaviour which can be measured or recorded via experiments or tests, and in turn, can be represented by an appropriate statistical distribution. For example, TV sets leaving a production line may be classified as correct or faulty with associated probabilities. In this case, the probability of a batch of 100 TV sets containing 5 faulty sets can be calculated using a specific distribution, namely the binomial distribution. In general, these different distributions assume certain circumstances to exist in the process under consideration and allow the decision maker to calculate the probability that a certain or desirable outcome will be achieved. A number of statistical distributions which are regularly applied to business related problems will be introduced in Chapters 7 and 8.

The contents of this chapter are essential in that they introduce the concept of probability. Specific applications of Excel in the area of probability will be provided in Chapters 7 and 8.

Examples of Classical Probability

In the next part of this chapter a number of examples involving the calculation of probabilities will be considered and a number of laws will be introduced. In order to illustrate these laws of probability, reference will be made to a number of gaming related problems involving coins, cards and dice. Relevant business related problems will also be considered.

Examples

What is the probability of recording a head when tossing a coin? In this example, the trial is throwing the coin and two possible events can take place, i.e. throwing a ***HEAD*** or ***TAIL.***

If the coin is unbiased, i.e. both alternatives have an equal chance of being selected, the probability of a *head* is 1 in 2, so the probability of recording a head is 0.5.

As indicated earlier, the probability of recording a head has a value lying in the range 0 to 1 inclusive.

What is the probability of recording a 6 when an unbiased dice is rolled? In this example, you have one trial, namely throwing a dice, and there are six possible events which may take place, i.e. scoring **1**, **2**, **3**, **4**, **5** or **6**.

The probability of recording a 6 is 1 in 6, so the probability of recording a head is 0.167 (3dp).

In general probabilities are expressed as fractions or decimal numbers and the **PROBABILITY OF EVENT 'X'** taking place, denoted by **P(X)** can be calculated using the formula:

$$P(X) = \frac{\text{Number of times you can record event X}}{\text{Total number of results possible}}$$

Laws of Probability

When dealing with probabilities there are certain laws which can be used:

Probability that an event does not occur

If the probability of an event X is represented by P(X), then:

P(X does not occur) = 1 - P(X does occur)

P(NOT X) = 1 - P(X), and therefore

P(X) + P(NOT X) = 1

Sum of probabilities

If two or more events cannot occur simultaneously they are called mutually exclusive. If p_1, p_2, ..., p_n represent the probabilities of a number of mutually exclusive events, where the events listed represent all possible events, then each probability can take on a value between 0 and 1 inclusive and the probabilities add up to 1. If you roll a dice, you have 6 possible events, i.e. the scores 1, 2, 3, 4, 5 and 6. These events are exclusive, i.e. you cannot score a 1 and a 6 with a single roll of the dice. The scores listed represent all possible events and are called exhaustive.

Expected number of occurrences

If you had a production process which resulted in **n units** of daily output, each with a probability of being faulty represented by **p**, you can measure the likely or expected number of faulty units, denoted by **E(f)**. This may be achieved using the equation:

Expected number of faulty units E(f) = n x p

For example, if you roll a dice 100 times, the expected number of sixes = 100 x 1/6 = **16.7 (1dp).** This simple example is useful because it shows that the expected value is not necessarily observable.

You can now apply these laws of classical probability to a business related example.

Example:

A sample of TV sets leaving a production line were classified as monochrome or colour and whether they Worked or were Faulty. The sample of data collected is shown in Figure 6.1.

	WORKS	FAULTY	TOTAL
MONOCHROME	36	14	50
COLOUR	104	46	150
TOTAL	140	60	200

Figure 6.1 - Status of TV sets leaving a production line

If a TV set is picked at random from the production line, find the probability that:

1. The TV set is colour.

   PROBABILITY OF EVENT 'X' taking place is given by the equation:

   $$\mathbf{P(X) = \frac{Number\ of\ times\ you\ can\ record\ event\ X}{Total\ number\ of\ results\ possible}}$$

   $$\mathbf{P(colour) = \frac{total\ number\ of\ colour\ sets}{total\ number\ of\ sets} = \frac{150}{200} = 0.75}$$

2. The TV set is faulty.

   P(faulty TV) = 60/200 = **0.3**

3. The TV is colour and works.

   P(Working and colour TV) = 104/200 = **0.52**

4. Find the expected number of times you would choose a faulty, monochrome TV if 50 different TV sets are selected randomly.

   P(faulty and monochrome TV) = 14/200 = **0.07**

   Expected number selected = np

where n is the number of TVs selected and p is the probability of the event taking place (i.e. the TV set being both monochrome and faulty).

Here n = 50 and p = 0.07.

Expected number = 50 x 0.07 = **3.5 faulty sets**. Thus, if 50 sets were selected randomly, you would expect to find (on average) 3.5 TV sets which are both monochrome and faulty.

Multiplicative Law of Probability

Quite often in applications of probability, it is necessary to consider two or more customers who may buy a particular product or items leaving an assembly line say, and in doing so, it may be desirable to calculate the probability of multiple events occurring together. In these examples you are considering two or more trials. If you have multiple trials to consider in this way, the probability of one or more events taking place can be calculated using the multiplicative law of probability. The actual method of calculating the probability of two events occurring depends on whether they are independent or dependent.

If X and Y are **independent** events, i.e. the fact that one event (X) has taken place has no impact on the other event (Y) occurring, then:

P(X and Y) = P(X) x P(Y)

where: P(X and Y) is the probability that both events take place

P(X) is the probability that event X takes place

P(Y) is the probability that event Y takes place

Example:

From a pack of cards, select an individual card, put this back in the pack and select a second card. What would be the probability of picking a DIAMOND and then a CLUB? In this example, you have two trials and are considering two events X and Y, where:

X = picking a diamond (there are 13 diamonds in a pack of 52 cards)

Y = picking a club (there are 13 clubs in a pack of 52 cards)

P(X) = ¼, P(Y) = ¼

$$P(X \text{ and } Y) = P(X) \times P(Y)$$
$$= \tfrac{1}{4} \times \tfrac{1}{4} = 1/16$$

These two events are independent because after the first card is selected, it is placed back in the pack. As a result, the selection of the second card is again from a pack of 52, and the subsequent probability of this event is not influenced in any way by the outcome of the first selection.

If X and Y are **not independent** but are **dependent**, i.e. the fact that one event (X) has taken place *does* have an impact on the outcome of the event other (Y), then:

$$\mathbf{P(X \text{ and } Y) = P(X) \times P(Y/X)}$$

where: P(X and Y) is the probability that both events take place

P(X) is the probability that event X takes place

P(Y/X) means the probability that event Y happens given that result X has already taken place.

The term **P(Y/X)** is also known as the conditional probability, i.e. event Y is conditional (or dependent) upon event X having already taken place.

Example:

From a pack of cards, you must select two cards, the second being selected **without** replacing the first. What is the probability that:

- You picked a diamond and then a club?
- You picked two diamonds?

X: the first card being picked is a diamond (there are 13 diamonds in a pack of 52 cards)

$$P(X) = \tfrac{1}{4}$$

Y: the second card is a club. There are now only 51 cards in the pack 13 of which are clubs, i.e. the outcome of the first card which has not been placed back in the pack has influenced the outcome of the selection of the second card since there are now only 51 cards to choose from.

$$P(Y/X) = 13/51$$
$$\text{So } P(X \text{ and } Y) = P(X) \times P(Y/X)$$
$$= \tfrac{1}{4} \times 13/51 = \mathbf{13/204}$$

X: first card is a diamond, 13 diamonds in a pack of 52 cards.

$$P(X) = \tfrac{1}{4}$$

Y: second card is a diamond. There are now only 51 cards in the pack, since the diamond selected first has not been placed back in the pack. Therefore, for the second selection there are only 12 diamonds left.

$$P(Y/X) = 12/51$$

$$\text{So } P(X \text{ and } Y) = P(X) \times P(Y/X)$$
$$= \tfrac{1}{4} \times 12/51 = \mathbf{3/51}$$

Tree Diagrams

A **tree diagram** can be used to display a number of trials where the corresponding probabilities will be calculated using the *multiplicative law*. This diagram is particularly useful since it gives you a way of displaying all *possible* events to the trials under consideration. The creation and application of the tree diagram is best shown by considering an example.

If a game involves throwing two coins you draw the tree diagram by considering the throw of each coin as two separate trials. By doing this, you display all possible events from the first coin as branches. The branches display the event and corresponding probability. Figure 6.2 depicts a tree diagram showing the outcomes from tossing the first coin, i.e. recording a head or a tail. The two respective branches display H(½) and T(½). Inspection of these branches show that the two probabilities add up to 1, since all possible events have been represented.

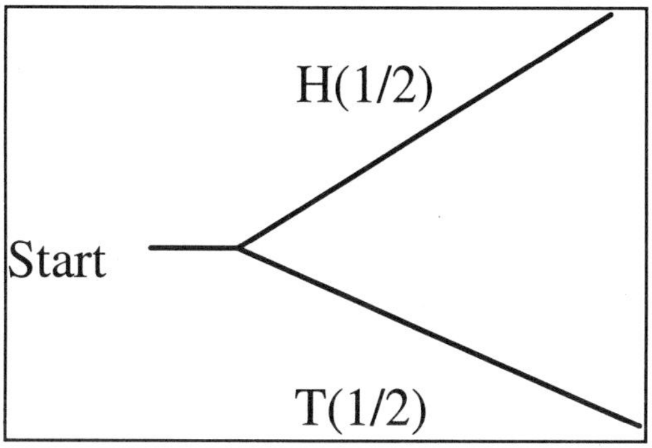

Figure 6.2 - Tree diagram illustrating the outcomes of tossing a coin

The tree diagram can now be further extended to show the possible events when the second coin is thrown.

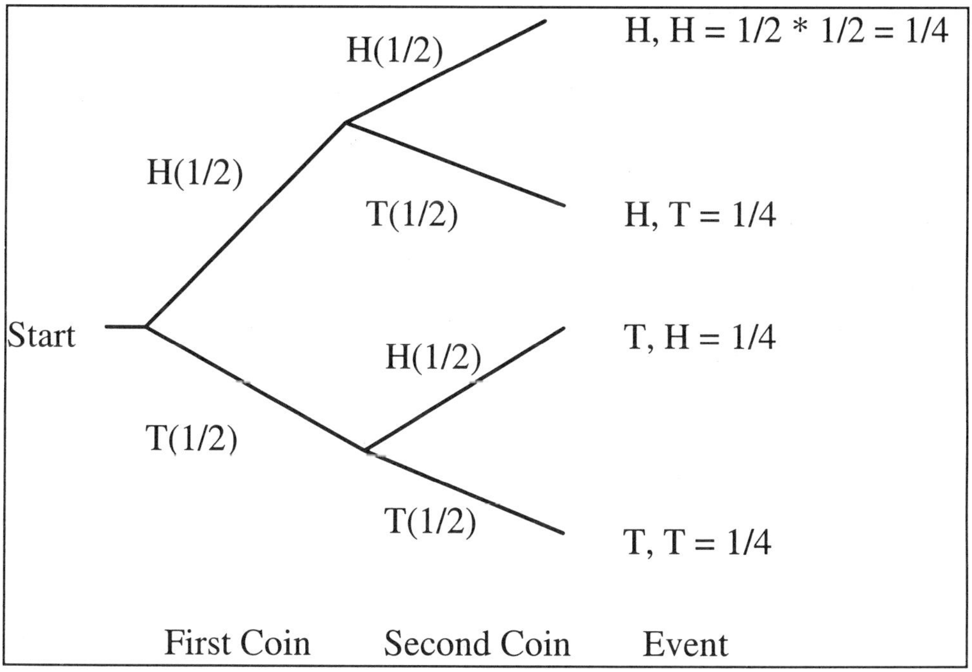

Figure 6.3 - Outcomes from tossing two coins

In Figure 6.3, the outcomes from tossing the second coin (i.e. the second trial) are represented by branches on the tree which extend from each outcome branch represents the events from the first trial. These branches display the event and corresponding probability (again each ***individual set of branches*** have probabilities which add up to 1). Before drawing a tree diagram, it is important to determine whether the events are independent or dependent. In the example above, the events are independent because the outcome from coin two is ***not*** influenced by the outcome of throwing the first coin.

To determine all possible outcomes and probabilities you must consider each branch for the combined events. The overall probability from throwing both coins can be calculated by multiplying probabilities along each identified branch. In the game shown in Figure 6.3, you are considering 4 outcomes in total.

The diagram can then be used to answer any questions relating to the whole game, e.g. the probability of recording two heads when tossing two coins is found by following the 'head, head' branch. The probability is given by the product of the two probabilities $\frac{1}{2} \times \frac{1}{2}$, i.e. $\frac{1}{4}$.

The diagram shows that to record one head and one tail can be achieved in one of two ways; "head then tail" or "tail then head" and the total probability recording one head and one tail is $\frac{1}{2}$ (i.e. $\frac{1}{4} + \frac{1}{4}$). Since all possible outcomes have been recorded on this tree diagram, the total of the corresponding probabilities is equal to 1, as expected.

In general by representing all possible outcomes to a problem using a tree diagram, you can ensure that the corresponding probabilities consider whether the events identified are independent or dependent. Figures 6.4 and 6.5 compare independent and dependent events displayed on a tree diagram by using the simple scenario of selecting two playing cards from a pack.

Tree Diagrams representing the selection of two playing cards

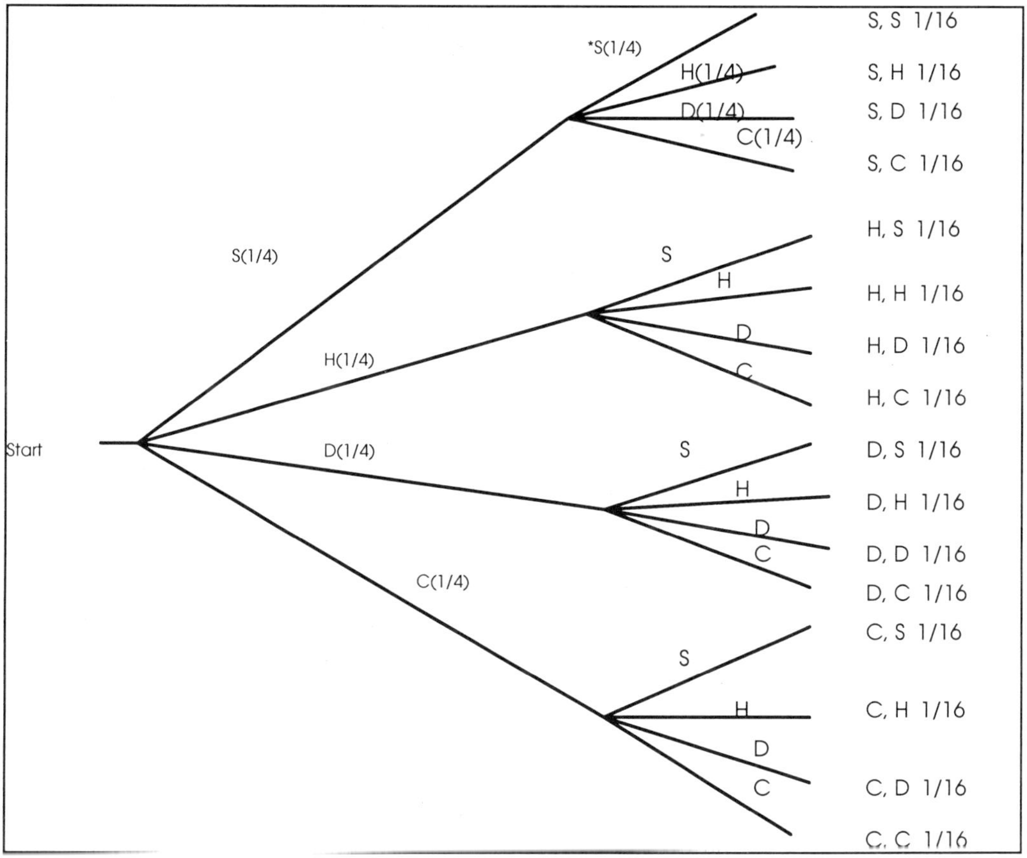

Figure 6.4 - When events are independent (i.e. a card is replaced after selection)

* The first card is replaced, so the second selection is again from 52 cards. As a consequence, the second outcome is ***independent*** of the first. That is, there are 52 cards of which 13 are spades. Therefore, P(S) = 13/52 = 1/4.

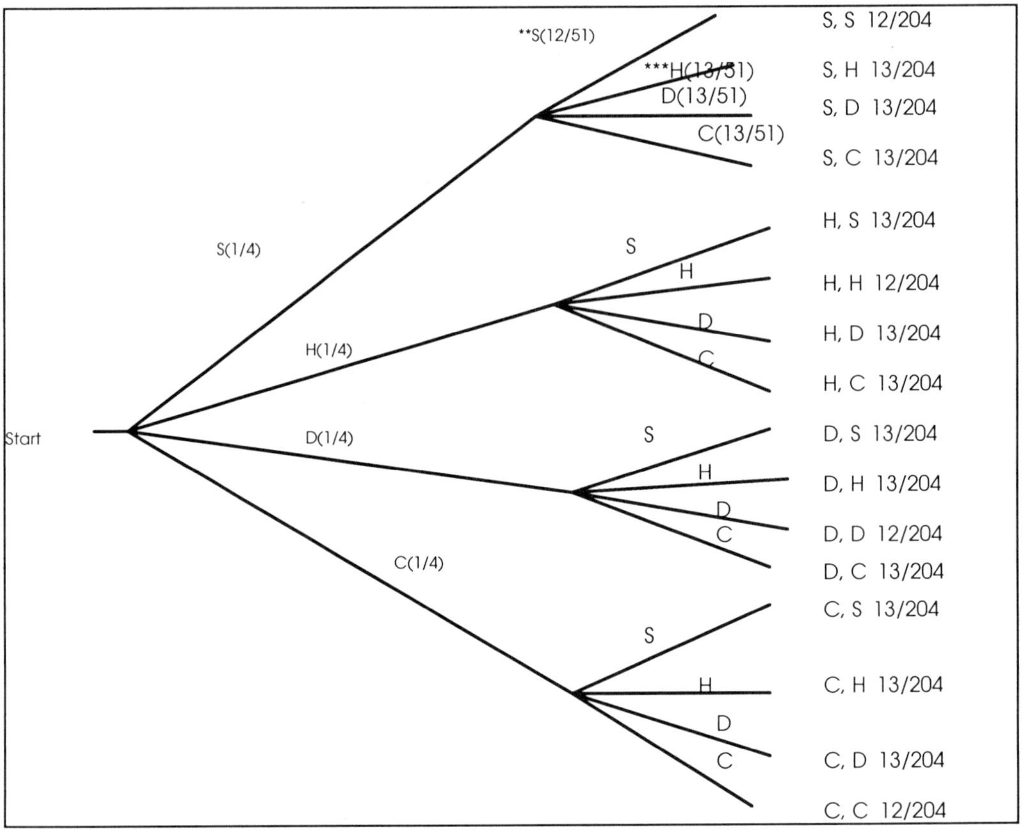

Figure 6.5 - When events are NOT independent (i.e. a card is NOT replaced after selection)

** After a spade has been selected as the first card and is not replaced, 51 cards are left in the pack, of which 12 are spades. Therefore, P(S) = 12/51. This probability is ***dependent*** upon the first event taking place.

*** After a spade has been selected as the first card and is not placed back in the pack, 51 cards are left in the pack, of which 13 are hearts. Therefore, P(H) = 13/51 and P(S,H) = ¼ x 13/51 = 13/204 (i.e. the probability of a spade which is not replaced followed by a head).

In both cases described in Figure 6.5, the second selection is ***dependent*** upon the first event taking place.

Now that you have considered the application of tree diagrams to independent and dependent events by making reference to playing cards, you can consider further examples which are business related.

Example:

A Northern engineering company produces lift cables for the commercial market. The lift cables have to undertake two tests; one for strength and one for elasticity. A cable has to pass both tests before being sent out to a customer. The test for strength is undertaken first. If the cable fails, the second test is not undertaken. The probability of failing with respect to strength is 0.2 and 0.3 with respect to elasticity. What is the probability that a cable selected at random will pass overall? If 20 cables are tested daily, what is the expected number of failures?

Figure 6.6 displays the tree diagram representing this problem. From the information provided, you can assume the outcome from the two tests are **independent**.

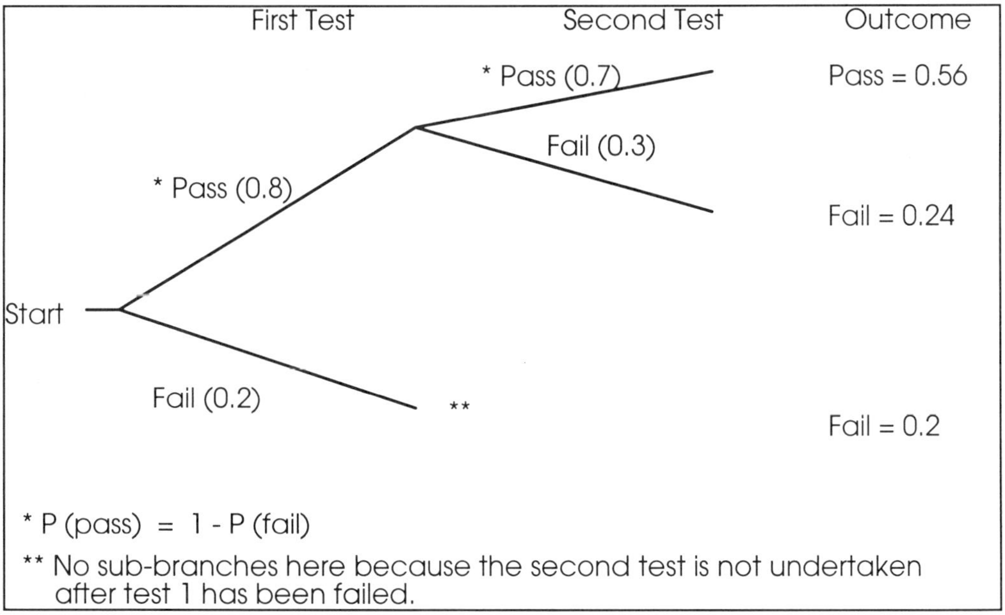

Figure 6.6 - Outcomes from the two cable tests

For Figure 6.6, P(cable passes tests) = 0.8 x 0.7 = **0.56**

P(cable fails) = P(fails test 1) + P(fails test 2)
= 0.2 + (0.8 x 0.3) = **0.44**

You should notice that these two probabilities, i.e. P(pass) + P(fail) = 1.

Expected number of daily failures = np = 20 x 0.44 = **8.8 failures**

Example:

Under a new EEC directive, a farmer has to carry out two tests on eggs produced at his farm. Eggs passing both tests are labelled category 'A', those passing one test are labelled category 'B', whilst those passing neither are labelled as category 'C'. The probability of an egg passing test 1 is 0.85. However, the outcome of test 2 is dependent upon the outcome of test 1. If the egg has passed the first test, it has a 90% chance of passing the second, but only a 60% chance of passing if it has failed test 1. If 5000 eggs are tested daily, what are the expected number falling into categories A, B and C?

The first part of the solution to this problem involves drawing a tree diagram. From the information provided, you are dealing with dependent events, i.e. the probability of passing test 2 is dependent upon passing of test 1. Figure 6.7 shows the resultant tree diagram.

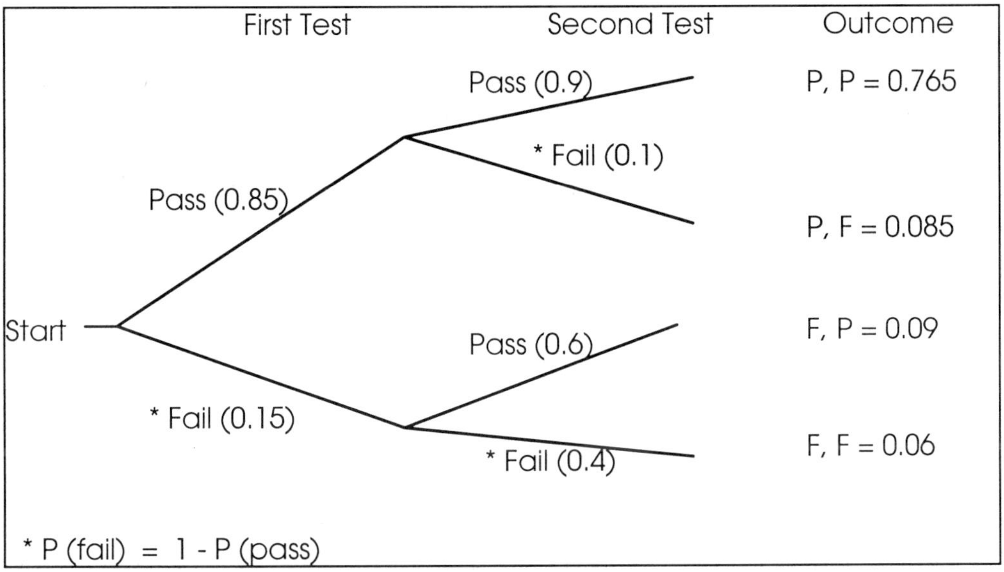

Figure 6.7 - Outcomes from the farmer's two tests

From Figure 6.7:

P(passing both tests) = 0.85 x 0.9 = **0.765**

P(passing 1 test) = P(pass test 1, fail test 2)
+ P(fail test 1, pass test 2)

= (0.85 x 0.1) + (0.15 x 0.6)
= 0.085 + 0.09 = **0.175**

P(failing both tests) = 0.15 x 0.4 = **0.060**

Note: P(pass both) + P(pass 1 from 2) + P(fail both) = 0.765 + 0.175 + 0.060 = 1, as expected since all possible events are listed.

The expected number of eggs from a batch of 5000 falling into the respective categories A, B and C is given by **np** where **n** is the number of eggs and p is the corresponding probability of falling into the relevant category.

Category A = np = 5000 x 0.765 = **3825 eggs**
Category B = np = 5000 x 0.175 = **875 eggs**
Category C = np = 5000 x 0.060 = **300 eggs**

Additive Law of Probability

Whilst the multiplicative law of probability can be used when you consider two or more trials, the additive law of probability can be applied to problems involving an ***individual*** trial where you need to determine the probability that one or more of a number of possible events take place. If events X and Y are **mutually exclusive**, i.e. events X and Y cannot occur together, then:

$$P(X \text{ or } Y) = P(X) + P(Y)$$

where: P(X or Y) is the probability that either event X only or event Y only or both X and Y take place
P(X) is the probability that event X takes place
P(Y) is the probability that event Y takes place

A simple example of two mutually exclusive events is the selection of a Labour or Conservative from a survey of voters at a general election. The respondent selected from the survey can be either Labour or Conservative but not both.

Example:

From a pack of cards, you need to pick one card randomly. Determine the probability that the selected card was a diamond or a club.

X = picking a diamond (there are 13 diamonds in a pack of 52 cards)
Y = picking a club (there are 13 clubs in a pack of 52 cards)

$$P(X) = \tfrac{1}{4},\ P(Y) = \tfrac{1}{4}$$

In this example the events are mutually exclusive, i.e. a card can be a diamond or a club but not both. As a consequence:

$$\begin{aligned} P(X \text{ or } Y) &= P(X) + P(Y) \\ &= \tfrac{1}{4} + \tfrac{1}{4} = \tfrac{1}{2} \end{aligned}$$

If events X and Y are **not mutually exclusive**, then the probability of either taking place is given by the equation:

$$\mathbf{P(X \text{ or } Y) = P(X) + P(Y) - P(X \text{ and } Y)}$$

where P(X and Y) is the probability that both events X and Y occur together.

Example:

From a pack of cards, you again pick one card randomly. Determine the probability that the card was an *ace* or a *club*.

X = picking an ace (there are 4 aces in a pack of 52 cards)
Y = picking a club (there are 13 clubs in a pack of 52 cards)

P(X) = 4/52, P(Y) = 13/52

In this example there is one card which is both an ace and a club, the ace of clubs, so events X and Y are not mutually exclusive.

P(X and Y) = $^{1}/_{52}$

So P(X or Y) = P(X) + P(Y) - P(X and Y)
= 4/52 + 13/52 - 1/52
= 4/13

Venn Diagrams

If you are considering an individual trial with multiple events, the trial can be displayed and probabilities calculated (in particular those involving the additive law) using a venn diagram.

You may wish to determine the probability that a card selected at random is a club or a diamond. This problem has been represented by the venn diagram in Figure 6.8.

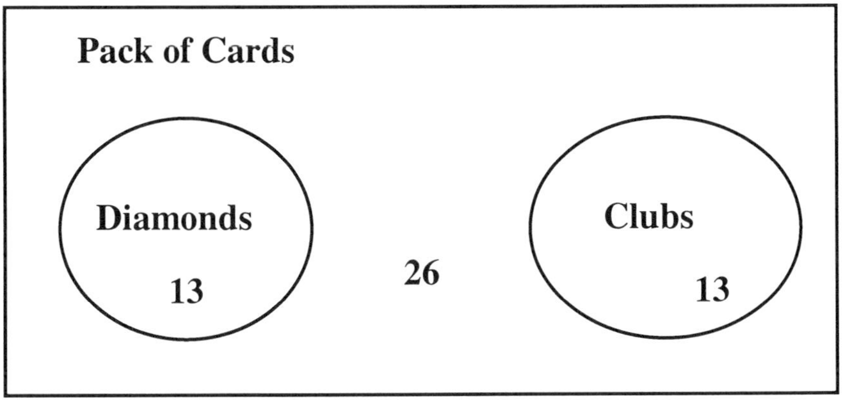

Figure 6.8 - A venn diagram representing card selection

In Figure 6.8, the individual events (i.e. diamonds and clubs) are represented by circles, whilst the outer rectangle represents all possible events from the trial including the circles enclosed within (i.e. the *whole* pack of cards). The numbers represented by each category are displayed in the respective circles, whereas the number representing the remaining cards in the pack is placed outside the circles but inside the rectangle. Since the two results, i.e. the selection of a diamond and the selection of a club are mutually exclusive (i.e. they cannot occur simultaneously), ***the two circles do not intersect.***

The probability required is then determined by:

$$\frac{\Sigma\text{Numbers in the circles}}{\Sigma\text{Numbers in the rectangle (including the circles)}} = \frac{13 + 13}{13 + 13 + 26} = \tfrac{1}{2}$$

i.e. the probability of selecting a diamond or a club is ½.

You may also wish to determine the probability that a randomly selected card is an ace or a club. This problem has been represented by the venn diagram in Figure 6.9. Unlike the venn diagram in Figure 6.8, the two events under consideration can both occur simultaneously, i.e. you can select the **ace of clubs**. As a consequence, the two circles have an intersection. The number written inside this intersection represents the number of possible ways both an ace or a club can occur together, i.e. 1. The total of the numbers in each individual circle when considered ***separately***, represent the number of possible way each event can occur, that is, there are $12+1 = 13$ clubs in the pack and $3+1 = 4$ aces. In particular, the value 3 in the last calculation tells us that there are 3 aces in the pack which are **not** clubs, whilst the number 12 tells us that there are 12 clubs in the pack which are not aces. These two numbers are written in the non-intersecting parts of the relevant circles.

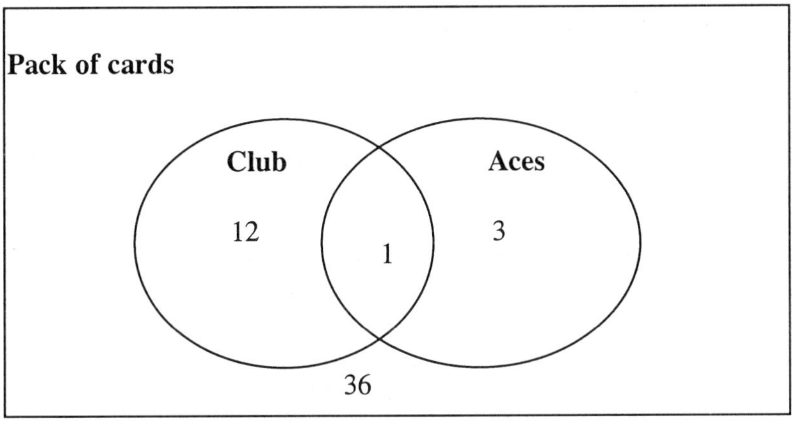

Figure 6.9 - A venn diagram for non-mutually exclusive events

The required probability is found by adding the numbers in the circles, including the intersection, and dividing this by the sum of all of the numbers in the rectangle including the circles. In this calculation you must ensure the numbers in the intersections are ***only counted once***. Moreover, the calculation of the various numbers is best achieved by entering the numbers in the intersections first, and then entering the values in the exclusive (non-intersecting) parts of the circles (after appropriate subtractions).

i.e. $$P(\text{Club or an ace}) = \frac{12 + 1 + 3}{12 + 1 + 3 + 36} = {}^{4}/_{13}$$

Example:

A part-time University course offers students three units; Information Technology (IT), Quantitative Methods (QM) and Business Studies (BS). One hundred and twenty students have enrolled. The Course Leader is concerned about failure rates and wishes to represent the data using a venn diagram and identifying the proportion of students failing. The University rules state that if a student fails two or units they have failed the year.

Analysis of the results shows that 20 students had failed IT, 30 had failed QM and 22 had failed Business Studies. From these students, 5 failed both IT and QM but not Business Studies, 8 failed QM and Business Studies but not IT and 2 students failed all three units. Using the venn diagram you can determine:

(a) How many students pass the year.

(b) How many students can resit one failed unit.

(c) How many students failed the course.

(d) Find the probability of a student selected at random failing the QM unit.

Figure 6.10 shows the venn diagram which represents this information. The diagram uses the following notation:

IT represents students failing the Information Technology unit.
QM represents students failing the Quantitative Methods unit.
BS represents students failing the Business Studies unit.

To draw this diagram, enter the 2 into the inter-section of all three circles first. When entering values onto a venn diagram, it is best to start in the "middle" (i.e. the intersection of the circles) and work "outwards". For the IT failures enter the 5 for those who also failed the QM unit. So far you have accounted for 7 students (i.e. 2 + 5) who have failed the IT unit. Therefore, 13 (i.e. 20 -7) have failed this unit only, and as a consequence, the 13 is placed in the exclusive part of the circle labelled IT. Using the same logic, 15 students fail the QM unit only (i.e. 30 - 2 - 5 - 8), whilst 12 (i.e. 22 - 2 - 8) students fail the Business Studies unit only. The numbers in the circles (counting them only once) add up to 55, hence 65 (120 - 55) pass the year. This number is written outside the circles but inside the rectangle.

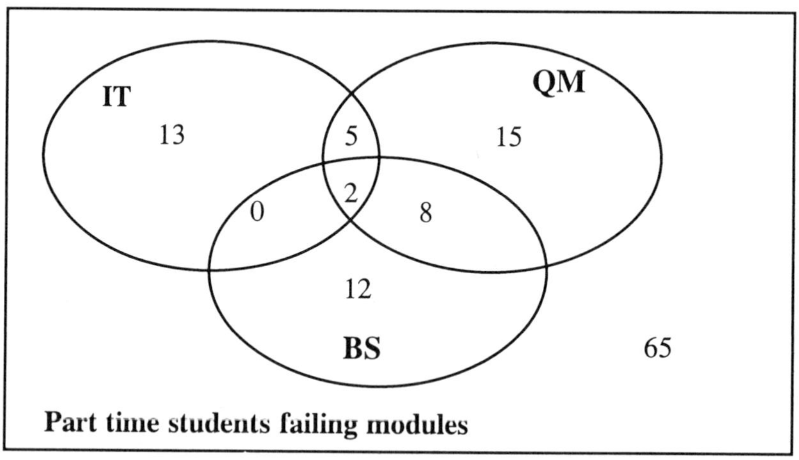

Figure 6.10 - A venn diagram representing students failing units

You are now in a position to answer the questions for the Course Leader.

(a) The number of students passing the year is **65**.

(b) The number of students who can resit one unit is 13 + 15 + 12 = 40.

(c) The number of students failing the course (i.e. two or more failed units) is 5 + 2 + 8 = **15**.

(d) Finally, the probability of a student selected at random failing the QM unit is **30/120**, i.e. **1/4**.

Conclusions

Many business problems involve uncertainty. Items leaving a production line have a probability of being faulty, whilst a company which has borrowed money from a bank may default on its repayments with a measurable probability based on the past performance of the economy and his business sector. The probability laws described in this chapter provide the decision maker with an opportunity to quantify the likelihood of these events taking place using a range of values between 0 and 1 inclusive.

At the start of the chapter, a set of laws were introduced which are used to calculate probabilities. In particular attention should be paid when calculating the probability of two or more events occurring, since the decision maker needs to decide whether the events under consideration are independent or dependent if they are from separate trials, or whether they exclusive or non-exclusive if they are from the same trial. There are two useful diagrams which can be used to represent different the possible events, namely the tree and venn diagrams. Using these diagrams to depict various events can greatly simplify the required probability calculations.

Learning Outcomes Checklist

After completing this chapter you should have an understanding of the following concepts, calculations and functions:

- The concept of probability, in particular the difference between classical and experimental probability.
- The terms probability, event and trial.
- Independent and dependent events.
- The multiplicative and additive laws of probability.
- The application of the multiplicative law to independent and dependent events.
- The application of the tree diagram to the multiplicative law.
- The application of the additive law to exclusive and non-exclusive events.
- The application of the venn diagram to the additive law.

Ensure that you understand these concepts before progressing to Chapter 7.

Chapter Case Question

The pub chain owns 700 houses nationally and these are categorised in the table below:

	Country	Town	Suburb	Total
Restaurant	32	43	25	100
Family Pub	38	85	77	200
Theme Bar	26	18	36	80
Sports	16	82	102	200
Traditional	2	58	60	120
Total	114	286	300	700

- Calculate the following probabilities:

  A public house selected at random is a theme bar.

  A public house selected at random is located in the suburbs.

  A public house selected at random is a sports or theme bar.

  A public house selected at random is not in the country.

  A restaurant selected at random is located in the suburbs.

  A traditional house selected at random is located in the town.

  A public house selected at random is not in the country.

  A public house is in the suburbs or the town given that it is a family pub.

- The probability of a public house in this chain appointing a new manager within the year is 20%. Three public houses are considered at random. Represent the outcome of all three events (i.e. whether they appoint a new manager within the next year) using a tree diagram. Determine the following probabilities together with any assumptions made:

  All three appoint a new manager.

  Two of the three houses appoint a new manager.

  One of the three houses appoints a new manager.

  None of the houses appoint a new manager.

Supplementary Questions

1. What is meant by the terms ‘event’, ‘trial’ and ‘probability’?

2. If the probability of the event Z is denoted by P(Z), what range of values can P(Z) take?

3. What do the extreme values in this range suggest about Z?

4. What is meant by the following terms in probability?

(a) mutually exhaustive

(b) mutually exclusive

(c) expected value

Give business related examples of all three.

5. What is the difference between independence and dependence? Give examples of both relationships.

6. As part of its staff development, a company surveyed its staff with regard to the time they have been employed by the company. The company employs 150 people and the results of the survey are shown below:

Length of service	Male	Female
< 1 year	35	10
1 year -	15	5
3 years -	8	12
5 years -	12	28
10 years +	10	15
TOTAL	**80**	**70**

Calculate the following probabilities:

(a) Selecting an employee appointed in the last year.

(b) Selecting a man appointed in the last 3 years.

(c) Selecting a woman appointed in the last 5 years.

(d) Selecting an employee appointed more than 5 years ago.

(e) Selecting an employee appointed more than 10 years ago given that the employee is female.

(f) Selecting an employee appointed in the last year given the employee is male.

(g) Selecting an employee appointed in the last year given the employee is female.

7. A small building society has decided to conduct a survey into the saving habits of different sections of its customers, based on age and sex. The results were based on a 1000 individuals and are shown below:

	Male			Female		
Savings	<30	30+	45+	<30	30+	45+
< £1000	100	100	70	100	70	30
£1000 -	60	60	30	40	20	40
£3000 -	40	10	30	30	50	20
£5000 +	10	10	40	10	10	20

Calculate the row totals, column totals and cross total for this table and determine the following probabilities:

(a) A customer selected at random is male.

(b) A customer selected has savings in excess of £5,000.

(c) A female is selected with savings of less than £3,000.

(d) A female over 30 is selected and has savings of less than £5,000.

(e) A male under 30 is selected.

(f) A customer aged 30 or over is selected.

8. An unbiased coin has been thrown three times. Draw a tree diagram to illustrate the different outcomes from the exercise, assuming that the coin is fair. Determine the probability that the trial will result in:

(a) Exactly two heads

(b) Three tails

(c) No tails

9. A manufacturer processes meat for the domestic market. The meat has to undergo two tests. If it passes both tests it can be sold for human consumption, if it passes one of the two tests it can be sold for animal consumption, but if it fails both tests it must be destroyed. The meat has a 90% chance of passing the first test, but its chances on passing the second test depend on the outcome of the first. If it passes the first, its chances of passing the second are 75%, but if it fails the first its chances of passing test two are only 60%. Represent this problem using a tree diagram and determine the following:

   (a) the probability that a case of meat passes both tests.

   (b) the probability that a case of meat passes one test only.

   (c) the probability that a case of meat passes neither test.

   (d) In one day 100 cases of meat were tested. What number would you expect to be fit for human consumption, animal consumption, neither?

10. Two cards have been selected from a pack **with** replacement and you are interested in selecting pictures. Draw a tree diagram to represent this problem. Use the tree diagram to calculate the following probabilities:

   (a) Two pictures are selected.

   (b) A picture is selected followed by a number.

   (c) A number is selected followed by a picture.

   (d) Two numbers are selected.

11. Repeat question 16 without replacing the first card.

12. A bank has recently located to a green-field site and wishes to invite applications for three types of job post from recent graduates in Business Information Technology. The bank's computer department consists of three sections; end-user computing, database development and IT trainers.

    At the close of applications, 30 people graduates had applied for the end-user computing posts, 40 applied for the database development and 15 applied for the IT training posts. For graduates submitting the applications, 10 applied for both end-user computing and database development, 10 applied for both end-user computing and IT training, 2 applied for database development and IT training only, but only 1 graduate applied for all three posts.

Represent the number of applications submitted using a venn diagram and determine the following:

(a) The number of graduates applied in total?

(b) The number of graduates applied for one post?

(c) The number of graduates applied for two posts?

(d) The probability of an applicant selected at random applying only for a post of IT Trainer.

(e) The probability of an applicant selected at random applying only for a post of Database Developer.

Chapter 7

Discrete Probability Distributions

Learning Outcomes

In Chapter 6 you were introduced to a number of probability laws. In this chapter the concept of probability will be extended and you will look at a number of statistical distributions often applied to business problems. You will be able to define the term 'distribution' and consider the features of certain discrete probability distributions. Reference will be made via worked examples to the relevant built-in facilities offered by Excel.

After completing this chapter you will be able to:

- Understand the term 'probability distribution'.
- Recognise the features of a discrete probability distribution.
- Recognise the properties of the discrete uniform, binomial and poisson distributions and apply them to a variety of relevant problems.
- Apply a number of relevant built-in facilities offered by Excel to solve problems involving the binomial and poisson distributions.

Introduction

In Chapter 6 you saw a number of ways in which the probability of a particular event taking place could be calculated. In short, the probability of event X taking place can be calculated using the equation:

$$P(X) = \frac{\text{Number of times you can record event X}}{\text{Total number of events possible}}$$

For example, you may wish to undertake an experiment which involves throwing two unbiased dice and calculating the total score. The table in Figure 7.1 indicates all possible scores and corresponding probabilities from the experiment, the first number in each permutation indicating the score recorded by dice one. By recording the possible outcomes of the experiment in this way, you can create a **probability distribution**.

Score	Possible Ways	Number	Probability
2	1,1	1	$^1/_{36}$
3	1,2 2,1	2	$^2/_{36}$
4	1,3 2,2 3,1	3	$^3/_{36}$
5	1,4 2,3 3,2 4,1	4	$^4/_{36}$
6	1,5 2,4 3,3 4,2 5,1	5	$^5/_{36}$
7	1,6 2,5 3,4 4,3 5,2 6,1	6	$^6/_{36}$
8	2,6 3,5 4,4 5,3 6,2	5	$^5/_{36}$
9	3,6 4,5 5,4 6,3	4	$^4/_{36}$
10	4,6 5,5 6,4	3	$^3/_{36}$
11	5,6 6,5	2	$^2/_{36}$
12	6,6	1	$^1/_{36}$
	Total	**36**	**1**

Figure 7.1 - A probability distribution

The example shown above in Figure 7.1 illustrates two laws of probability:

- Each individual probability p has a value between 0 and 1 inclusive.
- If the outcomes under consideration are exhaustive (i.e. all possible outcomes are considered) and exclusive (i.e. the outcomes are distinct), then the probabilities add up to 1.

The probability distribution is useful because they indicate the likelihood of various outcomes taking place. For example, the most likely score when throwing two dice is 7, because this outcome has the highest probability. The probability of scoring 10 or more can be determined by adding the appropriate probabilities together, i.e. $P(X \geq 10) = P(X = 10) + P(X = 11) + P(X = 12) = {}^3/_{36} + {}^2/_{36} + {}^1/_{36} = \mathbf{{}^6/_{36} = {}^1/_6}$.

The concept of a probability distribution extends beyond throwing a pair of dice and recording the possible scores. There exist a number of theoretical probability distributions which can be applied to a variety of business problems. In general, these formal probability distributions fall into one of two categories:

- Discrete probability distributions
- Continuous probability distributions

In the next two chapters you will be made aware of the difference between the two types of distribution, and with reference to appropriate business related examples, will consider specific discrete distributions in detail.

The distributions considered in this Chapters 7 and 8 are neither exhaustive in terms of probability distributions applied by decision makers in business nor in the facilities offered by Excel. They are, however, the distributions which are most often used and are regularly featured on Business Statistics courses.

Discrete Probability Distributions

A variable is said to be discrete if you can only record specific values over a given range. If you can measure the respective probabilities for each value of the discrete variable you can determine its probability distribution. This probability distribution is also discrete. Throwing two dice and recording the total score is an example of a discrete variable, since the score recorded can only be an integer in the range 2 to 12 inclusive, but cannot have other (non-integer) values in this range such as 5.9 or 11.46. The resulting probability distribution pictured in Figure 7.1 is an example of a discrete probability distribution. The probability distribution is discrete since probabilities exist for certain scores (i.e. the whole numbers 2 to 12) but not other numbers such as scores 0.6 or 4.7. In the remainder of this chapter, you will consider three important discrete probability distributions in detail:

- Discrete Uniform
- Binomial
- Poisson

In particular, the last two distributions will be applied to relevant business related problems and you will see how to undertake the relevant calculations both manually and using the relevant facilities provided by Excel.

Discrete Uniform Distribution

In a discrete uniform distribution, each of the possible events have an *equal probability of taking place*. The simplest example of this kind of distribution are the possible outcomes when throwing one unbiased coin. Figure 7.2 illustrates this probability distribution both graphically and by table.

Face (X)	Probability (X)
Head	$^1/_2$
Tail	$^1/_2$

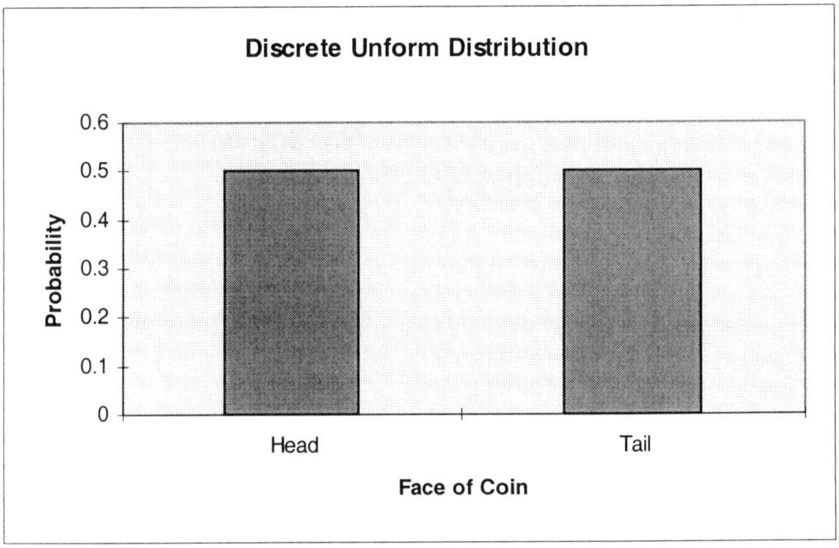

Figure 7.2 - Graphical display of a discrete uniform distribution

The presentation of the probability distributions shown in Figures 7.1 and 7.2 is similar to the frequency distribution described in Chapter 2.

Binomial Distribution

Let us consider a quality control exercise which may be carried out on an assembly line. The factory produces alarm systems and every hour a number of systems are selected at random and tested. Recent production records show that an individual alarm system has a 20% probability of failing the test. If three alarm systems are selected at random, you may wish to determine the probability of one failing and two passing.

The problem described above has a number of important features:

- The events are independent, i.e. the status of system 1 has no effect on the status of systems 2 and 3. In other words, if system 1 fails, this will not have any impact on the probability that a subsequent system passes or fails.

- The status of the systems falls into one of two separate categories, i.e. Pass or Fail. These two categories are:

    - mutually exclusive, i.e. a system cannot Pass and Fail, it must be one or the other.

    - exhaustive, i.e. P(Pass) + P(Fail) = 1

- The distribution of failures is discrete, since for one set of quality control trials, the number of failing systems can be 0, 1, 2 or 3 but not say 2½ or 1.675.

Because the problem under consideration involves calculating the number of independent incidents (often known as 'successes') from a specified number of trials, where each success has a constant probability of taking place, the required probabilities can be calculated using a discrete probability distribution called the binomial distribution.

The two categories in a binomial distribution are often called *SUCCESS* and *FAILURE*, where:

$$P(\text{SUCCESS}) + P(\text{FAILURE}) = 1$$

Example:

In our quality control problem, an individual alarm system has a 20% probability of being faulty. Therefore, if 'success' involves selecting a system which passes:

$$P(\text{success}) = 0.8, \; P(\text{failure}) = 0.2$$

What is the probability when selecting two systems at random:

(a) Both pass.

(b) 1 system fails.

(c) Both systems fail?

Let Pass = success, Fail = failure

p = P(success) = 0.8, q = P(failure) = 1 - p = 0.2

This can be illustrated using a tree diagram as shown by Figure 7.3 given that we are dealing with events concerning two separate systems.

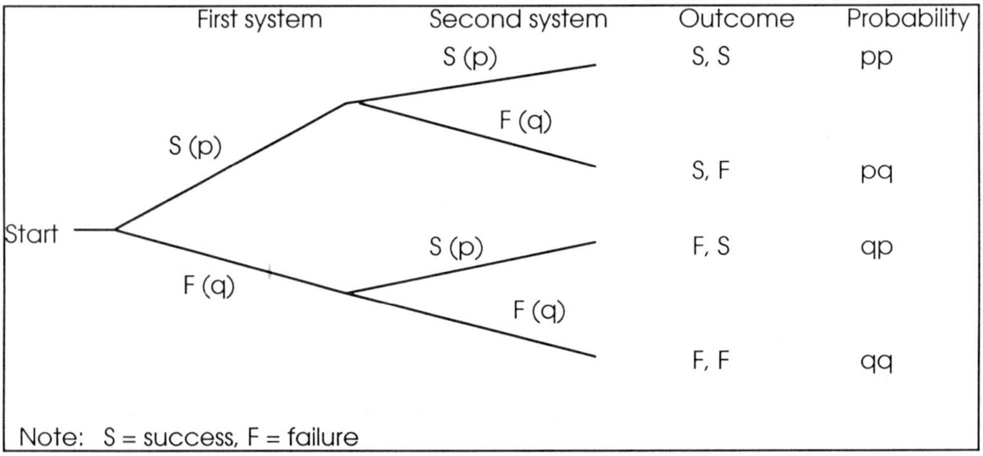

Figure 7.3 - Tree diagram for alarm system problem

Considering the four branches of the tree diagram, you should see:

P(2 Pass) P(S,S) = p^2 = 0.8^2 = **0.64**

P(1 Pass, 1 Fails) P(S,F) + P(F,S) = 2pq = 2 x 0.2 x 0.8 = **0.32**

P(2 Fail) = P(F,F) = q^2 = 0.2^2 = **0.04**

It can be seen from the tree diagram in Figure 7.3 all possible outcomes are shown and the sum of the corresponding probabilities add up to 1.

The quality control exercise at the alarm system factory involves selecting and testing three systems at random. In this case you can extend the tree diagram and determine the probability of having two failing systems when three alarm systems are selected randomly. The extended tree diagram is shown below in Figure 7.4.

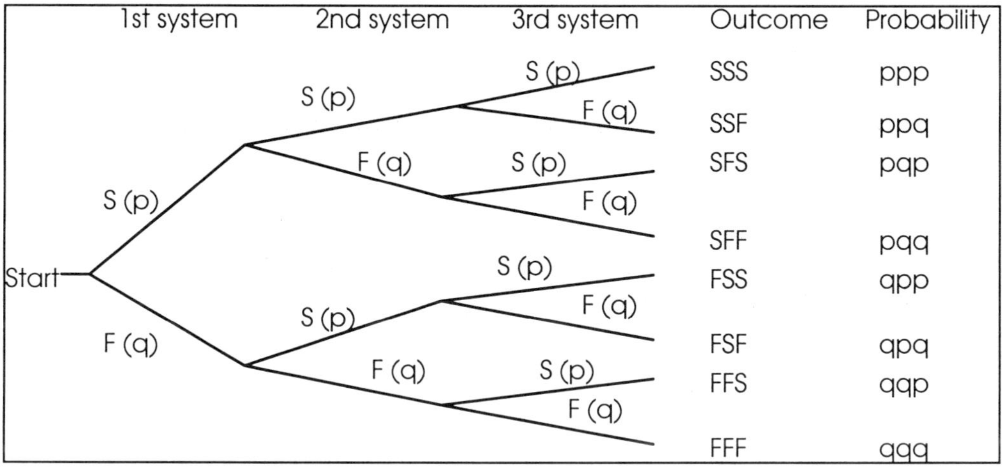

Figure 7.4 - Tree diagram for selection of three alarm systems

If you want to determine the probability of exactly two failing, you must identify all events from the tree diagram whose probability calculations include one 'p' term for the system which passes and two 'q' terms for the two systems which fail. This happens three times, i.e. outcomes pqq, qpq and qqp.

The required probability is $3pq^2$

$$= 3 \times 0.8 \times (0.2)^2$$

$$= \mathbf{0.096}$$

As indicated, you have multiplied the term pq^2 by 3, because there are three ways in which two of the three systems selected at random can fail, i.e. SFF, FFS and FSF.

In general, the number of ways of recording **r successes** (in this instance the term success refers to the selection of a alarm system which passes the test) from **n trials** (the total number of alarm systems randomly selected in one quality control exercise) is given by the combination formula which is displayed below:

$$\frac{n!}{r!\,(n-r)!}$$

In this formula, n, r and (n -r) are all integer values, where:

n! (n factorial) = n x (n - 1) x (n - 2) .... x 2 x 1 (e.g. 4! = 4 x 3 x 2 x 1) and 0! = 1 and 1! = 1

A combination is used to determine the number of ways in which a desired outcome can be achieved because order (of say, failures from a batch of tested systems in the quality exercise) doesn't matter, you are interested instead in counting the number of successes and failures in one group of trials (i.e. an individual quality control test). Since the individual events within the trial are independent, you must multiply the combination by the relevant probabilities.

Therefore, P(r successes in n trials) =

$$\frac{n!}{r!\,(n-r)!} \times p^r \times q^{n-r}$$

where:

r is the number of successes or events you are interested in

n is the total number of items or trials considered

$\frac{n!}{r!\,(n-r)!}$ counts the number of ways of achieving r successes from n trials

p^r measures the probability of achieving **r independent successes**

q^{n-r} measures the probability of achieving **n-r independent failures**

Example:

You can now consider the following example that will be used to answer a series of questions and demonstrate a number of ways of limiting the number of calculations when applying the binomial distribution formula.

Crystal glasses produced by a company based in Dublin are packed in sets of 6 for the domestic and European market. It is found that 10% of these individual glasses are sub-standard and are classed as *Class B* products. Glasses which meet the quality standard are labelled as *Class A* products.

If the crystal glasses are packed in gift sets of containing 7 glasses.

(a) Find the probability that a set contains exactly 4 glasses that are Class A.

$n = 7$, $p = 0.9$, $q = 0.1$, $r = 4$, where p is the probability that an individual glass is Class A

P(4 glasses out of 6 being Class A) = (r = 4)

$$P(r = 4) = \frac{n!}{r!\,(n-r)!} p^r q^{n-r}$$

$$= \frac{7!}{4!3!} (0.9)^4 (0.1)^3$$

= 35 x 0.6561 x 0.001 (note: there are 35 ways of selecting 4 Class A glasses from 7) (0.9^4 = 0.9 x 0.9 x 0.9 x 0.9 and 0.1^3 = 0.1 x 0.1 x 0.1)

= 0.0230 (4dp)

Therefore, there is a **2.30%** probability of exactly 4 glasses being Class A in a set of 7.

(b) The probability that a set contains 4 Class B glasses.

In this example you are interested in Class B glasses rather than glasses which are Class A. As a consequence, you can define p = 0.1 and q = 0.9 instead, since p is the probability of an individual glass being Class B. In this example, n = 7 and r = 4.

$$P(r = 4) = \frac{7!}{4!3!} (0.1)^4 (0.9)^3$$

= 35 x 0.0001 x 0.729 (note: there are 35 ways of selecting 4 Class B glasses from 7)

= 0.0026 (4dp)

This probability indicates that there is a **0.26%** probability of exactly 4 Class B glasses being found in a set of 6.

(c) The probability that in a set of 7 glasses *at most one* crystal glass is Class B.

Because of the wording of this problem (i.e. *at most one*) you need to calculate the probability of no Class B glasses and exactly one Class B glass. Therefore,

P(at most one item is Class B) =

P(no items are Class B) + P(exactly one item is Class B)

The two events above are mutually exclusive, i.e. no Class B and one Class B exactly cannot occur within the same set of crystal glasses. As a result, the individual probabilities corresponding to these two exclusive events can be added together to give the required probability.

$n = 7, \; p = 0.1, \; q = 0.9, \; r = 0 \text{ or } 1$

$$P(r \leq 1) = P(r = 0) + P(r = 1)$$

$$= \frac{7!}{0!7!}(0.1)^0(0.9)^7 + \frac{7!}{1!6!}(0.1)^1(0.9)^6$$

$$= (1 \times 1 \times 0.4783) + (7 \times 0.1 \times 0.5314)$$

$$= \mathbf{0.8503 \; (4dp)}$$

In conclusion, there is an 85.03% probability of at most 1 Class B glass appearing in a set of 7.

(d) Find the probability that at most 5 glasses in a set are Class B standard.

$n = 7, \; p = 0.1, \; q = 0.9, \; r = 0, 1, 2, 3, 4 \text{ or } 5$

Using the same argument as shown in part c), that is the events are mutually exclusive:

$$P(r \leq 4) = P(r = 0) + P(r = 1) + P(r = 2) + P(r = 3) + P(r = 4) + P(r = 5)$$

This particular problem is starting to involve a lot of calculations because you now have to apply the complex binomial distribution formulae 6 times. However, the crystal glasses are packed six into a set, you can have either 0, 1, 2, 3, 4, 5, 6 or 7 Class B standard glasses. Since these number of Class Bs are exclusive and exhaustive events:

$$P(0) + P(1) + P(2) + P(3) + P(4) + P(5) + P(6) + P(7) = 1$$

Comparison of the equation above and the required probability shows us that:

$$P(r \leq 5) = 1 - [P(r = 6) + P(r = 7)]$$

This rearranged formula is an improvement because you only have to apply the binomial distribution formula twice rather than six times.

$$P(r \leq 5) = 1 - [0.000006 + 0.0000001]$$

$$= 1 - 0.0000061$$

$$= \mathbf{0.9999\ (4dp)}$$

Since this value is almost equal to 1, it shows you that there is a very high probability that a set of 7 contains at most 5 Class B glasses.

Like all probability distributions, it is possible to calculate a mean and variance for the binomial problem under consideration. The mean and variance are given by the formulae:

MEAN = np and VARIANCE = npq or np(1 - p)

(e) If the Dublin glass manufacturer has a contract to supply a department store with a 1000 sets of crystal glasses, what is the expected number of Class B standard glasses? In other words, you need to determine the mean number of Class B glasses in 1000 sets.

In 1000 sets there are 7000 glasses, i.e. **n = 7000**
P(single glass being Class B standard) = p = 0.1

Expected number of Class B glasses in **1000 sets**

$$= np = 7000 \times 0.1 = \mathbf{700\ glasses}$$

Variance $= npq$
$= 7000 \times 0.1 \times 0.9 = 630$

Standard deviation $= \sqrt{630}$ = **25.1 glasses (1dp)**

Obviously, the bigger the number of trials (glasses packed into a gift set in this example), the more difficult this type of calculation becomes if performed using a calculator. Fortunately, the process is relatively straightforward if Excel's **BINOMDIST()** function is applied. This facility will be described shortly.

Poisson Distribution

Earlier in the chapter an example referred to a alarm system factory which operates a quality control system on its production line. This factory also produces security lights for the domestic market which are tested for quality. Again, you have a number of exclusive events (the test for each individual security light), whose outcome falls into one of two categories and so you can measure the required probabilities as previously demonstrated. However, you are now looking at a problem where the value of **'n'** (the number of security lights produced in one shift) is big and **'p'** (the probability of an individual security light failing the test) is small. As a consequence, you can calculate the required probabilities using another discrete probability distribution which is called the **poisson distribution**.

Inspection of the formula indicates this distribution can be used where the number of trials is unknown or cannot be measured, but assumes the **average** number of failures per shift say, can be quantified. Because of this, the poisson distribution is often applied to production problems where output is high within 'a pre-defined time period' (such as a single shift at our security light factory) and where the probability of a specific event **'p'** is small. You can also use this distribution to calculate the probabilities of events such as the probability of PC network failure occurring more than twice in a university term.

The Poisson Distribution is found by using the formula:

$$P(\text{'r' events}) = \frac{e^{-(np)}\,(np)^r}{r!}$$

where:

e = 2.71828 (this is a constant value)
np = mean or average number of outcomes say, in a defined time interval such as a shift or a university term

The label 'μ' (mu) can also be used as notation instead of 'np' in the poisson formula, giving:

$$\textbf{P('r' events)} = \frac{e^{-(\mu)}(\mu)^r}{r!}$$

Example:

The mean number of **failing** security lights leaving a production line has been calculated from recent shift records by the production manager as 3 faulty lights per shift. For any given shift, you can use the poisson formula to find the probability that:

(a) Eight failing lights are produced in a shift.

(b) Between 1 and 5 (inclusive) failing lights are produced in a shift.

(c) At least one failing light is produced in a shift.

(d) Ten failing lights being produced in one week.

The most cumbersome part of any calculation involving the poisson distribution is the calculation of $e^{-\mu}$. If you are using a calculator, it is best to determine this value separately and record it for use in other calculations. Alternatively, by using Excel's built-in **POISSON()** command, no explicit calculation of this value will be needed. This command will be described shortly, by reference to a specific example.

(a) The probability that 8 failing lights are made can be calculated as:

$$P(r = 8) = \frac{e^{-3}\, 3^8}{8!} = \mathbf{0.0081\ (4dp)}$$

Therefore, there is a **0.81%** probability of producing exactly 8 failing lights on an individual shift at the factory.

(b) To calculate the probability that between 1 and 5 failing lights (inclusive) are identified, requires you to use the poisson distribution formula three times. As demonstrated with the binomial distribution, remember to consider the exact wording of this problem. The required probability is given by the sum:

$$P(1 \le r \le 5) = P(1) + P(2) + P(3) + P(4) + P(5)$$

(since the word inclusive has been used)

$$= \frac{e^{-3}\,3^1}{1!} + \frac{e^{-3}\,3^2}{2!} + \frac{e^{-3}\,3^3}{3!} + \frac{e^{-3}\,3^4}{4!} + \frac{e^{-3}\,3^5}{5!}$$

$$= 0.1494 + 0.2240 + 0.2240 + 0.1680 + 0.1008$$

$$= \mathbf{0.8663\ (4dp)}$$

In conclusion, there is a **86.63%** probability of producing between 1 and 5 failing lights (inclusive) in an individual shift.

(c) At least one failing light is made:

Here you are required to calculate P(1) + P(2) + ... etc., because of the wording '*at least*'. As demonstrated with the binomial distribution, simple rearranging of the formula makes this sum of probabilities easy to evaluate. The required probability can be written as:

$$P(r \geq 1) = 1 - P(r = 0)$$

$$P(r \geq 1) = 1 - 0.0498 = 0.9502$$

where 1 represents the sum of the probabilities of all the exclusive probabilities.

There is a **95.02%** probability of at least one failing security light being identified in a given shift.

(d) Find the probability in one week that 10 failing lights are found. You can assume that one working week consists of 6 shifts. Therefore, the mean number of failing security lights is given by:

μ = 3 per shift, so per week μ = **3 x 6 = 18**

$$P(r = 10) = \frac{e^{-18}\,18^{10}}{10!} = \mathbf{0.0150\ (4dp)}$$

Therefore there is only a **1.50%** probability of detecting exactly 10 failing security lights at the factory in a typical working week.

Using Excel to Solve Discrete Distribution Problems

By considering the examples described above, it should be apparent that using the formulae for the binomial and poisson distributions can prove difficult and time consuming, especially in scenarios when you have to calculate probabilities such as between 12 and 16 faulty parts. Fortunately, Excel provides a built-in function for both distributions which are described below with reference to worked examples. Both functions can be used to determine either individual or cumulative probabilities, which respectively lend themselves to questions using phrases like 'exactly' and 'at most'.

Binomial Distribution

The probability of **'r'** successes from **'n'** trials and the probability of between **0** and **r** (inclusive) successes (individual and cumulative respectively) can be calculated quickly and accurately using Excel's built-in **BINOMDIST()** function. The structure of this function is:

BINOMDIST(r,n,p,cumulative)

where:

r, **n** and **p** have already been defined.

cumulative indicates whether an individual (FALSE) or cumulative (TRUE) probability is required.

Example:

Circuits for PCs are packed in boxes of 6 from sales to specialist PC retailers. The probability that individual circuit works is 30%. What is the probability of exactly 3 circuits in a pack being in working order and what is the probability of at most 4 working circuits? To answer these questions, Excel has been used and the relevant calculations are shown below in Figure 7.5.

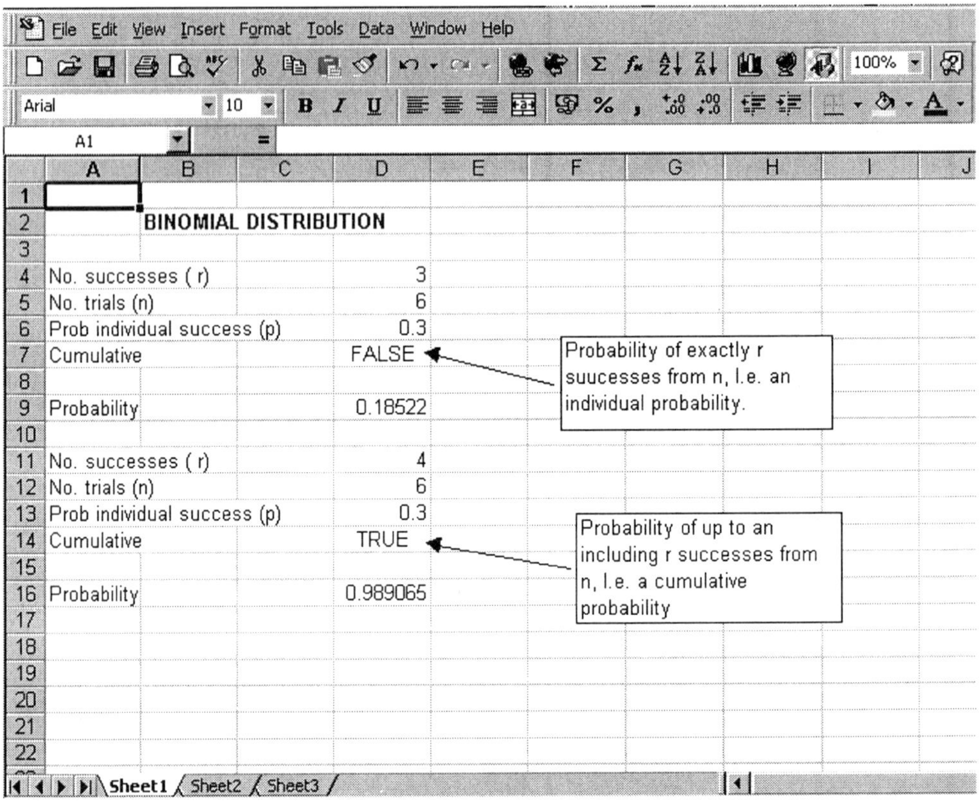

Figure 7.5 - Excel output for a binomial problem

To calculate the probability of exactly 3 working circuits, you have typed into cell **C9** the formula:

=BINOMDIST(D4,D5,D6,D7)

The value of **D7** is '*FALSE*' which indicates an individual or single probability rather than a cumulative probability is required. The value returned is 0.18522, which indicates that the probability of receiving exactly three working circuits is **18.5%**. To determine the probability of receiving at most 4 working circuits i.e.

$$P(0) + P(1) + P(2) + P(3) + P(4)$$

The formula typed into cell **D16** is:

=BINOMDIST(D11,D12,D13,D14)

In this example, the value of **D14** is '*TRUE*' indicating a cumulative probability is required, as indicated by the wording 'at most' in the problem description. Inspection of Figure 7.5 suggests that there is a **98.9%** probability of receiving at most 4 working circuits from a pack of 6.

In certain business applications the number of trials (n) may be very large, and as a consequence, the calculations may be impossible to perform using a calculator. In such situations an approximation to the binomial distribution (provided by the normal distribution) is required. Fortunately, the built-in **BINOMDIST()** function can operate for large scale applications, hence simplifying the calculation process. The method of approximation will not be considered in this book.

Poisson Distribution

The probability of **'r'** events taking place within a given interval of time and the probability of **r** events or between **0** and **r** (inclusive) events (i.e. individual and cumulative) can be calculated quickly and accurately using Excel's built-in **POISSON()** function. The structure of this function is:

POISSON(r,μ,cumulative)

where:

r and **μ** have already been defined
cumulative indicates whether an individual (FALSE) or cumulative (TRUE) probability is required.

Example:

The billing department at a self assessment centre at a city tax office records an average of 20 incomlete tax forms each week. To calculate the probability of a certain number of incpomplete forms appearing, you can use Excel's **POISSON()** command. Figure 7.6 indicates how the probability of exactly 25 incomplete forms in a week has been calculated as well as the probability of between 15 and 20 incomplete forms errors and the probability of more than 20 forms which are incomplete.

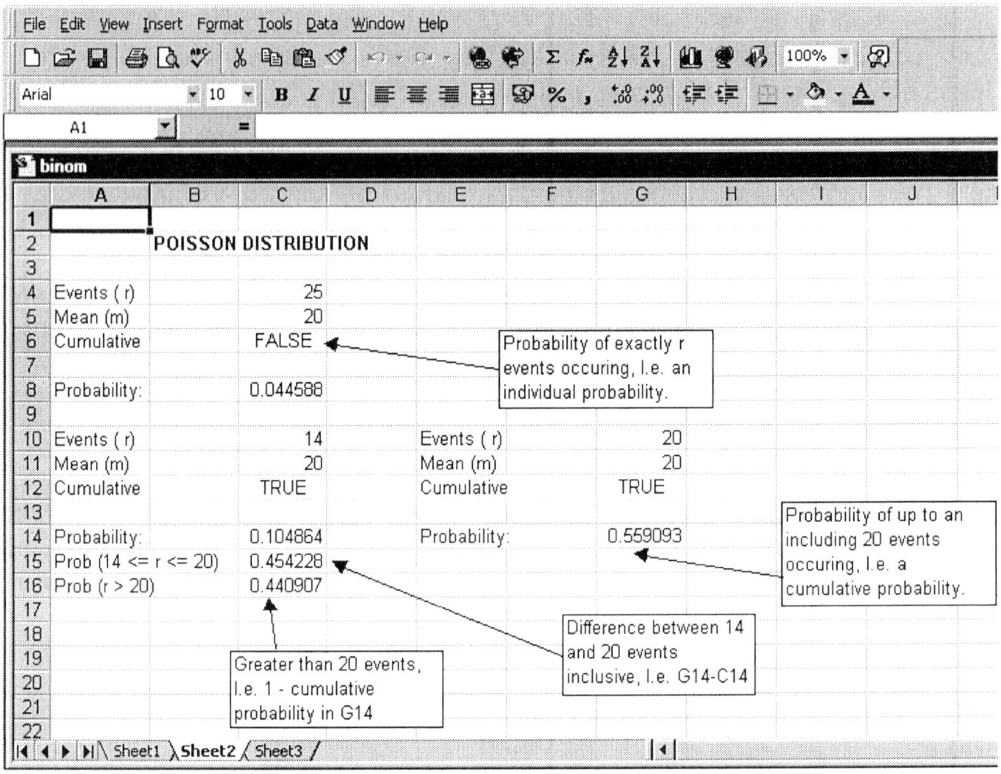

Figure 7.6 - Excel output for a poisson problem

To calculate the probability of exactly 25 incomplete tax forms being returned, you have typed:

=POISSON(C4,C4,C6)

into cell **C8**. The value of **C6** is '*FALSE*' which indicates an individual rather than a cumulative probability is required. The value returned is 0.0446, which indicates that the probability of getting exactly 25 incomplete forms is **4.46%.**

To determine the probability of receiving at most 20 incomplete forms i.e.

$$P(0) + P(1) + P(2) + \ldots\ldots\ldots\ldots + P(19) + P(20)$$

you have typed the following command in cell **G14**:

=POISSON(G10,G11,G12)

whilst, the formula in cell **C14** is:

=POISSON(C10,C11,C12)

which has been used to determine the probability of 14 incomplete forms. The difference between the two (given by the formula **=G14-C14** in cell **C15**) indicates the probability of between 15 and 20 incomplete forms inclusive.

Finally, the formula housed in cell **C16**:

=1-G14

gives the probability of more than 20 incomplete forms returned to be **44.09%**. Again 'FALSE' and 'TRUE' have been used as appropriate in these calculations. In the cumulative calculations for both binomial and poisson calculations, the probabilities calculated correspond to *up to and including r successful outcomes*. If the probability of more than r events is required, simple manipulation of the output, as shown, provides the required probability.

Conclusions

If the outcomes for a variable are identifiable and the corresponding probabilities quantified, the resultant display of outcomes and corresponding probabilities can be referred to as a probability distribution. The **probability distribution** is a useful display useful because it indicates the likelihood of various events taking place.

Probability distributions have various forms such as experimental distributions which are calculated from the outcomes of throwing dice or the profile of sales recorded by a number of consultants. In general, two additional types of experimental probability distribution can be applied to various business problems. These are **discrete probability distributions** and **continuous probability distributions**.

A variable is said to be **discrete** if you can only record specific values within a given range. If you can record the corresponding probability for each discrete value, it is possible to a determine a probability distribution which is also discrete. Examples of discrete probability distributions which are widely used in business decision making in business are the **binomial** and **poisson** distributions.

To apply either of the distributions described above, characteristics of the problem must first be identified and these must be compared with those characteristics which define the probability distributions. In particular, the two main statistical distributions which are listed above can be identified by the following features:

- The **binomial distribution** measures the probability of achieving **'r'** successes from 'n' trials where each trial is independent and the probability of an individual success at a trial can be measured and assumed to have a constant value.

- The **poisson distribution** measures the probability of a specified number of events taking place over a fixed, pre-defined length of time where the number of trials is big and the probability of an individual event (such as a light or system failure) is small.

Learning Outcomes Checklist

After completing this chapter you should have an understanding of the following concepts, calculations and functions:

The properties of a discrete data set.

- The probability distribution.

- The properties of the discrete uniform, binomial and poisson probability distributions.

- The use of the **BINOMDIST()** and **POISSON()** functions available within Excel.

Ensure that you understand these concepts before progressing to Chapter 8.

Chapter Case Question

The public house chain are interested in selling off part of their estate. A property agent believes that a country located public house has a 25% probability of selling within six months of being on the market. Ten public houses located in this country have become available for sale.

- Explain why the distribution of probabilities is binomial.

- Using the **BINOMDIST()** function, create the following table:

Sales	Probability	Cumulative Probability
0		
1		
2		
3		
4		
5		
6		
7		
8		
9		
10		

- What is the probability of exactly 3 public houses out of the 10 being sold within six months?

- What is the probability of between 2 and 4 (inclusive) of the 10 public houses being sold within six months?

- What is the probability that at most 4 of the 10 are sold in this time?

- What is the probability that at least 7 of the 10 properties are sold within six months?

For the whole pub chain for a given year, 15 public houses on average will be refurbished. Explain why this probability distribution is poisson.

- What is the probability that 20 houses exactly will be refurbished?

- What is the probability that more than 30 will be refurbished?

- What is the probability that less than 10 will be refurbished?

- Save the file as **CHAP07.XLS**

Supplementary Questions

1. What is meant by the term 'probability distribution'?

2. 1000 CD players were assembled at a North East factory in one week. The time of assembly is given below:

Time (minutes)	12	14	16	18	20	22
Number of CD players	50	300	335	195	65	55

   (a) Using this information create a probability distribution.

   (b) From the distribution, what is the most likely assembly time?

   (c) What is the probability that the assembly time exceeds 18 minutes?

   (d) What is the probability that the assembly time is at most 16 minutes?

3. Three dice are rolled at the same time and a score is recorded by adding all three values together.

   (a) Create a probability distribution to represent this game.

   (b) Using the distribution, what is the most likely score?

   (c) What is the probability that the score exceeds 14?

   (d) What is the probability that the score is at most 8?

   (e) What is the probability that the score is between 10 and 13 inclusive?

4. What are the main features of a discrete probability distribution?

5. Describe briefly the main features and applications of the following discrete probability distributions:

   (a) discrete uniform

   (b) binomial

   (c) poisson

6. CD players leaving a production line have a 12% probability of being faulty. Every hour, 6 CD players are selected randomly and tested. Find the probability that:

   (a) All 6 CD players work.

   (b) Two CD players are faulty.

   (c) At least 4 CD players work.

   (d) If 2000 CD players are made every week, what is the expected number of faulty players?

   (e) Check the answers obtained using the relevant facilities offered by Excel.

7. A University network manager has set up 15 stand-alone PCs for an IT examination. He believes that the probability of a machine crashing during the examination to be 0.075. Determine the probabilities below:

   (a) No PCs will crash during the examination.

   (b) One PC will crash during the examination.

   (c) At least two machines will crash.

   (d) Check the answers obtained using the relevant facilities offered by Excel.

   (e) If the machines were networked instead of stand-alone, what impact, if any, would this have on your calculations?

8. A factory processes meat for domestic animal consumption. The meat is stored in large cans which are tested for quality. Those failing the test are incinerated. Recent production records show that 25% of cans are destroyed per day. If a random batch of 12 large cans are selected randomly for testing, calculate the probabilities below:

   (a) All 12 cans are destroyed.

   (b) Six cans exactly are destroyed.

   (c) More than four cans are destroyed.

   (d) Between 1 and 3 cans (inclusive) are destroyed.

9. At a plant producing dog meat, any punctured tins are automatically destroyed. On average, it is estimated that 50 tins are destroyed per day.

   (a) Why would you apply the poisson distribution to this problem?

   (b) Calculate the probability that exactly 60 tins are destroyed in a single shift.

   (c) Calculate the probability that between 50 and 55 tins are destroyed.

   (d) Check the answers obtained using the relevant facilities offered by Excel.

10. A University Business School runs a computer network. The network manager estimates that the files server fails on average once every two weeks. The faculty examinations are taking place soon over a two week period. Determine the following probabilities:

    (a) The network does not fail during the examinations.

    (b) The network fails exactly twice during the examination period.

    (c) The network fails more than twice.

    (d) Check the answers obtained using the relevant facilities offered by Excel.

    In the summer, the examinations take place over a period of three weeks. Determine the following probabilities:

    (e) The network fails once exactly during the summer examinations.

    (f) The network fails exactly twice during the summer examination period.

    (g) The network fails more than three times.

    (h) Check the answers obtained using the relevant facilities offered by Excel.

Chapter 8

Continuous Probability Distributions

Learning Outcomes

In this chapter you will consider the features of a number of continuous probability distributions and will apply these distributions to relevant business related problems.

- After completing this chapter you will be able to:
- Recognise the features of a continuous probability distribution.
- Recognise the properties of the continuous uniform, exponential and normal distributions and apply them to a variety of relevant problems.
- Apply a number of relevant built-in facilities offered by Excel to solve problems involving exponential and normal distributions.

Introduction

In Chapter 7 you considered discrete probability distributions, where the variable under consideration can only record certain values within a pre-specified range. A variable is said to be continuous if you can measure any value (or at least a very large number of values which may be grouped into continuous intervals) within a pre-specified range. If you can calculate the corresponding probabilities for these intervals, you can create a probability distribution. This probability distribution will also be continuous over the range of values under consideration. For example, the time between two machine breakdowns in a factory can be any value within a pre-defined scale, and as a result, is a continuous variable. Moreover, you may wish to determine the probability of this interval being more than a certain length of time.

In the next section of this chapter, you will consider three important continuous probability distributions in detail, namely:

- Continuous Uniform
- Exponential
- Normal

These distributions will be applied to relevant business related problems.

Continuous Uniform Distribution

Like the discrete uniform distribution, the possible outcomes or values for this variable have an equal probability of taking as long as these values are between two values a and b. The probability of an individual value being recorded is zero if the value is found outside this range. The continuous uniform distribution is shown graphically by Figure 8.1.

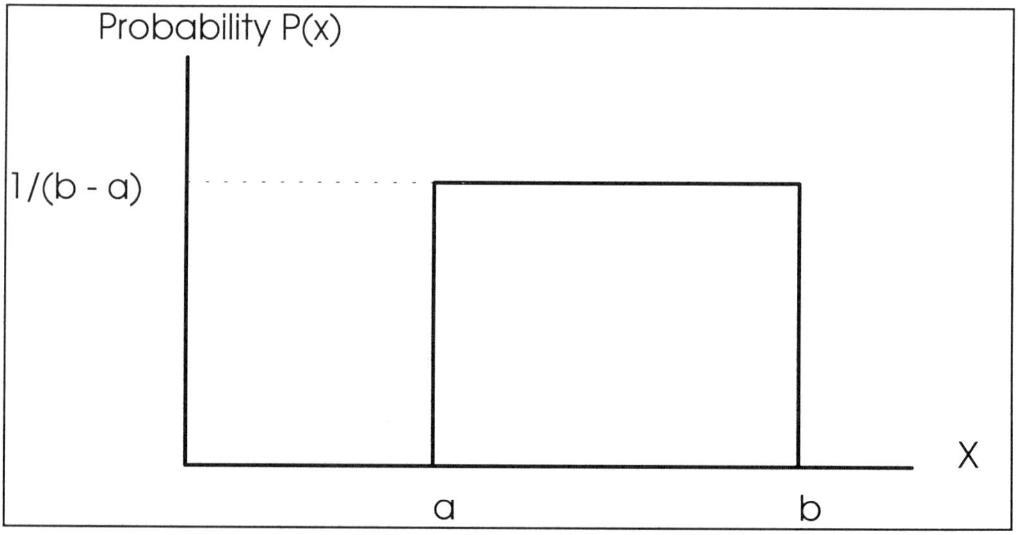

Figure 8.1 - Continuous uniform distribution

Between the values a and b, (which depend upon the process under consideration) the probability of all values being measured is the same. This probability is **1/(b - a)**. Inspection of the graph in Figure 8.1 indicates that the area of the rectangle is equal to 1, as expected for a probability distribution and it is impossible for values of x which are less than a or exceed b to exist, hence their corresponding probabilities are zero. Company figures 7.2. and 8.1 will indicate the difference between a discrete uniform and a continuous uniform distribution, where the observation in the former are distinct.

Finally, the mean and variance for a continuous uniform distribution can be calculated using the formulae:

Mean = (a + b)/2 and Variance = (b - a)^2/12

and the probability distribution is given by:

$$p(x) = {}^{1}/_{(b - a)} \qquad a \leq x \leq b$$

$$= 0 \qquad x < a \text{ or } x > b$$

Example:

A city council runs a help desk in a local shopping centre to allow the public to register concerns on matters such a waste removal, payment of local taxes and to report problems relating to theft and vandalism. It has been suggested that the rate at which the public register complaints is evenly distributed between 5 and 25 minutes. It would be reasonable to assume that the distribution is continuous, because the time between individual complaints can be any value between 5 and 25 minutes. Find the probability that:

(a) Less than 7 minutes elapses between two people using the facility.

(b) The time between two customers is between 8 and 14 minutes.

From the information provided:

$$p(x) = {}^{1}/_{(25 - 5)} = {}^{1}/_{20} \qquad 5 \leq x \leq 25$$

$$= 0 \qquad x < 5 \text{ or } x > 25$$

(a) The probability of less than 7 minutes elapsing is shown by the labelled area under the curve in Figure 8.2.

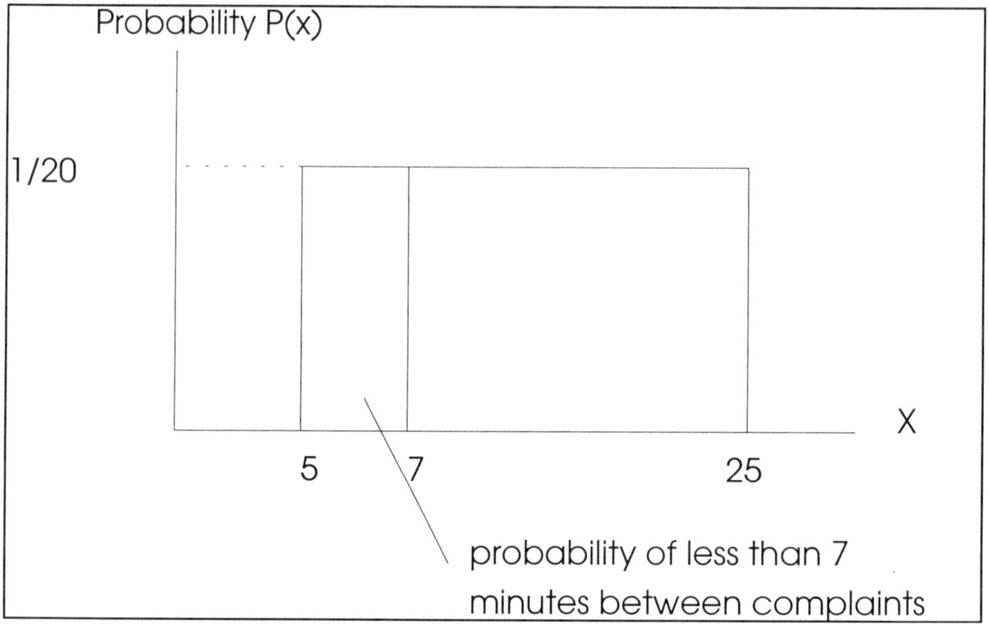

Figure 8.2 - Probability of less than 7 minutes between complaints

Since the distribution is rectangular, the area corresponding to the required probability is equal to *width x height*, i.e. (7 - 5) x $^1/_{(25\ -\ 5)}$ = $^1/_{10}$. Therefore, there is a 1 in 10 (i.e. 0.1 or 10%) probability of less than 7 minutes elapsing between two members of the public registering a complaint.

(b) The probability of between 8 and 14 minutes elapsing between two people using the help desk is shown by the indicated area under the probability function in Figure 8.3.

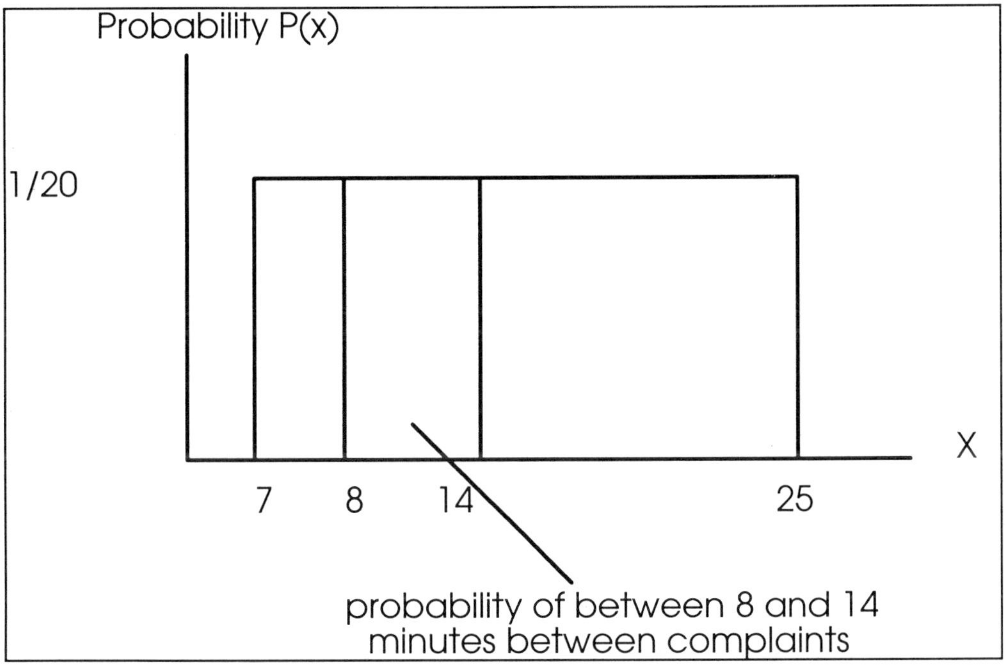

Figure 8.3 - Probability of between 8 and 14 minutes from one complaint to another

The required probability is given by area indicated, i.e. $(14 - 8) \times {}^{1}/_{(25 - 5)} = {}^{\mathbf{3}}/_{\mathbf{10}}$.

In addition, you can calculate the mean time between complaints being registered at the help desk as **(5 + 25)/2** or 15 minutes.

Exponential Distribution

In the last chapter, you saw how the poisson distribution could be used to calculate the probability of a number of events taking place within a given time period. The poisson distribution represented a *discrete probability distribution* since the number of events taking place within the specified time interval could be 0, 1, 2, etc., but not, say, 1.6 or 2.8. The poisson distribution is applied to problems where the number of trials is big (i.e. security lights leaving a mass production environment) or cannot be measured and where probability of a individual event (such as a security light failing a test for quality) taking place is small. This distribution lends itself to problem where you consider specified periods of time. The distribution can be used to calculate the probability of events such as PC failure taking place on a university campus.

However, you may not only be interested in the number of PC failures over a specified length of time, say during the university's examination period, *but also the actual length of time between each recorded failure*. Measuring time in this way involves considering continuous data (since time is a continuous variable), and by doing so, you will be considering a continuous probability distribution. This distribution of such times can be calculated using the **exponential distribution** and this is typically used by business decision makers who need to measure the life between machine failures to plan repairs and shut-downs or work study engineers who may want to measure the rate at which customers join a queue in a high street bank during peak working hours in order to determine the number of cashiers required.

As suggested, on an assembly line the number of breakdowns is obviously important because subsequent maintenance and plant shut-downs have to be planned. By measuring the time between breakdowns useful information is generated which may allow the manager to schedule any preventative maintenance in response to the predictions made. To predict the number of machine failures, say, in a month, the poisson distribution can be used (because individual machine failures are discrete events), whilst the probability that the time between failures (a continuous variable) is of a certain length can be measured using the exponential distribution. Figure 8.4 illustrates a typical exponential distribution.

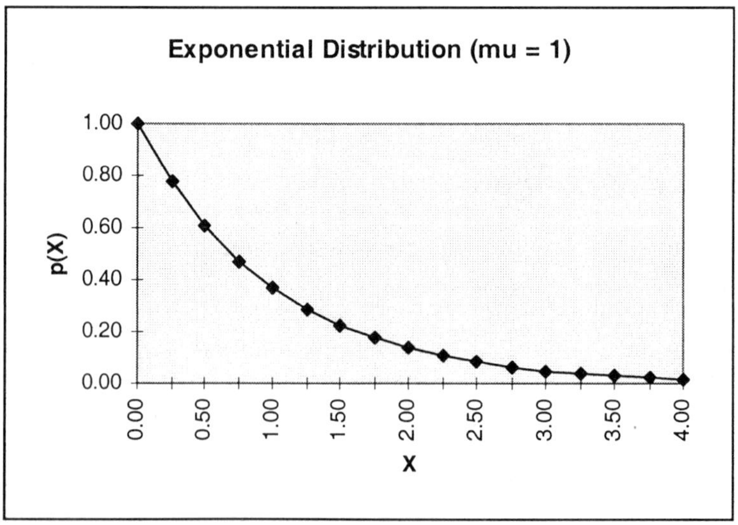

Figure 8.4 - Exponential distribution

The distribution shown in Figure 8.4 shows a declining curve which is reasonable because much larger time intervals (measured in weeks say) between PC failure are much less common than the smaller time intervals between machine failures, hence the former have much smaller probabilities. The probability distribution for the exponential distribution is given by:

$$\mathbf{p(x) = \mu e^{-\mu x} \qquad x, \mu > 0}$$

$$\mathbf{= 0 \qquad x < 0}$$

In the formula for the probability distribution p(x) above, x represents the time between two events such as machine failures. The constant μ is calculated from the mean time between two events. The value of μ = **1/mean**.

Example:

Time between PC network failure at a large university is estimated to be on average 40 days. Calculate the following:

(a) The value of μ.

(b) The probability that the time between two network failures is exactly 30 days.

(c) The time between two failures is less than 25 days.

(d) The time between two failures is greater than 50 days.

(a) $\mu = 1/\text{mean} = 1/40 =$ **0.025**

(b) $P(x = 30) = \mu e^{-\mu r}$, where r = 30 and $\mu = 0.025$

$= 0.025e^{-(0.025 \times 30)} =$ **0.0118** (4dp)

Therefore, there is a **1.18%** probability of exactly 30 days between two network failures.

To calculate the probability of time between two failures being less than or greater than a certain amount of time x, you can use the formulae:

$$P(X > r) = e^{-\mu r}$$

and

$$P(X < r) = 1 - e^{-\mu r}$$

where μ = **1/mean** and **r** is the time between two events. These formulae will be used in parts c) and d).

(c) $P(x < 25) = 1 - e^{-(0.025 \times 25)}$

$= \mathbf{0.4647}$ (4dp)

Therefore, there is a **46.47%** probability of the network lasting at most 25 days between two successive network failures.

(d) $P(X > 50) = e^{-(0.025 \times 50)}$

$= \mathbf{0.2865}$ (4dp)

In conclusion, there is a **28.65%** probability of the network lasting more than 50 days between two successive network failures.

Using Excel to Solve Exponential Distribution Problems

Excel offers a built-in facility, **EXPONDIST()**, which can be used to determine the required probabilities. The structure of this function is:

EXPONDIST(r,μ,cumulative)

where:

r and **μ** have already been defined (μ = 1/mean)
cumulative indicates whether an individual (FALSE) or cumulative (TRUE) probability is required.

Example:

A machine part has an average estimated life of ten working days. The production engineer has fitted a new part in response to a new production run which is planned to last 7 working days. As a consequence, he is interested in determining the following probabilities:

(a) The machine part lasts exactly 7 working days.

(b) The part lasts less than or equal to 7 working days.

(c) The machine part lasts at least 7 working days.

Given that the average working life of the part is 10 working days, you may wish to assume that the average time between replacement is also 10 working days. As a consequence, the mean time is 10 working days, and μ= 1/mean, i.e. 1/10 or 0.1. Figure 8.5 illustrates the application of Excel's **EXPONDIST()** command.

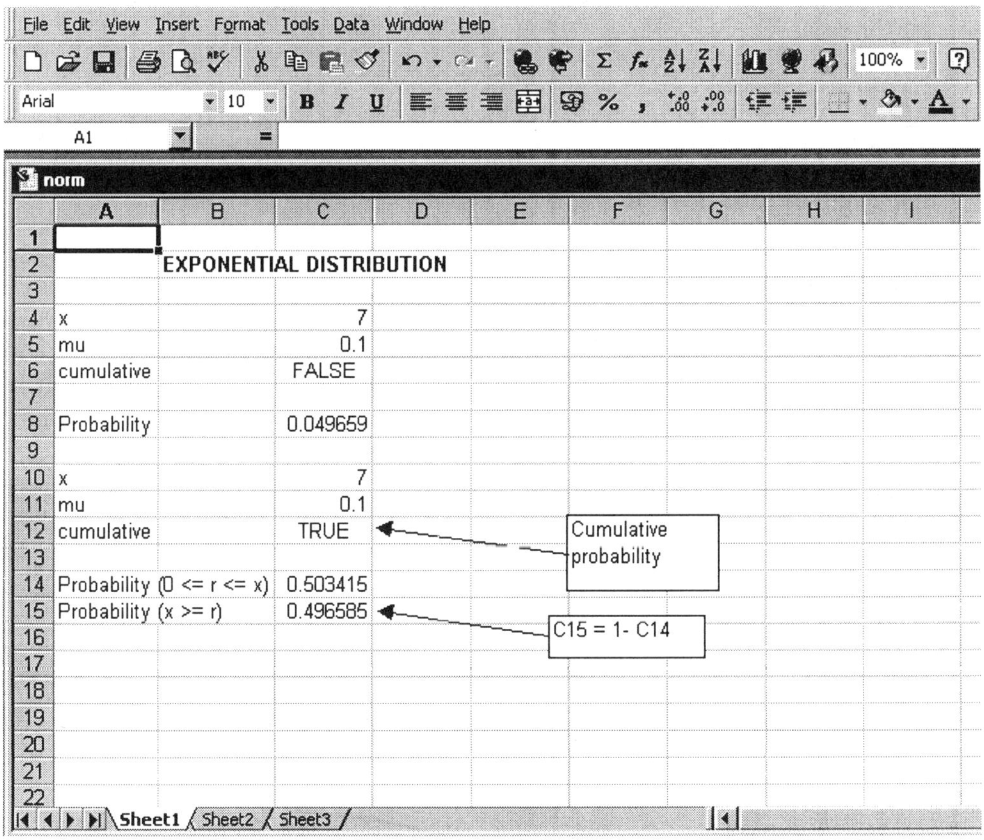

Figure 8.5 - Calculating Exponential distribution probabilities using Excel

(a) To determine the probability the part lasts exactly 7 working days, you must use the formula:

=EXPONDIST(C4,C5,C6)

where **C6** contains the term '*FALSE*'. The value of the probability in cell **C8** is **0.0497**, which indicates **4.97%** of parts are should last exactly 7 working days.

(b) To calculate the probability the part lasts at most 7 working days, the same term is used again except the cumulative parameter '*TRUE*' is referenced instead. Cell **C14** contains the value **0.5034** which indicates **50.34%** of parts are expected to last at most 7 working days. This indicates the probability that the production run will be interrupted so that maintenance can take place.

(c) Finally, to determine the probability that a part lasts at least 7 working days, the formula:

=1-C14

has been typed into cell **C15** indicating the proportion of parts lasting at least this length of time is **49.66%.**

Normal Distribution

Suppose the weight of 1000 boxes of tea selected at random were measured and displayed using a frequency polygon, it would be reasonable to expect the graph to resemble Figure 8.6 below. This graph is appropriate because the variable under consideration is continuous, i.e. the weight measured can be any value within the pre-defined range.

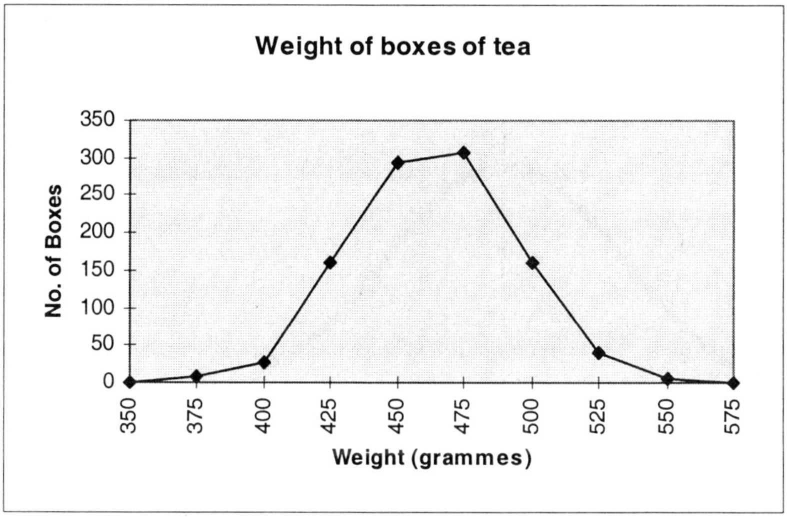

Figure 8.6 - Weight of 100 boxes of tea

More importantly, the distribution of weights measured may take the form of a symmetrical curve which peaks around its 'middle' value, where the mean and median values and the modal class will be very similar in value. Also, the more distant an individual weight is compared to the mean of 450g, the less chance it has of being recorded (i.e. its probability is much smaller).

To calculate the probabilities for a variable which is distributed in this way, you can make reference to a theoretical distribution which is known as the **normal distribution**. The normal distribution is given by a complex formula which is beyond the scope of this book, and as a consequence, will not be stated. However, the shape of this distribution is indicated by two parameters; its middle or **mean** value around which the distribution peaks and is symmetrical, and its spread or variability, which is determined by its **standard deviation**.

This type of distribution can also be used to represent everyday features such as heights, shoe size and weights (which will have impact in the retail sector for products such as clothes and shoes) as well as business related variables such as the number of defectives recorded each day in a high volume production process or salaries awarded in a particular business sector. It should be obvious that the height or weight of a group of adults is likely to be normally distributed, with only a small proportion of big and heavy people, a small proportion of small and light people with a peak in the distribution caused by the biggest proportion being of average height and weight.

The corresponding theoretical curve is shown by Figure 8.7.

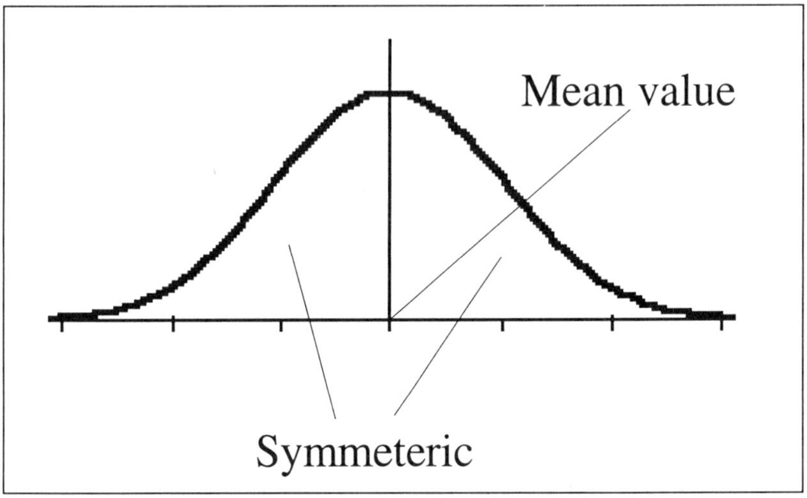

Figure 8.7 - The theoretical normal distribution curve

You can assume that a variable **x** relating to a particular business problem or process is **normally distributed** with a mean value μ and standard deviation σ then it can be presented mathematically using the notation:

$$x \sim N(\mu,\sigma^2)$$

Given that the formula for calculating probabilities from the normal distribution is awkward to use, an alternative method for calculating probabilities from a given normal distribution is required. To determine the required probabilities, you must use statistical tables instead of manipulating the formula and these tables will be introduced shortly.

Since the mean and standard deviation of this type of distribution are not going to be 0 and 1 respectively, the actual values of these parameters depending upon the individual distribution being considered, it is necessary to **standardise** the distribution before undertaking any probability calculations. This is achieved by making reference to one particular distribution which is known as the **standard normal distribution**.

The Standard Normal Distribution and Normal Tables

The standard normal distribution is the curve which may be generated by transformation from any normal distribution. This distribution forms the basis of the normal distribution tables which will be used to evaluate the required probabilities. The mean of the standard normal distribution is equal to 0 and a standard deviation equal to 1, and is represented by the notation:

$$z \sim N(0,1^2)$$

where z denotes the standard normal variable instead of the notation x, which is used to define the normal distribution which represents the business process under consideration. This distribution is symmetric around its mean value of zero, and given that the curve represents a probability distribution, the area either side of the mean value of zero are equal to ½. To determine the areas to the left, right or between values of z you can use the standard normal tables listed in Appendix I.

The standard normal tables are straightforward to use. The three examples pictured in Figure 8.8 (which are not to scale) show the following areas:

- $P(z < 1.54)$
- $P(z > 1.72)$
- $P(-1.65 < z < 1.54)$

For those students with no experience of using the normal distribution, it is generally a good idea to sketch the distribution to show the shaded area before using the tables to evaluate the corresponding probability. Your sketch will give you an immediate indication that the probability you need to calculate is greater than or less than 0.5.

The examples listed are useful because they demonstrate all possible scenarios you are likely to encounter with the standard normal tables; namely determining the areas to the left, right or between values of z and dealing with negative values of z.

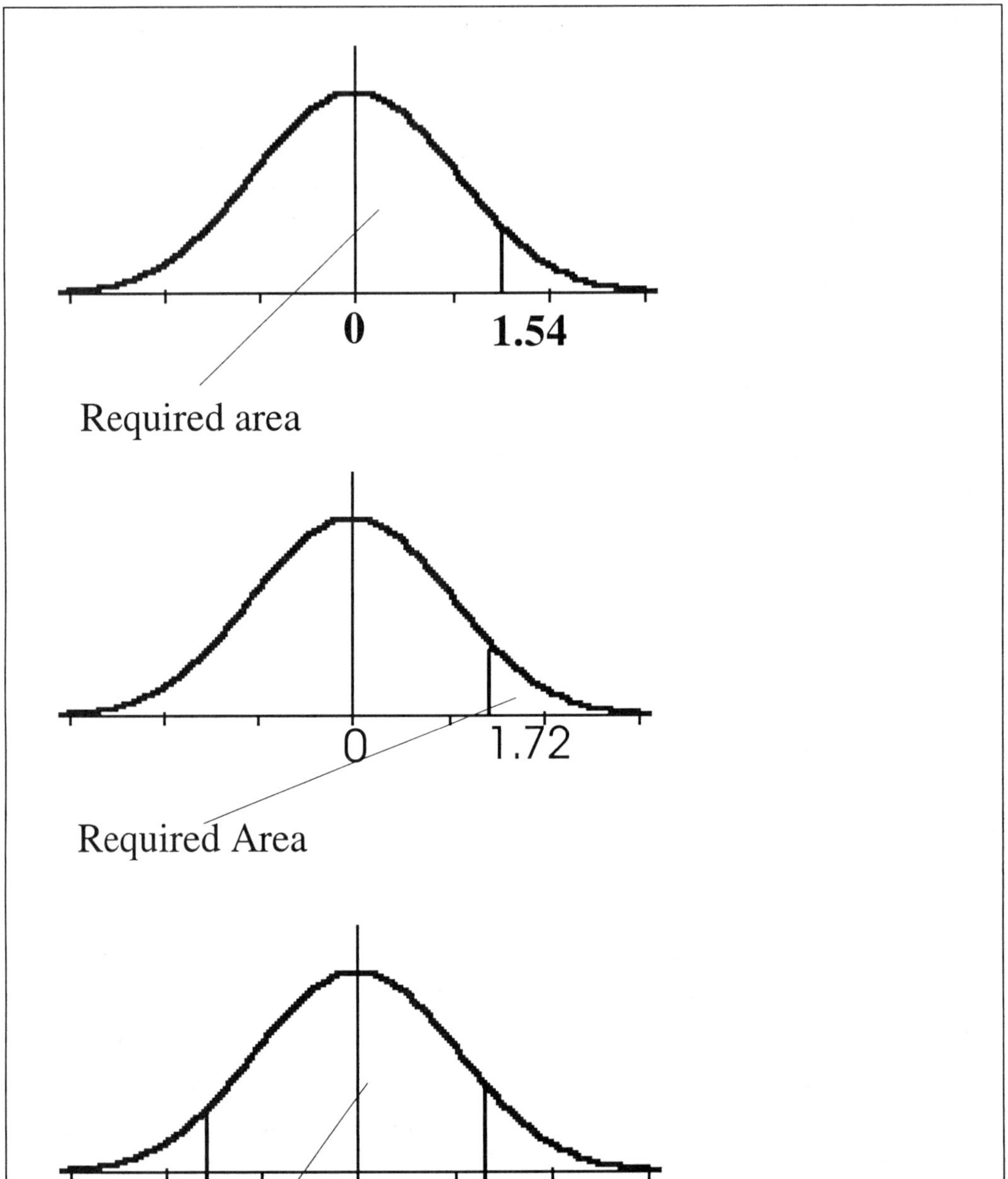

Figure 8.8 - Determining the areas under the standard normal curve

To determine the area under the standard normal curve which is situated to the left of z = 1.54, i.e. to evaluate P(z < 1.54), you must:

- Pick the relevant table from Appendix I. To do this notice the required area is situated to the left of z on the diagram in Figure 8.8. Compare this to the tables on the top of each normal distribution table. In this case you need the table labelled P(Z < z)

- Read down the left hand side of the table to the row valued **1.5**, as shown in Figure 8.9.

- Read across the top of the table to the column valued **0.04**.

- Read off the value at the intersect of this row and column to determine the area under the curve, i.e. **0.9382**.

This tells us that **93.82%** of the area under the standard normal curve is situated to the left of z = 1.54.

					(Column)	
z	0.00	0.01	0.02	0.03	**0.04**	0.05
0.0						
0.1						
0.2						
0.3						
0.4						
.						
.						
1.0						
1.1						
1.2						
1.3						
1.4						
1.5	**(Row)**				**0.9382**	
1.6						
.						
.						

Area to the right of **Z = 1.72:**

			(Column)							
z	0.00	0.01	**0.02**	0.03	0.04	0.05	0.06	0.07	0.08	0.09
0.5										
0.6										
0.7										
0.8										
0.9										
1.0										
.										
1.5										
1.6		.								
1.7	**(Row)**		**0.0427**							
.										
.										

Figure 8.9 - Example of how to read from the standard normal tables

Using the same process, you will determine $P(z > 1.72) = 0.0427$. In this case you should refer to the second set of tables in Appendix I and in Figure 8.9 because you wish to determine the area to the right of 1.72.

To evaluate $P(-1.65 < z < 1.54)$ is more complicated.

Inspection of the area under the curve tells us that:

$$P(-1.65 < z < 1.54) = P(z < 1.54) - P(z < -1.65)$$

Now $P(z < 1.54)$ can be evaluated easily from tables as 0.9382, as shown earlier. In contrast, $P(z < -1.65)$ is initially more difficult because z is negative in value. To overcome this problem, you can consider the symmetry of the distribution, i.e.

$P(z < -1.65) = P(z > 1.65)$, the latter can be found from tables. Using this information:

$$P(-1.65 < z < 0) = P(z < 1.54) - P(z < -1.65)$$
$$= 0.9382 - 0.0495$$
$$= \mathbf{0.8887}$$

Therefore, **88.87%** of the area under the standard normal curve is situated between the values $z = 1.54$ and $z = -1.65$.

In general on a normal distribution curve, the area between values a and b (where b is greater than a), can be written as $\mathbf{P(a < x < b)}$ and is equal to $\mathbf{P(x < b) - P(x < a)}$.

Applying the Normal Distribution to Business Problems

Before applying the normal distribution to a business problem, one question which you may need to answer is 'When can you assume that the distribution you are dealing with is normally distributed'? This question can be answered by plotting a graph to represent the data and if it roughly resembles the symmetrical curve presented in Figure 8.7, then the normal distribution can be applied to determine the relevant probabilities. If any asymmetry exists, it can be quantified using the skewness coefficient described in Chapter 5. Once you are satisfied that the curve is *roughly* symmetrical, you can confidently apply the normal distribution to the problem under consideration.

The next characteristics of our data set to consider are its mean and standard deviation. You would not expect that for any particular normal distribution encountered within business, the mean and standard deviation to be 0 and 1 respectively. Therefore, to apply the tables considered above, you must **transform** the normal distribution representing your business problem, i.e. $\mathbf{x \sim N(\mu,\sigma^2)}$, into the standard normal distribution $\mathbf{z \sim N(0,1^2)}$. This can be achieved using the transformation:

$$\mathbf{z = (x - \mu)/\sigma}$$

As a consequence, the value of interest x and $P(X < x)$ on the normal distribution under consideration are equal to z and $P(Z < z)$ under the standard normal curve. To evaluate probabilities for a distribution exhibiting normal properties, the following steps must be undertaken:

- Identify the mean and standard deviation of the distribution under consideration.
- Transform the value x into z using the equation listed above.
- Use the tables to determine the required probability.

You can also start with a specified probability instead and 'work back' to evaluate the corresponding value x. Both types of calculation are presented below using a specific business example.

Example:

At a 'temping' agency dealing with data processing workers, the weekly salaries for advertised posts are normally distributed with a mean of £275 and a standard deviation of £35. Find the proportion of posts where the salary paid is less than £240 per week, and determine the minimum salary for the best paid 20% of jobs.

To calculate the proportion of posts which pay less than £240 per week, you must first transform $x = 240$ into an equivalent value of z using the normal transformation.

x = distribution of weekly wages at the 'temping' agency, $x \sim N(275, 35^2)$
z = standard normal distribution, $z \sim N(0,1)$

To transfer x into z, you can use:

$$\begin{aligned} z &= (x - \mu)/\sigma \\ &= (240 - 275)/35 \\ &= -1 \end{aligned}$$

Therefore: $P(x < 240) = P(z < -1)$

You now use the fact that the distribution is symmetrical and use:

$P(z < -1) = P(z > 1)$.

From tables, this area is equal to **0.1587**. As a consequence, **15.87%** of advertised posts pay less than £240 per week. This area is depicted in Figure 8.10.

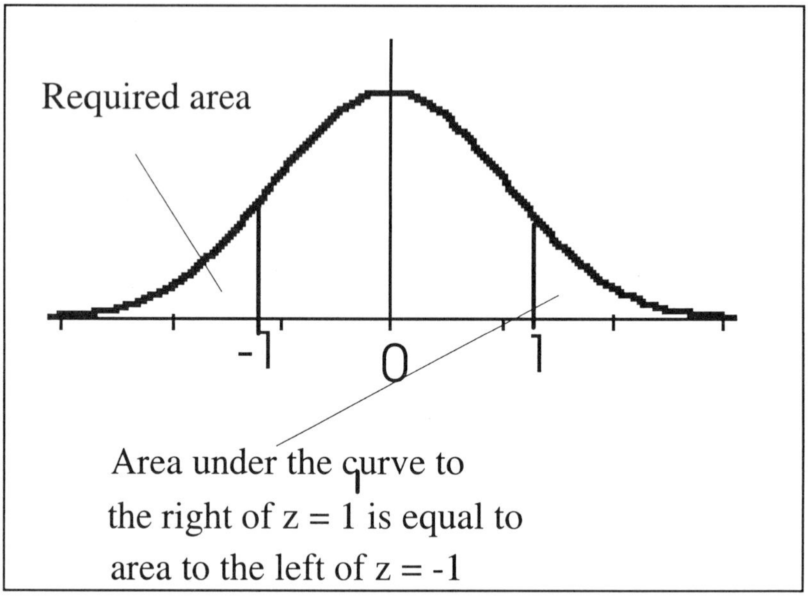

Figure 8.10 - The standard normal distribution

In the second part of the question, you are given the probability and are required to 'work back' to determine the corresponding value of x. Moreover, the probability provided corresponds to the best paid 20% of jobs, and inspection of the appropriate normal table shows us that the value of z is **0.84**. This is found by identifying the nearest probability to **0.20** in the table of standard normal probabilities and reading back up the relevant column and row to find z. It should be apparent that a z value corresponding to the top of the distribution must be positive since it is situated to the right of the mean value of zero. If you were interested say in the **worst paid** 10% of jobs instead, the corresponding value of z would have to be **negative**, since the lower 50% of values on the standard normal distribution are situated to the left of z = 0. In general, the 'heaviest' and the 'biggest' tails have positive z values, whilst the 'lightest' and the 'smallest' tails have negative z values. Figure 8.11 shows how to work back to z from the tables and the relevant area under the normal curve.

z	0.00	0.01	0.02	0.03	**0.04**	0.05	0.06	0.07	0.08	0.09
0.5										
0.6										
0.7										
0.8					**0.2005** (nearest probability to **20%**)					
0.9										

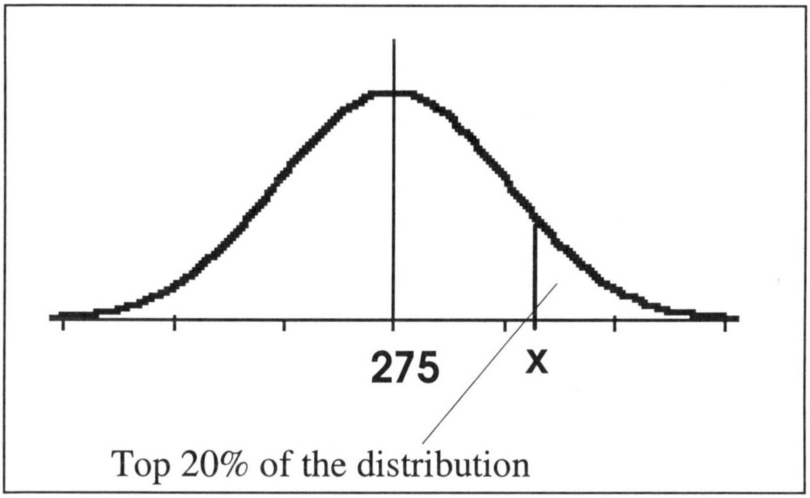

Figure 8.11 - The best paid 20% of advertised jobs

Re-arranging the normal transformation equation $z = (x - \mu)/\sigma$ gives:

$$x = \mu + z\sigma$$

Now you can substitute in the values:

$$= 275 + 0.84(35)$$
$$= \mathbf{£304.40}$$

where x and z represent the variables defined previously.

Therefore, the best paid 20% of jobs at the agency pay at least £304.40 per week.

Example:

At the same agency, the daily number of applications received for all posts is normally distributed with a mean of 1000 and a standard deviation of 120. What is the proportion of days where the number of applications is between 900 and 1100 inclusive?

Because the actual number of applications is discrete, i.e. 1, 2, etc. but not say 1½ or 25.63, you must make a **continuity correction**, given that the normal distribution is not a discrete but a continuous distribution. Therefore, you need to determine:

$$P(899.5 \leq x \leq 1100.49)$$

since 889.5 is the lower bound of those values which can be rounded to 900 as the nearest integer and 1100.49 is the upper bound of those values which can be rounded to 1100 as the nearest integer.

Using the transformation $\mathbf{z = (x - \mu)/\sigma}$, you get:

$$P(x < 899.5) = P(z < -0.8375)$$
$$P(x < 1100.49) = P(z < 0.8375)$$

Thus, $P(899.5 < x < 1100.49)$
$$= P(-0.8375 < z < 0.8375)$$
$$= P(z < 0.8375) - P(z < -0.8375)$$
$$= 0.7995 - 0.2005$$
$$= \mathbf{0.5990}$$

Therefore, on **59.90%** of days, the number of applications received by the agency is between 900 and 1100 inclusive.

Using Excel to Solve Normal Distribution Problems

Even though the statistical tables simplify the process of using the Normal distribution, the process can be simplified even further using the various commands related to this distribution which are offered by Excel. In particular, the two functions **STANDARDIZE()** and **NORMSDIST()** calculate the standard normal distribution value z and the corresponding probability for the area *is situated to the left of z under the standard normal curve*. The structure of the two functions are:

STANDARDIZE(x,μ,σ)

where:

x, **μ** and **σ** have already been defined

and

NORMSDIST(z), where z is the equivalent value from the standard normal distribution.

Example:

The price of a three bedroom house in a Northern City are normally distributed with a mean of £56,500 and a standard deviation of £8,100 What is the probability that a house selected at random has a value:

(a) less than £60,000

(b) less than £50,000

In this example, x = the prices of the houses.
$x \sim N(56{,}500,\ 8100^2)$
z = is the standard normal distribution, $z \sim N(0,1)$

Figure 8.12 shows how these probabilities can be calculated:

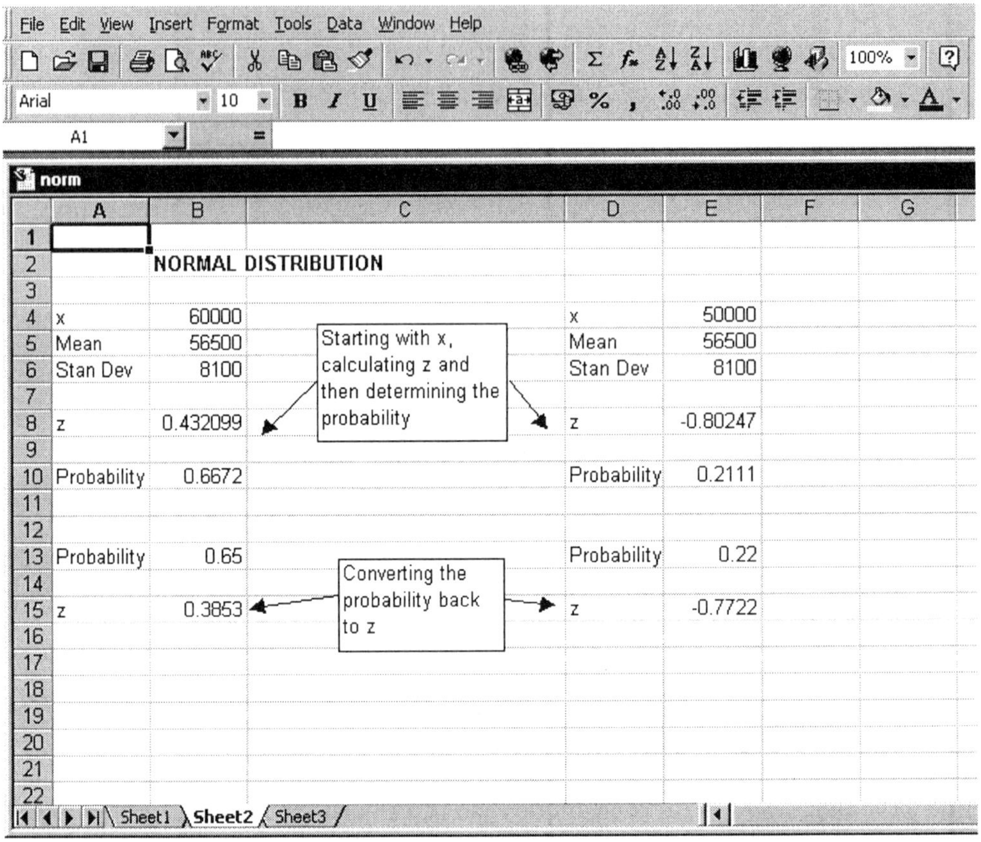

Figure 8.12 - Using Excel's STANDARDIZE() and NORMSDIST() functions

The cells B8 and E8 contain the respective standard normal value corresponding to house valuations of £60,000 and £50,000. Cell **B8** contains the formula:

=STANDARDIZE(B4,B5,B6).

To convert these standard values into probabilities, the cells **B10** and **E10** contain the formulae:

=NORMSDIST(B8) and =NORMSDIST(E8)

respectively. Inspection of this output suggests that the probability that a house is valued at less than £60,000 is **0.6672 (4dp)** and less than £50,000 is **0.2111 (4dp)**.

It is sometimes necessary to start with a probability and convert back to z. This may be achieved using the **NORMSINV()** function. In Figure 8.12, the cell B15 contains the formula:

=NORMSINV(B13)

and this suggests that **65%** of the area under the curve (the value in B13) is situated to the left of **z = 0.385** (the value returned to cell B15). Additionally, the same command has been used to indicate that 22% of the area under the standard normal curve is situated to the left of z = -0.77.

The **NORMSINV()** command returns the value z corresponding to the area situated under the normal curve to the left of it. If you wish to determine probabilities or values at the top (or right hand end) of the distribution, then you must first consider what is the most appropriate value of z to use in the Excel function. For example, if the value of z for the top 10% is required, then the value 0.9 (or 90%) should be used instead because the area under the probability curve is equal to 1.

Additionally, it is possible to start with the parameters of a normal distribution and calculate directly the relevant probabilities using Excel's **NORMDIST()** function. The structure of this function is:

NORMDIST(x,μ,σ,cumulative)

where:

x, **μ** and **σ** have already been defined
cumulative indicates whether an individual or single probability (FALSE) or a cumulative (TRUE) probability is required. The latter indicates the proportion of the normal curve which is situated to the left of x. Practically all examples will involve using the TRUE command.

Again, considering the valuations of the three bedroom houses which a normally distributed with a mean of £56,500 and a standard deviation of £8,100. You may wish to determine the proportion of houses are valued at less than £60,000.

The relevant details to this problem are pictured below in Figure 8.13.

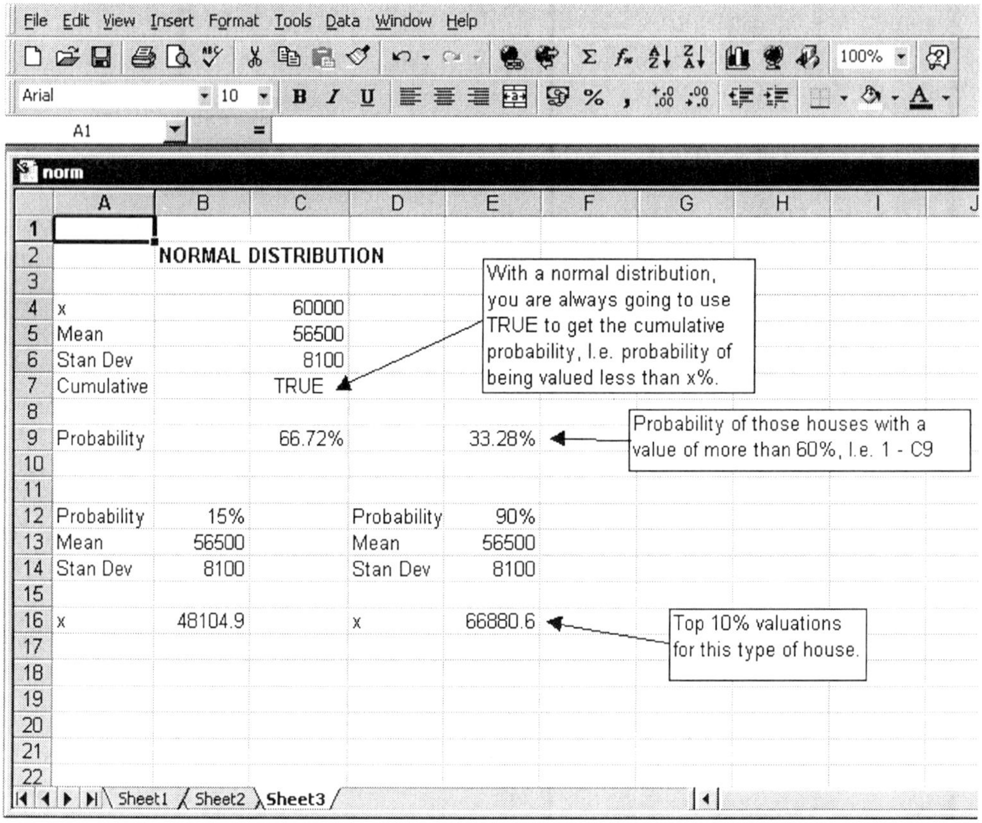

Figure 8.13 - Applying Excel's normal distribution functions

To determine the proportion of houses with this valuation,

=NORMDIST(C4,C5,C6,C7)

has been typed into cell C9. The logical statement '*TRUE*' has been used to determine all houses with a valuation of less than £60,000, i.e. the cumulative probability. As shown by Figure 8.13, this proportion is 66.72% of those houses in this category. Additionally, cell E9 contains the simple formula:

=1-C9

which indicates 33.28% of houses have a valuation of at least £60,000.

As indicated earlier in the chapter, it may be necessary to convert a proportion back into a value from the distribution. Supposing the cheapest 15% of houses receive only two displays in the local advertising paper, whilst the most expensive 10%

receive four advertising slots. You may wish to determine the highest price for the former and the lowest valuation of the latter.

In both cases, you are starting with a percentage and wish to work back to a house price x. To do this automatically using Excel, you must apply the **NORMINV()** command. The structure of this function is:

NORMINV(p,μ,σ)

where:

p represents the area to the left of x under the normal curve
μ and σ have already been defined

Figure 8.13 illustrates the application of this function. In particular, cell **B16** contains the formula:

=NORMINV(B12,B13,B14)

and this suggests that the highest valuation of the cheapest 15% of houses is **£48,105**. To determine the lowest valuation of the most expensive 10% of houses, the value 90% has to be used when applying this function because it assumes all proportions relate to the area which is situated *to the left of x* under the normal curve. Inspection of Figure 8.13 indicates that all houses which are valued at least **£66,881** fall into this category.

Conclusions

A variable is said to be **continuous** if you can measure any value within the pre-specified range. If you can measure the corresponding probability for each possible value, you can determine a probability distribution which is also a continuous distribution. Examples of continuous variables which are widely applied to business problems are the **exponential** and **normal distributions**.

To apply either of the distributions described above, characteristics of the problem must first be identified and these must be compared with those characteristics which define the theoretical probability distribution. In particular, the two statistical distributions which are listed above can be identified by the following features:

- The **exponential distribution** can be used to determine the probability that the time interval between two events (such as successive breakdown of a computer) is of a certain duration. Since time is a continuous variable, the exponential distribution represents a continuous probability distribution.

- The **normal distribution** is used to determine probabilities for events whose values peak around their mean and where these values occur with less regularity as you move away from the centre of the distribution.

Excel offers easy to use built-in functions pertaining to each of the widely used distributions which removes the need for lengthy calculations. In order to use these functions, you must simply identify or define the necessary distribution parameters, e.g. referring to the last Chapter, the number of trials **n**, number of successes **r** and the probability of success **p** are the parameters for the binomial distribution, and then apply the relevant built-in functions as demonstrated.

Learning Outcomes Checklist

After completing this chapter you should have an understanding of the following concepts, calculations and functions:

- The properties of a continuous data set.
- The properties and application of the exponential distribution.
- The application of Excel's **EXPONDIST()** function.
- The properties of the normal distribution.
- The features of the standard normal distribution.
- How to transform to the standard normal distribution.
- How to use standard normal tables to calculate probabilities.
- How to undertake inverse calculations for a normal distribution.
- The application of Excel's **NORMDIST(), STANDARDIZE(), NORMSDIST(), NORMINV()** and **NORMSINV()** functions.

Ensure that you understand these concepts before progressing to Chapter 9.

Chapter Case Question

- Open the file **CHAP05.XLS**

Assume the values of mean and standard deviation for the four categories of public house represent the population parameters.

- Determine the probability of a country restaurant selected at random having a monthly turnover of more than £125000 firstly by calculation and tables and then using the relevant Excel tools.
- Determine the probability of a town family pub selected at random having a monthly costing less than £60000, again using both methods described in the previous question.
- Determine the probability of a town family pub with a monthly turnover of less than £90000.
- What proportion of town family pubs have a monthly turnover between £60000 and £90000?
- What is the greatest monthly turnover that can be recorded by one of poorest 20% of town restaurants? Use both methods to determine your answer.
- Save your Excel file as **CHAP08.XLS**

Supplementary Questions

1. What are the main features of a continuous probability distribution?
2. Describe briefly the main features and applications of the following continuous probability distributions:

   (a) continuous uniform

   (b) exponential

   (c) normal
3. A newsagent considers the number of people buying lottery tickets from his shop on a Saturday is uniformly distributed between 100 and 250. Find the probability that:

(a) The number of sales is less than 200.

(b) The number of lottery tickets sold exceeds 175.

(c) The number of ticket sales is between 130 and 205.

4. The time between customers arriving at a cashier's window in a high street bank is evenly distributed between 12 and 45 every hour. Find the probability that:

(a) More than 20 customers arrive in a given hour.

(b) Less than 15 customers arrive in a given hour.

(c) The number of customers in one hour exceeds 30.

(d) The number of customers is between 15 and 27 in one hour.

In a working day consisting of 6 hours, find the probability that:

(e) Less than 100 customers arrive.

(f) The number of customers in one day exceeds 225.

(g) The number of customers is between 150 and 200 in one day.

(h) State any assumptions made.

5. The time between services for a cable testing machine is exponentially distributed with an average of 50 days. Find the probability that:

(a) The machine will have to be repaired exactly 27 days after maintenance was last undertaken.

(b) The machine will last at most 60 days.

(c) The machine will last between 25 and 55 days inclusive before its next service.

(d) Check the answers obtained using the relevant facilities offered by Excel.

6. In a city centre bank, the time between re-fills for the cash machine has an average of 60 hours. If it is filled on a Friday night, find the probability that:

(a) The machine will have to be re-filled exactly 40 hours after it was last re-filled.

(b) The machine will last at most 70 hours before needing to be re-filled.

(c) The money in the machine will last between 25 and 45 hours inclusive.

(d) What distribution have you assumed? Why?

(e) Check the answers obtained using the relevant facilities offered by Excel.

7. What is the difference between the normal distributions $\mathbf{x} \sim \mathbf{N(\mu,\sigma^2)}$ and $\mathbf{z} \sim \mathbf{N(0,1^2)}$?

8. State the transformation equation for standardising a normal distribution.

9. Using the standard normal distribution table, determine the following probabilities:

   (a) $P(z > 1.34)$

   (b) $P(z < 1.77)$

   (c) $P(z > -1.56)$

   (d) $P(z < -0.25)$

   (e) $P(1.75 < z < 2.21)$

   (f) $P(-1.15 < z < 0.65)$

   (g) $P(-2.32 < z < -0.58)$

   (h) Check the answers obtained using the relevant facilities offered by Excel.

10. The daily weight of parcels arriving at a small midlands sorting office have weights which approximately follow a normal distribution with a mean of 16.5 hundred weights and a standard deviation of 2.5 hundred weights. Calculate the probabilities that on a particular day:

    (a) The weight of parcels will be over 18 hundred weights.

    (b) The weight of parcels will be below 13 hundred weights.

(c) The weight of parcels will be between 10 and 15 hundred weights.

(d) Check the answers obtained using the relevant facilities offered by Excel.

11. At a college offering a combined Statistics and Operational Research degree, overall examination marks on the final paper are understood to be normally distributed with a mean of 52% and a standard deviation of 7.2%. The degree is graded First, Upper Second, Lower Second, Third and Fail. By presenting your answers to the nearest 0.5%, calculate the following band of marks:

(a) The lowest passing mark (Third Class) if the lowest 3% of students are awarded a Fail.

(b) The highest mark for an Upper Second, if the top 8% of students are awarded a First.

(c) The lowest mark for an Upper Second, if the top 8% are awarded a First and the next 35% are awarded an Upper Second grade.

(d) The minimum mark for a Lower Second if the next 42% of students are awarded this grade.

(e) How many students in a degree class of 150 would you expect to be awarded each of the possible grades listed above?

(f) Check the answers obtained using the relevant facilities offered by Excel.

12. The price of Victorian conservatories in a Northern town is considered to be normally distributed with a mean of £4,500 and a standard deviation of £750.

(a) What is the minimum price of a conservatory in the most expensive 15% of all conservatories built in the town?

(b) What is the maximum price of a conservatory in the cheapest 25% of all conservatories built in the town?

(c) What is the probability that an individual conservatory will be priced less than £3,800?

(d) If 100 conservatories have been built in the town, how many would you expect to be priced at least £5,750?

(e) Check the answers obtained using the relevant facilities offered by Excel.

Part 4
Statistical Inference and Tests for Independence

Chapter 9

Introduction to Statistical Inference

Learning Outcomes

In this chapter you will be introduced to the concept of statistical inference. Statistical inference involves making and testing statements about one or more populations via the collection and analysis of representative samples of data from the population(s) under consideration. Moreover, you will distinguish between point and interval estimates of population parameters, and in this chapter you will be introduced to the 'confidence interval'. Where appropriate reference will also be made to the relevant facilities offered by Excel.

After completing this chapter you will be able to:

- Understand the term 'statistical inference'.
- Recognise the difference between a population and a sample.
- Understand the concept 'sampling distribution of the mean'.
- Understand the principles of the central limit theorem.
- To calculate a point estimate for a population parameter.
- Calculate an interval estimate for a population parameter.
- Understand the term 'confidence interval'.
- Calculate a confidence interval for a population mean.
- Recognise the difference between a large and small sample.

- Use the Students' t-distribution to calculate the interval coefficients for a small sample.

- Calculate a confidence interval using the built-in facilities offered by Excel.

Introduction

In chapter one you were introduced to two concepts; the **population** and the **sample**. As a reminder, a population consists of all observations in which you are interested. To understand the properties of a **population**, it would be useful to consider all of its members, but for reasons of cost and practicality, this is often impossible. Instead, you consider a **sample**, which is a representative sub-set of the population of interest.

Statistical inference is the process whereby samples of data from one or more populations are analysed and statements (or ***inferences***) are made corresponding to the populations which are represented by these samples. Two aspects of inference will be considered in this book. In this chapter, **estimation** will examined, in particular you will see how the population mean can be estimated from sample data. In Chapter 10 you will be introduced to **hypothesis testing**. Figure 9.1 depicts the relationship between a sample and population by means of a simple diagram.

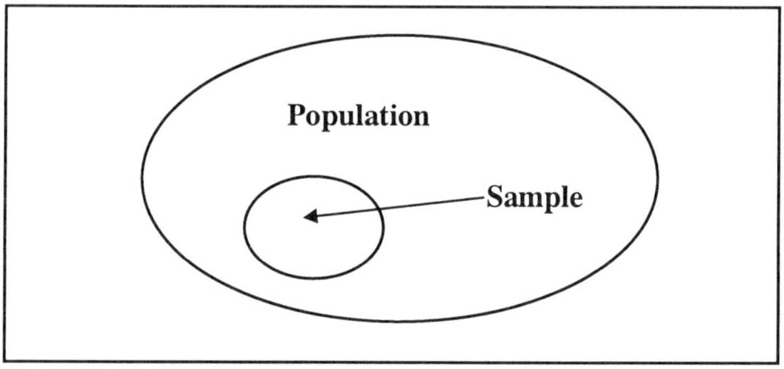

Figure 9.1 - Diagram representing the relationship between sample and population

It is obvious that the most accurate estimates and statements would be made about a population if all members of that population are targeted. This would involve undertaking a census to collect all of the relevant data, which is both costly and time consuming. In practice, data is much more often only collected from a sample or sub-set of this population, using one or more of the techniques described in Chapter 1. Once the sample of data has been analysed (in particular statistics such as its mean, standard deviation and size may be computed), this data can be used to make statements or test beliefs about the population.

Saving time and money are the obvious advantages, and moreover, collecting data from a sample rather than a population is much more practical in many cases because it may be neither possible or realistic to collect data from an entire population. For example, if a factory produces domestic vacuum cleaners, it would be totally impractical to test every single cleaner leaving the factory in order to determine the average life for the whole population, for fairly obvious reasons! In practice, only a small proportion of vacuum cleaners leaving the production line will be tested, and subsequent statements regarding all cleaners (i.e. the population) can be made and evaluated.

By undertaking tests for statistical inference certain terminology and notation is used which are listed below in Figure 9.2. In general, the population measures are called **parameters**, whilst the sample measures are known as **statistics**.

	Population parameters	**Sample statistics**
Mean	μ (mu)	$\bar{x}$ (x bar)
Standard deviation	σ (sigma)	s
Size		n

Figure 9.2 - Notation used in statistical inference

The degree of variability and uncertainty in any inferences or statements made about a population of interest can be accounted for by the normal distribution, as long as the sample of data is sufficiently large. If the sample has at least 30 observations it is assumed to be a large sample and the distribution of values around the population mean is assumed as normal. This feature is known as the sampling distribution of the mean, and this concept is described below, by means of a worked example.

The Sampling Distribution of the Mean

The welfare officer at a university student's union wishes to estimate the average overdraft amongst the university's undergraduates. She decides to sample 160 students and from this sample has calculated the following statistics:

Mean $\bar{x}_1$ Standard deviation s_1

The mean calculated can be used as an estimate of the population mean overdraft amongst the university's undergraduates. However, the welfare officer may also sample another 160 students, calculating sample statistics:

Mean $\bar{x}_2$ Standard deviation s_2

The second set of statistics are likely to be different to the statistics calculated for the first sample. Since each of the possible sample means are potentially different in value, there is a variance (i.e. spread of values) in the set of sample means. The difference between any of the sample means and the actual population mean μ they represent are known as **sampling errors**. Therefore, any measure of variance is a measure of the sampling error and in particular you can calculate a specific measure of variation known as the standard error. This is given by the formula:

$$\text{Standard Error} = \sigma/\sqrt{n}$$

and the distribution of sample means are governed by two parameters; the mean μ and the standard error $\boldsymbol{\sigma/\sqrt{n}}$.

Normality and the Central Limit Theorem

If you are considering a population which is normally distributed, you can also assume that the distribution of sample means is also normal, the sample means having the distribution $\mathbf{N(\mu,\sigma/\sqrt{n})}$.

However, the population may not display the properties of the normal distribution. To counter this problem, you can use the **Central Limit Theorem**. This theorem suggests that the distribution of sample means will display normal properties with a mean value μ and standard deviation $\boldsymbol{\sigma/\sqrt{n}}$, for any population whatever its distribution, if the samples are **large**.

Example - Uniform distribution:

Consider a continuous uniform distribution with values ranging from 0 to 1. This is a useful example to consider because the population from which the samples are to be selected is clearly ***not*** normally distributed. The population mean for such a distribution is **0.5** and variance is **0.0833** (4dp) using the formulae listed in Chapter 8.

To generate random values from such a distribution, you can make use of the **RAND()** function provided by Excel. By selecting 50 random samples of size 1, 2, 4 and 8 respectively and calculating their mean values, the histograms presented in Figure 9.3 were generated. As suggested, the greater the sample size, the easier it is for you to observe a greater convergence towards normality for the sampling distribution of the mean. The shape of the final chart in Figure 9.3 can be readily compared to the shape of the theoretical normal distribution introduced in Chapter 8. On each of these graphs the number of samples considered is the same. The scales on each graph changes as the mean values begin to group around the value 0.5.

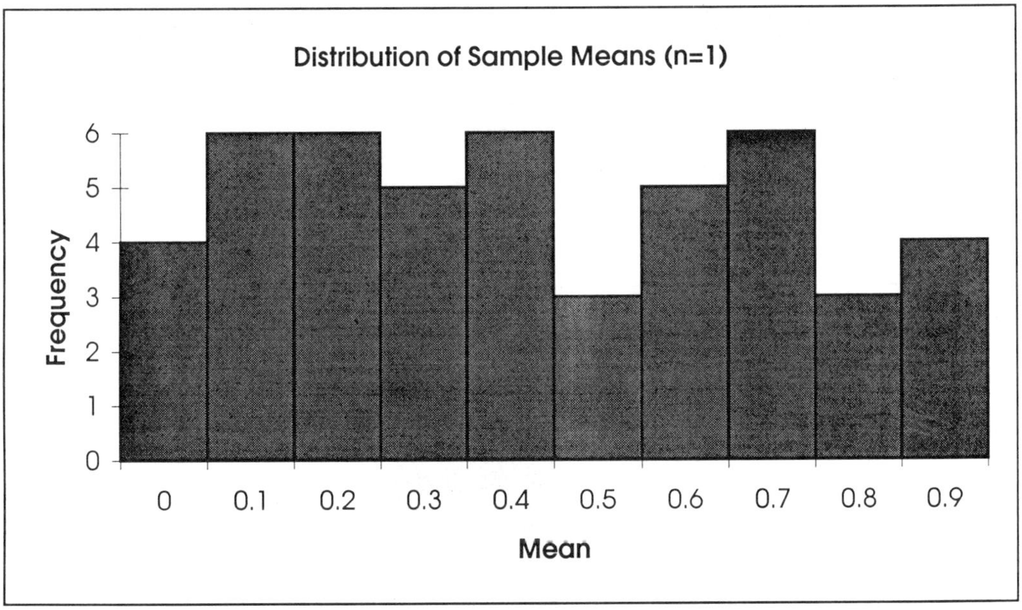

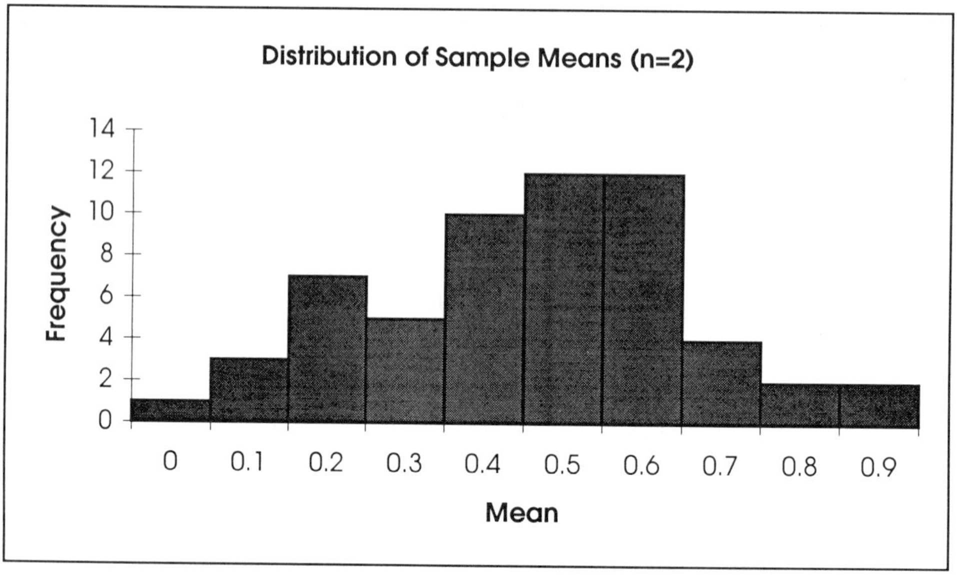
Distribution of Sample Means (n=2)
Frequency
14
12
10
8
6
4
2
0
0
0.1
0.2
0.3
0.4
0.5
0.6
0.7
0.8
0.9
Mean

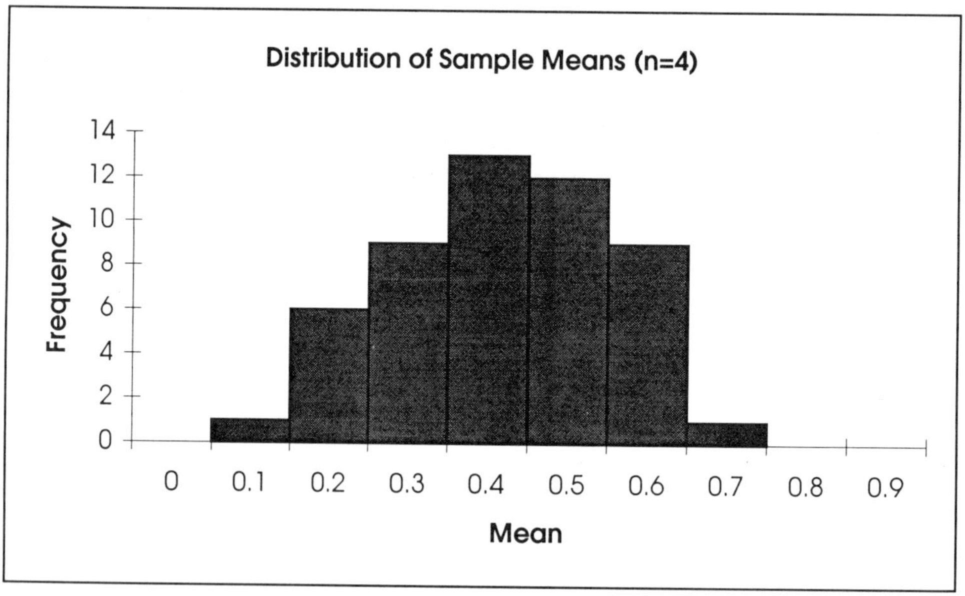
Distribution of Sample Means (n=4)
Frequency
14
12
10
8
6
4
2
0
0
0.1
0.2
0.3
0.4
0.5
0.6
0.7
0.8
0.9
Mean

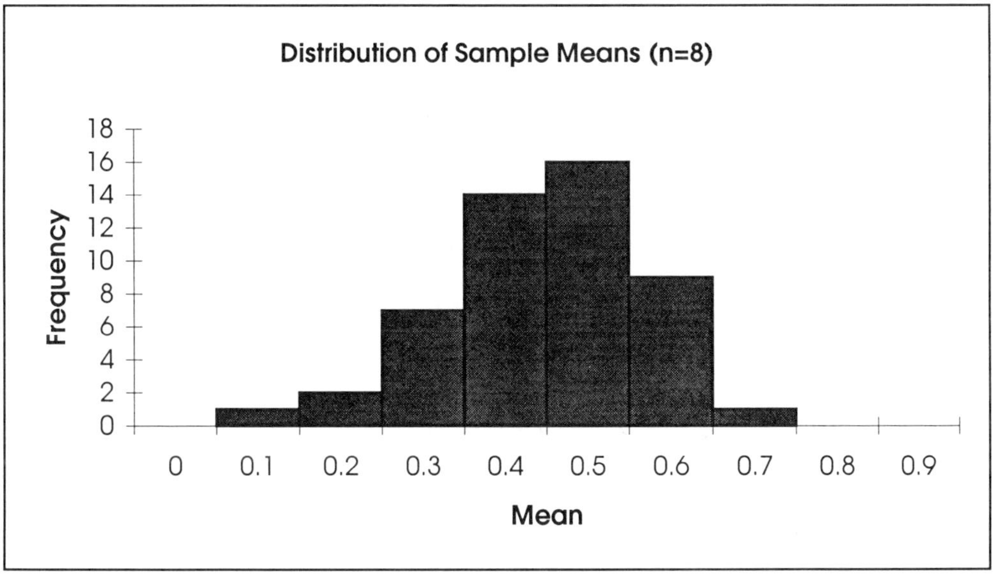

Figure 9.3 - Graphical presentation of sample mean distributions (50 samples)

One of the main points of statistical inference is that you consider a sample of data in order to make inferences or statements about their population. It would therefore make sense to assume that bigger samples will provide more accurate inferences. If you wish to estimate the population mean μ, then it can be estimated by the mean of a representative sample. Also, these sample means have variability measured by the standard error. Inspection of this formula suggests that the bigger the sample size n, the smaller the standard error, and hence the smaller the variability.

To prove this, the mean and variance for the sampling distributions represented graphically above are shown in Figure 9.4. As suggested, the mean of each sample mean is approximately equal to the population mean (which is 0.5) and by increasing the size of the sample, the variance of the sample means, and in turn, the value of the standard error is reduced.

Sample Size (n)	Mean	Variance
1	0.5102	0.0897
2	0.5261	0.0412
4	0.4848	0.0180
8	0.5037	0.0133

Figure 9.4 - Sampling distribution statistics

Using the assumptions listed above, you can transform the sampling distribution of the mean into the distribution Z (see Chapter 8), where Z represents the standard normal distribution with a mean of 0 and a standard deviation of 1.

This standard normal distribution can be written as: $Z \sim N(0,1)$

You were introduced in Chapter 8 to a transformation equation for the standard normal distribution. This transformation used the equation:

$$\mathbf{z = (x - \mu)/\sigma}$$

From the theory of the **sampling distribution of the mean**, the estimate of x and σ are given by x bar and $\boldsymbol{\sigma/\sqrt{n}}$ respectively. Moreover, from the standard normal distribution tables, 95% of the area under the standard normal curve is located between Z = -1.96 and Z = 1.96. Therefore:

$$P(-1.96 < Z < 1.96) = 0.95\ (95\%), \text{ where } \mathbf{Z = (\bar{x} - \mu)/(\sigma/\sqrt{n})}$$

$$-1.96 < (\bar{x} - \mu)/(\sigma/\sqrt{n}) < 1.96$$

Re-arranging the probability equation stated above, gives you a range of values known as the confidence interval which will be introduced shortly. Returning to the welfare officer's calculation of the average overdraft amongst the university's undergraduates, she can select a representative sample of students. From this sample, she can calculate:

Sample mean $\bar{x}$ standard deviation s standard error $s/\sqrt{n}$

The statistics listed above are known as **point estimates**.

The Confidence Interval

Rather than use a point estimate of a population parameter, it is more reliable to provide a **range of values** instead within which you can define the probability that the value of the corresponding population parameter is actually located. This range of values is known as a 'Confidence Interval'. By providing a range of values, you are not suggesting that the population parameter (specifically the mean in this chapter) takes any value within the range, but is a **fixed**, **single** value which has a corresponding, pre-defined probability of falling within the calculated range. In the example considered, this will overcome any problem of estimating the population average overdraft from a relatively small sample of students.

In calculating a range of values, you need to define the percentage of confidence which is sufficient for the decision or process under consideration. It should therefore be obvious that the higher the percentage you specify, then the wider the range of values in the interval.

Generally, business decision makers will apply the **95% level of confidence** for most applications. This range considers the 'middle' 95% of values in the distribution. However, certain decision makers may require a greater level of confidence, and in turn, will use the 99% confidence interval which considers the 'middle' 99% of values.

According to the central limit theorem, you can assume that the mean of any large data set (where $n \geq 30$), whatever the properties of its population, displays normal properties. Figure 9.5 displays a confidence interval by means of a diagram. Inspection of this diagram shows that the interval is symmetrical around the 'middle' value of the data set, i.e. its mean value.

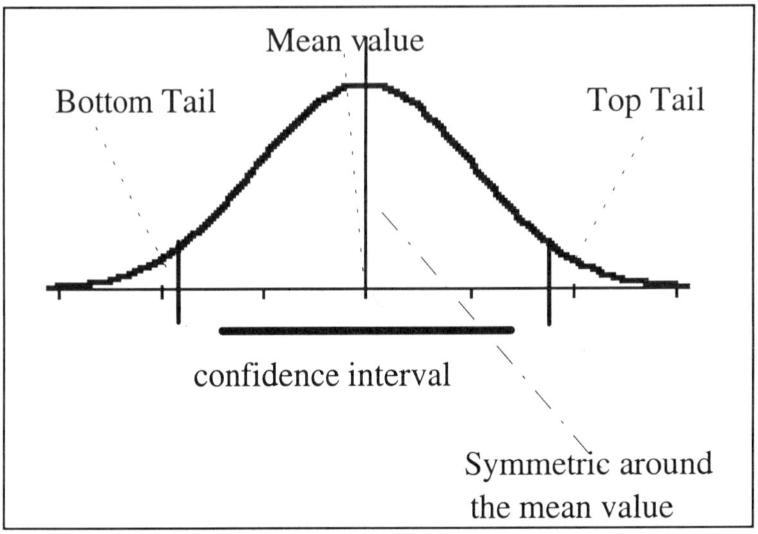

Figure 9.5 - Pictorial representation of a Confidence Interval

The confidence interval around the mean is defined by two values; an upper value which takes the form ***sample mean + increment***, and a lower value of the form ***sample mean - increment***. It will become apparent that the size of this increment will take into account the spread or variability of the data (as indicated by its standard deviation) and the size of the sample considered.

Confidence Intervals for large samples (30 or more observations)

The central limit theorem tells you that for data sets with 30 or more observations, you can assume it shows behaviour similar to the normal distribution. Using the relevant statistical theory, you can assume 68.3% of the area under the curve is within ± one standard error of the mean, whilst 95.4% of the area under the curve is located within ± 2 standard errors of the population mean. Business decision makers typically use the 95% Confidence Interval and as can be seen from the diagram in Figure 9.6, this can be calculated by considering the area under the curve which is within ± 1.96 standard errors of the mean. The value 1.96 is known as the *interval coefficient*. Inspection of the normal distribution tables show you that 2½% of the curve is situated to the right of $z = 1.96$ and the same amount (by symmetry) is situated to the left of $z = -1.96$, and as a consequence, the 'middle' 95% of the distribution is located between $z = -1.96$ and $z = +1.96$. Moreover, if a 99% confidence interval is required, the relevant interval coefficient would be 2.58, since 99% of the area under the standard normal curve is located between $z = -2.58$ and $z = 2.58$.

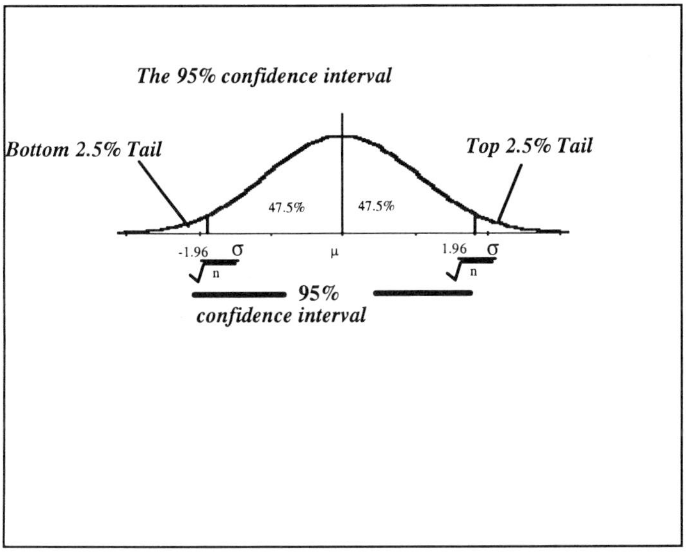

Figure 9.6 - Normal distribution curve and interval coefficients

Since $\bar{\mathbf{x}}$ (x bar) is used as the best sample estimate of the population mean μ and $s/\sqrt{\mathbf{n}}$ is used as the best sample estimate of $\boldsymbol{\sigma}/\sqrt{\mathbf{n}}$, the 95% Confidence Interval for the population mean is given by the equation:

$$95\% \text{ Confidence Interval} = \bar{x} \pm \frac{1.96\, s}{\sqrt{n}}$$

Therefore, you can be 95% confident that the population mean has a **fixed**, **single** value which is located within the range given by the two extreme points in the interval stated above.

Example

A student's union welfare officer wishes to estimate the average overdraft amongst the university students. A sample of 160 students was selected randomly and the average overdraft was found to be £1450 with a standard deviation of £230. The welfare officer is interested in determining the 95% confidence interval for all overdrafts (i.e. the population mean). The sample statistics provided are:

$\bar{x} = 1450 \qquad s = 230 \qquad n = 160$

Since you are dealing with a large sample (n = 160), you can use the equation displayed above to determine the 95% confidence interval.

$$95\% \text{ Confidence Interval} = 1450 - \frac{1.96 \text{x} 230}{\sqrt{160}} \quad - \quad 1450 + \frac{1.96 \text{x} 230}{\sqrt{160}}$$

$$95\% \text{ Confidence Interval} = £1414.36 - £1485.64$$

In conclusion, the welfare officer can be 95% confident that the population average overdraft amongst the university's students is a **single**, **fixed** value between £1414.36 and £1485.64. It is important to note that the population mean is a single point value which has a pre-defined probability (i.e. 95% in this case) of falling within a given range. The population mean does not take on the whole range of values, it is a unique value somewhere within the range identified.

Suppose instead, the welfare officer wanted to estimate the population mean to within ± £10. This can be achieved by reducing the size of the standard error ($s/\sqrt{n}$). Since the standard deviation measures the spread of the sample data and must be assumed constant, the standard error can be reduced by increasing the size of the sample n. In this example you must find **n** so that:

$$1.96\ s/\sqrt{n} = 10, \text{ i.e. } \sqrt{n} = 1.96\ s/10$$

$$= 1.96 \text{ x } 230\ /10$$

$$= 45.08$$

Squaring gives: **n = 2032.2**

Thus, to determine a 95% confidence interval which has values covering a range between ± £10 from the sample mean, the size of the sample must consist of 2033 students.

Confidence intervals for small samples (less than 30 observations)

If you consider large samples of data, you can use the central limit theorem to assume that the data shows the properties of the normal distribution. However, there will be occasions where you may have to consider much smaller data sets. If quality control measures are introduced into a factory producing vacuum cleaners, the cost of sampling and testing cleaners for the length of working life may be large and as such you may only be able to consider a small number of cleaners.

Specifically, the number considered may well be less than 30, and as a consequence, the normal distribution cannot be applied.

However, there is another distribution known as **Students' t-distribution** which can be used to provide interval coefficients which account for the size of the sample, as long as it is reasonable for you to assume that the **population** from which the sample is selected is **normally distributed**. Tables corresponding to the Students' t-distribution can be found in Appendix II of this book. The equation for the confidence interval for the small sample is the same as described for a large data set except the interval coefficient of 1.96 will now be replaced by a suitable value which considers the size of the sample.

The size of the interval coefficient is determined by the number of degrees of freedom, which is equal to **n - 1**, where n is the size of the sample. Therefore, if your sample size is 15, the number of degrees of freedom will be 14. To determine the coefficient using this sample for a 95% confidence interval, you need to inspect the column labelled *0.025* (since you ignore the top and bottom 2½% of population values in this particular interval) and the row labelled 14, i.e. the number of degrees of freedom. The interval coefficient can be found at the intersection of the selected column and row, as shown in Figure 9.7. For a 95% Confidence Interval based on a sample size of 15 observations, the interval coefficient is **2.15**. This value indicates that 95% of the area under the t-distribution with 14 degrees of freedom is located between t = -2.15 and t = 2.15. Equally, if a 99% Confidence Interval was required, it would be necessary to inspect the column labelled *0.005* (since you consider the 'middle' 99% of values in this interval).

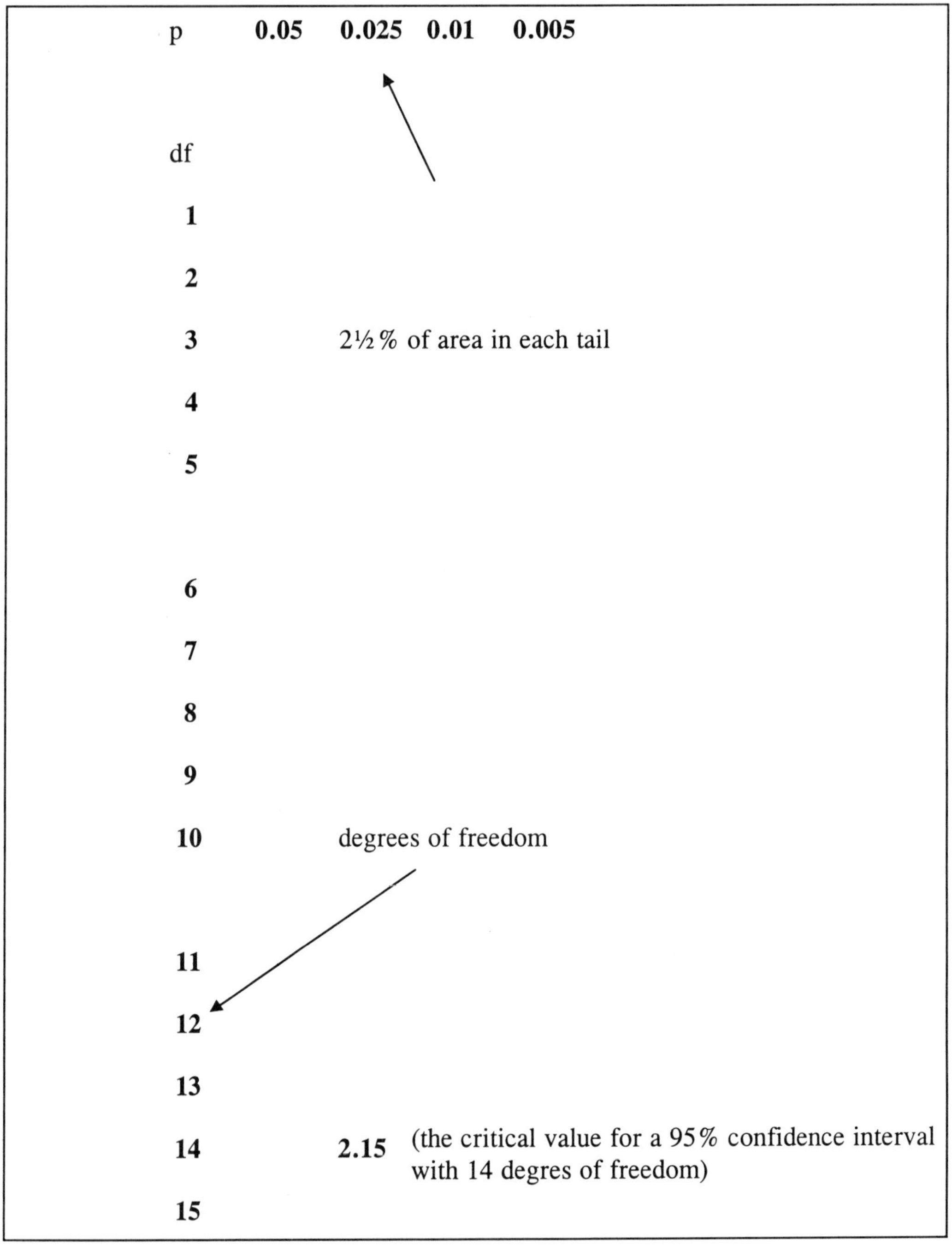

Figure 9.7 - Determining an interval coefficient from the t-distribution

Further inspection of the t-tables show that the smaller the sample size, the bigger the interval coefficient and as a consequence, the wider the confidence interval. This means that to ensure a pre-defined level of confidence that the population mean is located within a given range of values, you must for a smaller sample of data provide a bigger range of values around the sample mean.

Example

Twelve machinists at a factory were randomly selected and the time they took to produce a set of chair covers was measured as part of an efficiency study. The mean time was found to be 30 minutes with a standard deviation of 6 minutes. The factory manager is interested in determining a 95% Confidence Interval for the population average machine time. The sample statistics provided are:

$n = 12$, $\bar{x} = 30$ minutes, $s = 6$ minutes

Since the sample is small, you must use Students' t-distribution, and the number of degrees of freedom is 11 (i.e. 12 - 1). This gives an interval coefficient of 2.20 for the 95% confidence interval.

$$95\% \text{ Confidence Interval is given by } \bar{x} \pm 2.20 \times \frac{s}{\sqrt{n}}$$

i.e. $$30 \pm 2.20 \times 6/\sqrt{12}$$

95% Confidence Interval is **26.2 minutes - 33.8 minutes**

Therefore, you can be 95% confident that the population average time is a single (fixed) value which is in the range 26.2 - 33.8 minutes. By using the t-distribution to provide the interval coefficients, you are assuming that the **population** of times required to make a set of seat covers is **normally distributed**.

Using Excel to Determine a Confidence Interval

So far you have applied the confidence interval formula to a variety of examples involving the calculation of an interval estimate for a population mean. Equally, these calculations can be undertaken both quickly and accurately using Excel's **CONFIDENCE()** command. The structure of this built-in function is:

CONFIDENCE(α,σ,n)

where:

α is the level of significance which determines the level of confidence. The value of α corresponding to the 95% confidence interval is 5%.

σ represents the population standard deviation. If this is unknown, you must reference the sample standard deviation **s**.

n represents the sample size.

Example

Boxes of tea leaving a production line are advertised as having a population mean weight of 454 g. In a quality control exercise, 30 boxes were randomly selected and weighed. The data is shown below in Figure 9.8.

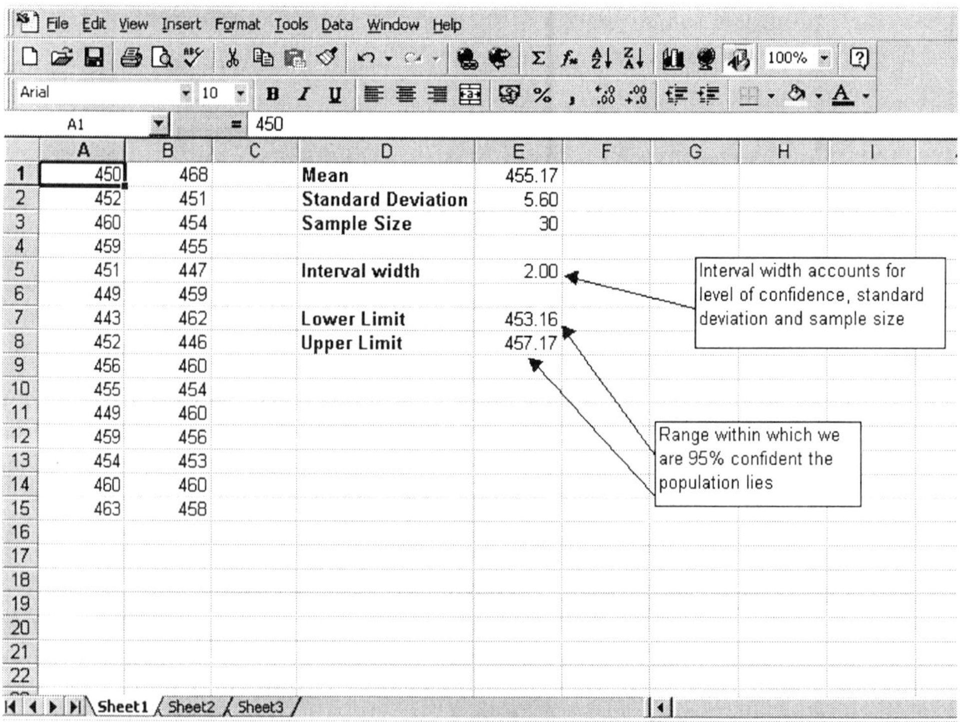

Figure 9.8 - Calculation of a confidence interval using Excel

In the worksheet in Figure 9.8, the mean weight in cell **E1** is calculated using:

=AVERAGE(A1:B15)

the sample standard deviation in cell E2 is evaluated using:

=STDEV(A1:B15).

and the sample size is calculated in cell **E3** using **=COUNT(A1:B15)**

To determine the 95% confidence interval width:

=CONFIDENCE(5%,E2,E3)

has been typed into cell E5. To calculate a 99% interval instead, 1% would be used in the **CONFIDENCE()** function.

Using these statistics, the lower limit of the confidence interval in cell E9 has been calculated using the formula:

=E1-E5

and the upper limit in cell E10 has been determined using the formula

=E1+E5

In conclusion, you can be 95% confident that the population average weight of the boxes of tea has a single, fixed value between 453.16 g and 457.17 g.

Conclusions

In this chapter you were introduced to the idea of statistical inference. Statistical inference is the process whereby a decision maker examines the statistics calculated from a sample of data, from which inferences or statements are made about the population. Obviously, the most accurate statements would be made if the whole of a population is examined, whereby the decision maker would carry out a **census**. Due to constraints of time and cost, a census is rarely undertaken, and as a consequence, a **survey** is carried out instead in which a representative **subset** or **sample** of the population is considered.

Once the sample has been analysed, estimates can be made for certain population parameters. Two types of estimate can be made:

- Point estimates
- Interval estimates

The point estimate is a single value estimate of the corresponding population parameter. For example, the mean from a representative sample of data is a single value which represents the best estimate for the population mean. The accuracy of this value will depend upon the size of the sample relative to the population and how representative that sample is. To counter these problems a **range** or **interval** of values may be used instead of a **single**, **point** value.

The confidence interval is a range of values, symmetrical around the point estimate of the parameter under consideration. The confidence interval is presented alongside a pre-defined percentage level, e.g. the 95% Confidence Interval. Within this particular range of values, you are 95% confident that the population parameter will occur. Obviously the higher the level of confidence, the bigger (or wider) this range of values, so the 99% confidence interval will be bigger than the 95% interval. The width of this range is influenced by the standard deviation and size of the sample data under consideration.

One final factor which has been stressed throughout the chapter is that the confidence interval does not suggest that the respective population parameter (specifically the population mean) can take any value within the calculated range. Instead, the interval indicates only that the population parameter has a **fixed**, **single** value which has a pre-defined probability (i.e. 95% or 99%) of occurring within the calculated range of values.

Learning Outcomes Checklist

After completing this chapter you should have an understanding of the following concepts, calculations and functions:

- The term 'statistical inference'.
- The difference between populations and samples.
- The calculation of a point estimate for a population parameter (specifically the population mean).
- The calculation of an interval estimate for a population parameter (specifically the population mean).

- Calculate a confidence interval for the population mean by considering a large sample of data.
- Calculate a confidence interval for the population mean by considering a small sample of data.
- An awareness of Excel's **CONFIDENCE()** function.

Ensure that you understand these concepts before progressing to Chapter 10.

Chapter Case Question

- Open the files **CHAP01.XLS** and **CHAP02.XLS**
- Copy the following table from **CHAP02.XLS** into **CHAP01.XLS** and close **CHAP02.XLS**

	Restaurant	**Family**	**Total**
Country			
Town			
Total			

- Sort the data by property type and then by location (i.e. Sort By and Then By fields).
- Create the following table with regard to monthly turnover:

Restaurant	**Restaurant**	**Family**	**Family**
Country	**Town**	**Country**	**Town**
Mean			
Standard Deviation			

- Using Excel's CONFIDENCE() command, calculate the following confidence intervals:

A 95% confidence interval for the average monthly turnover for a country restaurant.

A 99% confidence interval for the average monthly turnover for a town restaurant.

A 99% confidence interval for the average monthly turnover for a town family pub.

A 95% confidence interval for the average monthly turnover for a country family pub.

A 95% confidence interval for the average length of service for the pub landlords.

- Save the amended file as **CHAP09.XLS**

Supplementary Questions

1. What is the difference between a sample and a population?

2. Explain the term 'statistical inference'.

3. Describe the main properties of the sampling distribution of the mean.

4. Describe the properties of the central limit theorem.

5. Why do decision makers analyse samples of data in order to make inferences about the population from which the sample is taken?

6. What is the difference between a point 'estimate' and an 'interval' estimate? Give examples of both estimates.

7. What is mean by the term 'confidence interval'?

8. State the formula for the confidence interval for the population mean.

9. Why is the Students' t-distribution used to determine the interval coefficient when you deal with small samples?

10. What assumptions are made about the population of interest when a t-distribution is used to find the interval coefficients for a small sample of data?

11. As part of a sensible drinking campaign, the Human Resources Manager at a construction company collected data from a representative sample of trades staff. Fifty employees responded in the survey and the mean number of alcohol consumed in the previous week was found to be 13.8 with a standard deviation of 2.8 units. Determine a 95% confidence interval for the population mean.

12. From a sample of 60 commuters, a bus company recorded the number of times each had been subject to a delay in the previous working week.

0	6	4	1	1	2	1	3	2	0
0	7	7	1	0	3	1	0	0	1
1	2	0	4	4	0	0	1	3	6
4	1	5	3	1	1	2	0	1	0
2	0	2	2	2	8	4	0	7	2
1	0	1	1	0	1	3	8	2	6

(a) Calculate the sample mean and standard deviation for the number of delays.

(b) Calculate the 95% confidence interval for the population mean number of delays.

(c) Calculate the 99% confidence interval for the population mean number of delays.

(d) Explain these results.

(e) Check your results using the relevant facilities provided by Excel.

13. The placements office at a University Business School was asked to comment on the weekly salary paid to placement students in the previous year. A sample of 40 students were selected at random and the following results and the salaries were:

300	180	175	200	240	198	225	230	165	190
250	191	200	195	160	220	230	190	185	210
227	300	215	210	155	210	250	180	215	185
325	200	200	180	200	175	200	200	165	215

(a) Calculate the sample mean and standard deviation by hand.

(b) Calculate the 95% confidence interval for the population average number of incidents by hand.

(c) Calculate the 99% confidence interval for the population average number of incidents by hand.

(d) Explain the meaning of the two intervals calculated.

(e) Check your results using the relevant facilities provided by Excel.

14. The head of personnel at a city council is concerned at the level of abuse received by staff in the housing claims department. A sample of 20 staff were selected at random and the number of incidents experienced by each member of staff over the 1st quarter of 1994 were:

5	2	0	1	2	1	4	1	2	3
2	1	4	0	4	10	2	1	1	12

(a) Calculate the sample mean and standard deviation by hand.

(b) Calculate the 95% confidence interval for the population average number of incidents by hand.

(c) Calculate the 99% confidence interval for the population average number of incidents by hand.

(d) Explain the meaning of the two intervals calculated.

(e) Check your results using the relevant facilities provided by Excel.

Chapter 10

Hypothesis Testing

Learning Outcomes

In this chapter you will see the application of specific techniques which can be used to test a belief concerning various populations of interest. You will gain an insight into how these beliefs can be tested by analysing samples of data, and an indication will be given regarding the level of confidence you can have in the conclusions made about the population(s) of interest. Hypotheses will be defined, made and tested for assumed values of population means, and where appropriate, reference will made to various facilities offered by Excel.

After completing this chapter you will be able to:

- Understand the term 'hypothesis'.
- Recognise applications of hypothesis testing in business.
- Understand the sequence of steps required to undertake a hypothesis test.
- Distinguish between a null and alternative hypothesis.
- Distinguish between a one-sided and two-sided alternative hypothesis.
- Use the normal distribution to determine the critical values for a test statistic used on a large data sample.
- Use the Students' t-distribution to determine the critical values for a test statistic used on a small data sample.
- Undertake a hypothesis test for a population mean.
- Undertake tests on one or two populations.
- Recognise the possible outcomes from a hypothesis test.

- Utilise the relevant facilities offered by Excel.

Introduction

As demonstrated in Chapter 9, statistical inference is the process which involves making statements about one or more population parameters (such as the mean), and these statements are subsequently tested by analysing representative samples of data from the population(s). From the samples of data, relevant statistics are calculated, and these are used in within specific statistical tests to determine if the statements made can be accepted. Examples of such statements or beliefs which can be tested are:

- The time between two computer network failures is on average six weeks.
- The average time taken to process a claim in a council's housing department is 20 days.
- There is a significant difference in the salary increases between workers in the public and private sectors in 1997.

In this chapter you will be looking at tests which involve evaluating either claims made about a single population or those made when comparing two populations and the tests will involve population means.

To carry out a test, you require two hypotheses, the null hypothesis denoted by H_0 and an alternative labelled as H_1. Suppose for example you are testing the reliability of an automatic filling machine which fills jars of coffee. You may believe that the jars are correctly filled so that they (the population) have a mean weight of 120g. This belief will represent your **null** hypothesis and will be written as:

$$H_0: \mu = 120$$

To test this belief, you will in practice assume that the filling machine is operating correctly unless there is sufficiently strong evidence to the contrary. You will test against onc of three alternative hypotheses:

$$H_1: \mu > 120$$
$$H_1: \mu < 120$$
$$H_1: \mu \neq 120$$

The first alternative suggests the mean weight of the jars is significantly greater than 120g (i.e. the machine is over-filling), the second alternative suggests the mean weight of the jars is significantly smaller than 120g (i.e. it is under-filling), whilst the last alternative suggests the population mean weight is significantly different to 120g. The first two are known as one-sided alternatives, whilst the last is a two-sided alternative. The choice of alternative will reflect the problems you are encountering with the filling machine.

As sample data is going to be used to test any hypothesis, then you can never have 100% confidence that a correct conclusion has been made regarding your belief about the population under consideration. Confidence of 100% can only be achieved by undertaking a census, i.e. considering all of the population.

Therefore, once you have undertaken your test, you may reject the null hypothesis H_0. If there are problems with your machine, then this will have been the correct decision. However, there will be occasions when you reject H_0 even though it was true.

Testing a Hypothesis - Possible Outcomes

There are four potential outcomes when undertaking a hypothesis test:

- Accept a true hypothesis (regarding the supposed value of a population parameter, specifically the mean in this chapter), in other words reach a correct conclusion.

- Reject a false hypothesis, again reaching a correct conclusion.

- Reject a true hypothesis, this time reaching an incorrect conclusion. For this type of outcome, you have encountered a TYPE I error. The probability of a TYPE I error occurring is given by α, which is also known as the level of significance for the test to be undertaken.

- The value of α will be defined shortly. In this chapter you will concentrate on this type of error and the associated level of significance.

- Accept a false hypothesis, again you will have reached an **incorrect** conclusion. If this type of decision is made, you have encountered a TYPE II error.

The probability of rejecting a correct null hypothesis results in a TYPE I error, the probability of which will be decided upon before undertaking the test. This value is called the significance level and represents the potential error in any conclusions made. The smaller the level of significance, the smaller the potential error. The chosen value is often $\alpha = \mathbf{0.05}$, and so the hypothesis test is undertaken at the 5% level of significance. Alternatively, you can say that you can be 95% confident that the decision made is the correct one.

Undertaking a Hypothesis Test for a Population Mean

The process of undertaking a hypothesis test is listed below:

- Define suitable null and alternative hypotheses regarding the hypothesised value of the population mean.

  The null hypothesis is that the population mean is equal to a particular value. The choice of H_1 will depend upon the population and decision under consideration and will be one of the three cases considered in the earlier example.

- Collect a representative sample of data and calculate the sample mean, standard deviation and sample size.

- Determine the appropriate formula to calculate the test statistic. Before listing the choices of test statistic, you will see how the general test statistic for one sample has been derived.

  Using the transformation equation for the normal distribution introduced in Chapter 8, you can state that:

  $$P(-1.96 < Z < 1.96), \text{ where } \mathbf{Z} = (\bar{\mathbf{x}} - \mu)/(\sigma/\sqrt{\mathbf{n}})$$

  Using the value of Z as a test statistic, you can be 95% confident that the hypothesised value of the population mean μ is correct based on the analysis of the representative sample if it falls within the limits $\pm$ 1.96. Conversely, you can assume that the extreme 5% of the distribution (i.e. 2½% in each of the top and bottom tails) are located outside this range. This test equation can be modified slightly based on the availability of sample statistics.

  If the sample size is at least 30 ($n \geq 30$), you can assume from the central limit theorem that the data set displays normal properties, hence the test statistic can be measured against critical values from the standard normal distribution, and you don't have to assume anything about the properties of the population from which the data is collected. The test statistic is given by:

$$z = \frac{\bar{x} - \mu}{s/\sqrt{n}}$$

If the sample is small (i.e. n < 30), you must use the test statistic:

$$t = \frac{\bar{x} - \mu}{s/\sqrt{n}}$$

You will measure this test statistic against critical values from the Students' t-distribution with *n - 1* degrees of freedom. By applying the t-distribution in this test, you are assuming that while the sample is small, the **population** from which it is collected is **normally distributed**.

- The value of the test statistic is found using either of the formulae listed above and measured against the relevant critical value. This critical value will consider whether the alternative hypothesis H_1 is one-sided or two-sided and the level of significance you have chosen. The critical values are presented as positive values in the statistical tables.

- Make the comparison below to determine the likelihood of the null hypothesis H_0 being correct.

  You can 'forget' the sign in front of the test statistic value, since the negative or positive sign only indicates whether you are dealing with the top or bottom of the distribution.

  If **test statistic** > **critical value** then **reject** null hypothesis H_0

  If **test statistic** < **critical value** then **accept** null hypothesis H_0

- Use the results of the hypothesis test to make decisions about the population of interest.

It is worth noting from the equation of the test statistic that if the sample and hypothesised population means are of similar value, relative to the distribution of the sample (which is measured by the standard error), then the value of the test statistic will be close to zero. Assuming that the sample of data is representative, this would suggest that H_0 is true, and it coincides with the test statistic's value lying in the "body" (or centre) rather than the extreme tails of the (test) distribution. In contrast, if the sample provides a mean value which is relatively different to that of the hypothesised population mean, then it is more likely that the null hypothesis is false which coincides with the test statistic lying in either the extreme lower or upper tail of the test distribution. In other words, H_0 is only rejected if reasonable doubt is demonstrated with regard to its validity.

Hypothesis tests for other population parameters are carried out using a similar approach to that described above.

Example (a large sample test):

A large public utility has introduced a new scheme for customer care. Under the pilot scheme the public affairs director claims there will be on average 120 complaints registered at each large city office every year. Results from the first year based on a sample of 35 offices, show an average of 115 complaints with a standard deviation of 15. The publicity director wishes to determine whether the number of complaints have changed significantly since the pilot study.

H_0: Average no. of complaints recorded per month is 120
i.e. $\mu = 120$

H_1: **$\mu \neq 120$**

In this example the test is **two-sided** because the publicity director is only interested in determining if the number of complaints have significantly changed. You are given the following statistics:

$\bar{x} = 115$, $s = 15$, $n = 35$

The sample size is greater than 30, so you should use the test statistic:

$$z = \frac{\bar{x} - \mu}{s/\sqrt{n}}$$

Calculating z gives:

$$z = \frac{115-120}{15/\sqrt{35}}$$

$$z = -1.9720$$

Inspection of the normal distribution tables in Appendix I show that 2½% of the area under the curve is located to the left of value Z = -1.96. You can now measure the value of the test statistic with this critical value.

The critical region for the two-sided test is shown under the normal and right distribution curve in Figure 10.1. You are considering the critical region at both the left sides because the alternative hypothesis is $\mu \neq 120$.

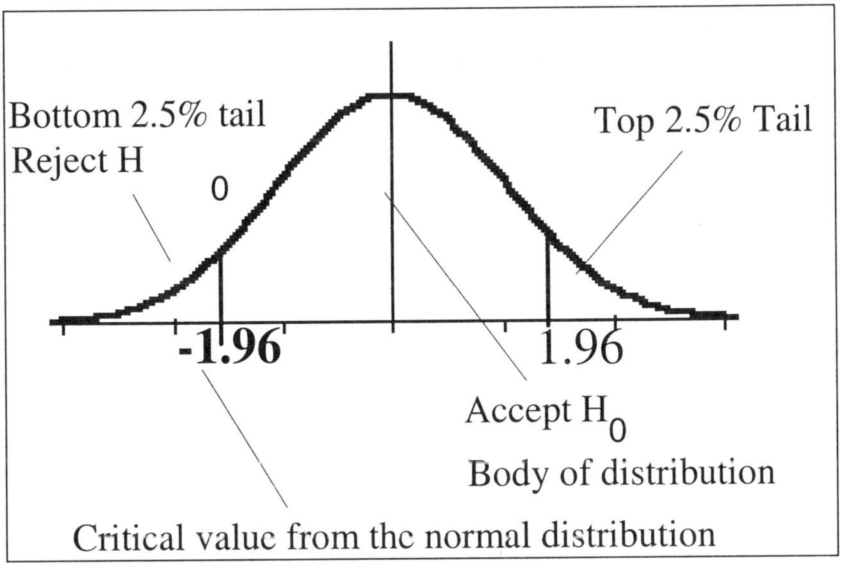

Figure 10.1 - Critical values from the normal distribution

Inspection of the absolute value of the test statistic z (i.e. removing the sign), you see that the test value is greater than the critical value. Therefore, you must reject H_0.

In conclusion, you can state that based on this sample of data, at the 5% significance level there is evidence to suggest that the average number of claims per month is significantly different to 120. Given the test is based on a 5% significance level, there is only a 5% probability of rejecting a correct statement about the population mean number of complaints.

Example (using the ZTEST() function offered by Excel):

Excel offers a built-in command **ZTEST()** which can be used to determine the level of significance in either a one-tailed or a two-tailed test. This command generates a P-value for the hypothesised population mean with respect to a sample of data rather than generating the value for the z statistic. The P-value is a probability value from the normal distribution. It represents the level of significance you must have chosen in order to reject H_0. Specifically, you will reject H_0 at the 5% level of significance if the P-value is less than 0.05. The structure of the function is:

ZTEST(data,μ,σ)

where:

> **data** represents the sample of data (referenced as block)which is used to test the hypothesis.
>
> **μ** and **σ** have already been defined. The latter is *optional.* If it this value is unknown and not referenced, Excel will calculate the sample standard deviation instead from the referenced sample data.

Boxes of tea leaving a production line are advertised as having a population mean weight of 454 g. The head of production control at the factory is aware of potential problems with the filling machine on the production line and wishes to test whether the machines are functioning properly. The null and alternative hypothesis are shown below:

$$H_0: \mu = 454 \text{ g}$$
$$H_1: \mu \neq 454 \text{ g}$$

In this example, a two-side alternative is used because the production control manager wishes to test that the filling machines are not producing boxes of tea which are too heavy or too light. Figure 10.2 displays the Excel worksheet showing the sample data and the hypothesis test result:

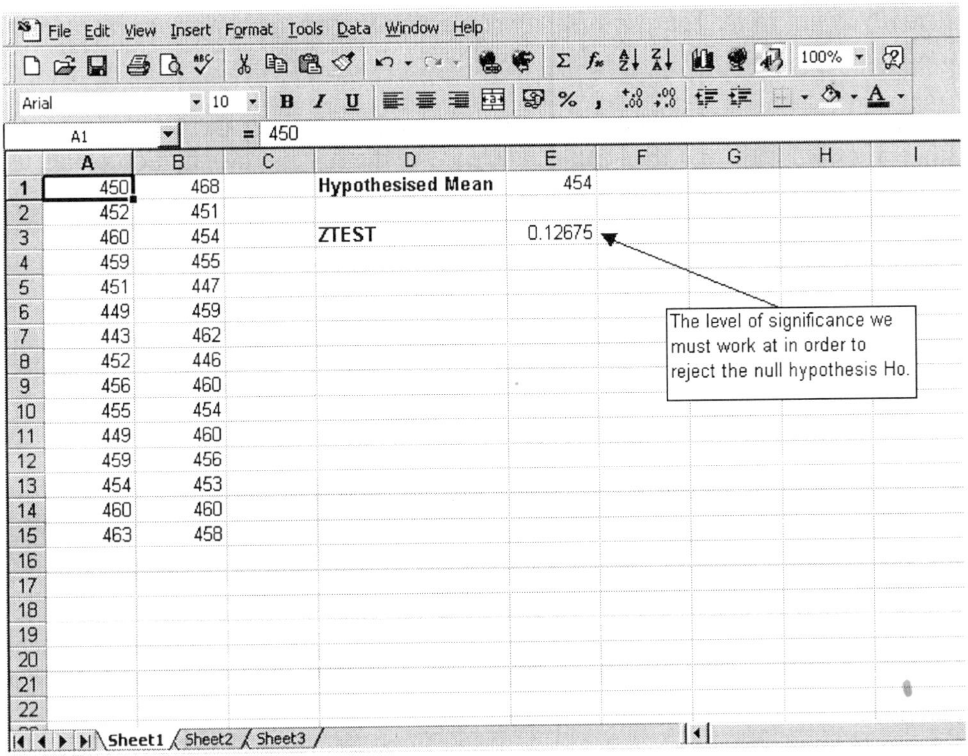

Figure 10.2 - ZTEST calculation using Excel

The calculation of the z test statistic has been undertaken using the formula:

=ZTEST(A1:B15,E1)

where the sample of data is stored in the block of cells **A1:B15** and the hypothesised population mean (454 g) is stored in cell **E1**. To obtain a critical result for a two-sided test at the pre-defined 5% significance level, the value returned by the **ZTEST()** command would have to be less than *0.05*. In this example, the value returned is 0.12675, which suggests that the null hypothesis H_0 cannot be rejected. In conclusion, at the 5% level of significance, there is no evidence to suggest that the filling machines are not functioning properly.

You must be aware that the statement listed above is quite different to saying that the population mean weight of boxes of tea leaving this production line is exactly 454g. In other words, the hypothesis test undertaken only permits us to say that the population mean weight is not significantly different to this hypothesised value, but not actually equal to it. You can also conclude that there is insufficient evidence to conclude that the mean filling weight is not 454g

It should be apparent that the use of this Excel function removes the need for you to calculate a test statistic and then make reference to the normal distribution tables to determine its critical values.

Example (a small sample test):

At the same factory, the production team wishes to check the automated packing equipment which is used to produce large packets of cocoa powder. The cocoa leaves the factory to be sold to hotels and restaurants in 1000g packets. A sample of 16 packets were weighed and the following results were recorded:

1008	998	1005	1013	1005	1017	1025	999
999	1010	998	1022	997	996	1001	1027

Again, the head of production control is interested in determining whether the filling machines are working correctly, i.e. on average are they over-filling each packet with cocoa weighing 1000g? Given the potential problem of over-filling, you must choose a one-sided alternative hypothesis.

The hypotheses are:

H_0: μ **= 1000g**
H_1: μ **> 1000g**

Analysis of the sample tells us that the mean sample weight is 1007.5g, the standard deviation is 10.48g and the sample size is 16.

Given that the sample size is small (i.e. less than 30 observations), the test statistic is given by:

$$t = \frac{\bar{x} - \mu}{s/\sqrt{n}}$$

Moreover, by undertaking a small sample t-test, you have assumed that the **population** of weights of cocoa boxes are **normally distributed**.

$$t = \frac{1007.5 - 1000}{10.48/\sqrt{16}}$$

$$\mathbf{t = 2.8626}$$

The critical region under the t-distribution curve and corresponding critical values are displayed in Figure 10.3. In the last chapter you saw how coefficients for a confidence interval based on a small sample of data were identified once you knew the pre-defined level of significance and the degrees of freedom. The approach for determining critical values is similar, you only have to consider whether the test is 1-sided or 2-sided. If you are working at the 5% level, you look down the column headed *0.05* for the critical values for a 1-sided test and down the column headed *0.025* for a two-sided test. These tables are shown in Appendix II.

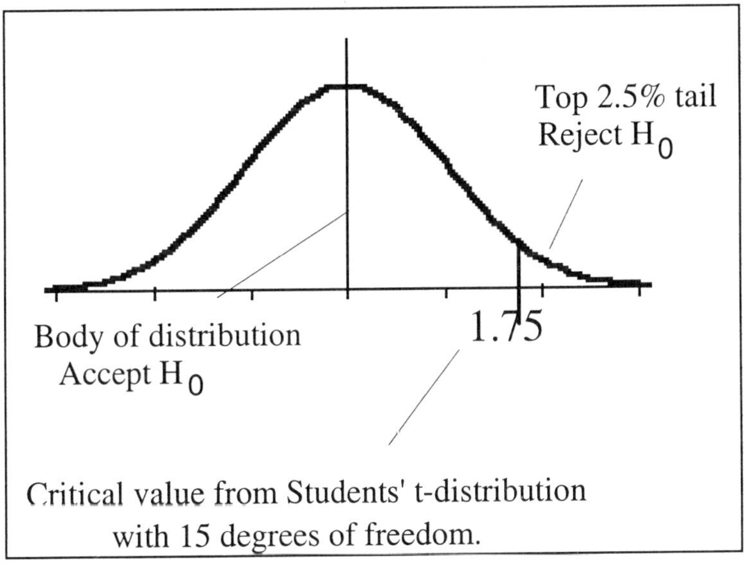

Figure 10.3 - Critical values from the Students' t-distribution

Inspection of the test statistic shows that its value is greater than the **critical value** 1.75. Therefore, at the 5% significance level you should reject the null hypothesis H_0. In other words, there is evidence at the 5% level to suggest that the population weight of the boxes of cocoa leaving the factory are significantly heavier than 1000g.

Testing the Difference Between Two Means

You have now considered tests concerned with individual population means. You may also be interested in determining if significant differences exist between the means of two populations. Examples of such tests include:

- A company may claim there is a significant difference in average output between two of their factories.

- An IT trainer may suggest that the average number of items processed by an administrative team is significantly greater once the staff have undertaken an in-house training course in word-processing.

In order to test these types of statement you need to sample from both populations and undertake a hypothesis test similar to those used to test the significance of a claim made about a single population.

The process of undertaking a significance test on two population means (labelled μ_1 and μ_2) is shown below:

- Define the null and alternative hypotheses. In general these are:

Null Hypothesis: $\mu_1 = \mu_2$ (i.e. the population means are the same)

with the alternative hypothesis taking the form of one of the following:

Alternative Hypothesis: $\mu_1 \neq \mu_2$

$\mu_1 > \mu_2$

$\mu_1 < \mu_2$

If you wish to test the belief that the difference between two means is a specific value, say d, then for a two-sided test the null and alternative hypothesis would be:

$$H_0: \mu_1 - \mu_2 = d$$
$$H_1: \mu_1 - \mu_2 \neq d$$

- Collect a representative sample of data from each population. From these samples determine the means, standard deviations and sample sizes.

- Determine the formula required to calculate the test statistic. Like the tests on single samples, the statistic calculated depends upon the sample data available and their populations. In this chapter you shall consider three possible tests, which will be introduced shortly.

- Calculate the value of the test statistic and measure it against the relevant critical value.

- Make the comparison below to determine the likelihood of the null hypothesis H_0 being correct. Again, you can remove the sign in front of the test statistic value for the reasons suggested earlier.

  If **test statistic** > **critical value** then **reject** null hypothesis H_0.

  If **test statistic** < **critical value** then **accept** null hypothesis H_0

- Use the results of the hypothesis test to make decisions about the two populations.

Again, it is worth noting from the equation of the test statistics that if the sample and hypothesised population means are of similar value relative to the distribution of the samples (which are measured by the respective standard errors), then the value of the test statistic will be close to zero. Assuming that the sample of data is representative, this would suggest that H_0 is true, and it coincides with the statistic's value lying in the "body" rather than the extreme tails of the (test) distribution. In contrast, if the samples provide mean values which are relatively different to that of the hypothesised population difference, then it is likely that the hypothesis is false which coincides with the test statistic lying in either the extreme lower or upper tail of the (test) distribution. Where the two samples are small, you can only apply the relevant tests if you are confident that the populations are both normally distributed.

The Test Statistics for a Two Sample Test

In this chapter you will be introduced to three tests. The selection of the test statistic will depend upon the size of the samples considered and the nature of the populations under consideration.

If the data is selected from two independent populations and the respective sample sizes n_1 and n_2 are both at least 30 (i.e. large samples), then you can use the respective standard deviations s_1 and s_2 in the test statistic:

$$z = \frac{\bar{x}_1 - \bar{x}_2}{\sqrt{\dfrac{s_1^2}{n_1} + \dfrac{s_2^2}{n_2}}}$$

The value of this test statistic will be measured against critical values from the standard normal distribution. If the null hypothesis is H_0: $\mu_1 - \mu_2 = d$, then you can modify the numerator of the statistic.

If the data is selected from two independent populations and either of the respective sample sizes n_1 and n_2 are less than 30 (i.e. one or both samples is small), then you can use test statistic:

$$t = \frac{\bar{x}_1 - \bar{x}_2}{\sqrt{\dfrac{s_p^2}{n_1} + \dfrac{s_p^2}{n_2}}}$$

$$\text{where } s_p^2 = \frac{(n_1 - 1)s_1^2 + (n_2 - 1)s_2^2}{(n_1 + n_2 - 2)}$$

The value of this test statistic will be measured against critical values from the Students' t-distribution with $n_1 + n_2 - 2$ degrees of freedom. The statistic s_p is called the pooled standard deviation and s_p^2 is the pooled variance. Using the pooled standard deviation in this way counters the problem of dealing with a small data set and the pooled standard error is a reasonable approximation to the standard error of the mean differences if the individual standard deviations have similar values. Again, by using a small sample t-test, you are assuming that the two populations under consideration are both normally distributed.

Finally, if the two samples represent 'pairs' of data values collected from the same population, for example, where a group of individuals who are delegates on a week's training programme who have been asked to award marks for their tuition on two courses, then you can use the test statistic:

$$t = \frac{\bar{d} - \mu_0}{s_d/\sqrt{n}}$$

where d represent the differences in the pairs of values ($\bar{d}$ and s_d being their mean and standard deviation) and μ_0 is the hypothesised mean difference in their opinion of the two training units.

Example - (Considering two large samples):

A leading manufacturer of children's clothes wishes to determine if there is a significant difference in monthly unit sales of its 'Baby Romper' range across the UK last winter. A random selection of 30 retail outlets were selected in Greater Manchester as well as 35 from the West Midlands the following statistics about the number of unit sales were collected:

Manchester: $\bar{x}_1 = 2813 \quad s_1 = 177 \quad n_1 = 30$

West Midlands: $\bar{x}_2 = 2748 \quad s_2 = 226 \quad n_2 = 35$

You can test the claim at the 5% level of significance that there is no difference in the average unit sales between the two regions.

The hypotheses are:

H_0: $\mu_1 = \mu_2$

Number of unit sales of the baby garment per outlet in Greater Manchester **is not significantly different** to as the number of unit sales of the garment in the West Midlands.

H_1: $\mu_1 \neq \mu_2$

Number of unit sales of the baby garment in Greater Manchester **is not the same** as the number of unit sales of the garment in the West Midlands.

From the sample statistics provided, you can see that the two samples contain more than 30 observations and the alternative hypothesis H_1 suggests that the test is two sided.

The test statistic is:

$$z = \frac{\bar{x}_1 - \bar{x}_2}{\sqrt{\frac{s_1^2}{n_1} + \frac{s_2^2}{n_2}}}$$

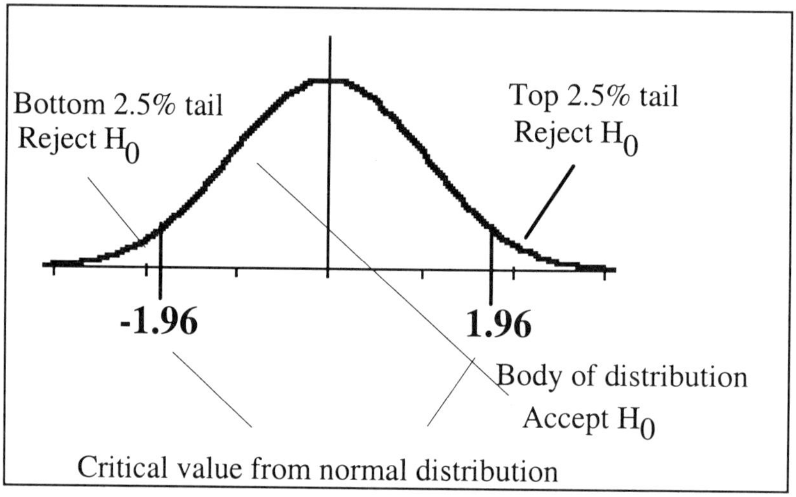

Figure 10.4 - Critical values from the normal distribution

Substituting the values into the test statistic gives:

$$z = \frac{2813 - 2748}{\sqrt{\left(\frac{[177^2]}{30} + \frac{[226^2]}{35}\right)}}$$

$$z = \frac{65}{\sqrt{(1044.3+1459.3)}} = \frac{65}{50.04}$$

$$z = 1.30 \text{ (2dp)}$$

Figure 10.4 illustrates the critical values for this two-tailed test.

Measuring the value of the test statistic with the critical value from the normal distribution, you should see that the value of the test statistic is less than the critical value. Therefore, you cannot reject the null hypothesis H_0.

In conclusion, at the 5% significance level, there is **no evidence** to assume that number of unit sales of the baby garment in Greater Manchester **is significantly different to** the number of unit sales of the garment in the West Midlands.

Example - (Considering two small samples):

The work study department for a Midlands Building Society has undertaken a project to measure the times taken by staff to process customer details via interview for mortgages. Two branches were considered and the following statistics were collected:

Branch 1: $\bar{x} = 40$ minutes, $s = 20$, $n = 9$

Branch 2: $\bar{x} = 60$ minutes, $s = 18$, $n = 7$

The staff at Branch 1 are using new documentation, whilst the staff at Branch 2 are using existing forms and procedures. The work study manager wishes to determine whether the new procedures have shortened the interview time. In view of this, your hypotheses are:

H_0: $\mu_1 = \mu_2$
(i.e. the interview times are the same using both procedures)

H_1: $\mu_1 < \mu_2$
(i.e. the interview times using the new procedures at branch 1 are significantly shorter)

Given both samples are independent, small and the standard deviations are similar, you can use the t test with a pooled standard deviation.

In this example there are 9 + 7 - 2, i.e. 14 degrees of freedom, and the critical value for the 1-tailed alternative is shown on the diagram in Figure 10.5.

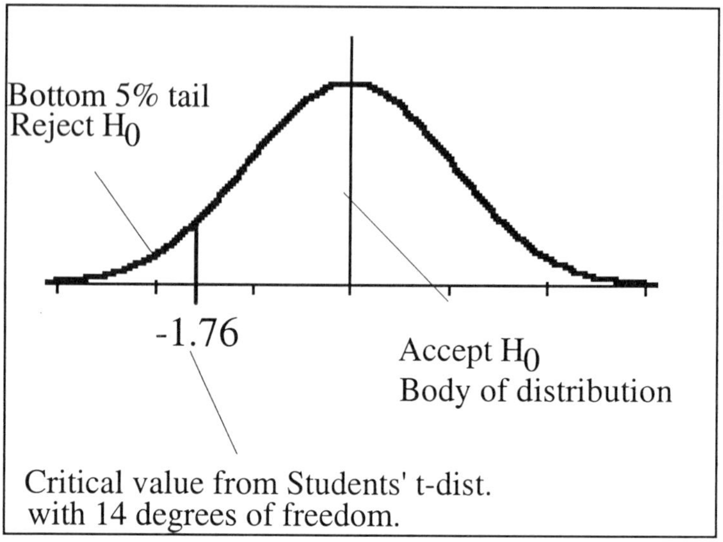

Figure 10.5 - Critical values from the t-distribution for a 1-tailed test

The pooled variance (s_p^2) is equal to:

$$s_p^2 = \frac{9\text{x}400 + 7\text{x}324}{14} = 367.43$$

Using the sample means, sizes and pooled variance in the test statistic gives:

$$t = \frac{40 - 60}{\sqrt{[367.43/9 + 367.43.14/7]}}$$

$$\mathbf{t = -2.07\ (2dp)}$$

The value of this test statistic is located in the critical region, therefore you must reject the null hypothesis H_0. At the 5% level, there is evidence to suggest that the new procedures have significantly reduced the customer interview time.

Example - (Two samples of paired data):

At a particular branch of this building society, the manager has decided to send 8 of her staff for word processor training using Windows software. The staff at the branch currently use a DOS package. It is hoped that this training will increase the number of customer letters they could process in 1 hour. The results for the 8 staff before and after training are shown below:

DOS:	15	9	6	7	5	9	7	10
Windows:	17	11	7	7	5	10	6	11

The manager wishes to determine if the chosen training course has significantly improved productivity. Since the productivity measures are paired, you must consider the mean differences in output (μ_d). The null and alternative hypotheses should reflect this:

H_0: $\mu_d = 0$ (the productivity is the **same** using the Windows software as it was using the DOS package)

H_1: $\mu_d > 0$ (the productivity has significantly **increased** using the Windows software compared to using the DOS package)

The differences in output (Windows - DOS) for the 8 sampled staff are:

2 2 1 0 0 1 -1 2

The mean and standard deviation for this sample are 0.75 and 1.04 respectively. The test statistic is:

$$\mathbf{t = \frac{\bar{d} - \mu_0}{s_d/\sqrt{n}}}$$

In this example $\mu_0 = 0$ since you not are looking for a specific difference in productivity.

$$t = \frac{0.75}{1.04/\sqrt{8}} \quad \mathbf{= 2.04\ (2dp)}$$

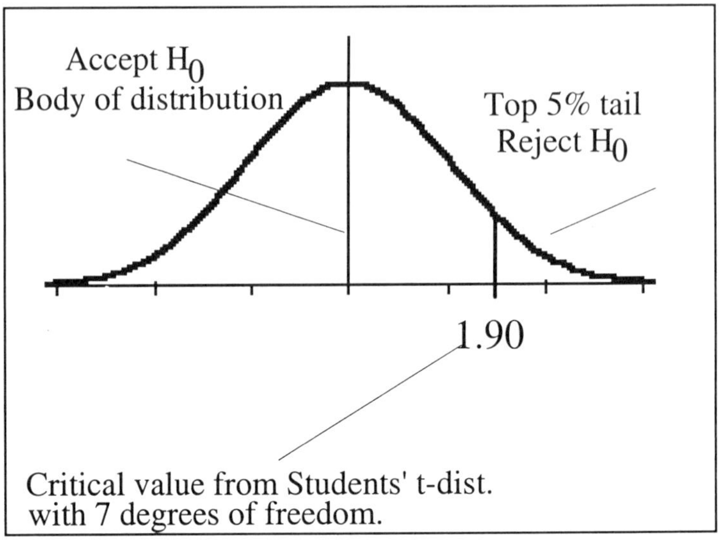

Figure 10.6 - Critical values from the t-distribution for a 1-tailed test

The critical value for a one-sided t test with 7 degrees of freedom at the 5% level of significance is 1.90, as shown in Figure 10.6. Inspection of the test statistic shows that its value is in the tail or critical region of the test distribution. Therefore, there is sufficient evidence to reject H_0 at this level. The manager can conclude that the conversion to the Windows software and subsequent staff development has led to a significant increase in productivity.

Using Excel to Test the Difference Between Two Means

The previous calculations can be simplified further with the use of various facilities offered in Excel's toolpak. In the next part of this chapter, two of these facilities will be considered by means of worked examples: The facilities to be considered are:

- t-Test: Paired Two-Sample for Means
- t-Test: Two-Sample Assuming Equal Variances

In order to activate these facilities, you must first type the sample data into Excel and then activate the relevant tool by clicking on:

Tools
Data Analysis

t-Test: Paired Two-Sample for Means

If you wish to compare performance say, **before** and **after** employee training or the installation of new technology, you can use **Excel's t-Test: Paired Two-Sample for Means** facility. For example, an office manager in the civil service has responsibility for a team of clerks who open and log mail for a large office site. A sample of the clerks were measured with regard to the number of letters opened using the old machines and were then re-assessed once new technology had been introduced into their office.

The corresponding dialogue box is shown in Figure 10.7. In this case, the decision maker has to define the variable ranges and the output range. Again, unless specified otherwise, the value of alpha, the pre-defined level of significance is taken as *0.05*. If you were testing the belief that productivity had increased by 15 letters per hour, the value 15 would be input into the box labelled **hypothesised mean difference**.

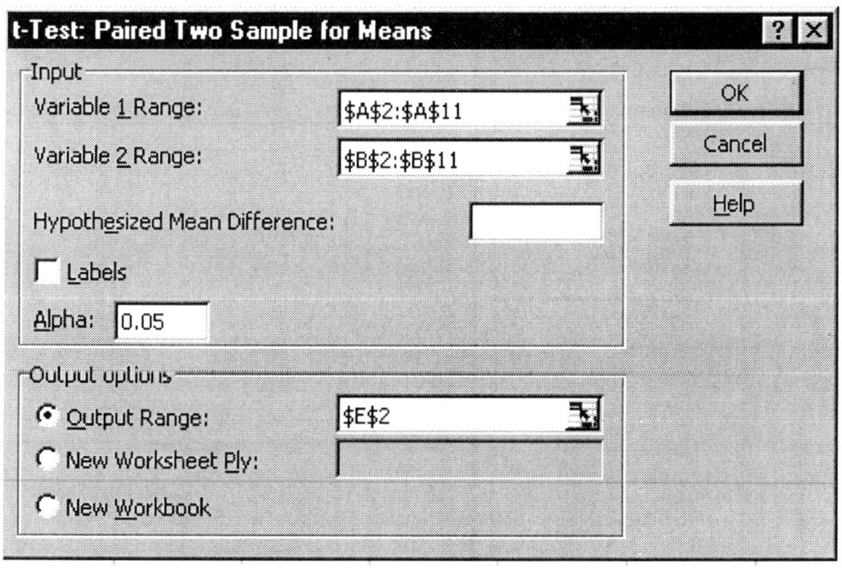

Figure 10.7 - Dialogue box for Excel's t-Test: Paired Two-Sample for Means facility

In this particular scenario, the following hypotheses should be defined:

H_0: $\mu_d = 0$
H_1: $\mu_d \neq 0$

where μ_d represents the mean of the differences in output for the group of staff.

In this case the null hypothesis states that the output with the old and new machines has remained the same, whereas the two-sided alternative tests whether the output has significantly increased or decreased. Figure 10.8 shows the output generated by Excel.

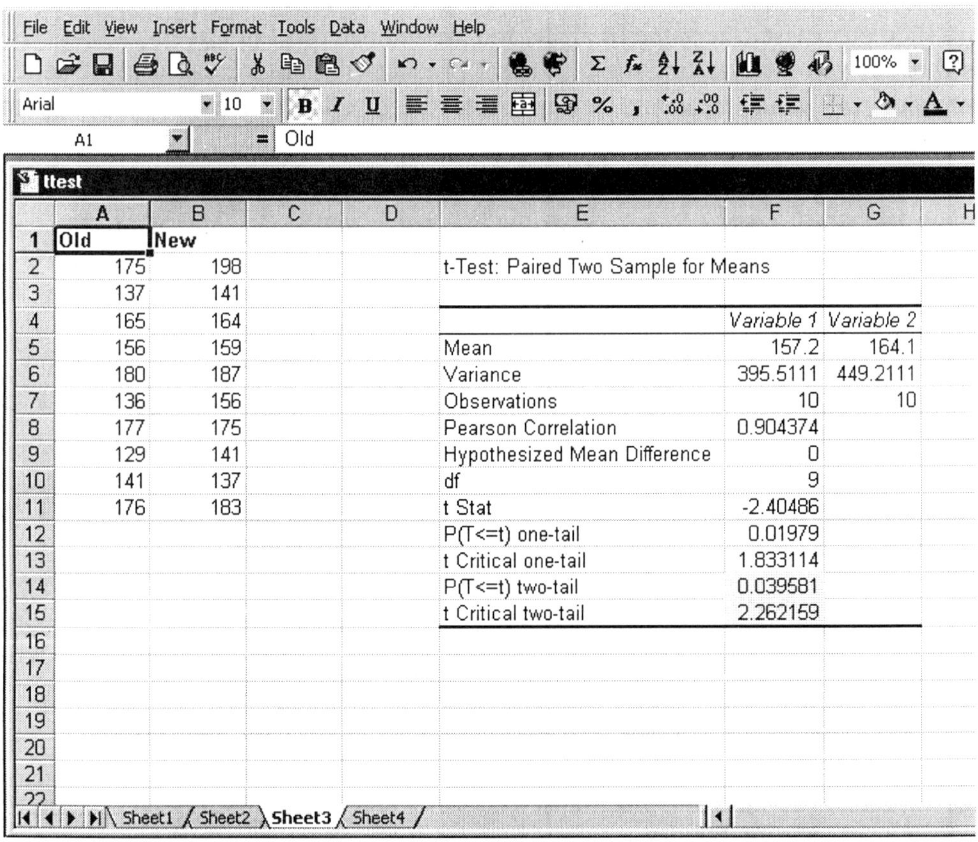

	A	B	C	D	E	F	G
1	Old	New					
2	175	198			t-Test: Paired Two Sample for Means		
3	137	141					
4	165	164				Variable 1	Variable 2
5	156	159			Mean	157.2	164.1
6	180	187			Variance	395.5111	449.2111
7	136	156			Observations	10	10
8	177	175			Pearson Correlation	0.904374	
9	129	141			Hypothesized Mean Difference	0	
10	141	137			df	9	
11	176	183			t Stat	-2.40486	
12					P(T<=t) one-tail	0.01979	
13					t Critical one-tail	1.833114	
14					P(T<=t) two-tail	0.039581	
15					t Critical two-tail	2.262159	

Figure 10.8 - Output from t-Test: Paired Two-Sample for Means facility

Inspection of the P-value (i.e. the level of significance required to reject H_0) corresponding to the two-tailed test can be found in cell **F14**. To be significant at the selected 5% level, you would need a value less than 0.05 for this type of alternative. The value (0.0395) is less than 0.05, which suggests at this level of significance, the null hypothesis should be rejected. In other words, there is sufficient evidence at the 5% level to claim that the new technology has lead to a change in productivity. The P-value described above can also be generated using:

=TTEST(A2:A11,B2:B11,2,1)

where the **2** indicates a two-tailed test and the 1 indicates the data corresponds to a paired sample.

t-Test: Two-Sample Assuming Equal Variances

A retail outlet specialising in sportswear owns a string of shops in Northern England, one with a head office in Newcastle, the other in Leeds. One worrying problem for the company is the drop-out rate of part-time retail staff. To determine whether there is a significant difference in regions a sample of 7 high-street shops were selected from the Newcastle area and 5 from the Leeds area and the number of staff leaving in the past three months were recorded. The null and alternative hypotheses are:

H_0: $\mu_n = \mu_l$
H_1: $\mu_n \neq \mu_l$

where μ_n and μ_l represent the mean number of staff leaving posts in Newcastle and Leeds respectively.

Again, a two-sided alternative has been selected because you are interested in seeing if the rates in the two regions are different, rather than one being significantly greater or smaller than the other. Given that the respective sample standard deviations are 20 and 19.3 (i.e. are similar), it is reasonable to assume equal variances. Figure 10.9 shows the dialogue box corresponding to the relevant toolpak facility. Inspection of this box shows that you must specify **both input ranges**, the **output range** and if necessary, a **level of significance**, (i.e. labelled as Alpha) if you are choosing one different to the default of 5%.

Moreover, if you were suggesting the difference in means between the two groups was say a loss of 10 staff, then this value would be entered in the box labelled **Hypothesised Mean Difference**.

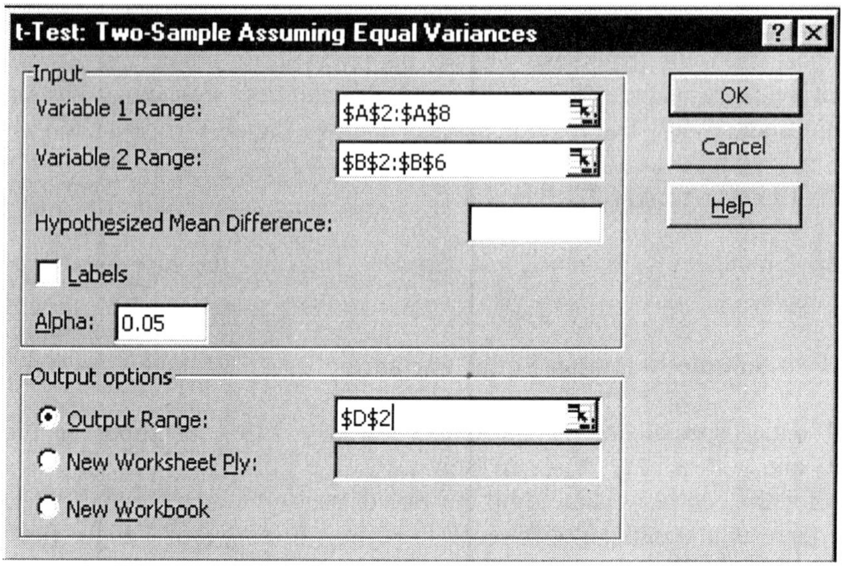

Figure 10.9 - Dialogue box for t-Test: Two-Sample Assuming Equal Variances tool

To determine the level of significance, you can use the P-value which is stored in cell E14 of the worksheet in Figure 10.10.

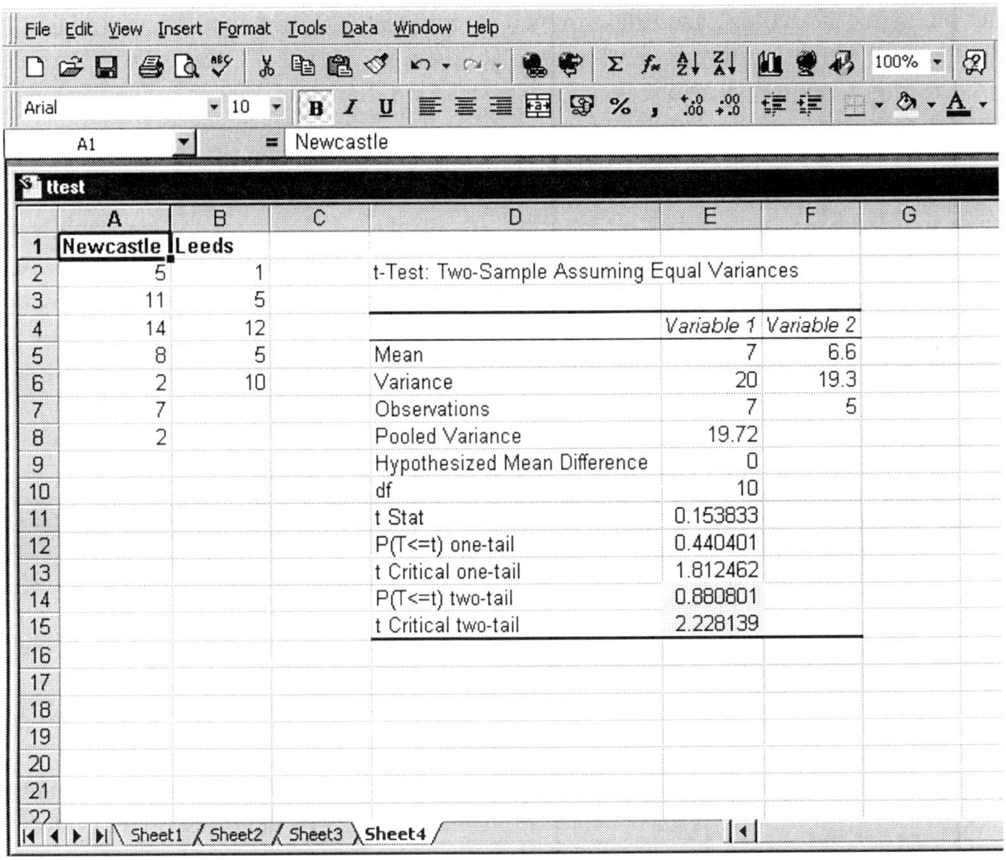

Figure 10.10 - Output from t-Test: Two-Sample Assuming Unequal Variances facility

Inspection of this output shows the P-value for the two-sided test to be **0.8808**. At the 5% significance level you would be looking for a P-value which is less than *0.05* in order to reject the null hypothesis H_0. Comparison with the value calculated suggests that the test is not significant, so you can accept the null hypothesis H_0. In conclusion, the loss of part-time retail staff from the chain in the Newcastle area is not significantly different to the number of part-time staff lost per store in the Leeds region. The P-value described above can also be generated using:

=TTEST(A2:A8,B2:B6,2,2)

where the first **2** indicates a two-tailed test and the second **2** indicates the data corresponds to two samples where you can assume equal variances.

When using the toolpak facilities for two sample tests the two input ranges must be defined as single columns. Two other facilities are offered **t test: Two Sample Assuming Unequal Variances** and **z test: Two Sample Means**. The dialogue boxes for these tests are similar to that displayed in Figure 10.9.

Finally, when you considered the manual calculations, you assumed that characteristics of the normal distribution are displayed. For smaller samples, you can only undertake t-tests if you are confident that the populations from which the individual samples collected are normally distributed. When normality cannot be assumed, the t-test should not be used and you must consider other, distribution-free tests. These tests are not considered in this book.

Conclusions

In this chapter you were introduced to a number of significance tests to test a decision makers beliefs or hypotheses regarding:

- Value of a single population mean.
- Difference in two population means.

Inspection of the various worked examples indicates that the steps required for testing a null hypothesis against an appropriate alternative are similar for both scenarios listed above. Excel provides a number of built-in facilities relating to the various hypothesis tests which further simplifies the numerical manipulation of the various sample data.

One important feature which is common to all significance tests is the level of significance you choose before testing the sample data. In business decision making, this level of significance is usually either 5% or 1%. This level of significance represents the probability of rejecting a correct statement about the population of interest, at the levels listed above. Therefore, you have either a 5% or 1% probability of making an incorrect decision based on the sample data available. Obviously, you can never have 100% confidence in the conclusions made if you are considering sample data, but you can reach these conclusions with an associated degree of confidence.

The final important feature of the significance test is the choice of the alternative hypothesis H_1. As demonstrated in this chapter, the alternative hypothesis can be either one-sided or two-sided. The choice depends very much on the situation under consideration. If you were measuring the average weight of boxes of tea as part of a quality control exercise, then you would need a two-sided alternative hypothesis to test that the filling machine isn't producing boxes of tea which are significantly lighter (because of trades description problems) or significantly heavier (because the company would be giving away free tea) than advertised. In contrast, if a factory produces industrial lighting which has an advertised life, then a one-sided test would be more appropriate because the manufacturer only really needs to test that the population mean life isn't significantly less than that advertised and assumed by its commercial users.

Learning Outcomes Checklist

After completing this chapter you should have an understanding of the following concepts, calculations and functions:

- The term 'hypothesis'.
- The process of taking a hypothesis test for a single population mean.
- The process of taking a hypothesis test for the difference between two population means.
- The terms 'null hypothesis' and 'alternative hypothesis'.
- The difference between a one-sided and two-sided alternative hypothesis.
- Identifying critical values for tests based on large or small samples of data.
- An awareness of Excel's **ZTEST()** function.
- An awareness of the hypothesis test facilities housed in Excel's **Analysis Toolpak**.

Ensure that you understand these concepts before progressing to Chapter 11.

Chapter Case Question

- Open the files **CHAP09.XLS**
- Using the relevant facility in Excel (i.e. **ZTEST()** or the facilities in the **Analysis Toolpak**) undertake the following hypothesis tests, writing down your proposed null and alternative hypotheses and test all at the 5% level of significance:

The average monthly turnover for a country restaurant is £113,000.

The average monthly turnover for a country family pub is less than £100,000.

The average monthly turnover for a country family pub is greater than that for a town restaurant.

The average monthly turnover for a country restaurant is at least £15,000 greater than that for a town family pub.

The average length of service for a pub landlord is 20 months.

There is a significant difference in length of service in landlords whose pubs have been decorated compared to those pubs which haven't been decorated.

- Provide a full interpretation for the **P-value** provided by Excel.
- Save the amended file as **CHAP10.XLS**

Supplementary Questions

1. Describe the main stages of a hypothesis test with reference to a one sample test.
2. What is the difference between a z-test and a t-test?
3. Describe the differences between a one-sided and two-sided test, giving business related examples to show when each would be appropriate.
4. State the test statistics for testing the significance of a single population mean, differentiating between z and t-test statistics.
5. What assumptions are made when small sample tests are undertaken?
6. At a factory packing catalogues for the mail order industry, the production manager believes the average number of catalogues packed per day by the packing staff is 1000. To test this belief, 40 staff were selected at random and the number of catalogues packed in one day were recorded as shown below:

1100	989	1001	977	1029	1212	868	929	782	804
1003	848	929	1007	1123	848	779	1221	839	1032
1321	887	798	1000	792	815	1005	1153	900	1321
954	903	1130	786	832	1065	965	756	1100	945

(a) Calculate the sample mean and standard deviation.

(b) Define an appropriate null and alternative hypothesis to test the production manager's belief about the average daily staff output.

(c) Test this belief using an appropriate statistic at the 5% significance level, stating your conclusions.

(d) Repeat the above test at the 1% level of significance.

(e) Check the results obtained using the appropriate facilities offered by Excel.

7. In a local council office problems of staff morale has lead to significant levels of absenteeism. To counter this problem, the Personnel Officer has decided to test whether the number of days of sick leave taken in the last year is significantly greater than 8.5 days, which was the population mean number of days lost per person in the previous year. Before taking action, the head of personnel will only issue a directive to staff if she is 95% certain that the actual number of days is greater than 8.5. To make this decision, the records of a random sample of 12 employees were considered and the number of days sick leave were:

9	1	12	5	3	15	18	14	3	15	14	4

(a) Calculate the sample mean and standard deviation.

(b) Define an appropriate null and alternative hypothesis to test the personnel manager's belief about the yearly level of sick leave.

(c) Test this belief using an appropriate statistic at the 1% significance level, stating your conclusions.

(d) Should the head of personnel take any action?

8. State the test statistics for testing the significance of the difference between two population means, differentiating between z and t-test statistics.

9. For small samples, what is the advantage of using a pooled standard deviation? When is it not appropriate to use the pooled standard deviation?

10. A furniture manufacturer contracts out to two upholsterers who make suite covers, one located in Port Talbot the other situated in Peterlee. He is wishing to review the contracts to both upholsterers based on the average time to complete an order. Thirty contracts from Port Talbot were considered and average time to complete the order was 17 days with a standard deviation of 5 days. In comparison, for the contractor Peterlee it was found that the average order time was 13 days with a standard deviation of 4 days, considering a sample of 40 orders.

    (a) Test at the 5% significant level if the average order times at the two upholsterers are significantly different.

    (b) Test at the 1% significance level, the claim that the average order times at Peterlee are significantly quicker than their counterparts at Port Talbot.

    (c) Check the results using Excel.

11. Staff working at a packaging factory have until recently been packing books and catalogues manually. Investment in new machinery has been supported by staff development and the average daily output on the old and new machinery has been recorded for a sample of ten packing staff. The results are:

Old:	978	994	1123	1005	787	1120	949	888	787	1102
New:	1003	1100	1232	979	800	1003	1000	992	868	1213

    (a) Set up the appropriate null and alternative hypothesis to test the production manager's belief that productivity has increased since the new machinery was introduced.

    (b) Test this belief at the 5% significance level using an appropriate test statistic.

    (c) Has productivity increased significantly?

    (d) Check the results obtained using the relevant facilities offered by Excel.

12. In a survey into health and safety amongst VDU operators, 10 people who had taken part in a health and safety course pertaining to RSI injuries in the last 3

years were asked how many referrals they had made to the company doctor in the last year because of this injury. The results were:

2 1 4 6 10 4 2 6 0 0

Another group of 12 operators who hadn't received training were asked the same question. Their responses were:

4 3 8 9 2 5 2 7 7 0 2 6

(a) Calculate the sample mean and standard deviation for each sample.

(b) Determine the pooled standard deviation.

(c) Set up the appropriate null and alternative hypothesis to test the health executive's belief that training and awareness of RSI has reduced the amount of referrals to the doctor caused by this condition.

(d) Test this belief at the 5% significance level using an appropriate test statistic.

(e) Has the attendance on the course had any significant impact on the amount of referrals?

(f) Check the results obtained using the relevant facilities offered by Excel.

(g) State any assumptions made about the populations of interest.

Chapter 11

Statistical Tests for Independence

Learning Outcomes

In this chapter you will be introduced to two-variable classification of data using a table from which the degree of association between two variables can be measured. In order to measure the degree of association between two categorical variables, a statistical test for independence, known as the chi-squared (X^2) test will be introduced. At the end of the chapter, the relevant facilities offered by Excel for tabulating categorical data and carrying out this test will be considered with reference to business related examples.

After completing this chapter you will be able to:

- Understand the term 'contingency table'.
- Distinguish between 'observed' and 'expected' values.
- Undertake a chi-squared (X2) test for independence between two categorical variables.
- Understand the term 'degrees of freedom' and calculate this statistic for a contingency table.
- Undertake a chi-squared test by hand.
- Undertake a chi-squared test using the built-in facilities offered by Excel.
- Interpret the meaning of the P-value generated by Excel when undertaking a X 2 test.
- Create a contingency tables using Excel's PivotTable Report facility.

Introduction

Many of the calculations you have considered so far in this book have involved individual variables. However, when you collect data to make decisions, for example during market research survey amongst the readership of a national newspaper or if you are assessing the degree performance of class of undergraduates, you are likely to consider a number of variables. In a market research survey for the newspaper, customer details such as age, sex and social class may be recorded alongside the number of times each customer buys the paper each week, whilst in the assessment of degree results, gender, course and classification may be considered.

Using the information collected for the relevant variables, you may wish to determine which of these variables show association, and if so, quantify the nature or strength of this association. The results of this analysis can then be used in the decision making process, say, to determine which age group, gender group or social class are more likely to buy the newspaper, which in turn may influence the nature of any future marketing.

In Chapter 1 you were introduced to two types of data; categorical and quantitative. Depending upon the type of data being considered, two different approaches will be taken to determine whether association exists. If you need to determine whether a relationship exists between two **quantitative** variables, you can calculate a statistic known as the **correlation coefficient.** The application of the correlation coefficient which will be introduced in the next chapter. In contrast, if **categorical** data is being considered, then an alternative approach is required. This approach will be considered in this chapter and is called the **chi-squared test for independence**.

Before introducing this test, initial inspection of the data in tabular form provides an easy way of identifying any potential association. This type of table is called a **contingency table**.

Example

The head of a University Business Department wishes to determine whether the application of its prospective students for the various courses is influenced by gender. To determine this, the records of 1997 applicants were considered and the table in Figure 11.1 was produced.

Course	Gender		
	Male	**Female**	**Total**
Business	95	103	198
Information Technology	37	25	62
Marketing	25	36	61
Logistics	20	12	32
Tourism	32	35	67
Finance	46	33	79
Total	255	244	499

Figure 11.1 - University applications by gender and course

To determine if any course has a greater proportion of male or female applicants compared to the department as a whole, you can calculate **expected values** and compare these with the observed values for each category shown in Figure 11.1.

By using column and row totals to calculate expected values, you are assuming that if the variables are independent, each category (there are 12 categories in Figure 11.1) will have a proportionate number of observations. That is, the number of male business applications will be in proportion both to the total number of business applications and the total number of male applications made to the department.

The **expected values** can be calculated from the row and column totals, e.g. the expected number of male applicants for the Business course is given by:

Row total x Column total / Cross-total

i.e. 198 x 255 / 499 = 101.18 (2dp)

This formula has been derived from the statistical law of independence and the formula for expected values, i.e.

P(A and B) = P(A) x P(B) and E(A and B) = np

Using these rules, gives: Expected number in a single category

$$= \text{Cross Total} \times \frac{\text{Row Total}}{\text{Cross Total}} \times \frac{\text{Column Total}}{\text{Cross Total}}$$

which simplifies to give the formula used. Figure 11.2 lists all of the expected values for each course by gender. Inspection of this table shows that the row and column totals are the same as those for the observed values shown in Figure 11.1. This will always be the case.

	Gender		
Course	**Male**	**Female**	**Total**
Business	101.18	96.82	198
Information Technology	31.68	30.32	62
Marketing	31.17	29.83	61
Logistics	16.35	15.65	32
Tourism	34.24	32.76	67
Finance	40.37	38.63	79
Total	255	244	499

Figure 11.2 - Expected values by gender and course

To determine the extent of the difference between observed and expected values, you can present the differences as a percentage of the expected values, i.e.

100% x (observed value - expected value)/expected value

The table in Figure 11.3 contains these percentage differences.

	Gender	
Course	**Male**	**Female**
Business	- 6.1%	6.4%
Information Technology	16.8%	-17.5%
Marketing	-19.8%	20.7%
Logistics	22.3%	- 23.3%
Tourism	- 6.5%	6.8%
Finance	13.9%	- 14.6%

Figure 11.3 - Percentage differences between observed and expected values

Inspection of this table indicates a number of large positive percentage differences exist. In particular, the number of males applying for Information Technology is 17% greater than expected, the number of females applying to the Marketing course is 21% greater than expected, whilst the number of male applicants to Logistics is 22% greater than expected. This information is useful because it may suggest that the Information Technology course is currently much more likely to attract male rather than female applicants, whilst the number of male and female applicants to Business and Tourism are more or less in proportion.

The application of the contingency table has been used to introduce the concept of measuring the association between two categorical variables. However, while simple percentage differences suggest likely relationships, it is possible to determine the significance of these differences using a formal statistical test. This test is called the **chi-squared test for independence**.

The Chi-Squared Test for Independence

As suggested earlier, the chi-squared (X^2) test allows us to measure the significance of the statistical association between two categorical variables. To determine the level of significance you can follow the steps shown below:

- Define the null (H_0) and alternative (H_1) hypotheses. In general, these hypotheses take the form:

H_0: *No association exists* between the two categorical variables.

H_1: *An association exists* between the two variables.

By defining H_0 and H_1 in this way, you are assuming no relationship exists between the two categorical variables until proven otherwise.

- Specify the pre-determined level of significance. Like the hypothesis tests described in Chapter 10, the pre-defined level of significance is either the 1% or 5% significance levels for business applications. The 5% indicates the probability of a Type I error (see Chapter 10), i.e. the probability of rejecting a correct null hypothesis.

- Determine the value of the test statistic. The chi-squared test statistic is:

$$X^2 = \Sigma[(\text{obs-exp})^2/\text{exp}]$$

where:

obs represent the observed values (i.e. the actual number of applicants for each course in the example described).

exp represents the expected values assuming the number of applicants are in proportion to the sub-categories they represent.

The differences calculated are then totalled.

To determine the expected values based on the above assumption, you can use the equation:

Row total x Column total / Cross-total

The only modification you need to make in this test are for categories where the **expected number** of observations is small. Specifically, if the **expected value** is less than 5, you should group categories appropriately (in the example above you could group all of the small courses together into a group called 'Others') and then carry out the test as shown below. Inspection of the expected values in this example indicates that this is not a problem.

Figure 11.4 lists the expected values and value of X^2 for this example involving the number of university applicants by gender and course.

	Gender		
Course	**Male**	**Female**	**Total**
Business	101.18	96.82	198
Information Technology	31.68	30.32	62
Marketing	31.17	29.83	61
Logistics	16.35	15.65	32
Tourism	34.24	32.76	67
Finance	40.37	38.63	79
Total	255	244	499

X^2 differences:

	Gender	
Course	**Male**	**Female**
Business	0.3777	0.3948
Information Technology	0.8922	0.9324
Marketing	1.2222	1.2773
Logistics	0.8135	0.8502
Tourism	0.1463	0.1529
Finance	0.7849	0.8203

Figure 11.4 - Expected values by gender and course and X^2 differences

The first X^2 difference (0.3777) has been calculated as $(95-101.18)^2/101.18$. The sum of all of the differences shown in Figure 11.4 is **8.6647**. This test statistic will always have a positive value because you have squared the differences between each observed and expected values.

- To determine the critical value, you must know the level of significance (which has been pre-defined as 5%) and the **number of degrees of freedom**. The number of degrees of freedom can be calculated as: **df = (r - 1) x (c - 1)**, where **r** and **c** represent the number of **rows** and **columns** respectively from the contingency table. In this example r = 6 (the number of faculties) and c = 2 (the gender of the applicants), therefore you have **5 degrees of freedom**. By taking into account the degrees of freedom, you are accounting for the number of categories on the contingency table. Inspection of the table listed in Appendix III suggests that $X^2_{(0.05,\ 5)} = 11.14$. Using this notation 0.05 represents the proportion of the curve in the critical tail (i.e. 5%) and 5 represents the number of degrees of freedom. Reading the X^2 table provided, we obtain the critical value by looking at the intersection of the column headed 0.05 and the row labelled 5.

- The next stage is to measure the test statistic against the relevant critical value. If association exists between the two variables, a pattern will be evident in the (categorical) data which causes large differences between observed and expected values. If the differences are statistically significant, then their total value will be situated in the critical tail of the chi-squared test distribution. To determine if this is the case, you must make the following comparison:

  If **test statistic > critical value** then **reject** null hypothesis H_0, since the test value will be situated in the critical tail of the chi-squared distribution. If **test statistic < critical value** then **accept** null hypothesis H_0, since the test value will be in the 'body' and not the tail of the chi-squared distribution. A 1-tailed test will always be carried out because the value of the test statistic is always positive. In this example the value of the test statistic 8.6647 is less than the critical value 11.14, hence the test statistic's value is located in the body of the X^2 distribution. Therefore, at the 5% level of significance, you must accept the null hypothesis H_0.

- The final part of the hypothesis test is to comment whether or not a statistically significant association exists between the two variables. In the example shown above, you can comment that at the 5% level of significance there is no evidence to suggest a association exists between gender and course amongst the university applicants. Whilst large percentage differences exist in gender amongst applicants for the Logistics course, this course has a relatively small number of applicants (32 is the smallest number of applications to an individual course in the department), and when compared to the total number of applicants to the whole faculty, these differences have been shown to be statistically insignificant.

Using Excel to Undertake Chi-Squared Tests

So far you have seen how a chi-squared test can be undertaken manually. In the next part of the chapter you will see how all of the necessary calculations can be undertaken both quickly and accurately using Excel. This will be achieved with reference to a business related example.

A company owns a chain of wholesale warehouses which are situated around the UK and deal in high turnover, low price merchandise. The marketing director of the company wishes to fix the advertising budgets for 1998 and wishes to determine what association exists, if any, between the sales of various canned alcoholic drinks and the location of the store. Figure 11.5 shows the observed number of different brands of canned drink sold in a particular month for each of the eight warehouses. You don't have to adjust this data because all of the expected values are at least 5.

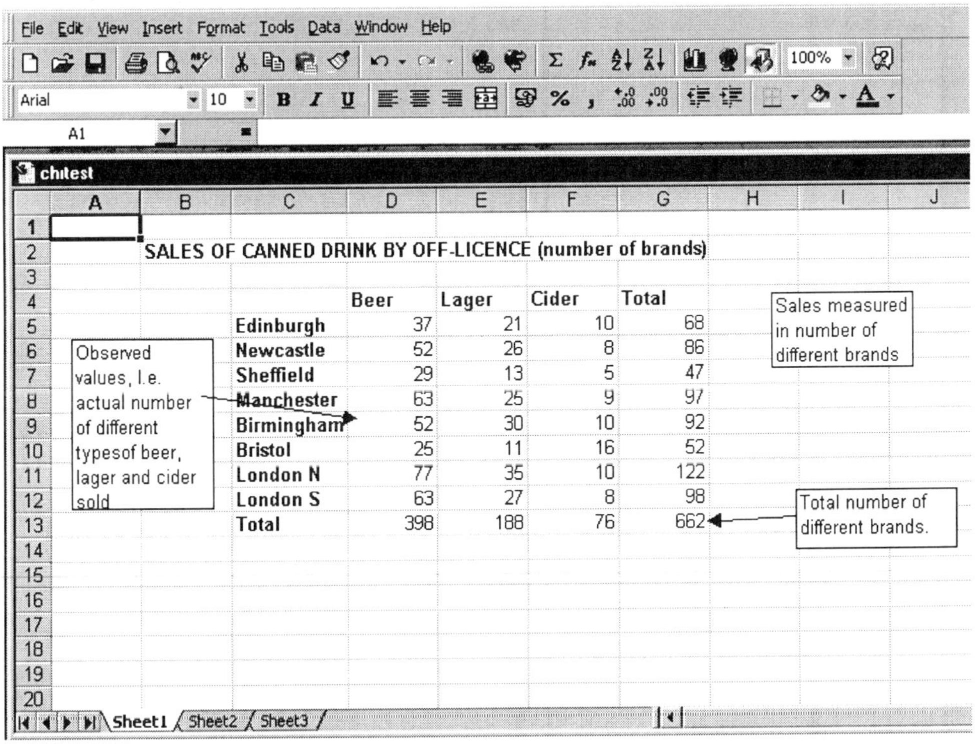

Figure 11.5 - Observed Sales Data

Before undertaking any calculations you must define an appropriate null (H_0) and alternative (H_1) hypotheses. For this problem, these hypotheses are:

H_0: *No association* between the sales of each type of drink and the location of the warehouse.

H_1: *An association* exists between the sales of each type of drink and the location of the warehouse.

The level of significance for this test will be pre-defined at the 5% level.

The next stage of the process is to calculate the expected values. Figure 11.6 shows the expected number of different brands sold for each of the eight warehouses.

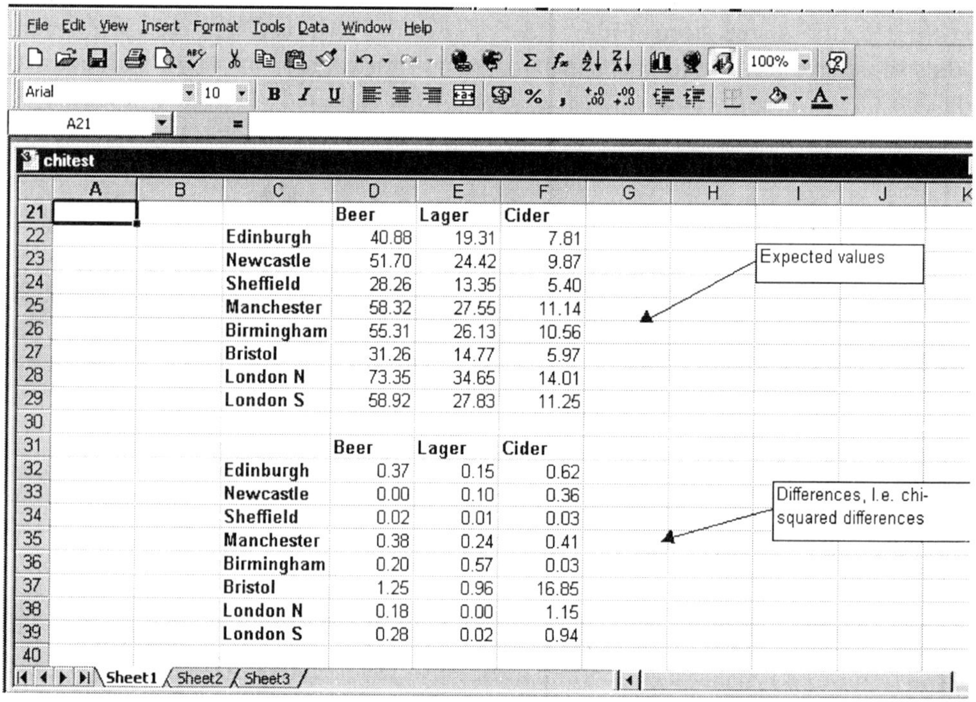

	Beer	Lager	Cider
Edinburgh	40.88	19.31	7.81
Newcastle	51.70	24.42	9.87
Sheffield	28.26	13.35	5.40
Manchester	58.32	27.55	11.14
Birmingham	55.31	26.13	10.56
Bristol	31.26	14.77	5.97
London N	73.35	34.65	14.01
London S	58.92	27.83	11.25

	Beer	Lager	Cider
Edinburgh	0.37	0.15	0.62
Newcastle	0.00	0.10	0.36
Sheffield	0.02	0.01	0.03
Manchester	0.38	0.24	0.41
Birmingham	0.20	0.57	0.03
Bristol	1.25	0.96	16.85
London N	0.18	0.00	1.15
London S	0.28	0.02	0.94

Figure 11.6 - Expected values and differences

These expected values are calculated by making references to the column and row totals shown in Figure 11.5. The first expected value in cell **D22** has the formula:

=D$13*$G5/$G$13

where:

D13 represents the column total

G5 represents the row total

G13 represents the cross-total

You should notice that the formula uses dollar ($) references to ensure that only one (formula) needs to be written, and this can be subsequently copied to the remainder of the block. In D13 the dollar is placed before the number so that the row reference (i.e. the column totals) remains constant. In the reference to G5, the dollar is written in front of the letter G so that the column reference (i.e. the row totals) remains constant. Finally, dollar signs are placed in front of both letter and number for the reference to the cross-total. This absolute reference ensures that whatever direction the formula is copied, reference will always be made to this cell.

In addition to the expected values, the X^2 differences have also been calculated. This calculation is purely optional when using Excel and reasons for this will be given shortly. The first difference has been calculated using the formula:

=(D5-D22)^2/D22 **(^2 means squared)**

which has been subsequently copied to the remainder of the block.

Given the information available, there are two ways in which you can use Excel to calculate the X^2 statistic. The first is to add up all of differences and use the **CHIDIST()** built-in function. The structure of this function is:

CHIDIST(sum,df)

where:

sum represents the sum of the X^2 differences.

df represents the number of degrees of freedom.

This command provides a probability value for the chi-squared distribution. In this example, the value of **x** has been found by typing **=SUM(D32:F39)** into the cell D41 as shown in Figure 11.7. The number of degrees of freedom can be found using the equation:

df = (r - 1) x (c - 1)

= 7 x 2 = 14

since there are 8 stores (i.e. r = 8 rows) and 3 types of canned drink (i.e. c = 3 columns) considered in the contingency table. This value is shown in cell **D42** in Figure 11.7

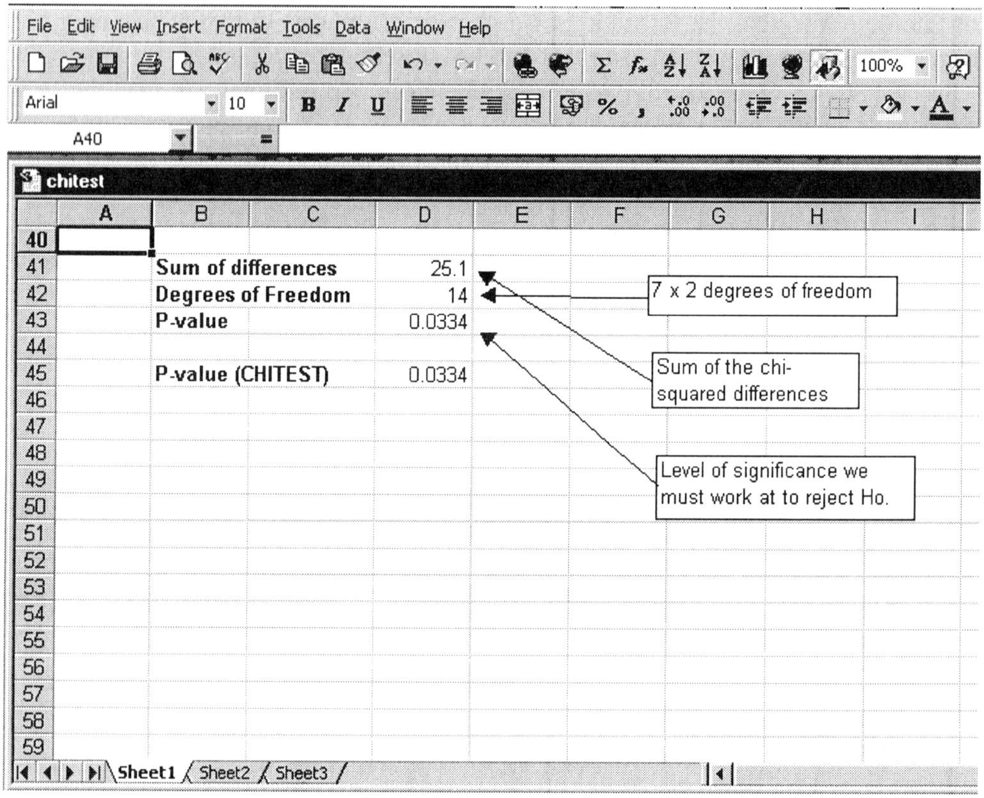

Figure 11.7 - Calculation of X^2 statistic using Excel

The cell **D43** contains the formula:

=CHIDIST(D41,D42)

and has returned the value **0.0334 (4dp)**. This P-value suggests the level of significance required to ensure that association can be assumed between the number of different brands of each drink sold and the location of the warehouse, i.e. the level of significance required so that you could reject H_0. Since this value is less than the pre-defined *0.05* (i.e. the 5% significance level), you should reject the null hypothesis H_0. In other words, since the P-value is less than 0.05, you can assume that the test statistic is critical at a smaller level of significance, and as a consequence, you could reject H_0 at the pre-defined 5% level.

To summarise, there is sufficient evidence at the 5% level to assume association exists between these two variables. That is, you can assume that store location and sales of different types of drink are influenced by the location of the warehouse.

Apart from using the **CHIDIST()** command provided Excel, you can also compare observed and expected values (without calculating the differences) using the built-in **CHITEST()** function. The structure of this function is:

> **CHITEST(observed values,expected values)**

where:

> **observed values** and **expected values** are the two sets of frequencies being compared. In this example, observed values represent the number of types of can sold at each of the various warehouses.

In Figure 11.7, cell D45 contains the formula:

> **=CHITEST(D5:F12,D22:F29)**

which yields the (same) P-value **0.0334 (4dp)**. Interpretation of this particular P-value has been provided already.

Building Contingency Tables Using Excel

The calculations shown above are based on a table of observed values known as a **contingency table**. In both examples, the tables had already been collated. If sample data has been collected, this data can be quickly assembled into a contingency table by making use of Excel's **PivotTable Report** facility. If you wish to determine as part of a market research exercise the relationship between daily newspaper purchase and voting intentions of a random sample of new voters, the sample data collected could be arranged in Excel as shown below in Figure 11.8.

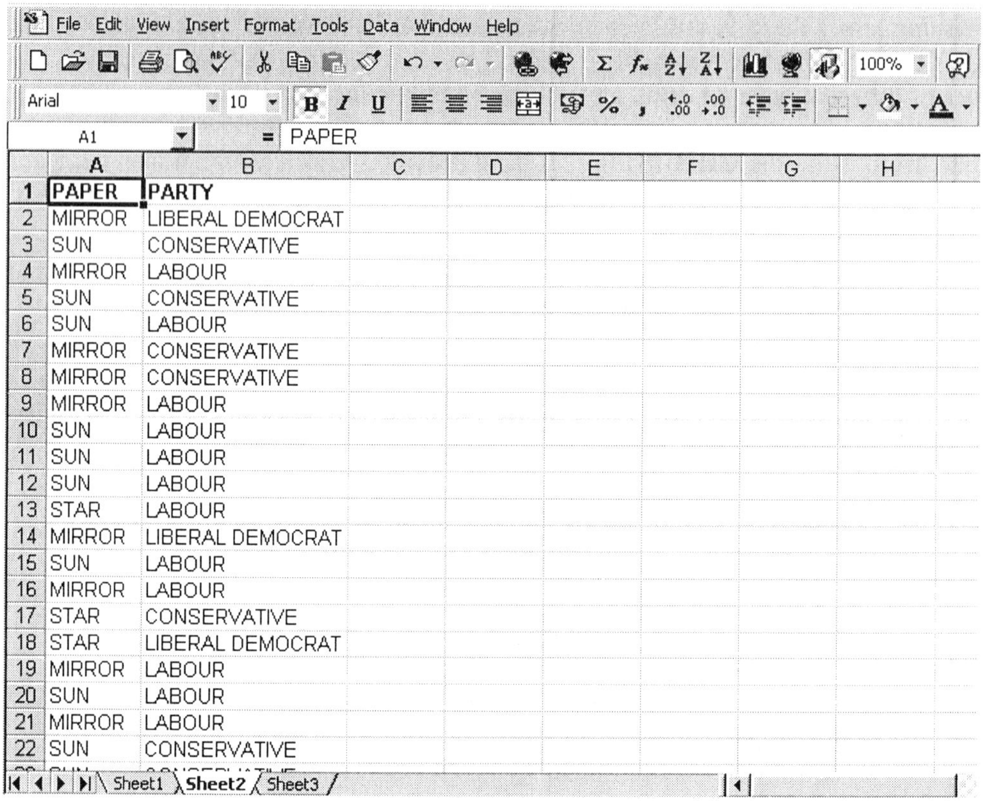

	A	B
1	PAPER	PARTY
2	MIRROR	LIBERAL DEMOCRAT
3	SUN	CONSERVATIVE
4	MIRROR	LABOUR
5	SUN	CONSERVATIVE
6	SUN	LABOUR
7	MIRROR	CONSERVATIVE
8	MIRROR	CONSERVATIVE
9	MIRROR	LABOUR
10	SUN	LABOUR
11	SUN	LABOUR
12	SUN	LABOUR
13	STAR	LABOUR
14	MIRROR	LIBERAL DEMOCRAT
15	SUN	LABOUR
16	MIRROR	LABOUR
17	STAR	CONSERVATIVE
18	STAR	LIBERAL DEMOCRAT
19	MIRROR	LABOUR
20	SUN	LABOUR
21	MIRROR	LABOUR
22	SUN	CONSERVATIVE

Figure 11.8 - Sample data from 100 tabloid readers listed in Excel

To create a table, you need to activate the **Data PivotTable** facility. Following the instructions provided in Chapter 2, you can create a two-variable contingency table like that shown in Figure 11.9.

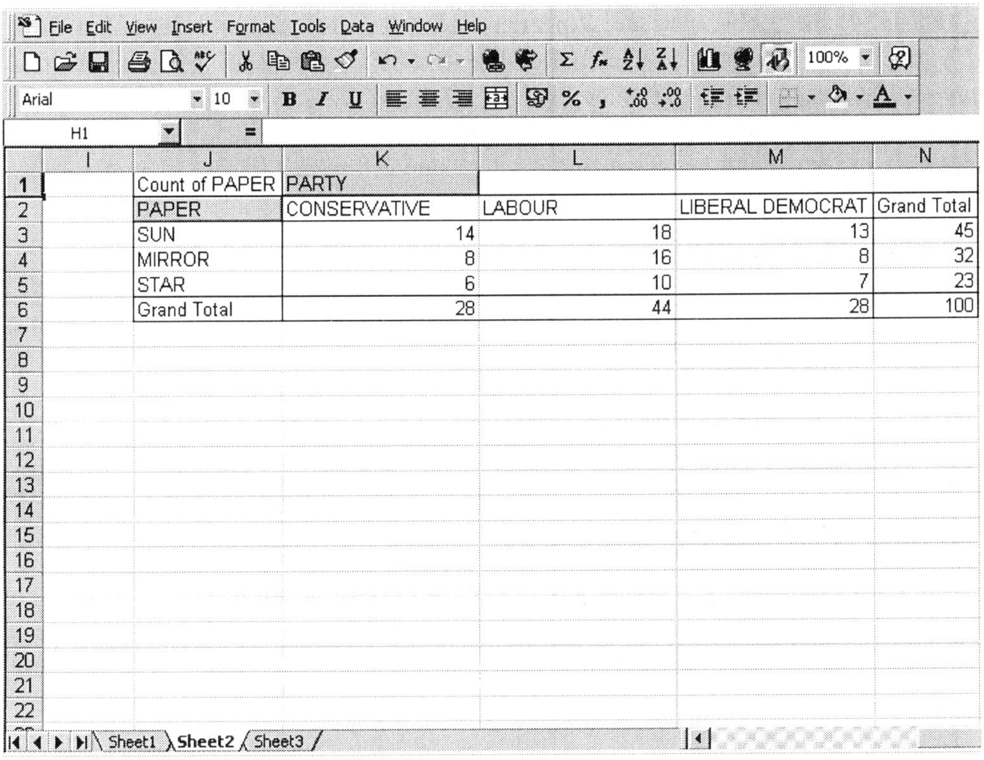

Count of PAPER	PARTY			
PAPER	CONSERVATIVE	LABOUR	LIBERAL DEMOCRAT	Grand Total
SUN	14	18	13	45
MIRROR	8	16	8	32
STAR	6	10	7	23
Grand Total	28	44	28	100

Figure 11.9 - Two-variable contingency table produced using PivotTable

From the table created you can calculate the expected values and then use Excel's **CHITEST()** command to determine the degree of association between choice of tabloid and voting intentions using the procedure demonstrated in the previous example. In this example, using the **CHITEST()** command should yield a P-value of **0.9275 (4dp),** which suggests that at the 5% level of significance, you should accept the null hypothesis that there is no association between these two variables. In other words, there is insufficient evidence at the 5% level of significance to assume there is a relationship between the newspaper purchased and the voting intentions of its reader.

Conclusions

In this chapter you have considered the chi-squared (X^2) test for independence between two categorical variables. The test requires you to compare observed and expected values. The expected values are based on the summary totals of each variable in the contingency table and when calculating their values you make the assumption that the two variables are independent, as indicated by the null hypothesis. If these observed and expected values are similar, this results in a small value for the X^2 statistic which implies that the null hypothesis of *no association* between the categorised variables is true. If large values of the individual X^2 differences, and in turn a large X^2 statistic is calculated, this indicates distinct values for observed and expected frequencies, suggesting that *association may exist*.

Learning Outcomes Checklist

After completing this chapter you should have an understanding of the following concepts, calculations and functions:

- Recognise a categorical data set.
- Construct a contingency table for two categorical variables either manually or using Excel's PivotTable facility.
- Understand the null and alternative hypotheses for a chi-squared test.
- Calculate expected values and percentage differences between observed and expected values.
- Calculate chi-squared differences between observed and expected values.
- Calculate the degrees of freedom for a contingency table.
- Measure the significance of the sum of the chi-squared differences using tables.
- Measure the significance of the sum of the chi-squared differences using Excel's **CHITEST()** and **CHIDIST()** functions.

Ensure that you understand these concepts before progressing to Chapter 12.

Chapter Case Question

The pub chain owns 700 houses nationally and these are categorised in the table below:

	Country	Town	Suburb	Total
Restaurant	32	43	25	100
Family Pub	38	85	77	200
Theme Bar	26	18	36	80
Sports	16	82	102	200
Traditional	2	58	60	120
Total	114	286	300	700

- Using Excel enter the table shown above.
- Calculate the expected values.
- Define the null and alternative hypotheses for a chi-squared test.
- Using the relevant command, determine whether the variables location and pub category are statistically independent.
- If a significant relationship exists, suggest which locations have a significantly greater proportion of certain types of public house?
- Save the file as **CHAP11.XLS**

Supplementary Questions

1. Describe the following terms:

   (a) Contingency table.

   (b) Observed values.

   (c) Expected values.

2. Describe how expected values can be calculated from a contingency table.

3. State the formula for the chi-squared (X^2) test for independence between two categorical variables.

4. What are the advantages of using this measure over simple percentage differences?

5. Typically, what are the null and alternative hypotheses for a X^2 test for independence between two categorical variables?

6. Why is the chi-squared test a 1-tailed test?

7. How do you calculate the number of degrees of freedom from the contingency table?

8. A newspaper proprietor owns 3 morning papers, a downmarket tabloid (paper X), a 'serious tabloid' (Y) and a broad sheet (Z). A proportionate number of readers of each paper were interviewed and their social class recorded. The information is show below:

Social Class

Paper	AB	C1	C2	DE	Unemployed/Retired/Student
X	7	32	39	71	19
Y	14	25	37	40	25
Z	35	19	10	5	22

(a) Is there any evidence at the 5% significance level to suggest that choice of paper and social class are associated. Explain your answer.

(b) Check the results obtained using Excel.

9. A University Business School has proposed to restructure its staff. Three possible structures have been created; A, B and C. The Dean has decided to consult amongst three groups of staff to determine their preferred structure. The following responses were collected:

	Faculty Structure		
Category of Staff	A	B	C
Academics	57	33	40
Administrators	21	24	10
Technicians	1	3	6

(a) Calculate the row and column totals for the observed values listed above.

(b) Calculate the expected values, and if appropriate group staff together to account for small values.

(c) State the null and alternative hypothesis for the chi-squared test for independence.

(d) Calculate the test statistic and the number of degrees of freedom.

(e) Can you suggest that the category of employee and preferred structure are independent? Explain your answer.

(f) Check the results obtained using Excel.

10. The marketing manager of a large record company wishes to determine what degree of association, if any, exists between the age of a customer and whether he or she purchases LPs, cassettes or CDs. One hundred customers were interviewed as part of a market research exercise and the following results were recorded:

Age	Purchase	Age	Purchase	Age	Purchase
63	CD	20	LP	36	CD
40	CD	53	CD	25	CD
71	CD	42	LP	52	CD
30	Cassette	40	CD	21	CD
46	CD	57	CD	18	CD
15	Cassette	38	CD	33	CD
22	CD	52	Cassette	57	CD
12	CD	36	CD	39	CD
14	CD	14	Cassette	38	Cassette
14	Cassette	46	Cassette	71	CD
21	Cassette	44	CD	45	LP
17	CD	10	CD	37	CD
65	CD	74	CD	74	CD
12	CD	15	CD	55	LP
10	CD	60	CD	18	CD
24	CD	28	CD	10	Cassette
24	CD	30	LP	20	Cassette
31	Cassette	34	CD	34	CD
31	CD	48	LP	55	CD
32	CD	67	CD	67	CD
65	CD	32	CD	49	Cassette
40	Cassette	69	CD	36	CD
11	Cassette	61	Cassette	15	CD
35	CD	52	CD	63	CD
35	CD	12	CD	66	LP
23	Cassette	59	CD	48	CD
46	CD	23	CD	32	CD
25	CD	37	CD	58	CD
54	CD	51	Cassette	13	CD
33	CD	41	CD	15	CD
41	CD	36	Cassette	22	Cassette
68	CD	69	Cassette	59	CD
55	Cassette	55	CD	47	Cassette
28	CD				

(a) By entering the data into two columns only (with one for age, the other for purchase), activate PivotTable Report to produce a contingency table. (Hint: convert your age data into categories, say Youth, Young Adult etc.)

(b) Undertake a chi-squared test to determine whether age and type of purchase are independent using the built-in facilities offered by Excel. Explain your answer.

Part 5

Measuring the Relationship Between Two Variables

Chapter 12

Correlation

Learning Outcomes

In this chapter, you will be made aware of how a relationship between two variables can be illustrated using a graph called a scatter diagram. If a straight line (or linear) relationship can be identified from the scatter diagram, you will see how its strength can be quantified using two statistical measures, the correlation coefficient and the coefficient of determination. The dangers of assuming the existence of certain 'relationships' between certain variables which actually may turn out to be false will be highlighted.

After completing this chapter you will be able to:

- Recognise how a scatter diagram may be used to identify if association exists between two numerical variables.
- Identify if a relationship is linear or non-linear.
- Determine the strength of a linear relationship using a suitable type of correlation coefficient and the coefficient of determination.
- Identify when a 'relationship' between two variables may be false.
- Calculate the correlation coefficient and the coefficient of determination using the built-in facilities offered by Excel.
- Determine the significance of the correlation coefficient.

Introduction

Most decision makers collect data either internal to or external to their organisation. This data may correspond to a production process, result from a market research survey or may even pertain to the staff working for the organisation. Whatever the origin of the data set, it may be fair to suggest that relationships exist between certain variables. For example, it could be reasonable to believe the volume sales of consumables such as food and drink are related to the level of advertising or external factors such as the weather.

In the last chapter you saw how association between two variables could be identified where at least one of these variables was categorical data.

It is also useful to be able to quantify the strength of any association between two numerical variables. If there was little association between expenditure on a certain method of advertising and unit sales of a particular item then the marketing group responsible may wish to review this particular advertising strategy. In this chapter you will see how this may be achieved by considering a statistic known as the **correlation coefficient**. This measure can be used to determine the strength of a linear (straight line) relationship which exists between two variables. Additionally, a second measure which is related to the correlation coefficient will also be described. This is called the **coefficient of determination**. As in previous chapters, you will follow examples which show firstly how manual calculations may be performed, and secondly, how the relevant facilities offered by Excel can be used to create scatter diagrams and compute the two coefficients.

The Scatter Diagram

Before determining the strength of any relationship between two variables, it is useful to produce a graphical presentation of the two variables in the data set. Depending upon the volume and accuracy of the data available, the graphical display can provide an indication of the type of relationship which may exist, if any, between the two variables. The type of graph used to illustrate such a relationship is known as a **scatter diagram**.

On a scatter diagram the variable you may be interested in forecasting is displayed on the **y axis**. This is often referred to as the **dependent variable**. In contrast, the **x axis** displays a variable which you can quantify within your organisation and this measurable variable is likely to affect the behaviour of the variable of interest. This is known as the **independent variable**. The corresponding pairs of x and y values are subsequently shown on the scatter graph by a set of points, but these points are *not* joined together. The graph will show indicate whether any changes in x cause a change in y, hence it may show if y is dependent upon x.

Figure 12.1 shows a scatter diagram produced using Excel. On this diagram the variable of interest is the new of new car insurance policies sold by county in 1997 and the measurable variable is the number of billboard adverts posted in the corresponding county. New policy sales and billboard postings have been recorded in 12 counties and each pair of x and y values are displayed on the graph by an individual point. The *whole of the pattern* on the scatter diagram indicates that association is likely to exist between the two variables. The shape of the points on the scatter diagram indicate that for a greater number of billboard postings, a higher number of new motor insurance sales in the corresponding county, and furthermore, the pattern displayed indicates the relationship is recognisably linear.

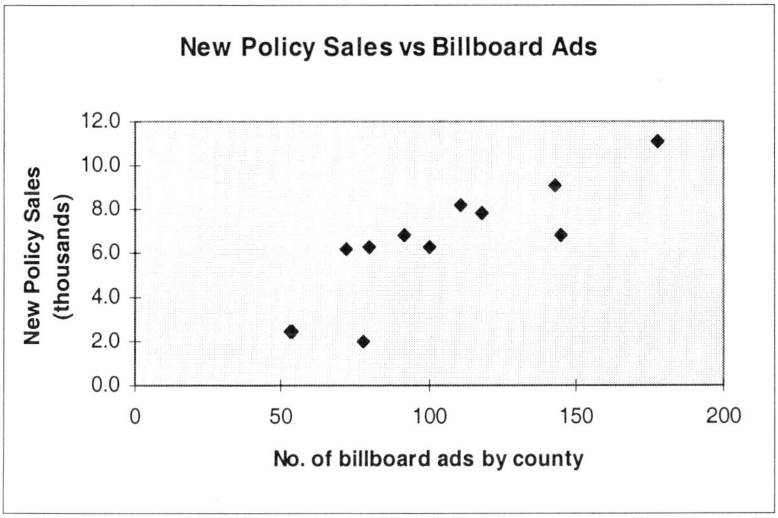

Figure 12.1 - Scatter diagram for insurance policy sales versus Billboard Advertisements

Figure 12.1 shows one type of relationship that may exist between two variables. Figure 12.2 shows a number of possible alternatives.

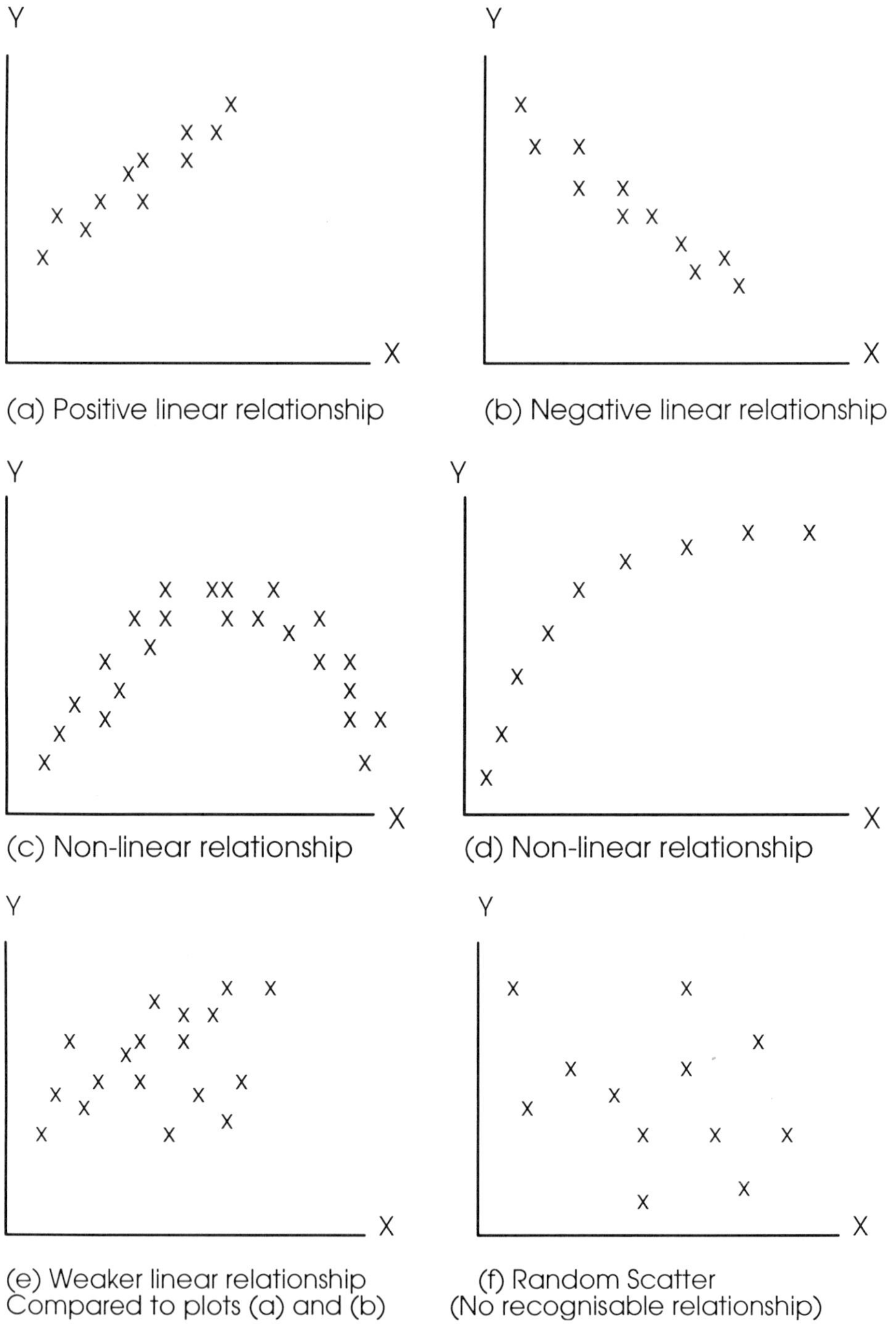

Figure 12.2 - Scatter diagrams illustrating various patterns

Examples (a) and (b) illustrate the difference between a positive and negative linear relationship. The latter may resemble the scatter diagram produced when considering the relationship between sales and price for a fast moving consumable. In this case, it would be fair to assume as price increases, sales decrease, and this relationship would be indicated by a scatter of points with a negative gradient.

In contrast, scatter diagrams (c) and (d) both suggest that relationships exist between two variables, but in a non-linear rather than linear manner. For example, diagram (c) suggests a non-linear relationship may exist due to the peak evident within the graph. A business scenario where a scatter diagram shows this type of relationship could be when the output from a market garden is recorded against the temperature of the greenhouses used in the production of fruit and vegetables. When the temperature of the greenhouses is either too hot or too cold, the output of fruit and vegetables is reduced. A 'best' temperature lying somewhere between these two extremes will yield a much higher output as illustrated by the turning point or peak on the scatter diagram. One common feature of both scatter diagrams (c) and (d) is that the points form a recognisable shape, which indicates a relationship may exist, albeit a non-linear relationship.

In comparison to diagram (a), diagram (e) illustrates a weaker linear relationship. This is evident because of the bigger spaces between the points on the graph. If the scatter diagram represented sales versus advertising exposure via magazine advertising for a package holiday, this suggests that only a moderate relationship exists between the variables. Moreover, it may be reasonable to suggest that sales could be influenced by other variables such as price, market share and the availability of credit.

Finally, scatter diagram (f) indicates that no relationship exists between two variables. This type of scatter is known as a random scatter, since the points displayed on the diagram contain no recognisable pattern.

In conclusion, the scatter diagram provides an indication whether a relationship may exist between two variables. If a scatter diagram is drawn which resembles either (a) or (b) in Figure 12.2, then it would be appropriate to measure the strength of such a relationship and perhaps forecast the value of one variable in terms of the other using the techniques to be described in the next two chapters. Scatter diagrams resembling (c) and (d) suggest a non-linear relationship exists between the variables. In both cases it is necessary to transform the data before measuring the strength of the relationship using the methods to be described. Transforming data is beyond the scope of this book. Finally, in the case of a scatter diagram (f) in Figure 12.2, the correlation coefficient would indicate that no association exists between the two variables. The scatter diagram is useful because it shows that it would be inappropriate to quantify the relationship between the two variables for the purpose of forecasting. The scatter diagram has shown the behaviour of variable y cannot be accurately described by the changes in variable x.

While the scatter diagrams shown so far have been presented in sketch form, a facility exists within Excel for creating this type of graph, and examples of Excel output incorporating scatter diagrams are provided later in the chapter. A detailed description on how to create any graph using Excel has been given in Chapter 3.

Determining the Strength of a Linear Relationship

In many cases, the scatter diagram may provide an initial indication that a relationship exists between two variables. However, it is likely that a decision maker may require an accurate measurement of the strength of such a relationship. This type of measurement is particularly useful when a decision maker wishes to develop a formal business model, say to forecast the behaviour of a particular variable of interest. For example, if a decision maker wishes to forecast value of sales for a certain item, then it may be useful to determine the degree of association between it and a number of identifiable variables such as advertising expenditure, market share and price.

One way of determining the strength of a relationship between sales and each of the variables listed above is by computing a statistic called the **correlation coefficient** between each pair of variables. Specifically, this is a statistical technique which can be used to quantify the strength of a **linear** relationship between two variables. This coefficient quantifies the scatter or distance between the points and a theoretical straight line. The more scattered the points are on the scatter diagram, the weaker the correlation is said to be between the two variables.

In practice, the correlation coefficient is represented by the letter **r**. In this chapter you will consider two methods of calculating **r**, namely:

- Spearman's rank correlation coefficient.
- Pearson's product moment correlation coefficient.

Both methods of calculating the correlation coefficient provide a measure of association which on a scale between and including -1 and +1. The value of r determined by either method can be interpreted in exactly the same way. The choice of correlation coefficient will depend upon the type of data under consideration and the subsequent examples provided in this chapter will indicate when each method is appropriate.

Interpretation of the Value of the Correlation Coefficient

The value of the correlation coefficient r provides an indication of the strength of relationship between two variables. However, the significance of the coefficient calculated will also depend upon the size of the data set considered. In general, the correlation coefficient may take on one of three 'extreme' values.

Any positive value of the correlation coefficient means that the general direction of the points on the scatter diagram is upwards, i.e. as variable x increases in value, y also increases. That is, a positive value of r indicates a positive linear relationship. If r is close to + 1 this suggests that a very strong positive relationship exists between the two variables.

If the correlation coefficient has a negative value, the general direction of the points on the scatter diagram is downwards, i.e. as variable x increases in value, y decreases. That is, a negative value of r indicates a negative linear relationship. Two variables which are likely to be negatively correlated are the value of sales and price of fast moving consumables, e.g. food and drink. If r is close to - 1, this suggests that a very strong negative relationship exists between the two data sets.

Finally, if r is close to zero in value, this suggests that the two variables are not linearly related. This could mean one of two things; either no relationship exists or if there is a relationship, it is not a straight line. The scatter diagram corresponding to the former would show a random scatter of points.

However, care should be taken in automatically assuming that certain values of the correlation coefficient mean that a relationship exists between two variables. You may also have to measure the significance of the value of r with respect to the size of the data set considered. This concept will be discussed at the end of the chapter.

Figure 12.3 below illustrates five scatter diagrams with a description of their shape and a suggestion of the likely value of r, assuming these data sets consist of about 10-20 pairs of observations.

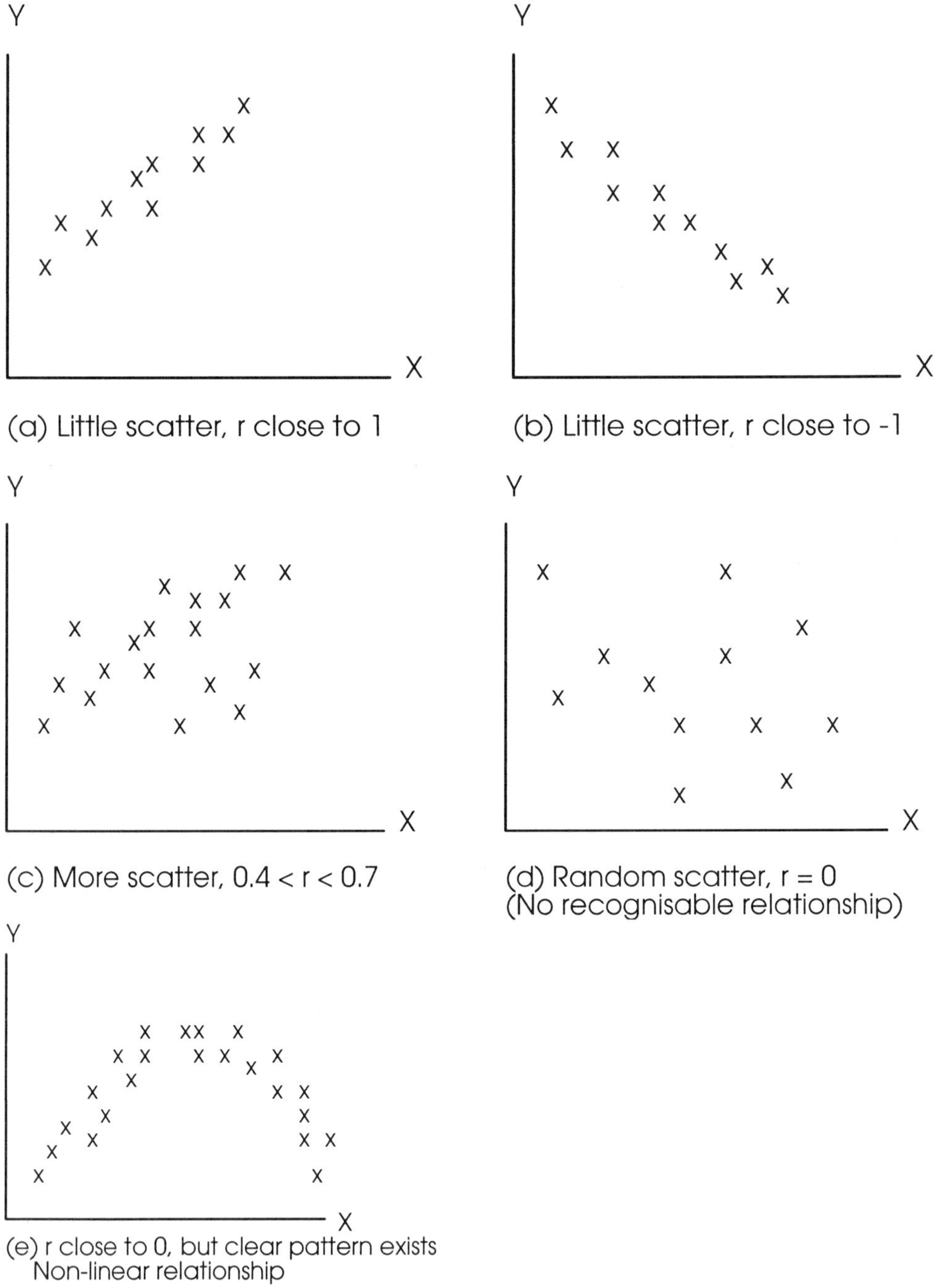

Figure 12.3 - Scatter diagrams and their likely values of r

Calculation of the Correlation Coefficient

As indicated already, the strength of a linear relationship can be measured by computing a correlation coefficient. The actual method of calculating this coefficient should reflect the type of data under consideration. In practice, this type of data can take two forms, non-numeric and quantitative. In the case of a non-numeric data set, ranks can be used to indicate order or position amongst a group of people or items. Despite the differences in application, the two formulae to be described are similar, although the rank correlation coefficient is easier to manipulate when performing calculations by hand. Pearson's method will be considered last because its application leads directly onto the concepts described in Chapter 13.

Rank Correlation Coefficient

The method of rank correlation uses the **ranks** of the values (these values may be numeric or non-numeric) found in a data set. This type of data consists of a set of values defined by their relative position within an ordered list. For example, the number 1 may represent the 'best' result and the number 10 the 'worst' result if ten candidates are ranked in their performance at a job interview. Ranks are considered to be particularly useful in market research surveys where respondents may be asked say to compare a number of bottled beers and place them in order of preference. In general, the rank correlation coefficient has two main applications:

- Measuring the correlation between non-numeric variables, like those described above.

- As an approximation to the product moment correlation coefficient (which is described later in this chapter). When a large data set needs to be analysed manually, the rank correlation coefficient can be used instead of the product moment correlation coefficient, since its formula is easier to manipulate. However, with the increased availability of computers and the provision of built-in statistical facilities within software such as Excel, it is very rare to have to use such an approximation.

To measure the rank correlation between two variables, **Spearman's rank** correlation coefficient formula should be used. This is represented by the equation:

$$\mathbf{r = 1 - \frac{6\sum d^2}{n(n^2 - 1)}}$$

where:

n = number of pairs of ranks

d = difference in value between the ranks of variables x and y

The evaluation and interpretation of Spearman's rank correlation coefficient is best illustrated by considering a specific business example.

Example 1: Measuring the relationship between ranked sales levels and league performance

The general manager of a national sportswear chain is interested in determining whether a relationship exists between the unit sales of football shirts and the league position of the club. Ten premier league clubs were selected at random, with their sales ranking within the chain and their final end-of -season league position recorded as ranks.

A rank of '1' in the table below represents the best performance both in terms of unit sales and final league standing, down to a rank of '10' which represents the poorest performance for both categories. The ranks awarded for each are recorded in the table shown in Figure 12.4.

Club	Volume sales **Rank**	Final league position **Rank**
Q	5	3
R	8	5
S	7	6
T	2	4
U	3	10
V	1	1
W	9	9
X	4	2
Y	10	8
Z	6	7

Figure 12.4 - Performance of each club in strip sales and league position

Each performance measure provided above represents a relative measure for each football club, i.e. '1' is a better performance than '2' but this doesn't necessarily mean that one club has performed twice as well as another. As a consequence, the most appropriate way of determining if a relationship exists between the performances of the clubs in both sales and league position is by using Spearman's rank correlation coefficient. As stated, this coefficient uses the formula:

$$r = 1 - \frac{6 \sum d^2}{n(n^2 - 1)}$$

For each applicant, **d** represents the difference in ranked performance in the two tests. The table labelled as Figure 12.5 shows the calculation of **d** and **d^2** for each football club.

Club	Volume sales	Final league position	**d**	**d^2**
	Rank	**Rank**		
Q	5	3	2 (i.e. 5- 3)	4 (i.e. 2x2)
R	8	5	3	9
S	7	6	1	1
T	2	4	-2	4
U	3	10	-7	49
V	1	1	0	0
W	9	9	0	0
X	4	2	2	4
Y	10	8	2	4
Z	6	7	-1	1
TOTAL (Σ)				76

Figure 12.5 - Calculation of difference in ranks

To determine the rank correlation coefficient the values of **n**, **n^2** and **d^2**, which has been calculated above, are substituted into Spearman's equation. Here, n is equal to 10 since we are considering 10 items, and therefore $n^2 = 100$.

$$r = 1 - \frac{(6 \times 76)}{10(100 - 1)}$$

$$r = 1 - \frac{456}{990}$$

$$r = 1 - 0.4606$$
$$r = 0.5394 \text{ (4dp)}$$

Given the value of the correlation coefficient (r = 0.5394), this suggests that there is only a moderate association between the volume of shirt sales and the final, end-of-season league position of the football club. This coefficient suggests the performance of the teams does not give a very strong indication of sales, despite the fact that the team who finished highest in the league also sold the most shirts. This may be explained by the behaviour of certain clubs in the data set. For example club U had the lowest league position but the third best level of sales.

Example 2: Measuring the relationship between percentage of supporters buying a shirt and league position

The sportswear company also conducted a survey with the permission of the clubs to see what proportion of supporters bought a club shirt. This survey was carried out by sending a questionnaire through the club to a representative sample of season ticket holders. The general manager of the sportswear chain wishes to determine whether the proportion of shirt ownership amongst season ticket holders is related to the final league position of their club. The data is shown in Figure 12.6 below:

Club	Percentage who own a club shirt	Final league position
		Rank
Q	50	3
R	60	5
S	55	6
T	55	4
U	50	10
V	55	1
W	65	9
X	70	2
Y	60	8
Z	45	7

Figure 12.6 - Percentage who own club shirt and final league position of club

Again, to determine the strength of the relationship between the percentage sales of shirts amongst each group of supporters and final league position, a suitable correlation coefficient must be calculated.

Inspection of the data shown in Figure 12.6, indicates that one variable (the final league position) has been recorded in ranked form, whilst the other data set (the percentage sales of shirts amongst each group of supporters) has been recorded in quantitative form. To measure the level of agreement between the two variables, they must first be presented in a **consistent** form. The only way this can be done is by ranking the quantitative data, i.e. the percentage sales of shirts amongst each group of supporters. When ranking this data, it is vital to use a method of ranking which is consistent with that used to rank their relative final league position, i.e. '1' represents the biggest percentage down to a rank of '10' for the club with the smallest percentage.

In ranking the percentage of shirt sales, it should be apparent that clubs R and Y both recorded 60%, S, T and V all recorded 55%, and Q and U both recorded 50%. When Spearman's coefficient is applied, these clubs must share the relevant ranks. To allocate ranks to each club the following calculations must be undertaken:

- List the clubs in descending order of sales, i.e. biggest percentage sales down to smallest. The order is:

X W (R Y) (S T V) (Q U) Z

Allocate ranks to the ordered list of football clubs.

Club:	X	W	(R Y)	(S T V)	(Q U)	Z
Rank:	1	2	(3 4)	(5 6 7)	(8 9)	10

In this example, clubs R and Y must share ranks 3 and 4, i.e. they are both allocated the rank 3½. In the same way, S, T and V share the ranks 5, 6 and 7 and as a consequence, each are awarded the rank 6, and finally, Q and U share the ranks 8 and 9, hence both are awarded the rank 8½. The ranks and differences for each club are shown in Figure 12.7.

Club	Percentage who own a club shirt	Final league position	Shirt ownership	**d**	$\mathbf{d^2}$
		Rank	**Rank**		
Q	50	3	8½	-5½	30¼
R	60	5	3½	1½	2¼
S	55	6	6	0	0
T	55	4	6	-2	4
U	50	10	8½	1½	2¼
V	55	1	6	-5	25
W	65	9	2	7	49
X	70	2	1	1	1
Y	60	8	3½	4½	20¼
Z	45	7	10	-3	9
TOTAL (Σ)					143

Figure 12.7 - Calculation of difference in ranks

In this example, Spearman's correlation coefficient takes the value:

$$\mathbf{r = 1 - \frac{6\,\Sigma d^2}{n(n^2 - 1)}}$$

$$r = 1 - \frac{(6 \times 143)}{10(100 - 1)}$$

$$r = 1 - \frac{858}{990}$$

$$r = 1 - 0.8667$$

$$\mathbf{r = 0.1333\ (4dp)}$$

Using Spearman's coefficient in this particular application, the general manager of the sportswear company can conclude there is little association between the proportion of season ticket holders owning a shirt and the final end-of-season position of their team.

Pearson's Product Moment Correlation Coefficient

When a decision maker is measuring the association between two quantitative variables, **Pearson's product moment** correlation coefficient should be used. This coefficient can be found using the formula:

$$\mathbf{r = \frac{n\Sigma xy - \Sigma x\Sigma y}{\sqrt{([n\Sigma x^2 - (\Sigma x)^2][n\Sigma y^2 - (\Sigma y)^2])}}}$$

where:

x and y represent the two variables under consideration, and

n represents the number of pairs of data points

In the same way as you considered Spearman's rank correlation coefficient, the application and interpretation of Pearson's product moment correlation coefficient is best illustrated by considering a specific business example.

Example 3: Measuring the association between new motor insurance policies and billboard advertisements over 12 counties.

A motor insurance company uses billboard advertisements as one method of advertising its products. Data has been collected for 12 English counties and the sales for 1997 (thousands of policies) and the number of billboard postings have been recorded in Figure 12.8 below. Unlike the data considered in Examples 1 and 2, the variable recorded in this example are both quantitative. As a consequence, Pearson's formula should be used to determine the degree of association between the number of new policies and the billboard postings. An indication of the likely values is given by the scatter diagram in Figure 12.1.

	Billboard Ads	**New Sales**			
	(x)	(y)	xy	x^2	y^2
	80	6.3	*504.0	**6400	***39.69
	92	6.8	625.6	8464	46.24
	143	9.1	1301.3	20449	82.81
	145	6.8	986.0	21025	46.24
	72	6.2	446.4	5184	38.44
	178	11.1	1975.8	31684	123.21
	100	6.3	630.0	10000	39.69
	53	2.5	132.5	2809	6.25
	118	7.8	920.4	13924	60.84
	54	2.5	135.0	2916	6.25
	78	2.0	156.0	6084	4.00
	111	8.2	910.2	12321	67.24
Total (Σ)	**1224**	**75.6**	**8723.2**	**141260**	**560.90**

Figure 12.8 - Insurance policy sales and billboard advertisements by county

Note:
* 504.0 = 80 x 6.3
** 6400 = 80 x 80
*** 39.69 = 6.3 x 6.3

The process is then repeated for all 12 pairs of observations. The columns are then totalled as shown above. From Figure 12.8, the following evaluations have been made:

$\Sigma x = 1224 \qquad \Sigma y = 75.6 \qquad \Sigma x^2 = 141260$

$\Sigma y^2 = 560.90 \qquad \Sigma xy = 8723.2 \qquad n = 12$ (12 English counties)

Substituting these values into the formula for Pearson's product moment correlation coefficient gives:

$$\mathbf{r = \frac{n\Sigma xy - \Sigma x\Sigma y}{\sqrt{([n\Sigma x^2 - (\Sigma x)^2][n\Sigma y^2 - (\Sigma y)^2])}}}$$

$$r = \frac{(12 \times 8723.2) - (1224 \times 75.6)}{\sqrt{([(12 \times 141260) - 1224^2][(12 \times 560.90) - 75.6^2])}}$$

$$r = \frac{(104678.4 - 92534.4)}{\sqrt{([1695120 - 1498176][6730.8 - 5715.36])}}$$

$$r = \frac{12144}{\sqrt{(199984815)}}$$

$$r = \frac{12144}{14141.6}$$

$$\mathbf{r = 0.859\ (3dp)}$$

In this example, the value of the correlation coefficient is much nearer to 1 than it is to 0. This indicates that there is reasonably strong positive linear association between the number of new policy sales and the number of billboard postings in each county. That is, the greater the number of billboard postings in an individual county, the higher the number of new motor insurance policies sold in that particular area. Therefore, for the service under consideration and the range of advertising exposure, you can conclude that sales seem highly influenced by the level of billboard postings recorded in the various counties, and importantly, the method of advertising may be assumed as effective.

The Coefficient of Determination (R^2)

An alternative measure of the degree of association between two variables is provided by the **coefficient of determination**. The coefficient of determination R^2 can be calculated by **squaring** the value of **r**.

The coefficient of determination provides a measure of the changes in the decision variable **y** which can be accounted for by the changes in the variable **x**. The value of this coefficient is usually displayed in percentage terms.

The correlation coefficient is measured on a scale between -1 and +1 inclusive, and so R^2 is measured on a scale between 0 and +1 inclusive. Given that the coefficient of determination R^2 is displayed in percentage terms, its value will be between 0% and 100% inclusive.

In particular, if R^2 = 100%, then for the sample of data considered, there will be perfect straight line association between the two variables. In other words, all of the changes in one variable can be accounted for by the changes in the other.

In Example 3 where the degree of association between motor insurance policy sales and the number of billboard postings was considered, the correlation coefficient r was computed to be **0.859**. Therefore, the coefficient of determination R^2 takes the value **0.7374** (i.e. 0.859 x 0.859). This tells us that **73.74%** of the changes in sales is accounted for by the changes in the number of billboards posted in each county. This indicates for the data set considered, a strong relationship exists between the two variables. However, you should be aware that 26.26% (.i.e. 100% - 73.74%) of the changes in sales may be accounted for by other variables such as price, market share and local competition which haven't yet been considered.

Using Excel to Determine the Correlation Coefficient

So far in the chapter, you have seen how a scatter diagram can be used to indicate the kind of relationship that exists between two variables, and also how the correlation coefficient can be used to quantify the relationship's strength. Both the scatter diagram and correlation coefficient can be generated quickly and accurately using Excel. The correlation coefficient can be generated by using the built-in function:

CORREL(y_data,x_data)

where y_data and x_data represent the observations of the two data sets under consideration.

In this part of the chapter, the application of Excel's **CORREL()** command to a pair of variables in a data set will be illustrated by reference to a number of specific examples.

Example 4: Measuring the degree of association between the performance of a group of students in an examination and their rate of absenteeism.

In this example, a group of 10 students sat an examination for which a mark was awarded as a percentage. Additionally, the rate of student absenteeism from seminars was also recorded. Figure 12.9 shows how this data was presented on the Excel worksheet. The scatter diagram included in Figure 12.9 indicates that a negative linear relationship exists between the two variables, i.e. as the level of absenteeism increases, the examination performance of the students decreases.

To measure the strength of this relationship, the **CORREL()** command has been used. On the worksheet illustrated, cell **E2** contains the formula:

=CORREL(A2:A11,B2:B11)

where:

A2:A11 represents the exam performance of each student in the data set
B2:B11 the corresponding rates of absenteeism

The value of the correlation coefficient r has been computed as **-0.83924**, which would support the assumption that a strong negative linear relationship exists between the two variables.

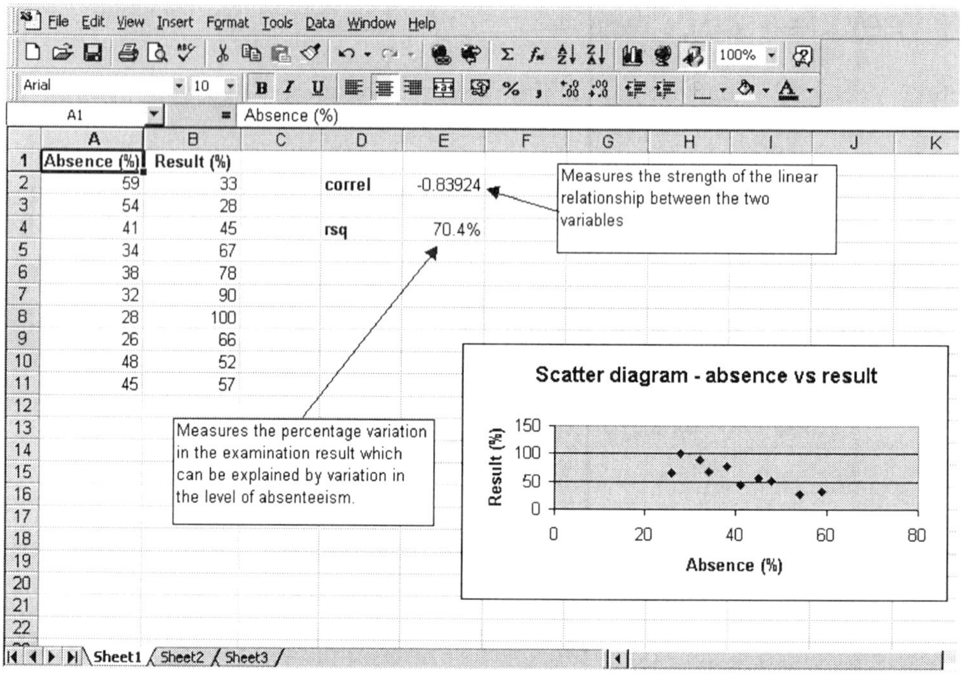

Figure 12.9 - Correlation output provided by Excel

Additionally, the coefficient of determination R^2 has been computed using the **RSQ()** command. In Figure 12.9, cell **E4** contains the formula:

=RSQ(A2:A11,B2:B11)

This calculation yields a value of **0.70433**, which suggests that just over 70% of the changes in examination performance is accounted for by changes in the rate of absenteeism.

Example 5: Measuring the degree of association between more than two variables using Excel.

So far, you have restricted the computation of the correlation coefficient to a pair of variables. However, there may be a number occasions when a you may wish to measure the degree of association between a greater number of variables in a data set. This can be achieved quickly using the **Data Analysis** facility offered by Excel.

To determine the correlation coefficient between a number of variables, you must select:

Correlation

from the toolpak. In Figure 12.10, the degree of association between four variables has been considered. The variables are student examination performance, rate of absenteeism, assignment performance and student age. When selecting the **Correlation** option from the toolpak, you are required to define the following ranges in the dialogue box as shown:

1. **The input range**. In the example below, the input range is represented by cells **A2:D11**. Selecting the data in this way, Excel assumes that four variables are under consideration, these being stored in columns A, B, C and D. **A1:D11** was defined as the range in the dialogue box, where row 1 houses the data labels. These are then used in the Excel output, and is indicated as such by **Labels in the First Row** being switched on.

2. **The output range**. This range should be defined so that it will not overwrite any of the original data set. In Figure 12.10, the output range was defined by cell reference **B13**.

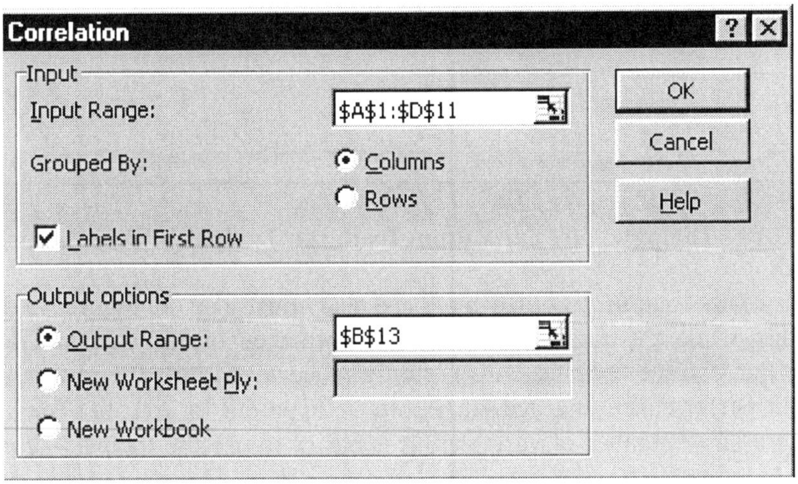

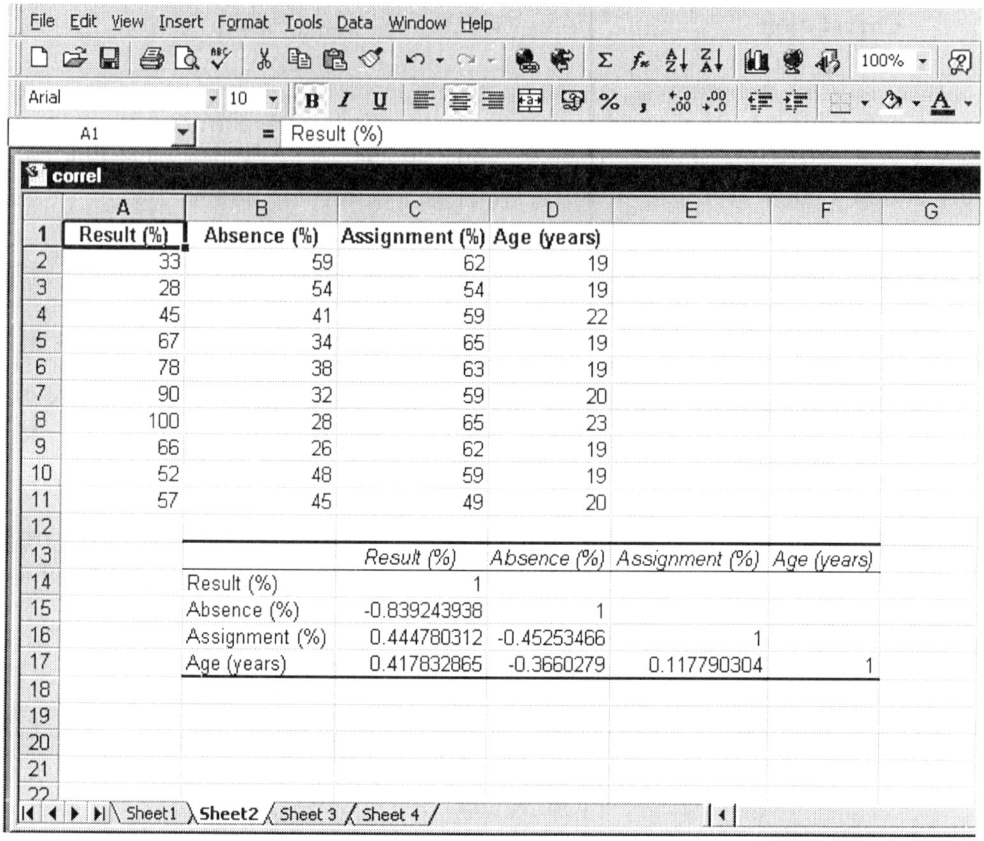

Result (%)	Absence (%)	Assignment (%)	Age (years)
33	59	62	19
28	54	54	19
45	41	59	22
67	34	65	19
78	38	63	19
90	32	59	20
100	28	65	23
66	26	62	19
52	48	59	19
57	45	49	20

	Result (%)	Absence (%)	Assignment (%)	Age (years)
Result (%)	1			
Absence (%)	-0.839243938	1		
Assignment (%)	0.444780312	-0.45253466	1	
Age (years)	0.417832865	-0.3660279	0.117790304	1

Figure 12.10 - Dialogue box and output from the Toolpak's Correlation facility

Inspection of the output provided by Excel and illustrated in Figure 12.10 would suggest that while the final examination performance of the students is strongly related to the level of absenteeism, it is only moderately correlated to the student's assignment performance and age. It should be apparent to you that for a data set containing a large number of variables, it is easier to use the toolpak's **correlation** than the individual **CORREL()** and **Copy** functions. However, when using the built-in CORREL() function, any changes made to the original data set, will result in automatic changes to the correlation coefficients calculated by Excel, whilst the toolpak facility generates numerical output only.

Example 6: Measuring the rank correlation coefficient using Excel

It is also possible to determine Spearman's rank correlation coefficient using Excel, although the spreadsheet doesn't provide an explicit rank correlation function. Since the formulae for Pearson's and Spearman's coefficients are similar, the **CORREL()** function can be used instead, for a data set displayed in rank form. For a large data set where one variable is ranked and the other is displayed in a quantitative form, the latter can be ranked by using the Excel command:

RANK(data_value,data_set,argument)

where the argument is **0** or **1** indicating ranks are descending or ascending respectively.

An example of this is shown in Figure 12.11 below.

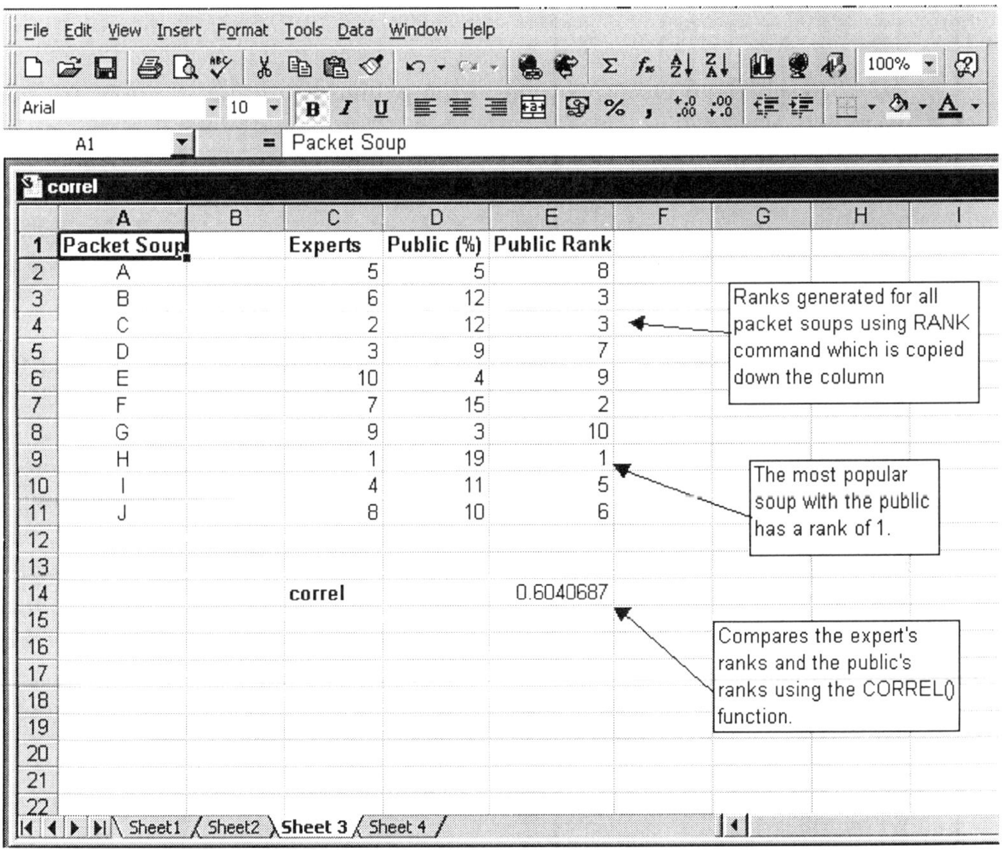

Figure 12.11 - Rank correlation calculation using Excel

In the example shown above, a panel of experts (drawn from restaurants and catering colleges) compared ten brands of packet soup by considering attributes such as taste and value for money. The soups have been ranked in preference, '1' representing the most preferred packet soup down by '10' representing the least preferred. A representative sample of the public have also been asked to select which soup they most prefer, and the percentages choosing each packet soup as their most preferred were shown in Figure 12.11.

To make the data comparative, the public responses have been ranked, from the soup with the greatest number of first preferences to the soup with the smallest percentage. This has been achieved using the **RANK()** command offered by Excel. Cell **E2** on the worksheet contains the formula:

=RANK(D2,D$2:D$11,0)

where:

> **D2** corresponds to the proportion of the public who prefer the first packet soup
>
> **D$2:D$11** corresponds to the public support for each of the ten packet soups
> This referenced has been fixed so that the formula can be copied down the column
>
> **0** will rank the soups in descending order of popularity, i.e. most popular to least popular. Alternatively, **1** would rank in ascending order.

One slight problem encountered when using the **RANK()** command offered command by Excel is that it doesn't share ranks for options with equal weighting. In the example above, both soups B and C should have been awarded the rank 3½ instead of rank 3. This slight difference should not however greatly affect the value of the subsequent correlation coefficient. After the ranks have been evaluated, the coefficient can then be calculated using the **CORREL()** command. Cell **D14** contains the formula:

=CORREL(C2:C11,E2:E11)

where:

> **C2:C11** contains the expert panel's ranks
> **E2:E11** contains the public's ranks

In this example, a correlation coefficient of **0.6041** has been computed, which suggests only a moderately high rather than extremely high level of agreement exists between the expert panel and the public. Nevertheless, inspection of the data set shows both the experts and the public actually agree in their choice of most preferred packet soup, namely soup H.

Identifying the True Cause and Effect Between Two Variables

In many applications of the scatter diagram and the correlation coefficient, it is reasonable for you to conclude that the two variables have association. In other words, the behaviour of one variable influences the behaviour of the other. In a number of cases, this conclusion may actually be false. The idea of making such a false assumption can be explained by considering the simple example provided below in Figure 12.12. Over number of years, the number of children per thousand suspended from primary schools has been recorded in two counties, one in the north, the other in the South. Drawing a scatter diagram like that in Figure 12.12 would suggest that a positive linear relationship exists between the two variables. However, it is highly debatable whether the rate of school suspensions in one county will have any influence on the rate in another county. This example shows the problem of false correlation or association being identified.

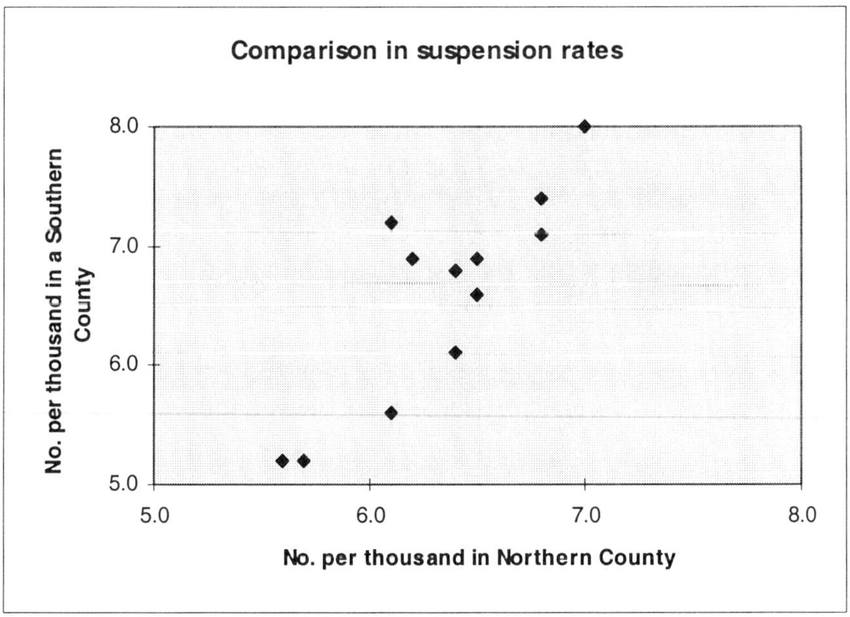

Figure 12.12 - Scatter diagram showing false correlation

In the example described above, the scatter diagram suggests an identifiable association because rates of school suspension in both counties are increasing in value with respect to time Specifically, both rates of suspension are increasing yearly, rather than the rate in one county increasing in response to increases in the other. More importantly, it should be apparent that measuring the rate of suspension in county X at a given time may not necessarily guarantee an accurate prediction for the rate of suspension in county Y in the future, given that different counties may introduce different policies to deal with the problems.

The example considered may be appear trivial, but it clearly illustrates the importance for you to be sure that a relationship is likely to exist between two variables and moreover, any relationship that you do identify is reasonable. For example, recent articles in the press have commented that people with certain first names in the UK pay less in car insurance than policy holders with other first names. In this business scenario, the true **'cause and effect'** of the association may not be immediately apparent, except consideration of the names connected would make you think association does exists, because certain first names are age related.

Determining the Significance of a Correlation Coefficient

Earlier in the chapter you were provided with a set of '*general*' guide-lines which may be used when interpreting the value of the correlation coefficient **r** (i.e. the 'extreme' values -1, 0 and +1). In many basic statistics courses delivered to Business Undergraduates, students do not consider the implications of the correlation coefficient beyond the explanation given above. In reality, you cannot necessarily say that a correlation coefficient of 0.8 between two variables is strong whilst a coefficient of 0.4 between two different variables indicates little association. If you have attempted Chapters 11 in this book, the concept described below should be straightforward. The coefficient determined is based on a data set of known size, and the significance of its value will also depend upon the size of the data set considered. If a small data set is being analysed, then a high value for the correlation coefficient must be determined in order to ensure that a significant relationship or association actually exists between the variables.

To measure the significance of the correlation coefficient r, an appropriate significance test can be undertaken. In measuring the statistical significance of the correlation coefficient, you must determine if it is significantly larger (or smaller) in statistical terms than zero if you want to confirm that a positive (or negative) relationship exists. In other words, by measuring the significance of this coefficient, you aim to provide evidence to suggest that a statistically significant relationship exists between two variables. You can assume that the correlation coefficients calculated for the various samples of data can be measured against critical values from the students' t-distribution.

From Example 3 described earlier in the chapter, the number of motor insurance policy sales in 1997 and billboard adverts were recorded for 12 English counties. For the twelve observations, a correlation coefficient of **0.859** was computed. Using the t-test statistic, it is possible to determine the significance of this correlation coefficient. The procedure for determining the significance of this coefficient is shown below.

- You must define an *appropriate* null and alternative hypothesis. In each hypothesis, r' has been used to denote the population correlation coefficient. The two hypotheses are shown below:

  H_0: r' = 0
  H_1: r' > 0

  In this test you will usually define a 1-sided alternative hypothesis. The reason for your choice is that from the sample of data considered, a positive correlation was calculated. The aim of the test (as illustrated by the choice of H_1) is to determine if the value of the correlation coefficient is *significantly* (statistically speaking) greater than zero. In contrast, for negative values of r, you would undertake a one-tailed test to determine if the true value of r was significantly smaller than zero and the alternative hypothesis would be H_1: r' < 0. The choice of the two hypotheses indicate that you believe no association exists unless there is significant evidence to the contrary. This concept is consistent with the tests considered in Chapters 11 and 12.

- The Marketing manager at the insurance company will only continue with billboard advertising campaign if it can be proven that the association between postings and new policy sales is highly significant. Given this requirement, you can work at the 1% level of significance, and you can obtain the critical value for the test statistic from the t-tables. The data set consisted of 12 observations. The test statistic for the correlation coefficient has *n-2* degrees of freedom. In this example, the number of degrees of freedom is 10. From tables, the critical value is:

  $$t_{0.05,10} = 2.76$$

- To determine the significance of the correlation coefficient, the following test statistic can be applied (this is derived from the test statistics you covered in Chapter 10):

  $$t = \frac{r}{\sqrt{((1-r^2)/(n-2))}}$$

where:

r represents the correlation coefficient determined from the sample of data, and

n is equal to the number of pairs of data points.

From Example 3, the correlation coefficient was calculated to be **0.859** for **12** data points. Substituting these values into the equation for the test statistic, gives:

$$t = \frac{0.859}{\sqrt{((1-0.859^2)/10)}}$$

$$= \mathbf{5.306\ (3dp)}$$

- Since 5.306 is greater than the critical value 2.76, the null hypothesis H_0 can be rejected, since the value of the test statistic lies in the critical region of the relevant t distribution. Therefore, at the 1% level of significance, you can conclude that the correlation coefficient is significantly larger than zero, and hence there is a statistically significant association between sales of new motor insurance policies and billboard postings by county.

Equally, you can determine the value of r which is significant for a data set of certain size. This can be calculated by rearranging the formula for the t statistic presented above. For the example above, where n is 12, and the corresponding critical value for t is 2.76, the critical value r, after substituting and re-arranging the formula is ± **0.6576** (4dp). This can be calculated using the rearranged equation:

$$t = t/\sqrt{(n - 2 + t^2)}$$

where t represents the critical value from the students' *t*-distribution which considers the size of the data set and the pre-defined level of significance.

Therefore, if the absolute value of r exceeds **0.6576** (i.e. r is between -1 and -0.6576 inclusive or between +0.6576 and +1 inclusive), the level of correlation between the two variables is statistically significant at the 1% level of significance.

Although Excel offers built-in facilities to determine the correlation coefficient, it doesn't offer an explicit facility for measuring its statistical significance. However, once **r** has been calculated using either the **CORREL()** command or the

Correlation facility from the toolpak, the steps outlined above should be easy to undertake semi-manually.

Review

In this chapter you have adopted a systematic approach which can be used when identifying and quantifying the strength of a linear relationship between two variables. The steps you should take are:

1. Draw a scatter diagram to represent the data set collected. Identify the nature of the relationship suggested by the scatter diagram.

2. Make sure that any association identified is reasonable, and not caused by the behaviour of an additional, perhaps unidentified variable.

3. Determine the strength of association between two qualitative variables using **Spearman's rank** correlation coefficient.

4. When considering quantitative variables, identify from the scatter diagram whether the relationship is linear or non-linear. Measure the strength of a relationship between two quantitative variables using **Pearson's product moment** correlation coefficient.

5. Use Excel to undertake the computation of the correlation coefficient both quickly and accurately.

Conclusions

Correlation offers you a way of measuring the strength of a linear relationship between two variables. The correlation coefficient can be used to identify which variable or variables best explain the behaviour of a particular variable of interest. A manufacturer of fast moving consumable products may be interested in which variables best explain the value of sales. Variables such as price, level of advertising and market share can be measured and their corresponding degree of association with sales can be quantified.

In determining whether relationships exist between variables in a data set, it is important to determine the true extent of any 'cause and effect' within these relationships. It may be necessary to identify whether any variables considered merely indicate false correlation.

In this chapter, you have been made aware of the application of two correlation coefficients by making reference to a number of worked examples. These examples include the necessary calculations and an interpretation of the results obtained. Additionally, reference has been made to the correlation facilities offered by **Excel**. In describing Excel's correlation facilities through specific worked examples, you have been provided with a clear indication of the ease at which correlation can be measured within a spreadsheet environment.

Learning Outcomes Checklist

After completing this chapter you should have an understanding of the following concepts, calculations and functions:

- How to determine whether a relationship may exist between two variables using a scatter diagram.
- Identify linear and non-linear relationships from a scatter diagram.
- How to measure the strength of a linear relationship between two variables using the correlation coefficient and the coefficient of determination.
- How to calculate the correlation coefficient manually for numerical and non-numerical data.
- Understanding that the correlation between two variables may be false.
- An awareness of the Excel functions **CORREL()** and **RSQ()** and the scatter graph facility present in **ChartWizard**.

Ensure that you understand these concepts before progressing to Chapter 13.

Chapter Case Question

- Open the file **CHAP01.XLS**
- Create scatter diagrams for the following relationships and comment upon the shape of the points:

  Turnover and number of guest beers
  Turnover and number of promotions
  Turnover and pub capacity

- Calculate the following correlation coefficients for the following using Excel's **CORREL()** function:

  Turnover and number of guest beers
  Turnover and number of promotions
  Turnover and pub capacity

- For the relationships listed, calculate the coefficient of determination using Excel's RSQ() function, presenting the values as a percentage formatted to one decimal place. Provide an interpretation of their value.

- Which variable provides the best explanation for turnover?

- Save the amended file as CHAP12.XLS

Supplementary Questions

1. What is a scatter diagram? Describe why this type of diagram is useful when identifying the degree of association between two variables.

2. Sketch the following scatter diagrams:

   (a) A random scatter.

   (b) A moderate positive relationship between two variables.

   (c) A strong positive relationship between two variables.

   (d) A moderate negative relationship between two variables.

   (e) A strong negative relationship between two variables.

Give examples of business data which may behave like those described above.

3. Describe briefly the difference between Spearman's Rank and Pearson's Product Moment correlation coefficients?

4. Describe briefly the term coefficient of determination.

5. A premier league football team has signed a new contract with a kit manufacturer. The manufacturer has produced seven designs for the team's new home kit. Representatives of the team's board were asked to rank these

kits in order of preference, '1' being the most preferred choice. Supporters representatives were asked to do the same. The following data was collected:

Kit	A	B	C	D	E	F	G
Club	2	6	1	4	3	5	7
Supporters	5	7	1	3	4	2	6

(a) Calculate Spearman's correlation coefficient manually.

(b) What does this coefficient suggest?

(c) Which kit should the club choose? Why?

(d) Check your results using Excel.

6. The same manufacturer produces kits for 10 English teams. The marketing team believes the number of shirts sold in the season 1996-97 is related to the number of the club's players appearing in the European Championship. The following data is available:

Club	A	B	C	D	E	F	G	H	I	J
Players	0	2	3	1	4	9	2	1	2	6
Sales (000s)	15.5	18.2	60.1	12.8	20.4	120.1	30.2	10.4	15.0	55.6

(a) Present the data using a scatter diagram.

(b) Does the scatter diagram indicate whether linear association exists?

(c) Calculate Pearson's Product Moment correlation coefficient and the coefficient of determination by hand.

(d) What do these coefficients suggest?

(e) Check your results using Excel.

7. A group of six applicants for an IT apprenticeship were ranked according to their performance in a numeracy test and a literacy test. Using the appropriate method, determine the correlation between their performance in these two tests.

Candidate	1	2	3	4	5	6
Numeracy test	4	2	3	6	1	5
Literacy test	1	6	4	5	3	2

Check your result using Excel.

8. A market research company compared the popularity of eight family cars with a group of experts and members of the public. The following data set was collected. The experts ranks are such that '1' represents the best car, down to '8' which represents the worst car. In contrast, the public's first choices are expressed as a percentage.

Car	A	B	C	D	E	F	G	H
Experts	3	4	8	5	1	7	2	6
Public	20	9	3	9	11	15	15	18

Using the appropriate method, determine the correlation between the opinions of the panel and the public and interpret the result.

Check your result using Excel. Why is there a slight difference in the results obtained?

9. The sales (thousands of bars) and price (pence) of ten bars of chocolate were recorded as follows:

Bar	1	2	3	4	5	6	7	8	9	10
Sales	125	78	224	67	130	55	91	43	77	49
Price	20	25	26	21	22	22	24	22	23	21

Present the data set above using a scatter diagram. What does this diagram suggest? Determine the correlation between sales and price of the chocolate bars and interpret this result. Also compute the coefficient of determination.

Again, check your results using Excel.

10. Explain the concept of false correlation. Provide business related examples when false correlation may occur.

Chapter 13

Simple Linear Regression

Learning Outcomes

In the last chapter, you saw how a linear relationship between two variables may be identified using a graph called a scatter diagram and how its strength could be measured using the correlation coefficient. If a linear relationship is suggested by this graph, you will see how it can be quantified using the equation of the straight line. In particular, you will describe and determine the 'best' straight line relationship between two variables using a technique known as least squares regression. Once this 'best' relationship has been determined, you will see how it can be used to describe a business situation and forecast values of the decision variable.

After completing this chapter you will be able to:

- Recognise whether a linear relationship exists from the appearance of the scatter diagram.
- Calculate the least squares regression equation manually.
- Calculate the least squares regression equation using the built-in facilities offered by Excel.
- Use the regression equation to predict values of the decision variable (variable of interest).
- Forecast from a time related data set.

Introduction

In the last chapter, you saw how a linear relationship between two variables can be identified using a graph called a **scatter diagram**. If a linear relationship was identified, you discovered how its strength could be measured by calculating a statistic called the **correlation coefficient**. In this chapter you will look in greater detail at the linear relationship which may exist between two variables.

In particular, if a linear relationship is suggested by the scatter diagram, it may be useful to quantify this using the equation of a straight line. Once the equation of the straight line has been determined, it may be used to describe the relationship that exists and also predict values of the decision variable. In quantifying a linear relationship, you will be able to define and calculate the equation of the 'best' straight line. This 'best' straight line is known as **least squares regression**. Using this straight line, y represents the dependent variable and x is the independent or measurable variable.

In this chapter, you will be provided with examples which demonstrate how the calculation of the regression equation may be undertaken manually, and secondly, how the relevant facilities offered by Excel can be used to create scatter diagrams and perform the necessary calculations.

The Least Squares Regression Equation

A linear relationship can be *approximated* for a scatter diagram displaying a recognisable straight line pattern by drawing a line on the scatter diagram as close as possible to the points. This method will have varying amounts of accuracy depending upon the shape and spread of the data points.

To counter the potential error in the process of estimating the straight line and its equation, a **'best line'** can be found using a formal statistical technique. This best possible line is called the **least squares regression equation**. In general, the equation of the straight line is given by:

$$y = a + bx$$

where:

a = intercept on the y-axis (i.e. the point where the line crosses the y-axis),

b = gradient (or slope) of the straight line.

When determining the regression equation, you need to calculate the most appropriate values for coefficients a and b. On the scatter diagram presented in Figure 13.1, for a given value of x, the actual value y has been indicated by **x**. Additionally, the corresponding predicted or fitted value of y (found using the regression equation) and is labelled **y'** is indicated by +. The difference between these two values is the potential error associated with the simple regression equation and is represented by the letter e. It follows that for each value x in the data set, you can expect to calculate a difference between the actual value of y and that predicted by the equation of the 'best' straight line.

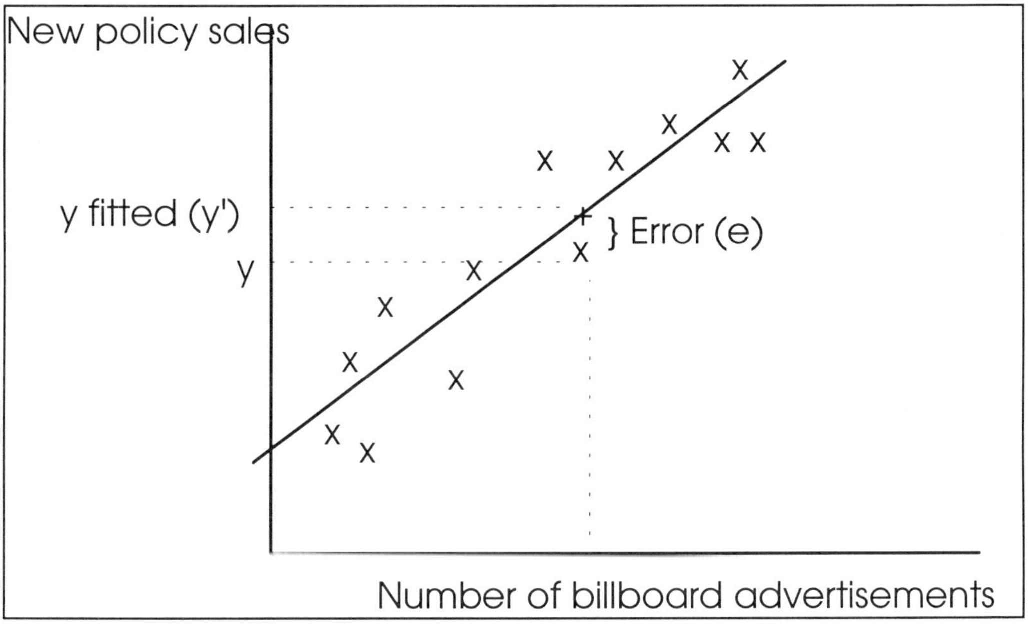

Figure 13.1 - Scatter diagram showing the 'best' straight line

When determining the 'best' or most accurate straight line relationship between y and x you need to minimise these errors or differences. If the errors are small, then the straight line can be considered as a 'good fit', i.e. it accurately describes the (straight line) relationship that exists between the two variables y and x in the sample of data. By minimising the sum of the squares of these errors so that the negative and positive errors are treated equally (hence the term 'the least squares regression line'), the equation of the 'best' straight line can be defined as:

$$\mathbf{y = a + bx}$$

where:

$$b = \frac{n\Sigma xy - \Sigma x\Sigma y}{n\Sigma x^2 - (\Sigma x)^2}$$

and $a = \bar{y} - b\bar{x}$

where:

x and y represent the two variables under consideration

$\bar{x}$ and $\bar{y}$ are the average values of x and y respectively

n is the number of points on the graph (i.e. pairs of observations)

Using the formula displayed above, you should be aware that *b is always calculated before a*, since the formulae for ***a*** depends upon the value of ***b***.

Inspection of the formula representing the gradient b in the straight line equation shows its value is calculated using two components, $n\Sigma xy - \Sigma x\Sigma y$ and $n\Sigma x^2 - (\Sigma x)^2$. Both of these components are used in the manual calculation of the correlation coefficient (as demonstrated in Chapter 12). Once this calculation has been undertaken, and its value indicates a strong linear association, the (justifiable) calculation of the gradient in the regression equation should be easy (i.e. divide the value of the first component by the value of the other).

Now that the 'best' straight line has been defined, you will identify how it can be determined for a particular data set. Once the equation of the straight line has been calculated, you can interpret the values of the coefficients a and b and demonstrate how the equation may be used to provide forecasts.

Example 1: Quantifying the linear relationship between the number of new motor insurance policies sold and the number of billboard advertisements for 12 English counties

A motor insurance company uses billboard advertisements as one method of advertising its products. Data has been collected for 12 English counties and the sales for 1997 (thousands of policies) and the number of billboard postings have been recorded in Figure 13.2 below. In chapter 12 you considered this data set and computed a correlation coefficient of **0.859** between new policy sales and the number of billboard postings by county. This suggested that a strong and recognisable linear relationship exists between the two variables. Moreover, because a linear relationship has been identified, it may be useful to determine the equation of the 'best' straight line. This straight line measures the impact of billboard postings on new insurance policy sales and may be used to forecasts sales for given levels of billboard advertising. Before calculating the equation, the variables y and x should be formally defined. In this example, you are interested in predicting the sales of new insurance policies, so this represents the y variable. Sales are influenced by the number of billboard advertisements, which in turn, can be measured by the insurance company. The latter represents the measurable or x variable. The calculation of the regression equation is shown below.

Billboard Ads		**New Sales**		
	(x)	(y)	xy	x^2
	80	6.3	*504.0	**6400
	92	6.8	625.6	8464
	143	9.1	1301.3	20449
	145	6.8	986.0	21025
	72	6.2	446.4	5184
	178	11.1	1975.8	31684
	100	6.3	630.0	10000
	53	2.5	132.5	2809
	118	7.8	920.4	13924
	54	2.5	135.0	2916
	78	2.0	156.0	6084
	111	8.2	910.2	12321
Total (Σ)	**1224**	**75.6**	**8723.2**	**141260**

Figure 13.2 - Insurance policy sales and billboard advertisements by county

Note: * 504.0 = 80 x 6.3

** 6400 = 80 x 80

From the table in Figure 13.2:

$\Sigma x = 1224$ $\Sigma y = 75.6$ $\Sigma x^2 = 141260$

$\Sigma xy = 8723.2$ $n = 12$

$\bar{x} = 102$ $\bar{y} = 6.3$
(i.e. 1224/12) (i.e. 75.6/12)

Substituting these values into the formula for the least squares regression line you get:

$$b = \frac{n\Sigma xy - \Sigma x \Sigma y}{n\Sigma x^2 - (\Sigma x)^2}$$

$$b = \frac{(12 \times 8723.2) - (1224 \times 75.6)}{(12 \times 141260) - 1224^2}$$

$$b = \frac{(104678.4 - 92534.4)}{(1695120 - 1498176)}$$

$$\mathbf{b = 0.0617\ (4dp)}$$

$$\mathbf{a = \bar{y} - b\bar{x}}$$

$$a = 6.3 - (0.0617 \times 102)$$

$$\mathbf{a = 0.0105\ (4dp)}$$

The regression equation which describes the relationship between the sales of new insurance policies and billboard postings is:

$$y = a + bx$$

New policy sales (000s) = 0.0105 + 0.0617 x Number of billboard postings

Interpreting the values of the coefficients in the regression equation

Once the regression equation has been determined, it can be used to forecasts sales of new insurance policies for different amounts of billboard postings. Before illustrating this, you will interpret the values of coefficients a and b in the equation determined above.

The regression line is given by the equation **y = a + bx**

- The value of a is referred to as the y intercept and is equal to the value of y (in this example sales of motor insurance) when x (i.e. number of billboard postings) is equal to zero. In the regression equation calculated, a is equal to 0.0105. This tells us that when no billboards are posted in a particular county, expected new sales of the motor insurance would be **10.5**.

- The coefficient b represents the gradient of the regression line and this tells you the change (i.e. increase or decrease) in the value of the decision variable (y) in response to unit changes in the measurable variable (x). As a consequence, the value of coefficient b is much more likely to be of greater interest to you than the value of coefficient a. The correlation coefficient calculated for this data set in Chapter 12 suggested that a recognisable positive relationship exists between sales of the motor insurance and the number of billboard postings. Therefore, you would expect a positive value for b. Specifically, the value of the coefficient b tells us the expected increase in sales for a unit increase in the number of billboard adverts. Therefore, for every additional billboard posting, you would expect the value of sales to increase by the value of b, namely 61.7.

Using the regression line for prediction

For a pre-defined level of advertising, you can forecast the expected value of sales by substituting the appropriate value into the regression equation. If you wish to predict sales for a particular county in which 60 billboard postings are planned, you should substitute 60 into the regression equation.

The regression equation is: y = 0.0105 + 0.0617x

i.e. **New policy sales (000s) = 0.0105 + 0.0617 x Number of billboard postings**

Substituting the value of 60 into the equation above:

Sales (1000's) = 0.0105 + (0.0617 x 60)
= 0.0105 + 3.6997
= 3.7102

Given that sales are measured in thousands, this forecast corresponds to 3,710 new insurance policies.

Therefore, for a county where 60 billboard advertisements are planned, you have forecast the number of new insurance policy sales to be 3,710 for the county under consideration.

You have now seen that forecasting using the simple regression equation is straightforward. However, you must be cautious when forecasting the expected value of sales for a level of billboard advertising exposure which is **outside** the range of values used to determine the regression equation. In the example, the number of billboard postings range between 53 and 178 for the counties considered, i.e. the lowest and highest values of x in the data set. For a number of postings inside this range, you have identified that a linear relationship exists between sales and billboard postings. You can assume that this relationship is representative for the counties in the population where the level of billboard postings lies inside this defined range. However, you cannot assume that the regression equation determined will still be the 'best line of fit' for levels of billboard posting which do not fall inside this range. This is illustrated by diagram in Figure 13.3.

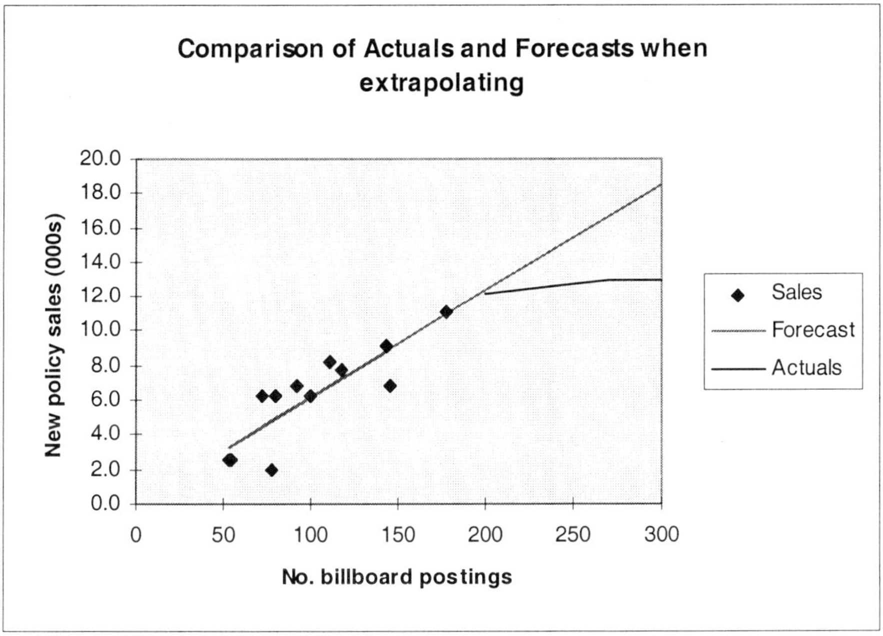

Figure 13.3 - Problems encountered by extrapolating the regression line

Over the range of values of x (number of billboard postings) contained in the data set, you can be confident about forecasting the value of sales because of the strength of the linear relationship (correlation coefficient **r = 0.859**, as shown in Chapter 12). However, if the number of billboard advertisements for a particular county is significantly bigger than those represented in the data sample, then it is unlikely that value of sales will simply increase in a linear manner (the opposite may also be true for a level of billboard advertising which is significantly lower than those found in the sample data). Demand for the motor insurance will have an upper limit and in particular, competition for sales exist from other products and companies. As a consequence, unit sales are likely to reach an optimum level, above which additional billboard advertising will have little or no influence on their value. The likely relationship between sales and billboard advertising for higher values of the measurable variable has been indicated by the dotted line in Figure 13.3.

Any forecasts corresponding to levels of billboard postings which do not fall inside the sample range are known as **extrapolations**, whilst forecasts corresponding to a number of billboard adverts inside the sample range are known as **interpolations**. For most data sets including the one under consideration, be cautious when extrapolating, and the more distant you are from this range, the less reliable the resultant forecasts are likely to be.

Using Excel to Determine the Regression Equation

So far in the chapter, you have seen how a scatter diagram can be used to indicate whether a linear relationship exists between two variables, and also how the least squares regression line can be used to quantify this relationship. Both the scatter diagram and the regression equation can be generated quickly and accurately using Excel. In particular, the coefficients a and b in the regression equation (intercept **a** and slope **b**) can be determined using the built-in functions:

INTERCEPT(y data, x data)
SLOPE(y data, x data)

In the next example, you will apply these two functions to a pair of variables and interpret the output. *It is important to note that the y data block must always be specified first and the x data block second within these two Excel functions.*

Example 2: Measuring the linear relationship between monthly attendance at an outdoor theme park and the number of days rain

The attendance (in thousands) at an outdoor theme park was recorded for 10 summer months. The manager of theme park is certain that the weather influences the level of attendance. For each month in the data set, the number of rainy days has been recorded. Figure 13.4 shows how this data was presented on the Excel worksheet. The scatter diagram included in Figure 13.4 indicates that a negative linear relationship exists between the two variables, i.e. as the number of rainy days increases, monthly attendance at the theme park decreases.

To quantify the linear relationship between the two variables, the **INTERCEPT()** and **SLOPE()** commands have been used. On the worksheet illustrated, cells **D17** and **D18** contain the formulae:

=INTERCEPT(D6:D15,C6:C15)
=SLOPE(D6:D15,C6:C15)

where:

range **D6:D15** represent the monthly attendance at the theme park (i.e. the y variable) and
range **C6:C15** represent the corresponding number of rainy days (the x variable)

As indicated above, the **y range** has been specified **first** (the level of attendance) and the **x range** (the number of rainy days) specified **second**.

For this data set, the value of the least squares regression line has been computed as:

$$y = 13.7275 - 1.0875\,x$$

i.e. **Attendance = 13.7275 - 1.0875 Days rain**

The negative value of the slope, i.e. -1.0875, supports the assumption that a negative linear relationship exists between the two variables. Specifically, this value suggests that for every additional rainy day, monthly attendance at the theme park falls by 1,088. Moreover, for a completely dry month, the expected attendance at the theme park is 13,728.

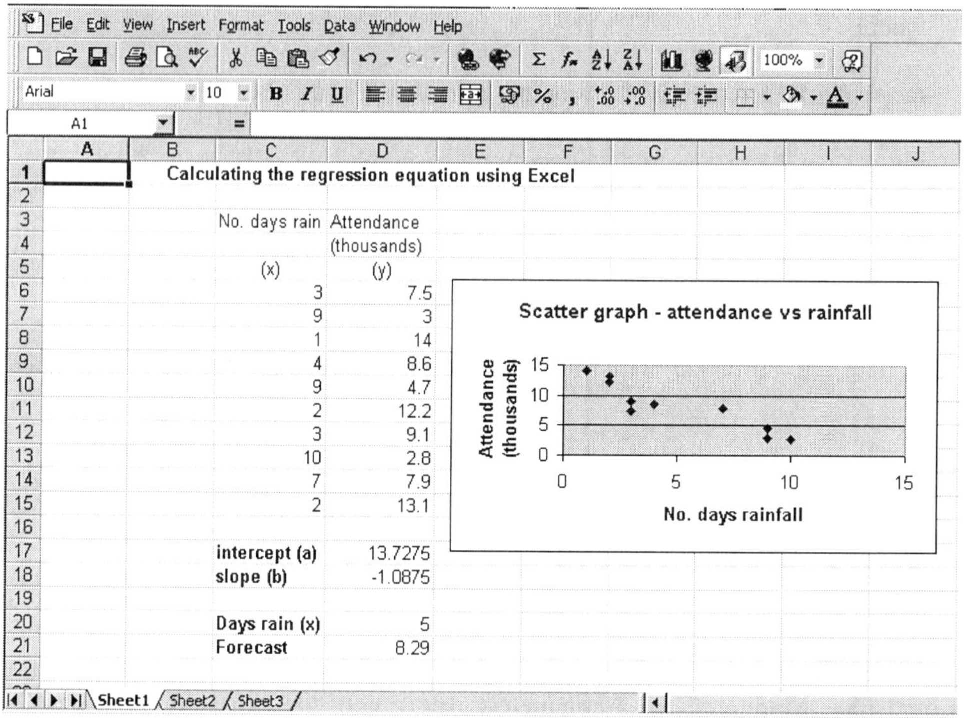

Figure 13.4 - Simple regression output and scatter diagram provided by Excel

In addition to the **INTERCEPT()** and **SLOPE()** command, the built-in **FORECAST()** facility can be used to forecast from a simple regression equation. In the example provided, you may be interested in determining the monthly attendance at the theme park when the number of rainy days is expected to be 5. The formula in cell **D21** is:

=FORECAST(D20,D6:D15,C6:C15)

where cell **D20** contains the value of x for which corresponds to the forecast. The result tells us that for a month containing five wet days, the expected attendance at the theme park is 8,290.

Example 3: Determining the regression equation using Excel'stoolpak.

An alternative way of determining the regression equation within Excel is by using the appropriate facility housed in the **Analysis Toolpak**. This facility is particularly useful because it can be used to develop multiple regression equations, where the behaviour of a decision variable y is explained by two or more x variables. The multiple regression equation is beyond the scope of this book and only simple regression will be considered.

To determine the linear relationship that exists between two variables, the decision maker must select the option:

Regression

from the **toolpak**. In Figure 13.5, you will see how we can quantify the linear relationship between the cost of materials used each day in a small dental practice (y) and the umber of patients attending (x). When selecting the **Regression** option from the toolpak, you are required to define the following in the dialogue box:

The y range. In this example, the y range is represented by cells **C6:C15**.

The x range. On the worksheet in Figure 13.5, the x range is represented by cells **E6:E15**.

The output range. This range should be defined so that it will not overwrite any of the original data set. For the data stored on the worksheet shown below, the output range was defined by entering cell reference **A20** before clicking **OK**. This cell reference represents the top left hand corner of the output generated.

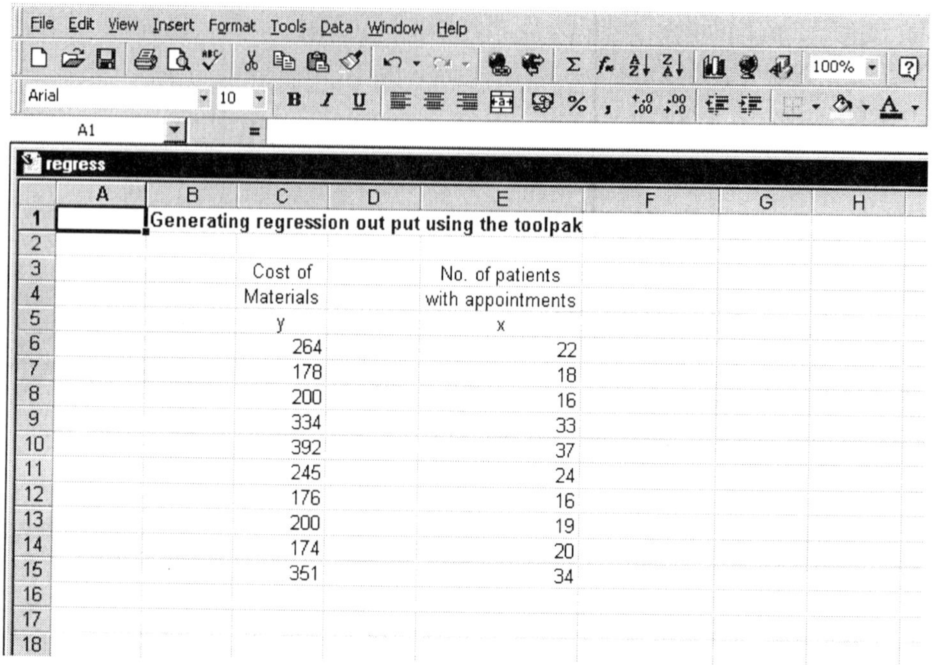
File Edit View Insert Format Tools Data Window Help
100%
Arial
10
A1
regress
Generating regression out put using the toolpak
Cost of Materials y
No. of patients with appointments x
264 22
178 18
200 16
334 33
392 37
245 24
176 16
200 19
174 20
351 34

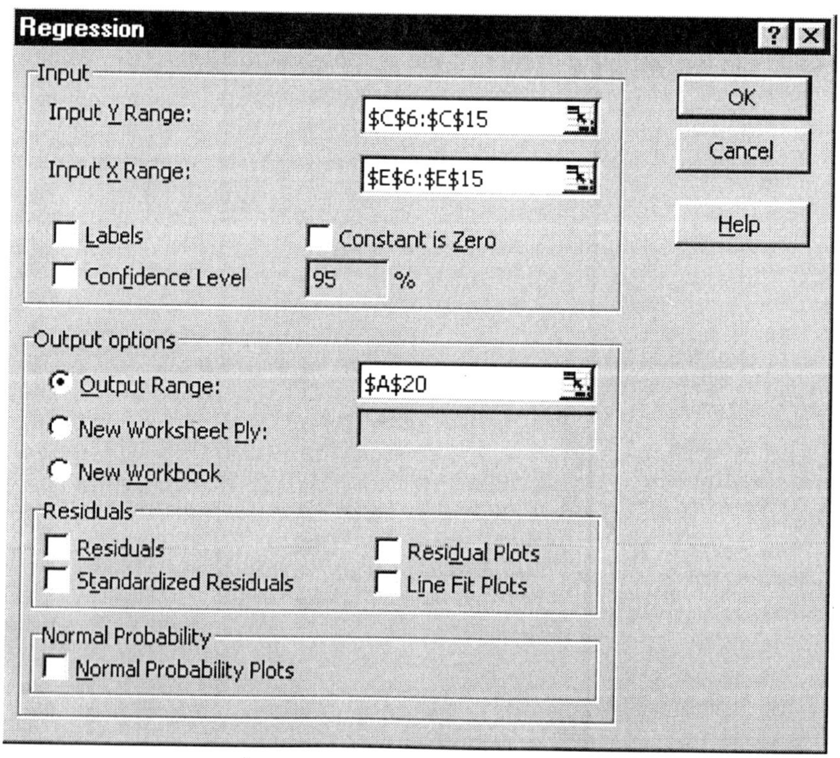
Regression
Input
Input Y Range: $C$6:$C$15
Input X Range: $E$6:$E$15
Labels
Constant is Zero
Confidence Level 95 %
OK
Cancel
Help
Output options
Output Range: $A$20
New Worksheet Ply:
New Workbook
Residuals
Residuals
Residual Plots
Standardized Residuals
Line Fit Plots
Normal Probability
Normal Probability Plots

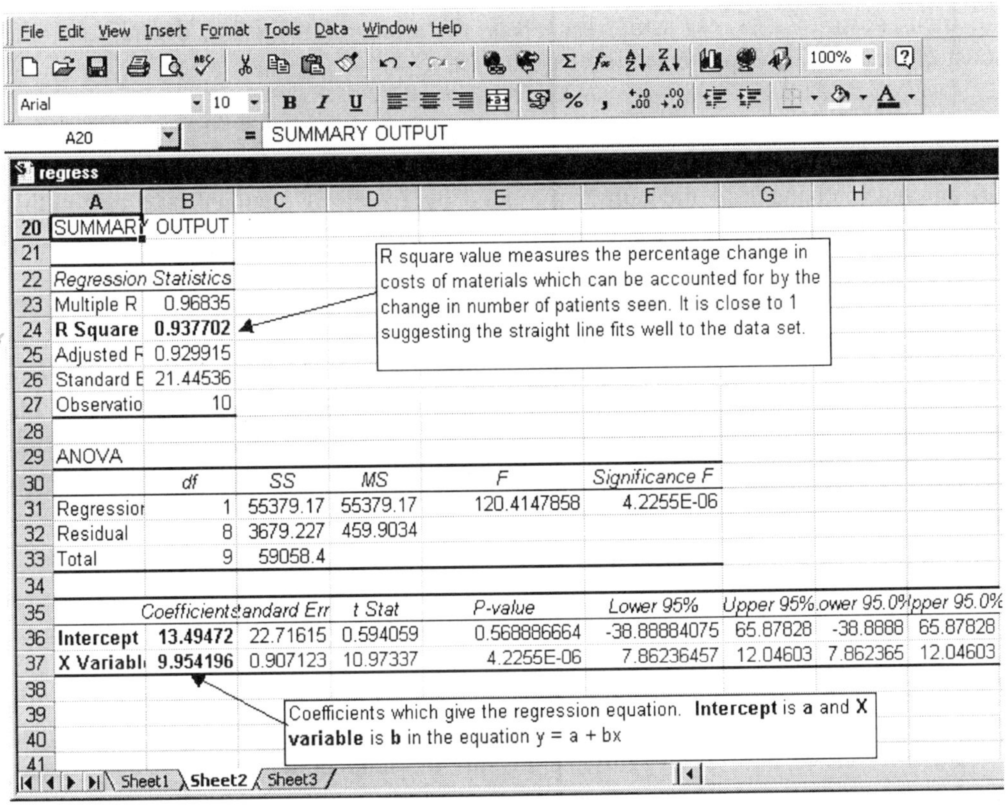

Figure 13.5 - Dialogue box and output from the Toolpak's Regression facility

Inspection of the output provided by Excel and illustrated in Figure 13.5 suggests that a strong positive linear relationship exists between the two variables, i.e. as the number of patients increases, the cost of material used by the dental practice also increases. This is supported by the high value of R^2 (0.937702 - suggesting 93.77% of the changes in cost is accounted for by changes in the number of patients) which is recorded in cell **B24**.

The regression line generated by Excel is:

$$y = 13.495 + 9.954\,x \quad \text{(3dp)}$$

Cost of materials (£) = 13.495 + 9.954 No. of patients

The coefficients a and b are recorded in cells **B36** and **B37** respectively. These coefficients respectively suggest that for a day with no bookings, you would expect to incur costs of £13.50, whilst for every extra patient receiving dental care, the cost of materials is expected to increase by £9.95.

If you decide to use the regression facility provided within the toolpak, it is important to understand that any alterations to the original data set, will **not** result in automatic changes to the output provided by Excel. If changes take place, this regression facility must be re-activated.

It should be apparent from inspection of Figure 13.5 that this regression facility produces significantly more output than that provided by the **INTERCEPT()** and **SLOPE()** functions. The output generated from the toolpak's regression facility can be used to both quantify the strength of a linear relationship (i.e. inspection of the R^2 value) and measure the significance of the corresponding regression equation (using the P values generated). The latter concept is beyond the scope of this book.

Forecasting From Time Related Data

In many business situations you may be presented with a data set, say consisting of volume sales, whose values may be time related. Specifically, the data values may be generally increasing with time and are said to show a positive trend, or alternatively, they may be generally decreasing with time and where they display a negative trend. In both cases, **time** represents the independent variable x. In these situations you may wish to forecast sales for future time periods. There are a number of approaches which can be taken, and these techniques are collectively referred to as the **time based models**. A number of time based models will be described in Chapters 14 and 15.

These techniques are generally more complex than the simple regression model and the choice of time based model used will depend upon you identifying specific features from the resultant time series graph. Nevertheless, if your sales data exhibits a trend over time, its behaviour may be adequately described by the regression equation described in this chapter.

An example of how to undertake the relevant analysis using Excel is shown below. The unit output from a cycle factory was recorded monthly throughout 1997 and is shown in Figure 13.6 on the Excel spreadsheet with its graphical display. The graph used to display this data is a line graph because time is a continuous variable. The graph indicates that the data shows a positive trend over the course of the year.

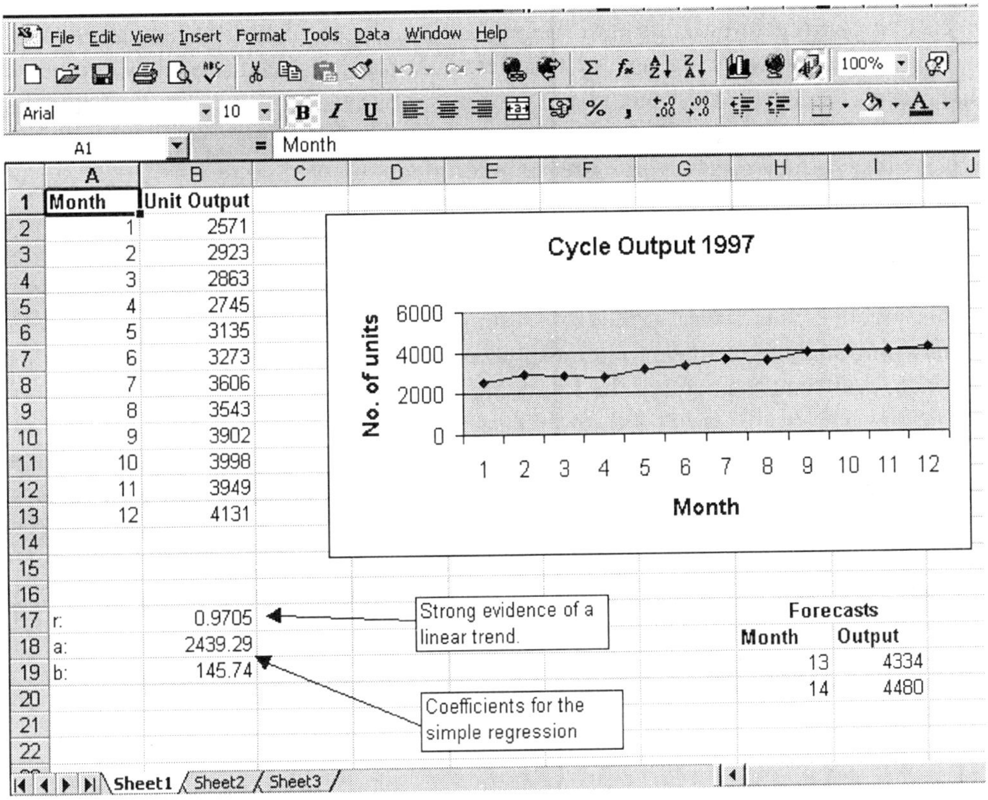

Figure 13.6 - Time related data presented by Excel

The regression equation is **y = 2439.29 + 145.74x**, where y = monthly output and x is time. The equation tells us that output is increasing on average by about 146 units per month. The line is a good fit, this being indicated by the correlation coefficient **0.9705**, which is stored in cell **B17**.

To forecast sales in months 13 and 14, the coefficients (a and b) for the regression equation have been created and stored in the block **B18:B19**. The forecast in cell **I19** contains the formula

=$B$18+$B$19*H19

where **H19** contains the value 13, which represents the time interval corresponding to the first forecast. The forecasts suggest the monthly output to be 4334 and 4480 units for the first two months of 1998.

Given that you are forecasting into the future, you are by definition **extrapolating**. As long as the forecasts are not for time intervals too far ahead, i.e. they represent **short term forecasts**, this should not be too problematic. However, it should be obvious that problems could occur if you forecast too far ahead, since it is highly unlikely that factory output will increase indefinitely at such a rate.

Review

In this chapter you have applied a systematic approach which can be used to identify and quantify a linear relationship between two variables. When using this approach, you should carry out the following steps:

1. Identify the decision variable (variable of interest) and a measurable variable which is likely to influence its behaviour. Label these variables y and x respectively.

2. Draw a scatter diagram to represent the data set collected. Identify the nature of the relationship suggested by the scatter diagram.

3. Ensure that any association identified is reasonable, and not caused by the behaviour of an additional, perhaps unidentified variable (see Chapter 12).

4. Determine the straight line equation, if appropriate, by using the least squares regression line.

5. Use Excel to undertake the computation of the regression equation both quickly and accurately.

6. Use the regression equation for prediction (either manually or by Excel), but be aware of the difference between interpolation and extrapolation.

Conclusions

Regression offers you a method of quantifying a linear relationship between two variables. In this chapter, you have seen how the regression equation may be computed by making reference to a number of worked examples. These examples include the necessary calculations and an interpretation of the results obtained. Additionally, the regression facilities offered by **Excel** have been described using specific examples.

Learning Outcomes Checklist

After completing this chapter you should have an understanding of the following concepts, calculations and functions:

- The best straight line relationship between two variables is given by the least squares regression line.

- That y represents the variable of interest and x the independent or measurable variable.

- How to calculate the regression line manually.

- An awareness of the Excel functions **INTERCEPT()** and **SLOPE()** functions and how they can be used to calculate the regression line.

- How to forecast from a regression line both manually or using Excel's **FORECAST()** function.

- The difference between interpolation and extrapolation when making forecasts from a regression line.

Ensure that you understand these concepts before progressing to Chapter 14.

Chapter Case Question

- Open the file **CHAP12.XLS**

- Using the 'best' relationship identified in the last part of the question, calculate the least squares regression line, where y is the monthly turnover and x is the variable which provides the strongest relationship. Use Excel's **INTERCEPT()** and **SLOPE()** commands to determine the straight line.

- Provide a full interpretation of the values of the coefficients **a** and **b**.

- Two additional public houses have been acquired by the chain:

  X: A country restaurant planning three guest beers and two promotions per month and has a capacity of 300.

  Y: A town family pub planning two guest beers and two promotions per month which has a capacity of 100.

Using the simple regression equation (and ignoring the irrelevant data provided), forecast the monthly turnover for the pubs X and Y.

- How much confidence can you have in the forecasts (Hint: Use **MIN()** and **MAX()** to determine the range of values for variable x in the sample of data).

- Save the amended file as **CHAP13.XLS**

Supplementary Questions

1. Sketch two scatter diagrams which demonstrate when a straight line can be used to represent a relationship between two variables.

2. Sketch a number of scatter diagrams which demonstrate that although a relationship exists between two variables, it should not be represented by a straight line Additionally, sketch a scatter diagram which displays a random scatter.

3. Describe briefly the term 'least squares regression line'. Use a diagram to support this description.

4. In the regression equation, which variables do the labels x and y represent? Illustrate your answer with a business example.

5. A sales manager wishes to predict value of sales for a certain level of advertising expenditure. Inspection of the data available at the company shows that the correlation between sales and TV advertising is 0.234, the correlation between sales and newspaper advertising is 0.871 and the correlation between sales and poster advertising is 0.525. If the manager wishes to predict sales using a simple regression equation, which measurable variable should be selected?

6. What is the difference between 'interpolation' and 'extrapolation'?

7. A supermarket sells iced drinks from a dispenser at the front of its store. The manager believes that either the temperature or the number of hours sunshine recorded in a particular day explain the daily sales. The following data was collected over a period of 10 days:

Day	1	2	3	4	5	6	7	8	9	10
Sunshine	2	1	2	0	1	3	2	4	1	3
Temp (^{0}C)	21	19	18	18	15	22	21	25	18	20

(a) Draw scatter diagrams to show the relationship between sales and sunshine and sales with temperature.

(b) Calculate Pearson's Product Moment correlation coefficient and the coefficient of determination by hand for these two relationships.

(c) Which relationship is the stronger? Why?

(d) Using the relationship identified in part c), determine the least squares regression equation to forecast sales.

(e) For the next weekend, the weather forecasts suggest:

	Sunshine	Temperature
Saturday	3 hours	22 ^{0}C
Sunday	5 hours	24 ^{0}C

Forecast the number of sales. Comment on the reliability of your forecasts.

8. A sales manager for a food company wishes to predict value of sales by the level of advertising expenditure. Currently, three types of advertising are used; advertising on local TV, advertising by newspaper and magazine and advertising by poster. The manager wishes to identify the best method of advertising the food products and determine a simple regression equation to predict sales. The following data (recorded in £000s) was collected:

Sales	77	65	56	72	80	85	57	62
TV adverts	2.8	2.5	3.1	3.2	3.4	3.3	2.7	2.8
Paper adverts	1.6	1.7	1.6	1.8	1.7	1.9	1.6	1.5
Poster adverts	0.8	0.6	0.3	0.7	1.1	1.1	0.5	0.7

Calculate the correlation coefficients between sales and each method of advertising. Which method of advertising best explains sales? Using this information, calculate the most suitable least squares regression line. For a particular month, a budget has been prepared allowing £3,000 to be spent on TV advertising, £1,500 on paper adverts and £750 on a poster campaign. Using the relevant information, estimate the value of sales, indicating whether interpolation or extrapolation has taken place. Check your answers using Excel.

9. The average price of a semi-detached house was recorded yearly over a period of six years in an English 'new town'.

Year:	1	2	3	4	5	6
Price: (£000s)	93	89	87	81	79	75

Present the data using a line graph and calculate the least squares regression line to describe price in terms of time. Using the regression equation, predict the house price for years 7 and 8. How confident are you in the forecasts?

10. The number of appointments booked into a hair salon over a two week period is shown below:

Working Day	1	2	3	4	5	6	7	8	9	10
Appointments	25	48	60	50	100	32	50	65	51	110

(a) Present this data using a line graph.

(b) Calculate the least squares regression equation to explain appointments in terms of time by hand.

(c) Calculate Pearson's Product Moment correlation coefficient and the coefficient of determination by hand for this relationship.

(d) What problems would you encounter when making forecasts from this straight line?

(e) What is causing the problems?

(f) Check your results using Excel.

Part 6

Forecasting from Time Related Data

Chapter 14

Introduction to Time Series Forecasting

Learning Outcomes

In this chapter you will be introduced to the concept of forecasting from time related data. Emphasis will be placed on the importance of undertaking an inspection of the data in order to identify its recent behaviour, and in turn, select an appropriate forecasting technique. At the end of the chapter forecasting from a stationary series will be considered. Like the previous chapters, reference will be made where appropriate to various facilities offered by Excel.

After completing this chapter you will be able to:

Understand the concept of time related data and describe the features of a time series plot.

- Recognise the importance of undertaking using a graph to assist in the selection of an appropriate quantitative model.
- Produce a time series plot for a business data set using the ChartWizard facility provided by Excel.
- Understand and recognise the properties of a stationary series and recognise a series containing trend or seasonal characteristics.
- Account for missing or extreme values in a time series.
- Recognise the scenarios in which quantitative forecasting models can be used.
- Forecast from a stationary series using one of three techniques; simple averages, moving averages and exponential smoothing.

Introduction

In this chapter you will see the importance of graphical presentation of past data in the selection and application of various quantitative forecasting models. The creation of the graphs featured in this chapter have been developed using Excel's ChartWizard facility.

The graphical presentation is an important stage in the selection of a quantitative forecasting model. It would be unwise for you to assume that certain patterns to exist without inspection of the recent data. The existence of such patterns in the data will be shown in the next two chapters and these features will influence the choice of forecasting model.

Quantitative forecasting involves examining a data set in order to identify a recognisable pattern or relationship which is measured. A useful set of quantitative forecasting models are the **time series** models. A time series is a data set which has been recorded at specific time periods or intervals (e.g. days, weeks, months etc.) in the recent past. The graphical representation of any time related data is known as a **time series plot**. On this graph. the variable of interest is plotted on the vertical or y axis, whilst time is plotted on the **horizontal** or **x axis**. The points are displayed using a line graph because time is a continuous variable (see Chapters 1 and 3). The past data may contain a pattern which can be identified and forecasts can be generated by assuming that this pattern is relevant to the future. The time based models provide an inexpensive approach to forecasting since the only data you have to consider is the single decision variable.

In analysing a time series, you have three tasks to undertake:

- To describe the past data by creating a time series plot and identifying any characteristics it displays. In the next two chapters, you will consider three patterns:
    - Trend
    - Stationary pattern
    - Trend and seasonality
- To build an appropriate forecasting model based on the recent pattern of the data identified from the time series plot.
- To forecast the future values for the data.

Throughout the next two chapters, you will apply these three steps to a variety of time related data.

When forecasting from past data, you will assume that the pattern you have identified will be repeated. Specifically, quantitative forecasts are most appropriate in the short term where the environment being considered is likely to be similar to that which influenced the past behaviour of the data. An example of a short term forecast may involve analysing sales of a particular family car by a motor dealer month by month in 1997. If the motor dealer forecasts sales in January and February 1998 based on the data collected in 1997, this represents a short term forecast.

Characteristics of a Time Series

There are a number of characteristics which may be identified from a time series plot. The existence of these characteristics will determine the selection of an appropriate forecasting model. This chapter considers three characteristics which may exist in a time series; namely a trend, a stationary pattern or time related data displaying seasonal characteristics.

Trend

A trend is present in a time series if the data typically increases or decreases with respect to time. If the value of the data values are increasing, the trend is positive, whereas if the values are typically decreasing, the trend is negative. Figure 14.1 below shows a time series plot featuring a positive trend. This data represents the number of complaints recorded weekly by an independent bus company. Inspection of this plot indicates that a positive trend exists from weeks 3 to 13 inclusive.

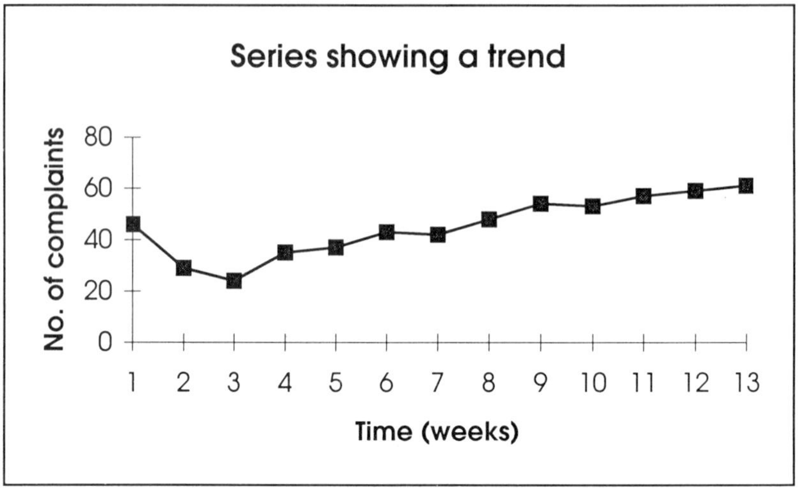

Figure 14.1 - Time series plot for a data set showing a trend

Stationary series

In contrast, a time related data set is called a stationary series if there is an absence of any trend, i.e. no typical increases or decreases are shown in the data with respect to time.

Figure 14.2 below shows a time series plot for a stationary series, which depicts the weekly output (in tonnes) recorded at an open cast mine which serves a local steel plant. Over a period of 3 - 4 months, the demand for coal is constant, and about 200 to 250 tonnes are produced each week. Inspection of the plot indicates the direction of the observations is parallel to the x axis rather than increasing or decreasing.

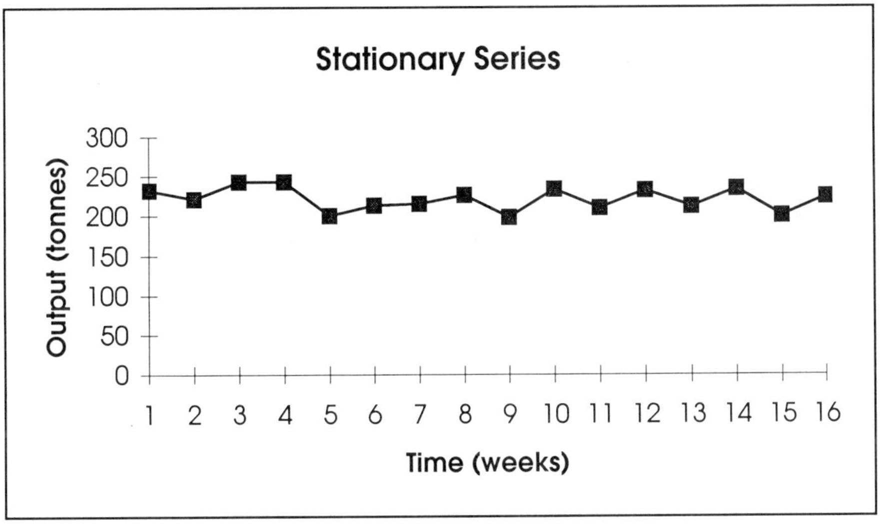

Figure 14.2 - A time series plot of a stationary series

Seasonality

Another feature seen in business data is seasonality. This seasonal characteristic is a pattern which is repeated periodically. In business applications, this seasonal pattern is often repeated yearly. If the variable of interest is monthly domestic consumption of electricity, then the pattern is likely to be seasonal, where the consumption is greater in the winter months and smaller in the summer months. This pattern is repeated each year and can be caused by events outside the control of the household using the electricity, i.e. changes in temperature and daylight. Since the time series observations are recorded monthly, it is reasonable in this example to assume that there are 12 seasons in each year. Other seasonal patterns may be caused by events inside an organisation, e.g. quarterly production at a factory may be seasonal and its behaviour could well be influenced by shift patterns, maintenance requirements and employee's holidays. The sales data recorded in Figure 14.3 is shown to have a pattern which is repeated every four time periods. This seasonal pattern shows a peak in every fourth quarter and a trough in every third quarter.

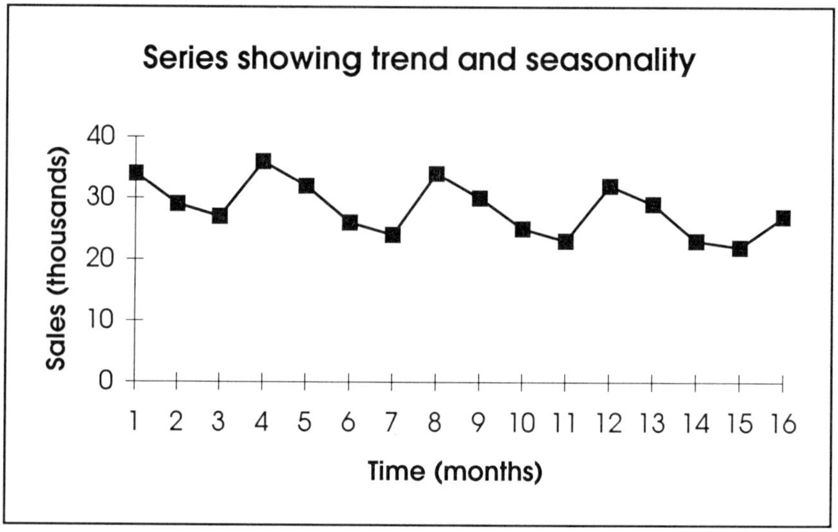

Figure 14.3 - Time series plot showing trend and seasonal characteristics

How Much Data is Required?

The process of forecasting from recent data will always raise the question 'How much data is required?' The answer to this question depends very much upon the features identified from the data. You only require small amounts of data to identify a trend or a stationary series. However, to properly identify a seasonal pattern, you will require enough data to ensure that seasonality actually exists, rather than being a pattern which occurs in one year only.

If you have enough recent data, you can forecast event when any of the following problems have occurred in the past provided the most recent data displays one of the three patterns displayed in Figures 14.1 to 14.3:

- Missing or non-recorded data.
- An alteration in the pattern of the data (e.g. a positive trend for sales data gradually turns into a stationary series).
- 'One-off' extreme values were recorded.

Forecasting from a Stationary Series

You will now consider an example of a stationary time series in which the number of computer services (including software installation and minor maintenance) required by a the Southern region of a bank weekly has been recorded over a 3 month time period. You will be required to forecast the number of services required each week for the next two weeks. This series can be assumed as stationary in the short term because the bank is using a particular computer system and a fixed number of related machines.

To provide short term forecasts from a stationary series you can use one of three models:

- simple averages
- moving averages
- exponential smoothing

The time series plot and the corresponding data values are displayed in Figure 14.4. Inspection of the plot indicates that the data is stationary since the values are not increasing or decreasing with respect to time.

Additionally, you can assume that in the following weeks, the volume of work performed on the computers will remain constant and the number of faults and corresponding services is expected to be similar to those recorded in the last three months. By ensuring this, it is assumed the models listed above can provide valid forecasts of the number of weekly computer services required.

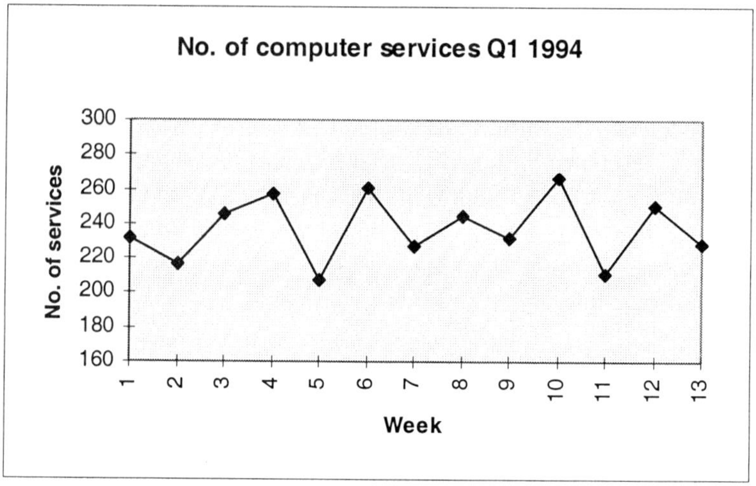

Week	1	2	3	4	5	6	7	8	9	10	11	12	13
Services	232	217	246	257	208	261	227	245	232	267	211	250	228

Figure 14.4 - Time series (and data set) of weekly computer services

The techniques listed are sometimes called 'smoothing models'. You are calculating various types of average in each of these three models and these averages 'smooth' the data, in order to exclude the randomness. By doing this, you can display the 'real' pattern beneath the data.

Simple Averages

Since the values of a stationary data set are not increasing or decreasing with respect to time, forecasts of its future values can be generated by calculating the average value of the recent data. The average or arithmetic mean of a data set was described in Chapter 4. For the number of services required, this can be calculated as:

$$(232 + 217 + 246 \ldots\ldots\ldots\ldots + 250 + 228)/13 = \mathbf{237.0\ services}$$

If Excel is being used the average of a data set can be generated using the built-in **AVERAGE()** command. For the data set under consideration, a comparison of actual and average number of computer services is shown by the graph displayed in Figure 14.5. Since you are dealing with computer services which will take integer values only, the forecasts should be presented accordingly. In this case, you are forecasting that the bank will require 237 computer services in weeks 14 and 15.

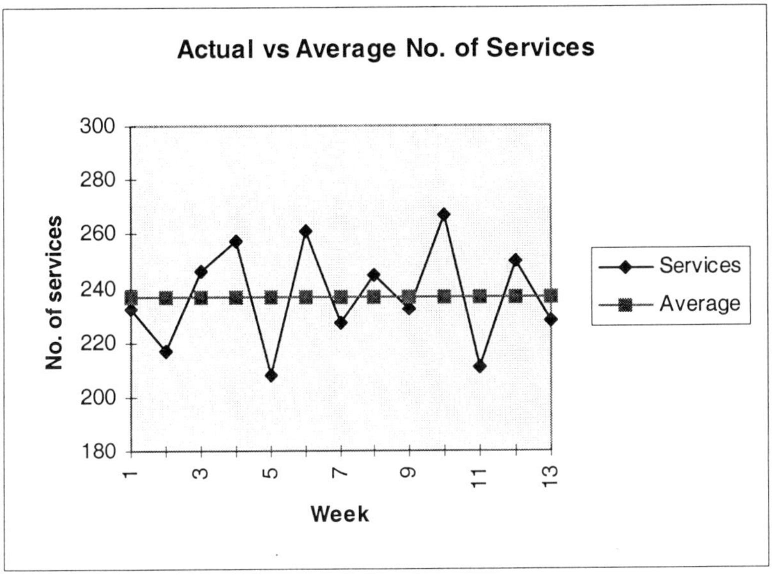

Figure 14.5 - A comparison of actual and simple average

The average calculated provides a measure of the 'real' value of the data set. In this example, the number of computer services range between 208 and 261 per week. Therefore, the average of 237 services provides a representative measure. It is useful to compare both the average and recent data on the same graph, as shown in Figure 14.5, since it shows that the average provides a reasonable estimate of the 'real' value of the past data. Since you are assuming that the series will behave in a similar manner in the future, you can use this average value as your forecast for the number of computer services for weeks 14 and 15.

The advantage of using the simple average to forecast is that the calculation is easy and most managers in business are comfortable with this particular measurement. However, by using an average value, all the values in the recent data are treated the same, i.e. the number of services in weeks 1 and 13 are averaged, despite time period one being three months in the past. If you are forecasting the number of computer services say for weeks 14 and 15, it would perhaps be appropriate to emphasise the more recent data.

Moving Averages

The moving average model only considers recent values on the time series and you 'move' through the data set with regard to the values you average. In general, two moving average models can be used, the three period moving average and the five period moving average. These are represented by the respective equations:

$$S_t = (A_{t-1} + A_t + A_{t+1})/3$$

and

$$S_t = (A_{t-2} + A_{t-1} + A_t + A_{t+1} + A_{t+2})/5$$

where:

S_t represents the value of the moving average model for time period t, i.e. the 'real' value of the series for time t, once any random component has been removed.

A_t represents the actual value of the series for time period t

In the first model, you consider weeks 1, 2, and 3 in the first calculation, weeks 2, 3 and 4 in the second average and so on, therefore the name 'moving' is used.

By creating this 'smoothed series', the latest averaged values are calculated only from the recent data, and as a consequence, this model is seen as an improvement compared to the simple averages. This argument would seem reasonable since the up to date values are likely to bear more relevance to the behaviour of the decision variable in the future than those values recorded in the distant past.

In general, *if the moving averages each consider n data values,* then the model created is called an *n period moving average model.* Figure 14.6 below shows the calculation of the three period moving and five period moving average models corresponding to the data set which records the weekly number of computer services.

Week	**Actual No. Services**	**3 period moving average model**	
1	232		
2	*217*	231.7	=(**232+217+246**)/3
3	*246*	240.0	=(*217+246+257*)/3
4	*257*	237.0	
5	208	242.0	**etc.**
6	261	232.0	
7	227	244.3	
8	245	234.7	
9	232	248.0	
10	267	236.7	
11	211	242.7	
12	250	229.7	
13	228		

Week	**Actual No. Services**	**5 period moving average model**	
1	**232**		
2	***217***		
3	***246***	232.0	=(**232+217+246+257+208**)/5
4	***257***	237.8	=(*217+246+257+208+261*)/5
5	***208***	239.8	
6	*261*	239.6	**etc.**
7	227	234.6	
8	245	246.4	
9	232	236.4	
10	267	241.0	
11	211	237.6	
12	250		
13	228		

Figure 14.6 - A 3 period and 5 period moving average

As well as describing the 'real' pattern the beneath the data using the moving average models, you also need to forecast the number of computer services required in weeks 14 and 15. **The forecasts of computer services are provided by the last value in the moving average model**. In the models illustrated in Figure 14.6, you can forecast **229.7** services if the 3 period moving average model is used or **237.6** services if the 5 period moving average model is applied. You would forecast that the bank requires **230** and **238 services** (respectively for the two models) for weeks 14 and 15.

The three period and five period moving averages are recognised as providing reasonable forecasts because they consider enough data values in each average calculation to identify the 'real' pattern in the past data. At the same time calculations involving either 3 or 5 data values are small enough to guarantee that the last average calculations in the model are relevant to the current and future behaviour of the data. The moving average models represent a big improvement on the simple average model, which in the example considered above, considered thirteen weekly values the same.

There is one major exception to the choice of moving average model. If a seasonal pattern exists in the past data, the de-seasonalised pattern can be identified by using an n period moving average where n is equal to the number of periods in the seasonal pattern. For example, a 4 period moving average would be used to de-seasonalise quarterly data where the pattern is seen year after year and a 7 period moving average should be used for daily sales data where the pattern is displayed week after week.

The quarterly data described above would be de-seasonalised using an even period moving average. To apply such a model to a time series, you must undertake an additional calculation. The moving average values initially generated do not correspond to actual time periods, but to periods of time which are situated in-between two actual periods. For example, if a 4 period moving average is calculated for quarterly data, the first value calculated is the average of actual values at quarters 1, 2, 3 and 4. This corresponds to quarter 2½. The next moving average will be the average of actual values at quarters 2, 3, 4 and 5 and corresponds to quarter 3½, as shown in Figure 14.7.

Time Period	1		2		3		4		5
Moving Average				2½		3½			
Centred Moving average					3				

Figure 14.7 - The relationship between moving and centred moving averages

By calculating the average of each adjacent pair of moving averages when you use an even period model, you create a **centred moving average**, whose values correspond to actual time periods, i.e. the average of the moving averages for quarters 2½ and 3½ provides a moving average corresponding to quarter 3.

Centred moving averages will be considered in Chapter 15 in relation to a data set with a quarterly seasonal pattern repeated yearly. An example of how to de-seasonalise data using a moving average is shown below.

The sales data corresponds to new cars sold each quarter over the last three years by one outlet. Inspection of the data shows the data is stationary but has a recognisable seasonal pattern. Specifically, sales peak in quarter three of each year, and show a trough in quarter 2. Given that there are 4 quarters in the seasonal pattern, the data can be de-seasonalised using a 4 period moving average. The centred moving average values then correspond to actual time periods, as displayed in Figure 14.8.

Quarter	Actual	4 period moving average		Centred moving average	
1	110				
2	78	120.25	=(110+78+195+98)/4		
3	195	121.25	=(78+195+98+114)/4	120.75	=(120.25+121.25)/2
4	98	120.25		120.75	=(121.25+120.25)/2
5	114	121.50	**etc.**	120.88	
6	74	122.25		121.88	**etc.**
7	200	121.75		122.00	
8	101	122.00		121.88	
9	112	121.00		121.50	
10	75	120.75		120.88	
11	196				
12	100				

Figure 14.8 - De-seasonalising sales data using moving averages

The typical value of the sales is 121 cars per quarter, ignoring any seasonality. The centred moving averages provide an estimate of the de-seasonalised sales. In order to forecast future quarterly sales, this value can be combined with appropriate estimates of the seasonal variation for each quarter. The method of calculating the seasonal estimates will be described in the next chapter. A comparison of actual and de-seasonalised data is shown in the graph in Figure 14.9 below.

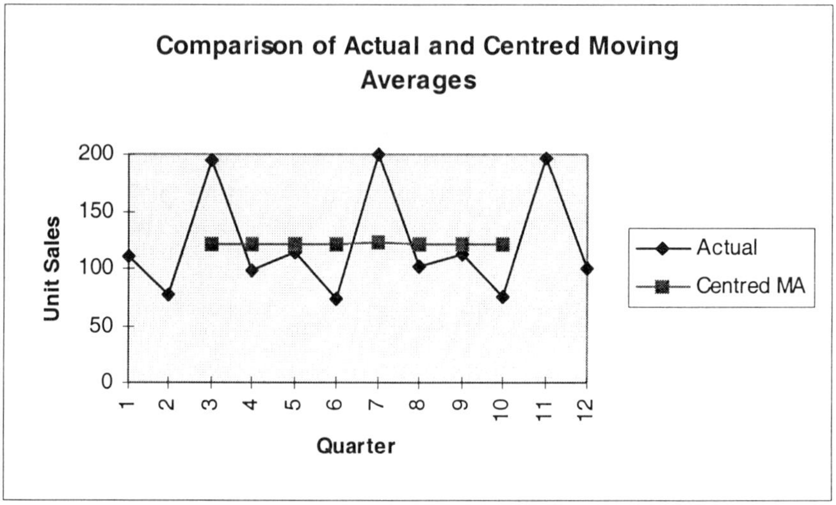

Figure 14.9 - A comparison of Actual and de-seasonalised data

This location of the moving average values is not a problem in the moving average models described in Figure 14.6. In the three period moving average for the weekly service data at the bank, the first calculation considers weeks 1, 2 and 3. The average calculated corresponds to the centre time period, i.e. week 2.

Exponential Smoothing

One common feature of both the simple average and moving average calculations are the past data used in the various averaging calculations are considered the same. The exponential smoothing technique provides a model in which a greater emphasis is placed on the latest data and less emphasis on the earlier data. This would seem a reasonable model because as more data is collected, the past data are likely to become less relevant to the future behaviour of the data.

The exponentially smoothed model is represented by:

$$S_t = (1 - \alpha)S_{t-1} + \alpha A_t$$

where:

S_t represents the value of the smoothed model for time period t, i.e. the 'real' value of the series for time period t, once the random component has been removed.

A_t represents the actual value of the series for time period t

α is a smoothing coefficient whose value lies between 0 and 1

Bigger values of α (in the range 0 to 1) put greater emphasis on the latest data. This could be inappropriate if the data has any 'one-off' high or low values, e.g. a peak in monthly sales data for one month during a year which is not caused by seasonal variation. Typically, the value of α is defined at the lower end of this range, i.e. between 0.1 and 0.3. The advantage of using low values of α in this range are that any 'one-off' changes in pattern represented in the data set are not over-emphasised in the smoothed model, and in turn, over-emphasised in any forecasts.

The data corresponding to the weekly number of computer services has been represented by an exponentially smoothed model and these values are shown in Figure 14.10. Initially, you can set S_1 equal to A_1, since S_0 is not defined.

Week	**Actual No. Services**	**smoothed model (α = 0.3)**	
1	232	232.0	$S_1 = A_1$
2	217	227.5	=(1 - 0.3) x 232+(0.3 x 217)
3	246	233.05	=(1 - 0.3) x 227.5+(0.3 x 246)
4	257	240.24	
5	208	230.56	etc.
6	261	239.70	
7	227	235.89	
8	245	238.62	
9	232	236.63	
10	267	245.74	
11	211	235.32	
12	250	239.72	
13	228	236.21	

Figure 14.10 - Exponential smoothed model

You have now calculated the 'real' values in the time series using the exponential smoothing model. The number of services forecast for weeks 14 and 15 are **provided by the last value in the exponential model**. From the calculations provided above, the forecasts for weeks 14 and 15 is **236.21**, which will be presented as **236 services** each week. This forecast is provided using the value α =

0.3. It should be apparent that different values of α will provide different forecasts of the number of computer services. Also, the larger the number of calculations undertaken, the larger the potential for problems to be encountered due to rounding. If these calculations are undertaken using a spreadsheet, then the accuracy provided by the software will help you avoid these problems.

Applying Excel's Built-in Forecasting Tools

To generate moving average values for a time series, the relevant built-in facility provided by Excel can be used. To select this you must activate:

Tools
Data Analysis

and select **Moving Average**. This results in the box shown in Figure 14.11.

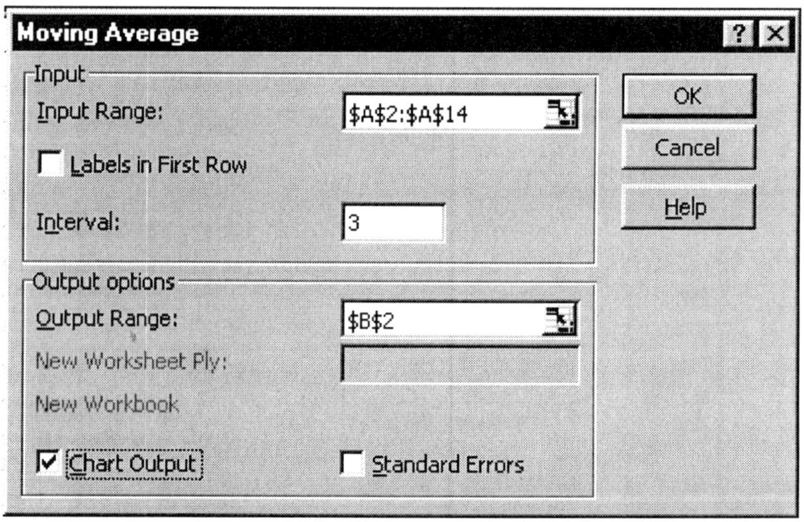

Figure 14.11 - Excel's Moving average Dialogue Box

The input range corresponds to the recent data regarding the number of weekly services required by the bank's Western region. You can define the **Interval** which is the number of periods considered in the moving average calculation. The output range can be entered as a single cell reference which is the first value in the moving average model. By selecting a cell reference next to the first value of the input range for the model's output, you will create a set of 1 period ahead forecasts using this facility rather than a moving average model. Specifically, the first average calculation (based on cells A2, A3 and A4) is located next to A4 rather than A3 (the centre period). By clicking on **Chart Output** (a tick appears next to this label), a graphical comparison is provided between the actual series and the series of moving averages. Figure 14.12 shows the moving average values and the graphical comparison generated by Excel. It should be clear that the value 157.3 represents the forecast of number of computer services required in weeks 14 and 15. This forecast would be presented as **157 services** each week.

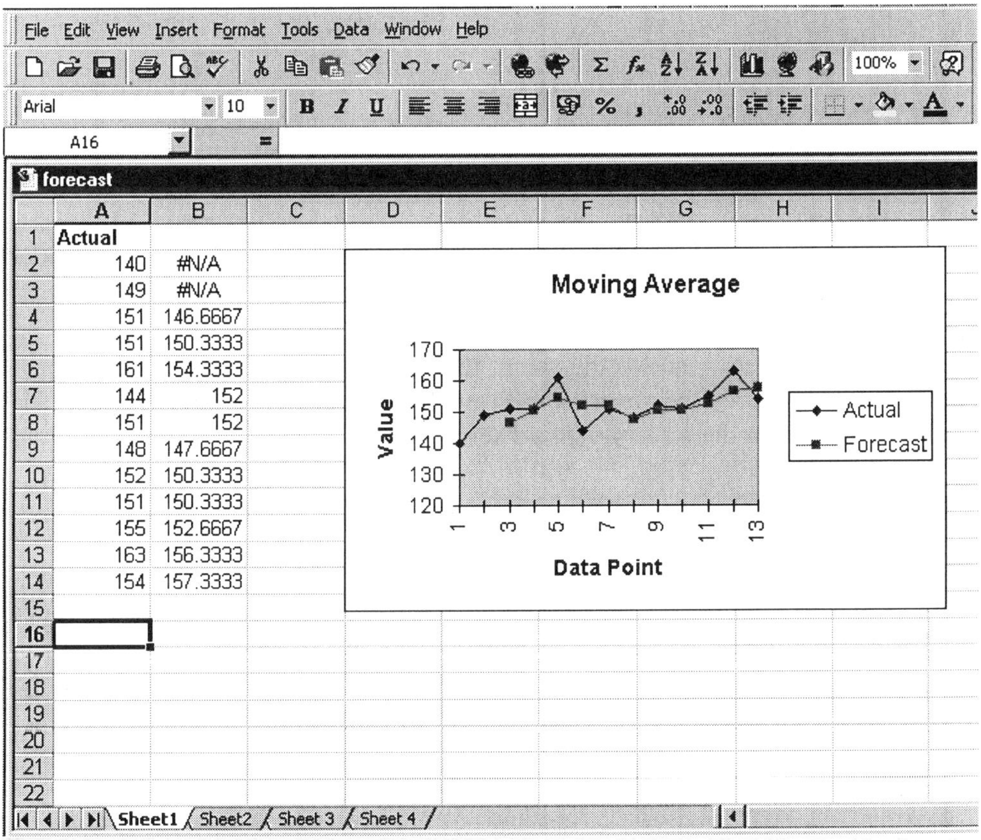

Figure 14.12 - Moving average output generated by Excel

Like the Moving Average model, Excel also provides a built-in Exponential Smoothing facility. To select this you must activate:

Tools
Data Analysis

and select **Exponential Smoothing**. This results in the box shown in Figure 14.13.

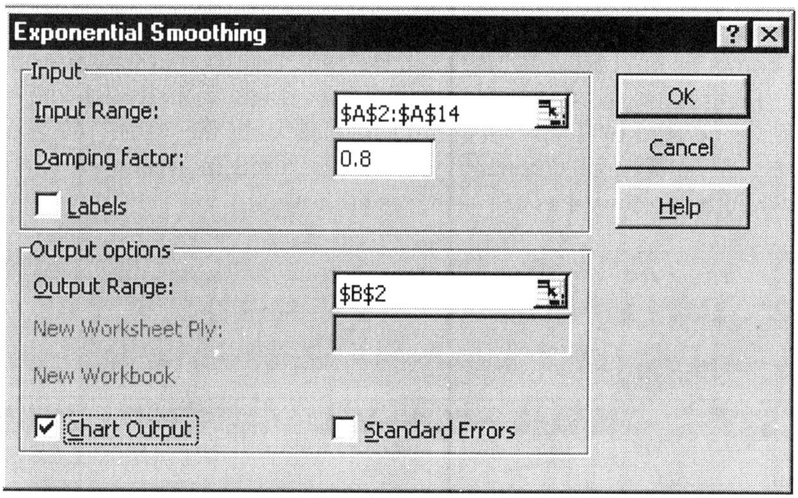

Figure 14.13 - Excel's Exponential smoothing Dialogue Box

The input range corresponds to the recent data. It is important also to be aware of the slight difference in the formula used by Excel and the one presented in this chapter. To generate the same smoothed series using this built-in Excel facility you must set the **Dampening Factor** to **0.8**. In general, the dampening factor is equal to ***1 - smoothing coefficient***. The output range can be entered as a single cell reference which represents the first value in the exponential smoothing model. By selecting a cell reference next to the first value of the input range for the model's output, you will create a set of 1 period ahead forecasts using this facility rather than model which describes the 'real' values of past data. Figure 14.14 shows the exponential smoothing values and the corresponding graphical comparison, which allows you to compare the actual data with its 'real' pattern.

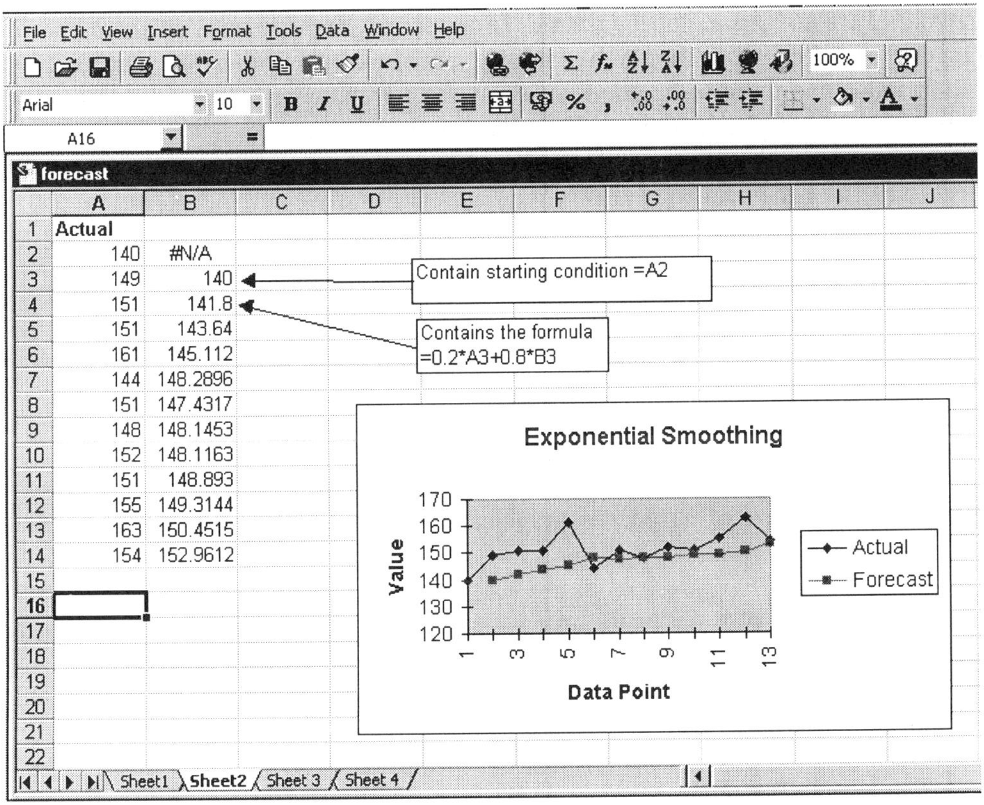

Figure 14.14 - Exponential smoothing output generated by Excel

Using this exponential smoothing model, the last average calculated is 152.96. Therefore, you would forecast **152** computer services are required in weeks 14 and 15 in the Western region of the bank.

Conclusions

The aim of the first part of this chapter was to demonstrate the importance of the graph in choosing an appropriate forecasting model. The creation of a time series plot is easy and it enables you to identify any patterns which may exist in recent data. Once an identifiable pattern has been recognised, you can then, where appropriate, select a suitable time based model. When forecasting using a quantitative model, you assume that the environment affecting the past data will be the same in the future.

In the second part of the chapter you considered three techniques for forecasting from past data which is stationary. The three techniques were simple averages, moving averages and exponential smoothing. It has been shown that these models range from the very simple averaging model to the relatively sophisticated exponential smoothing technique. However, the advantage of using the latter model is that greater emphasis is placed on the latest data, and as a consequence, the forecasts generated will hopefully prove more responsive to any changes in the 'real' pattern of the data.

Learning Outcomes Checklist

After completing this chapter you should have an understanding of the following concepts, calculations and functions:

- The existence of time related data.
- The application of a specific graphical display; a line graph known as time series plot.
- The existence of a stationary time series.
- How to forecast from a stationary time series using three techniques; simple averages, moving averages and exponential smoothing.
- The availability of the **Moving Average** and **Exponential Smoothing** facilities from Excel's toolpak.

Ensure that you understand these concepts before progressing to Chapter 15.

Chapter Case Question

The public house chain also run a conference centre. Over a ten month period, the number of conferences hosted at the centre were recorded and are shown below:

Month	1	2	3	4	5	6	7	8	9	10
Properties	56	52	55	59	53	57	53	54	56	52

- Enter this data into Excel using one column for the month number and an adjacent column for the number of conferences.
- Create a time series plot using **ChartWizard** for the data and confirm that it represents a stationary series.

- Calculate a three-month moving average (either by building the formulae using the **AVERAGE()** command or by using the relevant **toolpak** facility), and in doing so forecast the number of conferences to be hosted in months 11 and 12.

- Build an exponential smoothing model (either by building the formulae or by using the relevant **toolpak** facility), and in doing so forecast the number of conferences to be hosted in months 11 and 12.

- Save your file as **CHAP14.XLS**

Supplementary Questions

1. Give a *brief* description of a time series.

2. Give a *brief* description of a time series plot.

3 What are the main tasks you have to undertake in the development of a time series model?

4. In using a time series model, what is the main assumption you are making?

5. Describe *briefly* the following terms:

   (a) Stationary series

   (b) Trend

   (c) Seasonality

   Sketch time series plots showing the features listed in a), b) and c).

6. Discuss the two types of causes of seasonality in a time series. Give examples of both categories.

7. Compare the methods of simple averages, moving averages and exponential smoothing for forecasting from a stationary series. What are the advantages and disadvantages of using each technique?

8. A customer service centre recorded the number of customer complaints over a period of 12 days:

1	2	3	4	5	6	7	8	9	10	11	12
98	92	102	106	101	95	100	104	100	106	97	100

(a) Confirm that the time series is stationary by producing a time series plot.

(b) Produce forecasts for days 13, 14 and 15 using simple averages.

(c) Repeat part b) using 3 period and 5 period moving averages.

(d) Build an exponential smoothing series using the smoothing coefficient $\alpha = 0.2$.

(e) Compare the forecasts generated by the three methods used.

(f) Produce a time series plot using Excel's ChartWizard facility and check the calculations undertaken by using the relevant facilities offered by the spreadsheet.

9. The number of new members recorded by a national car insurance company were recorded monthly in 1994:

JAN	FEB	MAR	APR	MAY	JUN	JUL	AUG	SEP	OCT	NOV	DEC
549	589	525	500	577	543	550	595	534	525	556	538

(a) Confirm that the time series is stationary by producing a time series plot.

(b) Produce forecasts for January to June 1995 using simple averages.

(c) Repeat part b) using 3 period and 5 period moving averages.

(d) Build an exponential smoothing series using the smoothing coefficient $\alpha = 0.1$.

(e) Compare the forecasts generated by the three methods used.

(f) Produce a time series plot using Excel's ChartWizard facility and check the calculations undertaken by using the relevant facilities offered by the spreadsheet.

Chapter 15

Forecasting from a Time Series Showing Trend and Seasonal Characteristics

Learning Outcomes

In this chapter, you will consider a forecasting model which will enable you to predict future values for time series showing both trend and seasonal characteristics. Again, you will see how Excel can be used to build the necessary formulae.

After completing this chapter you will be able to:

- Recognise if a time series shows trend and seasonal properties.
- Distinguish between additive and multiplicative seasonality.
- Forecast from a time series showing these properties using an appropriate decomposition model.

Introduction

In Chapter 14 the concept of a time series was introduced, and a step by step method was taken to forecast the future values of the series. In this chapter, you will consider an additional model, which will enable you to forecast from past data showing both trend and seasonal properties.

A time series can be assumed to have a trend if the data typically increases or decreases with respect to time. If the data increases, it has a positive trend, whilst decreasing data has a negative trend. Moreover, you will assume in this chapter that any trend identified will be linear.

Additionally, a time series is considered to feature **seasonality** if there is a pattern in the recent data which is repeated periodically. As suggested in Chapter 14, this seasonal feature in the past data may be influenced by events inside or outside of an organisation. The amount of money spent monthly by a high street clothes store on wages and salaries might be seasonal, caused by company policy regarding pay rises, the payment of bonuses and the use of casual labour. This is an example of seasonality caused by decisions made inside a business. The sales of beachwear by the same clothes store is likely to be seasonal, influenced by the holiday and leisure plans of its customers. In this case, the seasonal differences in sales are caused by events outside the control of the store.

In many business applications, the seasonal pattern can be assumed to last one year, The number of seasons is determined by the number of observations in the repeating pattern, e.g. data recorded monthly will produce 12 seasons in one year, whereas sales data recorded daily whose periodic pattern is repeated every week will have 7 seasons (here 1 season represents an individual working day).

If the seasonal variations increase in size, then the seasonal pattern is **multiplicative**. This is illustrated by the time series plot in Figure 15.1 which shows a time series where the seasonal pattern of four periods becomes bigger each year. Inspection of the series shown in Figure 15.1 shows that the seasonal pattern in year 4 (quarters 13 to 16) is recognisably bigger than the seasonal pattern in year 1 (quarters 1 to 4).

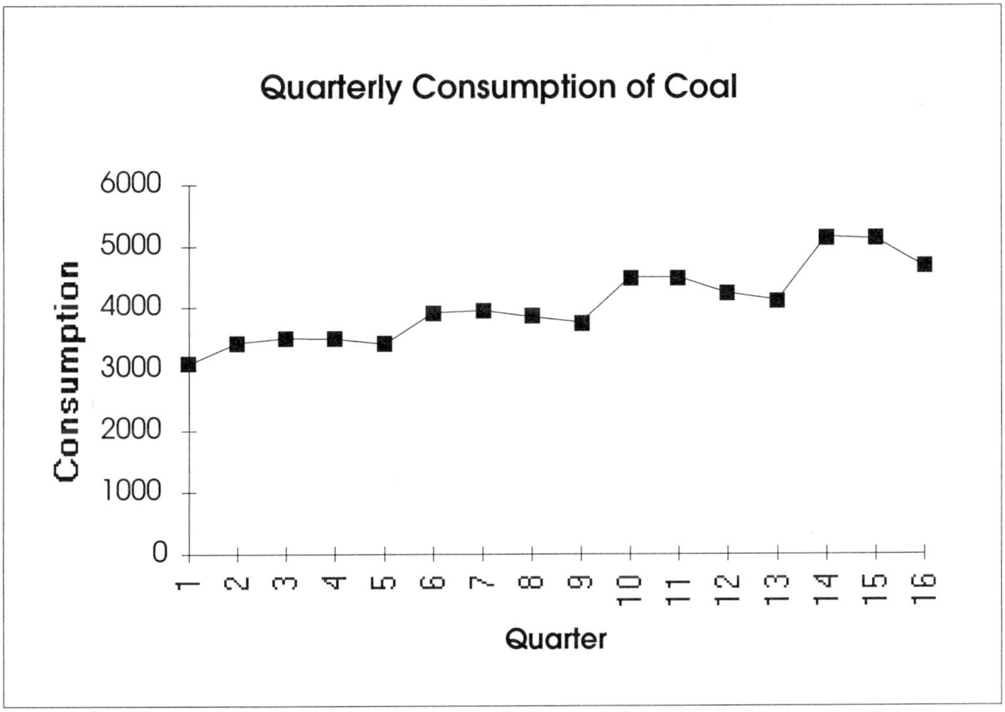

Figure 15.1 - Time series plot illustrating multiplicative seasonality

If the seasonal pattern remains constant with respect to time, the seasonality is considered to be **additive**. Figure 15.2 shows a time series plot which displays an additive seasonal pattern. In particular, the seasonal pattern in year 4 (quarters 13 to 16) is similar in size to that shown in year 1 (quarters 1 to 4).

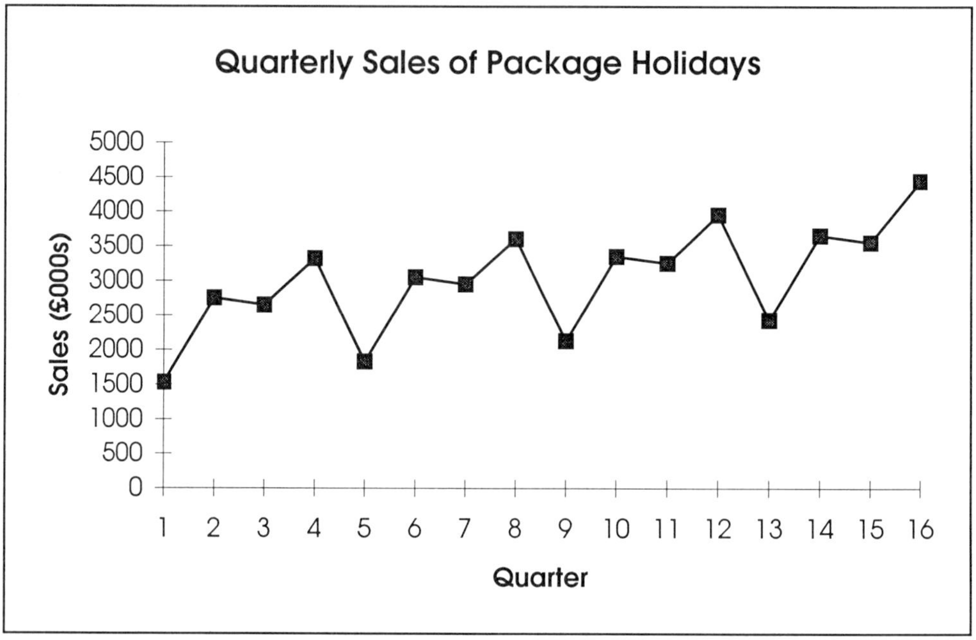

Figure 15.2 - Time series plot illustrating additive seasonality

Once the nature of the seasonal pattern has been identified, you can then select an appropriate time series model. One model which can be used in both situations entails 'decomposing' the time series into its component parts.

The Decomposition Model

Forecasting using a decomposition model involves splitting the past data into three exclusive component parts, namely trend, seasonal variation and randomness.

The trend and seasonal components, which form the 'real' pattern in the data can then be appropriately 're-composed' to produce the required forecasts. The random component of each past observation represents 'one-off' differences in the past data from the 'real' pattern which can not be described by the trend and seasonal behaviour. As a consequence, you don't use the random component as part of any subsequent forecast, but you can quantify this randomness as a measure of the potential accuracy of your forecasts.

Like the forecasts from a stationary series in Chapter 14, the resultant forecasts produced by the decomposition method assume that the 'real' pattern in the past data will be repeated in the future, which is reasonable in the short term. If you consider four years of data which shows a trend and seasonal pattern, you may consider the short term corresponds to 1 year in the future.

Since the seasonal pattern identified may be multiplicative or additive, two decomposition models are required.

The first is the multiplicative model where the time series data are represented by:

Actual data = Trend x Seasonal Variation x Randomness

and the second is the additive model where the time series data are represented by:

Actual data = Trend + Seasonal Variation + Randomness

The multiplicative model is applied to the series where the seasonal pattern is increasing year by year, whilst the additive model is applied to the time series where the seasonal pattern remains constant.

After collecting the data, you must decide whether the data contains a seasonal characteristic, and whether this is either additive or multiplicative. In the example below, the consumption of coal at a small steel works has been recorded over 4 years (figures in tonnes). The data is displayed in Figure 15.3.

		Quarter		
Year	1	2	3	4
1991	3077	3422	3500	3492
1992	3411	3920	3956	3850
1993	3758	4500	4502	4245
1994	4133	5160	5129	4677

Figure 15.3 - Coal consumption (tonnes) recorded quarterly 1991 - 1994

Using the spreadsheet, the time series data can be entered as shown in Figure 15.4. The spreadsheet is ideal for time series calculations. Each time period can be represented by a row, whilst the different columns on the spreadsheet can be used to calculate the trend, seasonal and random components. The spreadsheet also ensures that you don't encounter rounding problems with any of the calculations undertaken. The time series contains 16 data values (4 quarters over 4 years), and these have been labelled 1 to 16 inclusive on the Excel worksheet.

Year	Quarter	Period	Consumption
1991	1	1	3077
	2	2	3422
	3	3	3500
	4	4	3492
1992	1	5	3411
	2	6	3920
	3	7	3956
	4	8	3850
1993	1	9	3758
	2	10	4500
	3	11	4502
	4	12	4245
1994	1	13	4133
	2	14	5160
	3	15	5129
	4	16	4677

Figure 15.4 - Time series data entered in the spreadsheet

To determine whether the most appropriate decomposition model is either multiplicative or additive, a time series plot should be created. This was illustrated for the coal consumption data in Figure 15.1 and the time series plot suggests that the seasonal pattern is multiplicative.

In the multiplicative model,

Actual Data = Trend x Seasonal Variation x Randomness

Now that you have chosen the relevant decomposition model, you can split the past data into the exclusive trend and seasonal components.

The Trend Component

In the example being considered, the consumption of coal at the steel plant is increasing with respect to time, i.e. the time series displays a positive trend. This positive trend can be split from the actual data using **moving averages**. In this example, a 4 period moving average would be appropriate, because the pattern in the past data is repeated every four quarters. By calculating 4 period averages (i.e. the first calculation will consist of averaging data corresponding to quarters 1, 2, 3 and 4, the second will average data values for quarters 2, 3, 4 and 5, and so on), you can remove the peaks and troughs in the data, and in doing so, calculate a measure of the 'real' trend.

Considering to Figure 15.6, the formula used for the first 4 period moving average stored in cell **E3** and displayed as **3372.75** is:

=AVERAGE(D2:D5)

When you considered moving average models in Chapter 14, the moving average calculation corresponds to a time period in the centre of the block of data values used in its calculation. The first moving average calculated and described above represents a time period in-between quarters two and three, i.e. quarter '2½'. In the same way, the second moving average calculated will correspond to quarter '3½'. If these two moving averages are then averaged, then the resultant moving average will correspond to quarter 3, this being demonstrated in the last chapter by Figures 14.7 and 14.8. This second averaging model is known as a **centred moving average**. The moving average is located in column **E** and the centred moving averages are in column **F**. The formula in cell **F4** is:

=AVERAGE(E3:E4)

The centred moving average described above only needs to be calculated if the number of seasons in the seasonal pattern is **even**, as in the quarterly data under consideration in this example. If the seasonal pattern covers an odd number of periods, e.g. daily data which is repeated week after week (e.g. value of sales recorded daily in a newsagents), where the appropriate moving average would consider 7 periods, the centred moving average calculation is not required since the moving average calculated corresponds to an exact period of time (i.e. the first calculation would involve days 1, 2, 3, 4, 5, 6 and 7 and the average calculated would be located in day 4). In this case, the moving average model can be used to determine the trend shown by the past data.

The 'real' pattern in the past data consists of trend and seasonal components in addition to randomness. The (centred) moving average consists only of the trend. In the multiplicative decomposition model, actual data divided by centred moving average will give a combined measure of seasonal variation and the randomness in the data, as shown below:

Actual Data = Trend x Seasonal Variation x Random

Rearranging this equation gives:

$$\frac{\textbf{Actual Data}}{\textbf{Trend}} = \textbf{Seasonal Variation x Random}$$

Figure 15.5 compares the actual data and the moving averages. This graph illustrates how the centred moving average model displays only the trend in the time series data. You can say that the data has been de-seasonalised when it displays only the trend in this way.

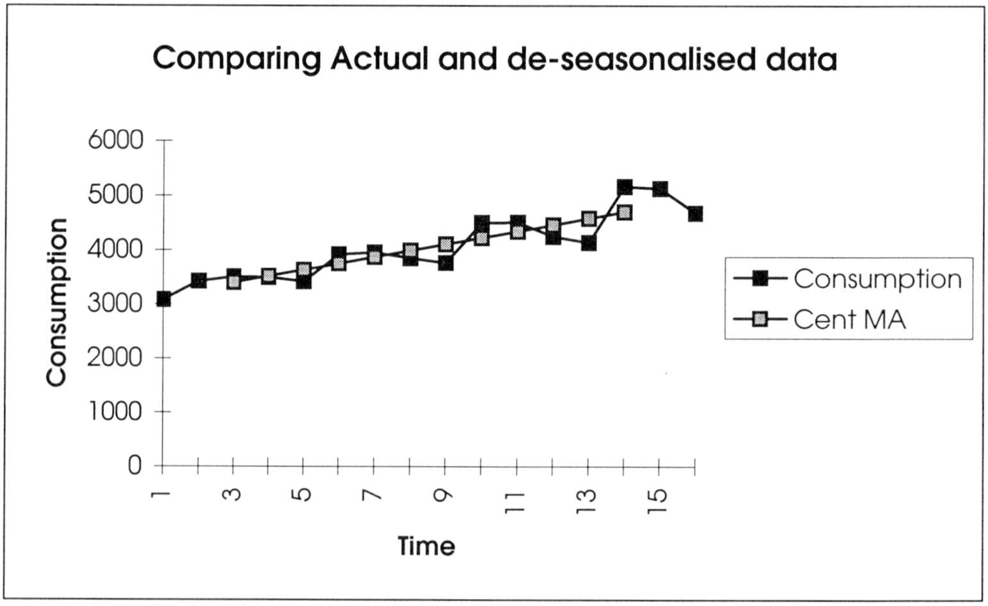

Figure 15.5 - Comparison of actual and de-seasonalised data

This trend can now be quantified using a simple linear regression equation where the x data is the quarter, i.e. quarters 3, 4, .. etc. and the y data is the centred moving averages. The regression equation is:

$$y = a + bx$$

where: y = trend estimated given by the centred moving average
x = corresponding quarter

Figure 15.6 below displays the trend estimate for each observation. The trend estimate can be generated using Excel's built-in **FORECAST()** facility (which has been described already in Chapter 13) for the first observation in the recent data and you can use Excel's **Copy** and **Paste** facilities to generate the trend estimate for quarters 2 to 16 inclusive.

File Edit View Insert Format Tools Data Window Help

A1 = Year

	A	B	C	D	E	F	G
1	**Year**	**Quarter**	**Period**	**Consumption**	**Mov Avg**	**Cent Mov Avg**	**Trend**
2	1991	1	1	3077			3152.9
3		2	2	3422	3372.75		3270.3
4		3	3	3500	3456.25	3414.50	3387.7
5		4	4	3492	3580.75	3518.50	3505.1
6	1992	1	5	3411	3694.75	3637.75	3622.5
7		2	6	3920	3784.25	3739.50	3740.0
8		3	7	3956	3871.00	3827.63	3857.4
9		4	8	3850	4016.00	3943.50	3974.8
10	1993	1	9	3758	4152.50	4084.25	4092.2
11		2	10	4500	4251.25	4201.88	4209.7
12		3	11	4502	4345.00	4298.13	4327.1
13		4	12	4245	4510.00	4427.50	4444.5
14	1994	1	13	4133	4666.75	4588.38	4561.9
15		2	14	5160	4774.75	4720.75	4679.3
16		3	15	5129			4796.8
17		4	16	4677			4914.2

Sheet1 / Sheet2 / Sheet 3 / **Sheet 4**

Figure 15.6 - Spreadsheet displaying the trend estimate

The trend estimates have been formatted to one decimal place. In the model displayed in Figure 15.6, the first trend formula is:

=FORECAST(C2,$F$4:$F$15,$C$4:$C$15)

where:

C2 is the quarter corresponding to the trend estimate, i.e. quarter 1.

$F$4:$F$15 is the y data in the regression equation, i.e. the centred moving averages which measure the trend in the data.

$C$4:$C$15 is the x data, i.e. quarters 3, 4, etc. which correspond to the centred moving average values described above.

Inspection of the trend values in column G indicate that the consumption of coal at the steel plant is increasing by about 117 tonnes per quarter.

The Seasonal Component

The data being considered involves coal consumption recorded quarterly each year and the time series plot indicates that a seasonal pattern exists. This seasonal pattern consists of four quarters. From the rearranged formula for the multiplicative decomposition model you have:

$$\frac{\textbf{Actual Data}}{\textbf{Trend}} = \textbf{Seasonal Variation x Random}$$

In Figure 15.7, the combined seasonal and random estimates (given by Actual/Centred Moving Average - the first formula being **=D4/G4**) are shown in column H of the spreadsheet. To calculate a seasonal estimate for each quarter, you must collect and average the appropriate estimates. For this data set, the following cells are averaged to calculate the four seasonal indices:

Q1	H6	H10	H14
Q2	H7	H11	H15
Q3	H4	H8	H12
Q4	H5	H9	H13

The resulting seasonal indices are housed on the Excel worksheet displayed in Figure 15.8. To obtain accurate seasonal estimates, you require more than one year of past data so you don't misinterpret any 'one-off' event as a seasonal pattern. In this example, the seasonal pattern is consistent and is repeated over four years.

	A	B	C	D	E	F	G	H
1	Year	Quarter	Period	Consumption	Mov Avg	Cent Mov Avg	Trend	Seasonal
2	1991	1	1	3077			3152.9	
3		2	2	3422	3372.75		3270.3	
4		3	3	3500	3456.25	3414.50	3387.7	1.0250
5		4	4	3492	3580.75	3518.50	3505.1	0.9925
6	1992	1	5	3411	3694.75	3637.75	3622.5	0.9377
7		2	6	3920	3784.25	3739.50	3740.0	1.0483
8		3	7	3956	3871.00	3827.63	3857.4	1.0335
9		4	8	3850	4016.00	3943.50	3974.8	0.9763
10	1993	1	9	3758	4152.50	4084.25	4092.2	0.9201
11		2	10	4500	4251.25	4201.88	4209.7	1.0710
12		3	11	4502	4345.00	4298.13	4327.1	1.0474
13		4	12	4245	4510.00	4427.50	4444.5	0.9588
14	1994	1	13	4133	4666.75	4588.38	4561.9	0.9008
15		2	14	5160	4774.75	4720.75	4679.3	1.0930
16		3	15	5129			4796.8	
17		4	16	4677			4914.2	

Figure 15.7 - Calculation of seasonal estimates

Cell **C21** in Figure 15.8 contains the average (i.e. the formula **=AVERAGE(H6,H10,H14)**), which is used as the first seasonal index. For those quarters with consumption above the trend, these indices are bigger than one in value, i.e. quarters 2 and 3. The indices corresponding to quarters 1 and 4 are below 1 in value, and as a consequence, this suggests consumption in these quarters is below the trend shown by the data.

However, because of the randomness which may exist in the past data, the average of the four seasonal indices **in the multiplicative decomposition model** will often not be exactly equal to one. It is reasonable to expect this since the values in column H of the spreadsheet measures both seasonal variation and randomness for each of the past data. If the seasonal indices calculated have an average greater than one, their use in the calculation of any forecast will result in overestimation (although only marginally in the example being considered). Calculating the average of the seasonal indices and **dividing** each index by this value will provide a set of adjusted indices whose average value is equal to one, as expected. The adjusted seasonal indices are also displayed in Figure 15.8.

The formula in cell **F21** is **C21/$C$26**, and this has been copied to the block of cells **F22:F24**.

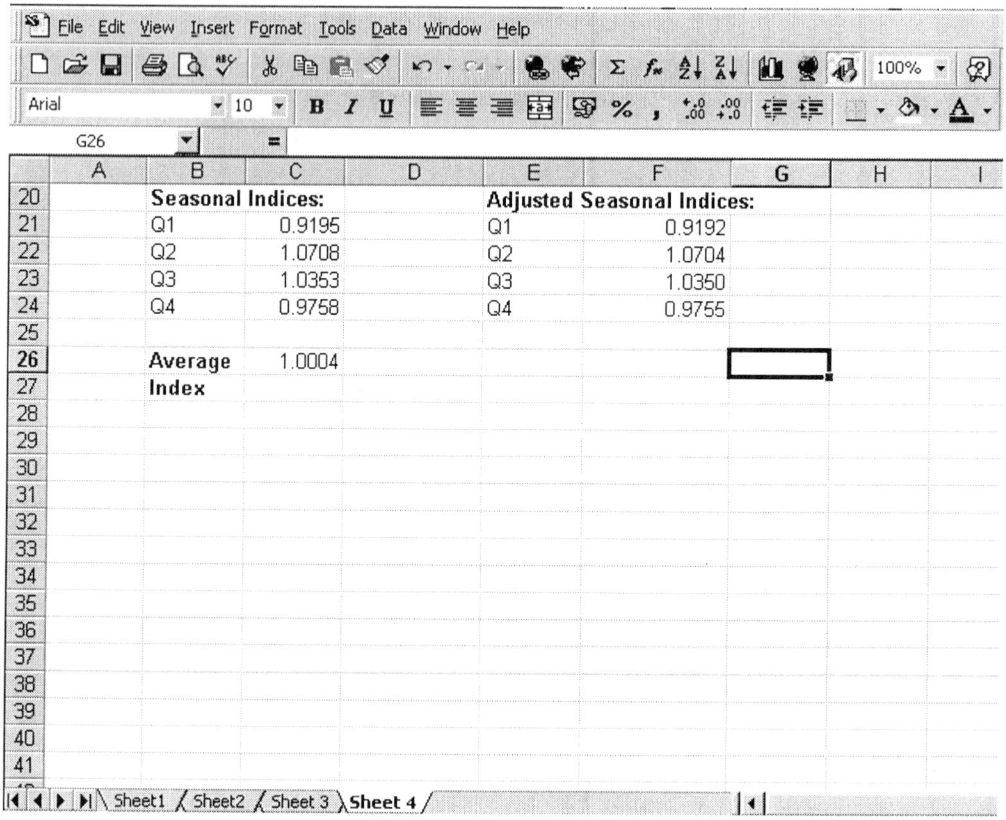

	A	B	C	D	E	F	G
20		**Seasonal Indices:**			**Adjusted Seasonal Indices:**		
21		Q1	0.9195		Q1	0.9192	
22		Q2	1.0708		Q2	1.0704	
23		Q3	1.0353		Q3	1.0350	
24		Q4	0.9758		Q4	0.9755	
25							
26		**Average**	1.0004				
27		**Index**					

Figure 15.8 - Calculation of (adjusted) seasonal indices

Inspection of the seasonal indices shown in Figure 15.8 suggests that peak consumption each year occurs in quarter 2 (the largest index), whilst the lowest consumption occurs in quarter 1 (the smallest seasonal index). Specifically, consumption of coal in quarter 2 is about 7% more than the yearly average, whilst coal consumption in quarter 1 is about 8% less than average.

Forecasting Using a (Multiplicative) Decomposition Model

The final calculation in the model is to forecast quarterly coal consumption for 1995. For the multiplicative decomposition model, you can calculate the forecasts by multiplying the relevant trend and seasonal estimates for each quarter. The formula used is:

Forecast = Trend x Seasonal Variation

In this forecasting equation, the seasonality component is given by the relevant adjusted factor shown in Figure 15.8. To determine, the trend, you can extend the trend values stored in column G of the screen shown in Figure 15.6. Since the past data were labelled 1 to 16 inclusive, the quarters in 1995 corresponding to the forecasts will be labelled 17 to 20, and are shown in Figure 15.9.

The forecast for quarter 17 is given by the equation:

=FORECAST(C32,$F$4:$F$15,$C$4:$C$15)*F21

where:

C32 is the quarter corresponding to the trend estimate, i.e. quarter 17.

$F$4:$F$15 is the trend estimate, i.e. the centred moving averages

$C$4:$C$15 is the time data, i.e. quarters 3, 4, etc. which correspond to the above moving averages.

FORECAST(C32,$F$4:$F$15,$C$4:$C$15) represents the trend estimate for quarter 17, i.e. quarter 1 1995.

F21 is the seasonal index for quarter 1.

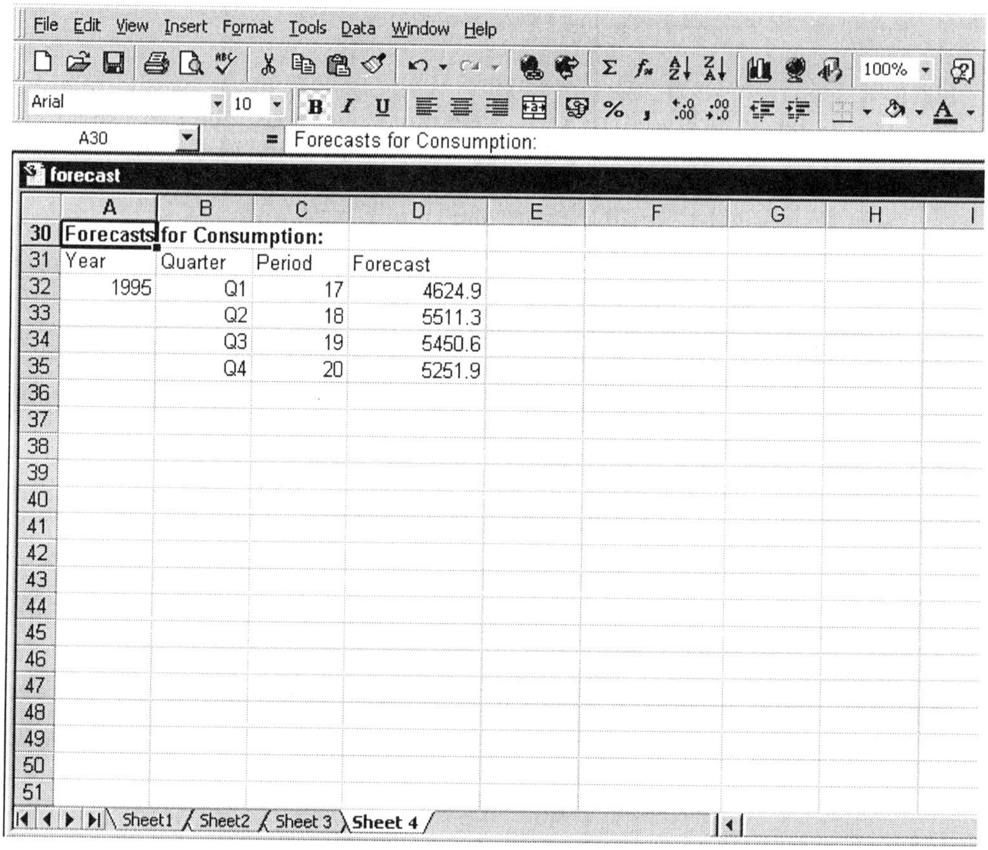

	A	B	C	D
30	**Forecasts for Consumption:**			
31	Year	Quarter	Period	Forecast
32	1995	Q1	17	4624.9
33		Q2	18	5511.3
34		Q3	19	5450.6
35		Q4	20	5251.9

Figure 15.9 - Calculation of forecasts for 1995

Inspection of the forecasts shown in Figure 15.9 indicates peak consumption for 1995 has been forecast to take place in quarter 2 and the lowest consumption has been forecast for quarter 1. The pattern repeated by these forecasts is consistent with that shown by the past data recorded from 1991 to 1994.

Measuring the Error in the Forecasts

Using the multiplicative model, you have assumed the actual data is given by:

Actual data = Trend x Seasonal Variation x Randomness

You now have the forecast equation (Forecast = Trend x Seasonal Variation) where the trend estimates are displayed on the spreadsheet and the appropriate adjusted seasonal indices represent the seasonal variation for each quarter. We can now measure the potential error in the quarterly forecasts for 1995. Figure 15.10 displays these calculations.

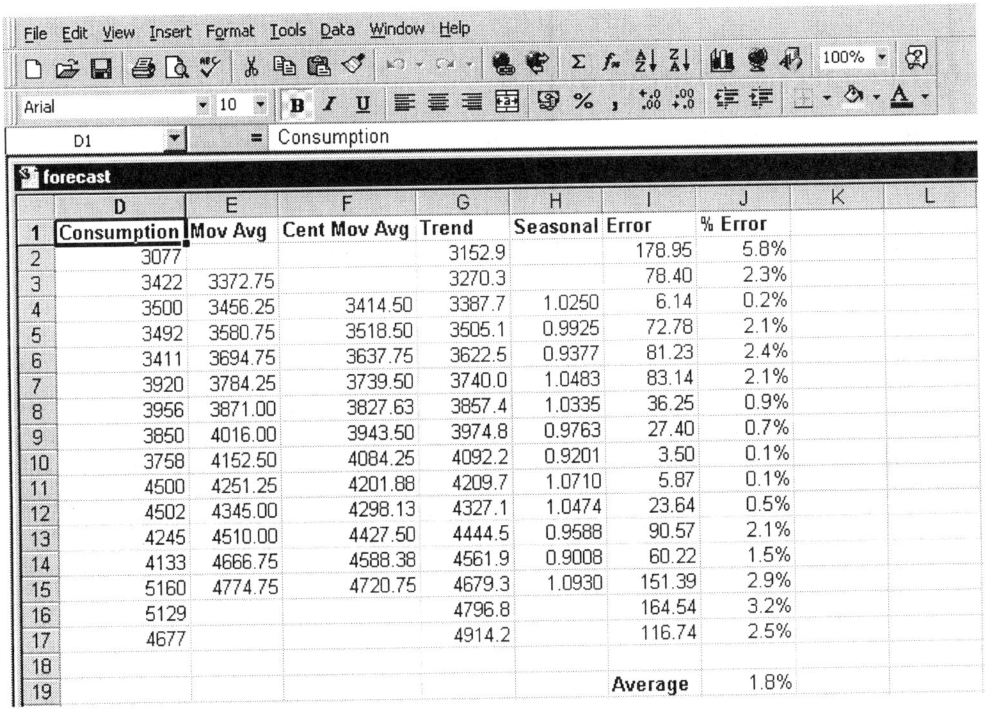

	D	E	F	G	H	I	J
1	Consumption	Mov Avg	Cent Mov Avg	Trend	Seasonal	Error	% Error
2	3077			3152.9		178.95	5.8%
3	3422	3372.75		3270.3		78.40	2.3%
4	3500	3456.25	3414.50	3387.7	1.0250	6.14	0.2%
5	3492	3580.75	3518.50	3505.1	0.9925	72.78	2.1%
6	3411	3694.75	3637.75	3622.5	0.9377	81.23	2.4%
7	3920	3784.25	3739.50	3740.0	1.0483	83.14	2.1%
8	3956	3871.00	3827.63	3857.4	1.0335	36.25	0.9%
9	3850	4016.00	3943.50	3974.8	0.9763	27.40	0.7%
10	3758	4152.50	4084.25	4092.2	0.9201	3.50	0.1%
11	4500	4251.25	4201.88	4209.7	1.0710	5.87	0.1%
12	4502	4345.00	4298.13	4327.1	1.0474	23.64	0.5%
13	4245	4510.00	4427.50	4444.5	0.9588	90.57	2.1%
14	4133	4666.75	4588.38	4561.9	0.9008	60.22	1.5%
15	5160	4774.75	4720.75	4679.3	1.0930	151.39	2.9%
16	5129			4796.8		164.54	3.2%
17	4677			4914.2		116.74	2.5%
18							
19						Average	1.8%

Figure 15.10 - Calculation of forecast errors

The formula for the first error measurement is stored in cell **I2** and represents the difference **Actual - Forecast**. The formula is:

=ABS(D2-(G2*F21))

where: **D2** represents the actual coal consumption
G2*F21 is the forecast
G2 is the trend estimate and **F21** is the seasonal component for quarter 1

The absolute value (given by the **ABS()** function) is used so any negative and positive errors do not nullify each other. To calculate the percentage error, J2 contains the formula:

=I2/D2

i.e. the error is expressed as a percentage of the actual consumption. The errors have been averaged, and this average is equal to **1.8%**. This measure will give an indication of the confidence you can have in the quarterly forecasts for 1995 and it shows that 98.2% of the pattern in the past data is accounted for by trend and seasonal variations.

Additive Decomposition Model

The example considered in this chapter has assumed that the seasonal pattern is multiplicative. In the case of additive seasonality, the decomposition equations are:

Actual data = Trend + Seasonal Variation + Randomness

Seasonal Variation + Randomness = Actual - (Centred) Moving Average

Forecast = Trend + Seasonal Variation

To adjust the seasonal indices in the additive model, the average value of the seasonal indices should be subtracted from each index to produce a set of adjusted indices. These adjusted indices should have an average value of zero. If the consumption of coal showed additive seasonality, those quarters with consumption exceeding the trend (i.e. the peaks) would have an adjusted seasonal index with a positive value, whereas those with consumption which is less than the trend (i.e. the troughs) would have an adjusted seasonal index with a negative value.

Review

1. A specific forecasting technique has been introduced to you in this chapter, which can be used to forecast from data with trend and seasonal characteristics. If you are going to apply any quantitative forecasting technique, a simple, step by step method can be used. The steps taken should include:

2. Draw a time series plot.

3. From the time series plot, identify whether a pattern exists. This pattern may include trend and seasonal properties.

4. If a seasonal variation exists, determine whether this is additive or multiplicative. Once this has been done, provide forecasts using an appropriate **decomposition** model, i.e. a multiplicative model if the seasonal variation becomes bigger with respect to time or the additive model if it remains constant.

5. The forecasts are calculated by estimating trend and seasonal characteristics in the past data.

6. Remember that by using a quantitative forecast, you are assuming that the environment which existed in the past will exist in the future. As a consequence, the forecasts should be provided for the short term only. In the coal consumption example, the behaviour of the past data is described more than adequately by trend and seasonal variation and it is reasonable to suggest that these will be displayed in 1995. However, production methods and markets for products change, and so you should be less confident in using the data to forecast quarterly consumption in 1996 and 1997.

Conclusions

Many decision makers in business collect time related data which may form a recognisable pattern. Three common patterns are positive and negative trends, stationary data, and trend and seasonality. In the last three chapters a number of forecasting techniques have been described which can be used to forecast from past data. The techniques and corresponding patterns are listed below:

Pattern	**Technique**
Trend	Linear regression
Stationary	Simple averages, moving averages, exponential smoothing
Trend and Seasonality	Decomposition (additive and multiplicative)

Each technique gives you a measure of the 'real' values of the data and can provide accurate forecasts in the short term. Equally, all three models can be used within a spreadsheet environment.

Learning Outcomes Checklist

After completing this chapter you should have an understanding of the following concepts, calculations and functions:

- The existence of trend and seasonal properties in a time series.
- That two types of seasonality exist; multiplicative and additive.
- Inspection of a time series plot will indicate the nature of the seasonal properties.

- How to forecast from a time series with trend and seasonal properties using a relevant decomposition model.

Chapter Case Question

The number of pub visits by the group's head office inspectorate were recorded daily, Monday to Friday over a period of five weeks. That data is shown below:

	Day				
Week	Mon	Tue	Wed	Thu	Fri
1	63	68	75	64	61
2	64	70	77	66	63
3	66	72	78	68	65
4	68	73	80	70	67
5	70	75	82	71	68

- Enter this data into Excel using one column for the day number (i.e. 1, 2, ..., 25) and an adjacent column for the number of pub visits.
- Create a time series plot using ChartWizard and confirm that trend and seasonal properties exist.
- Determine the exact nature of the seasonality.
- Build a relevant decomposition model for the data, and in doing so, forecast the number of daily visits for week six.
- Save your file as **CHAP15.XLS**

Supplementary Questions

1. What is meant by 'trend'?
2. Sketch time series which show positive and negative trends.
3. What is meant by the 'seasonality'?

4. Give examples of events inside and outside a particular organisation which may cause certain business data sets to show seasonal characteristics.

5. What is the difference between additive and multiplicative seasonality? Sketch time series which consist of:

   (a) A positive trend and additive seasonality.

   (b) A positive trend and multiplicative seasonality.

   (c) A negative trend and additive seasonality.

   (d) A negative trend and multiplicative seasonality.

6. A fast food store manager has recorded the daily value of sales (£) over the last five weeks. The data is stored below:

Week	Mon	Tue	Wed	Thu	Fri	Sat	Sun
1	7434	6973	7133	7522	8195	7806	6847
2	7261	6777	6962	7330	8015	7627	6659
3	7075	6620	6798	7164	7826	7469	6494
4	6904	6436	6614	6994	7660	7291	6315
5	6748	6254	6443	6808	7497	7107	6139

   Using Excel perform the following tasks:

   (a) Use ChartWizard to create a time series plot. What pattern is suggested by the past data?

   (b) On which days do the peak value of sales occur? Which days do the smallest value of sales occur each week?

   (c) What type of seasonality exists in this data set?

   (d) Forecast the value of sales for each day during week 6 using an appropriate decomposition model. State any assumptions made when computing these forecasts.

7. The unit quarterly sales of soups and hot snacks have been recorded over the last eight years by a supermarket manager. The volume of sales are shown below:

Year	Q1	Q2	Q3	Q4
1990	888	189	388	1632
1991	1352	651	872	2085
1992	1781	1098	1334	2565
1993	2229	1568	1793	3031
1994	2703	1986	2250	3479
1995	3185	2454	2694	3920
1996	3631	2949	3132	4386
1997	4068	3412	3638	4872

Using Excel perform the following tasks:

(a) Use ChartWizard to create a time series plot. What pattern is suggested by the data set?

(b) In which quarter does the peak sales occur? In which quarter does the smallest sales occur?

(c) What type of seasonality exists in this data set?

(d) Forecast the sales for each quarter of 1998 using an appropriate decomposition model. State any assumptions made when computing these forecasts.

8. The proprietor of a local daily newspaper has recorded the number of daily sales for the last four weeks. The results are tabulated below:

Week	Mon	Tue	Wed	Thu	Fri	Sat
1	7502	8275	9116	9269	11472	13283
2	7341	8040	8870	9024	11235	12984
3	7144	7838	8690	8801	10919	12626
4	6957	7655	8440	8583	10666	12325

Using Excel perform the following tasks:

(a) Use ChartWizard to create a time series plot. What pattern is suggested by the data set?

(b) On which days do the peak number of sales occur? On which days do the smallest number of sales occur?

(c) What type of seasonality exists in this data set?

(d) Forecast the number of sales for each day during week 5 using an appropriate decomposition model. State any assumptions made when computing these forecasts.

Appendix I

Normal Distribution Tables

$p(Z < z)$

z	0.00	0.01	0.02	0.03	0.04	0.05	0.06	0.07	0.08	0.09
0.0	0.5000	0.5040	0.5080	0.5120	0.5159	0.5199	0.5239	0.5279	0.5319	0.5359
0.1	0.5398	0.5438	0.5478	0.5517	0.5557	0.5596	0.5636	0.5675	0.5714	0.5753
0.2	0.5793	0.5832	0.5871	0.5910	0.5948	0.5987	0.6026	0.6064	0.6103	0.6141
0.3	0.6179	0.6217	0.6255	0.6293	0.6331	0.6368	0.6406	0.6443	0.6480	0.6517
0.4	0.6554	0.6591	0.6628	0.6664	0.6700	0.6736	0.6772	0.6808	0.6844	0.6879
0.5	0.6915	0.6950	0.6985	0.7019	0.7054	0.7088	0.7123	0.7157	0.7190	0.7224
0.6	0.7257	0.7291	0.7324	0.7357	0.7389	0.7422	0.7454	0.7486	0.7517	0.7549
0.7	0.7580	0.7611	0.7642	0.7673	0.7704	0.7734	0.7764	0.7794	0.7823	0.7852
0.8	0.7881	0.7910	0.7939	0.7967	0.7995	0.8023	0.8051	0.8078	0.8106	0.8133
0.9	0.8159	0.8186	0.8212	0.8238	0.8264	0.8289	0.8315	0.8340	0.8365	0.8389
1.0	0.8413	0.8438	0.8461	0.8485	0.8508	0.8531	0.8554	0.8577	0.8599	0.8621
1.1	0.8643	0.8665	0.8686	0.8708	0.8729	0.8749	0.8770	0.8790	0.8810	0.8830
1.2	0.8849	0.8869	0.8888	0.8907	0.8925	0.8944	0.8962	0.8980	0.8997	0.9015
1.3	0.9032	0.9049	0.9066	0.9082	0.9099	0.9115	0.9131	0.9147	0.9162	0.9177
1.4	0.9192	0.9207	0.9222	0.9236	0.9251	0.9265	0.9279	0.9292	0.9306	0.9319
1.5	0.9332	0.9345	0.9357	0.9370	0.9382	0.9394	0.9406	0.9418	0.9429	0.9441
1.6	0.9452	0.9463	0.9474	0.9484	0.9495	0.9505	0.9515	0.9525	0.9535	0.9545
1.7	0.9554	0.9564	0.9573	0.9582	0.9591	0.9599	0.9608	0.9616	0.9625	0.9633
1.8	0.9641	0.9649	0.9656	0.9664	0.9671	0.9678	0.9686	0.9693	0.9699	0.9706
1.9	0.9713	0.9719	0.9726	0.9732	0.9738	0.9744	0.9750	0.9756	0.9761	0.9767
2.0	0.9772	0.9778	0.9783	0.9788	0.9793	0.9798	0.9803	0.9808	0.9812	0.9817
2.1	0.9821	0.9826	0.9830	0.9834	0.9838	0.9842	0.9846	0.9850	0.9854	0.9857
2.2	0.9861	0.9864	0.9868	0.9871	0.9874	0.9878	0.9881	0.9884	0.9887	0.9890
2.3	0.9893	0.9896	0.9898	0.9901	0.9904	0.9906	0.9909	0.9911	0.9913	0.9916
2.4	0.9918	0.9920	0.9922	0.9924	0.9927	0.9929	0.9931	0.9932	0.9934	0.9936

2.5	0.9938	0.9940	0.9941	0.9943	0.9945	0.9946	0.9948	0.9949	0.9951	0.9952
2.6	0.9953	0.9955	0.9956	0.9957	0.9959	0.9960	0.9961	0.9962	0.9963	0.9964
2.7	0.9965	0.9966	0.9967	0.9968	0.9969	0.9970	0.9971	0.9972	0.9973	0.9974
2.8	0.9974	0.9975	0.9976	0.9977	0.9977	0.9978	0.9979	0.9979	0.9980	0.9981
2.9	0.9981	0.9982	0.9982	0.9983	0.9984	0.9984	0.9985	0.9985	0.9986	0.9986

These tables represent the area under the standard normal curve which is situated to the left of z.

Normal Distribution Tables

p(Z > z)

z	0.00	0.01	0.02	0.03	0.04	0.05	0.06	0.07	0.08	0.09
0.0	0.5000	0.4960	0.4920	0.4880	0.4841	0.4801	0.4761	0.4721	0.4681	0.4641
0.1	0.4602	0.4562	0.4522	0.4483	0.4443	0.4404	0.4364	0.4325	0.4286	0.4247
0.2	0.4207	0.4168	0.4129	0.4090	0.4052	0.4013	0.3974	0.3936	0.3897	0.3859
0.3	0.3821	0.3783	0.3745	0.3707	0.3669	0.3632	0.3594	0.3557	0.3520	0.3483
0.4	0.3446	0.3409	0.3372	0.3336	0.3300	0.3264	0.3228	0.3192	0.3156	0.3121
0.5	0.3085	0.3050	0.3015	0.2981	0.2946	0.2912	0.2877	0.2843	0.2810	0.2776
0.6	0.2743	0.2709	0.2676	0.2643	0.2611	0.2578	0.2546	0.2514	0.2483	0.2451
0.7	0.2420	0.2389	0.2358	0.2327	0.2296	0.2266	0.2236	0.2206	0.2177	0.2148
0.8	0.2119	0.2090	0.2061	0.2033	0.2005	0.1977	0.1949	0.1922	0.1894	0.1867
0.9	0.1841	0.1814	0.1788	0.1762	0.1736	0.1711	0.1685	0.1660	0.1635	0.1611
1.0	0.1587	0.1562	0.1539	0.1515	0.1492	0.1469	0.1446	0.1423	0.1401	0.1379
1.1	0.1357	0.1335	0.1314	0.1292	0.1271	0.1251	0.1230	0.1210	0.1190	0.1170
1.2	0.1151	0.1131	0.1112	0.1093	0.1075	0.1056	0.1038	0.1020	0.1003	0.0985
1.3	0.0968	0.0951	0.0934	0.0918	0.0901	0.0885	0.0869	0.0853	0.0838	0.0823
1.4	0.0808	0.0793	0.0778	0.0764	0.0749	0.0735	0.0721	0.0708	0.0694	0.0681
1.5	0.0668	0.0655	0.0643	0.0630	0.0618	0.0606	0.0594	0.0582	0.0571	0.0559
1.6	0.0548	0.0537	0.0526	0.0516	0.0505	0.0495	0.0485	0.0475	0.0465	0.0455
1.7	0.0446	0.0436	0.0427	0.0418	0.0409	0.0401	0.0392	0.0384	0.0375	0.0367
1.8	0.0359	0.0351	0.0344	0.0336	0.0329	0.0322	0.0314	0.0307	0.0301	0.0294
1.9	0.0287	0.0281	0.0274	0.0268	0.0262	0.0256	0.0250	0.0244	0.0239	0.0233
2.0	0.0228	0.0222	0.0217	0.0212	0.0207	0.0202	0.0197	0.0192	0.0188	0.0183
2.1	0.0179	0.0174	0.0170	0.0166	0.0162	0.0158	0.0154	0.0150	0.0146	0.0143
2.2	0.0139	0.0136	0.0132	0.0129	0.0126	0.0122	0.0119	0.0116	0.0113	0.0110
2.3	0.0107	0.0104	0.0102	0.0099	0.0096	0.0094	0.0091	0.0089	0.0087	0.0084
2.4	0.0082	0.0080	0.0078	0.0076	0.0073	0.0071	0.0069	0.0068	0.0066	0.0064

2.5	0.0062	0.0060	0.0059	0.0057	0.0055	0.0054	0.0052	0.0051	0.0049	0.0048
2.6	0.0047	0.0045	0.0044	0.0043	0.0041	0.0040	0.0039	0.0038	0.0037	0.0036
2.7	0.0035	0.0034	0.0033	0.0032	0.0031	0.0030	0.0029	0.0028	0.0027	0.0026
2.8	0.0026	0.0025	0.0024	0.0023	0.0023	0.0022	0.0021	0.0021	0.0020	0.0019
2.9	0.0019	0.0018	0.0018	0.0017	0.0016	0.0016	0.0015	0.0015	0.0014	0.0014

These tables represent the area under the standard normal curve which is situated to the right of z.

Appendix II

Student's T-Distribution Tables

p	0.05	0.025	0.01	0.005
df				
1	6.31	12.71	31.82	63.66
2	2.92	4.30	6.97	9.93
3	2.35	3.18	4.54	5.84
4	2.13	2.78	3.75	4.60
5	2.02	2.57	3.37	4.03
6	1.94	2.45	3.14	3.71
7	1.90	2.37	3.00	3.50
8	1.86	2.31	2.90	3.36
9	1.83	2.26	2.82	3.25
10	1.81	2.23	2.76	3.17
11	1.80	2.20	2.72	3.11
12	1.78	2.18	2.68	3.05
13	1.77	2.16	2.65	3.01
14	1.76	2.15	2.62	2.98
15	1.75	2.13	2.60	2.95
16	1.75	2.12	2.58	2.92
17	1.74	2.11	2.57	2.90
18	1.73	2.10	2.55	2.88
19	1.73	2.09	2.54	2.86
20	1.73	2.09	2.53	2.85
21	1.72	2.08	2.52	2.83
22	1.72	2.07	2.51	2.82
23	1.71	2.07	2.50	2.81
24	1.71	2.06	2.49	2.80
25	1.71	2.06	2.49	2.79

26	1.71	2.06	2.48	2.78
27	1.70	2.05	2.47	2.77
28	1.70	2.05	2.47	2.76
29	1.70	2.05	2.46	2.76
30	1.70	2.04	2.46	2.75
40	1.68	2.02	2.42	2.70
60	1.67	2.00	2.39	2.66
100	1.66	1.98	2.37	2.62

The values listed represent the value of t above which the indicated percentage area of the curve is situated, e.g. for a t-distribution with 15 degrees of freedom, 2½% of the area is situated to the right of t = 2.13. Alternatively, for a t-distribution with 15 degrees of freedom, 2½% of the area is situated to the left of t = -2.13.

Appendix III

Chi-Squared Distribution Tables

p	**0.05**	**0.025**	**0.01**	**0.005**
df				
1	3.84	5.02	6.63	7.88
2	5.99	7.38	9.21	10.60
3	7.81	9.35	11.34	12.84
4	9.49	11.14	13.28	14.86
5	11.07	12.83	15.09	16.75
6	12.59	14.45	16.81	18.55
7	14.07	16.01	18.48	20.28
8	15.51	17.53	20.09	21.95
9	16.92	19.02	21.67	23.59
10	18.31	20.48	23.21	25.19
11	19.68	21.92	24.72	26.76
12	21.03	23.34	26.22	28.30
13	22.36	24.74	27.69	29.82
14	23.68	26.12	29.14	31.32
15	25.00	27.49	30.58	32.80
16	26.30	28.85	32.00	34.27
17	27.59	30.19	33.41	35.72
18	28.87	31.53	34.81	37.16
19	30.14	32.85	36.19	38.58
20	31.41	34.17	37.57	40.00
21	32.7	35.5	38.9	41.4
22	33.9	36.8	40.3	42.8
23	35.2	38.1	41.6	44.2
24	36.4	39.4	43.0	45.6
25	37.7	40.7	44.3	46.9

26	38.9	41.9	45.6	48.3
27	40.1	43.2	47.0	49.6
28	41.3	44.5	48.3	51.0
29	42.6	45.7	49.6	52.3
30	43.8	47.0	50.9	53.7
40	55.8	59.3	63.7	66.8
60	79.1	83.3	88.4	92.0
80	101.9	106.6	112.3	116.3
100	124.3	129.6	135.8	140.2

The values listed represent the value of the chi-squared distribution above which the indicated percentage area of the curve is situated, e.g. for six degrees of freedom, 5% of the curve is situated to the right of $X^2 = 12.59$.

Index

Excel functions and facilities are indicated by **bold text**.